ALIAS SMITH & JONES

The Story of Two Pretty Good Bad Men

by Sandra K. Sagala & JoAnne M. Bagwell

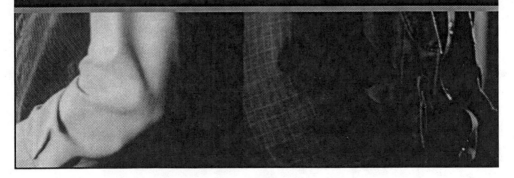

Alias Smith and Jones
The Story of Two Pretty Good Bad Men
© 2005 Sandra K. Sagala and JoAnne M. Bagwell

Published in the USA by:

BearManor Media
PO Box 750
Boalsburg, PA 16827
www.BearManorMedia.com

Library of Congress Cataloging-in-Publication Data

Sagala, Sandra K.
  Alias Smith & Jones : the story of two pretty good bad men / by
  Sandra K. Sagala & JoAnne M. Bagwell.
      p. cm.
  Includes bibliographical references and index.
  ISBN 1-59393-031-3
  1. Alias Smith and Jones (Television program) I. Title: Alias Smith
  and Jones. II. Bagwell, JoAnne M. III. Title.

  PN1992.77.A4826S24 2005
  791.45'72--dc22
                              2005018688

Printed in the United States.

Front cover photo courtesy of Jerry Ohlinger's Movie Materials Store.

Design and Layout by Valerie Thompson.

TABLE OF CONTENTS

INTRODUCTION

Smith and Jones. Could two more generic, all-purpose names be found in American society? Good, solid-sounding, easy-to-remember, easier-to-forget names were important to Hannibal Heyes and Kid Curry, "the two most successful outlaws in the history of the West." Porterville Sheriff Lom Trevors didn't have to think too long or too hard to come up with them. In fact, they were a desperate spur-of-the-moment inspiration.

But just who were those guys?

Their ancestry harkens back to romantic tales of highwaymen on fiery steeds who urged traveling coaches to stop, stand and deliver. Whether silk handkerchiefs or coarse linen covered their faces, the Robin Hoods excited in their victims a willingness to hand over their goods. In stories told about the legendary bandits, the marauders then fled, leaving behind passengers eager to share word of their encounter with the noble thieves. Heyes and Curry were born of this tradition.

They can count among their forefathers a young man named Robert Leroy Parker who, in the summer of 1889, joined three or four other desperadoes in robbing the Telluride, Colorado, bank of $10,000. Shortly afterward, he adopted the name Cassidy to honor his friend Mike Cassidy and took on the first name of Butch from butcher, a trade in which he had briefly been engaged.[1] Under his alias, he led a gang who called themselves the Wild Bunch or the Hole-in-the-Wall Gang. Numbering at times from a handful of outlaws to a small regiment, the gang included Harry Longbaugh, known as the Sundance Kid, and Harvey Logan, a.k.a. Kid Curry. Despite his acquaintance with Sundance, who could draw "as fast as a snake's tongue," and Curry, who was reputed to be a vicious "tiger of the Wild Bunch,"[2] Butch's reputation included his never having killed anyone.

Three years of frequent bank and train robberies brought the gang to the attention of the Pinkerton Detective Agency. Before the Civil War, Allan Pinkerton founded the company of dogged and rugged men. He instituted the Rogues Gallery, demanding that his operatives obtain photos of criminals and list all known aliases, nicknames, hangouts and associates.[3] After the telephone and telegraph increased cooperation between law enforcement agencies, the Wild Bunch realized their days were numbered. When the gang split up, Butch and Sundance fled the country via New York City. While in the Big Apple, the pair, with girlfriend Etta Place, proudly sat for photographs. The Pinkertons flooded western towns with these photos and used them to trace the pair to South America. For six years, Butch and Sundance practiced American-style Wild West outlawry in Bolivia. Finally the Bolivian army tracked them down and reportedly killed them in a bloody shootout in 1908. Another version contends that only three troopers cornered them and, realizing that the end was near, Butch shot Sundance and then himself. Still a third account has Cassidy returning to the U.S. and living under the alias of William T. Phillips in Spokane, Washington. Allegedly, he died there in 1937.[4]

George Roy Hill brought the story of the popular American outlaws to the big screen in 1969. For his screenplay, William Goldman won an Academy Award. Paul Newman (as Butch Cassidy) and Robert Redford (as the Sundance Kid) starred in the film that was one of Hollywood's first to depict bad guys as good guys, turning "Old West bandits into modern folk heroes."[5] The audience was advised at the beginning of the film that "most of what follows is true" and it mostly was.

The film depicted the events of August 1900 when the Wild Bunch stopped a Union Pacific Railroad train after it passed Tipton, Wyoming. Woodcock, a railroad employee, refused to open the door, so the gang dynamited the railroad car. The Union Pacific management decided this was the last straw and a few hours later, a special train was dispatched from Cheyenne carrying Pinkertons and a special posse.[6] Unable to shake them, Butch and Sundance decided to head for South America. Once there, under the aliases Smith and Jones, they continued their bank and train robbing careers and soon were enthusiastically hunted by the Bolivian authorities who knew them as the *bandidos Yanquis*. Director Hill went with the more dramatic of the death scenes, having the outlaws killed by scores of Bolivian soldiers.

It is difficult not to deduce that the film had some bearing on Glen Larson's inspiration to create a western television series based on the two lovable outlaws attempting to outrun the law. Larson's script for the pilot contained several mirroring scenes. In both, the outlaw gang uses dynamite to blast a safe being transported in a railroad car they've stopped. Something goes wrong and apprehension grows. A little old lady passenger approaches, fearless of the Wild Bunch. "I'm not afraid of you, I'm not afraid of anything," she shrieks. "I'm a grandmother and a female and I've got my rights." The Sundance Kid dismisses her with the observation, "We got no time for this." When a similar, but kindlier, grandmotherly old lady hands outlaw Kid Curry of the Devil's Hole Gang a pamphlet at the site of their failed train robbery, it starts him and partner Hannibal Heyes thinking about amnesty. Before either scene can develop further, the posse dispatched to chase them down gallops into view.

In another scene in the film, a card sharp who doesn't know Sundance suspects him of cheating. When Butch uses the Kid's name in conversation, the man is shocked for he instantly realizes that he will die if Sundance draws his pistol. Saved from his fatal error by an amiable Butch, the man wonders how close he came to death. "How good are you?" he asks Sundance, who answers by shooting the gun belt off the man's hips, sending it skittering across the floor. Hannibal Heyes's accomplice has the same quick-draw talent. When Wheat Carlson of Heyes and Curry's Devil's Hole Gang challenges Heyes during a bank robbery, Heyes refers Wheat to the loaded six-gun in the hand of Kid Curry. Wheat is immediately cowed.

Dismayed at modern technology that has made their "jobs" so much harder, both Butch Cassidy and Hannibal Heyes lament the improvements. When Butch inspects a refurbished bank, he is overwhelmed by the new bars, bolts, alarms, and safes. He asks the guard what happened to the beautiful old one. "People kept robbing it," the guard responds laconically. Butch muses that it was "a small price to pay for beauty." Heyes, unable to open the Brooker 202 safe in the train they've stopped, is doubly confounded by the Brooker 404 newly installed in the Porterville Bank. His nimble fingers are stymied by the locks built into the newer models. He concedes that "the banks they're building today are unrobbable."

There is dissension in Cassidy's gang, the Wild Bunch. With him and Sundance frequently absent, Harvey Logan takes charge and defies Butch for supremacy. In his own mind, Butch is, and always will be, leader. "I don't mean to be a sore loser," he whispers to Sundance as he's about to engage in a knife fight with Logan, "but when it's done, if I'm dead, kill him." Similarly, Wheat Carlson challenges Heyes for leadership. When Heyes's brilliant scheme to escape with the unopenable safe goes awry, Wheat insists that he could have done it better. When pushed further to detail how he would do it, he cryptically remarks, "Smarter." Heyes doesn't worry about a physical confrontation with his subordinate; Wheat's ideas usually fizzle out long before they come to fruition.

Despite the challenges aimed at the leaders of the Hole-in-the-Wall and Devil's Hole Gangs, their partners respect their brains, however sarcastically they may express it. Sundance laughs at Butch Cassidy's latest ideas. "You just keep thinkin', Butch, that's what you're good at." Curry depends on Heyes's wider vocabulary and wisdom, asking him to define "amnesty," and defers to him as leader of their gang.

In a way, they are all still boys at heart. Butch is fascinated with the newly-invented bicycle, tooling around a pasture with Etta Place to the tune of "Raindrops Keep Fallin' on My Head." Heyes, invited to the back room of the saloon by Deputy Harker, is entranced by the music emitted by a band organ, a gaudy, calliope-sounding music box.

When things get too hot for them, Butch and Sundance visit a lawman they know to find out about enlisting in the Spanish war, hoping to clear their names.

A week or so after the concept test was done, Isenberg relayed the bad news. *Alias Smith and Jones* failed. ABC's interest was wavering. The very low score it received from the focus group indicated that no one would be interested in watching two outlaws trying to earn an amnesty. Price was amazed. He began his Hollywood career as a script reader and story analyst and he knew a good concept when he saw it. Unable to believe *Alias Smith and Jones* fared so poorly, he asked Isenberg if he could read the summary they used in the test. "I read what they had and I said, 'This isn't what the show is, so you're testing something that we don't plan to do.'" Price asked if he could submit a summary of his own and have the concept retested. Isenberg agreed. "So I wrote a paragraph and gave it to them. They tested it and it came back with the highest concept [score] they had tested. You just had to tell it right." ABC gave the greenlight to proceed with the pilot. Frank Price, still with one foot in the production end of the business, would serve as the executive producer of the film, wielding creative control over the project. The third man had come into the West.

By the early summer of 1970, ABC had given Universal the order for fourteen episodes to begin airing at mid-season. Glen Larson began writing the pilot script. *Alias Smith and Jones* was Larson's first foray into the world of series creator, so a collaborator was brought in to help fine-tune the script. The collaborator was Douglas Heyes, a writer known for his deft touch with humorous Westerns, a skill developed during his stint writing and directing for *Maverick*.[5] While Heyes was perfectly happy to collaborate on the script, he had a policy of not putting his name on anything where he did not get sole writing credit; for *Alias Smith and Jones* he used the pseudonym Matthew Howard.

Larson was pleased to be working with a man who was one of his favorite writers, as well as something of a mentor. In 1959, Douglas Heyes was one of the core group of writers working with Roy Huggins on *Maverick*. Larson was a musician who decided to try his hand at writing a television script. He wrote a spec script for *Maverick* and, hoping to sell it, submitted it to Heyes, who read it and was impressed enough to give it a table reading with James Garner, Heyes and his wife all playing parts, much to the delight of the fledgling writer. Unfortunately, there was a writers' strike going on at the time which made it impossible for Heyes to buy Larson's script. Larson missed out on making his first sale, but was encouraged enough by Heyes's response to stick with writing.

Larson continued to write spec scripts while touring with his musical group The Four Preps. The group had been discovered at a high school talent contest in 1956 and signed to a long-term contract with Capitol Records. They enjoyed a long string of hits including "26 Miles," a song celebrating the island of Santa Catalina, located twenty-six miles off the coast of Southern California, and written by Larson and fellow group member Bruce Belland. That song set the tone for the West Coast beach sound of the sixties. "I wish we'd been as smart as Brian Wilson and the Beach Boys," Larson muses, "because we figured one song and that's over, you got to find something else." The Four Preps traveled the world, further, the posse dispatched to chase them down gallops into view.

In another scene in the film, a card sharp who doesn't know Sundance suspects him of cheating. When Butch uses the Kid's name in conversation, the man is shocked for he instantly realizes that he will die if Sundance draws his pistol. Saved from his fatal error by an amiable Butch, the man wonders how close he came to death. "How good are you?" he asks Sundance, who answers by shooting the gun belt off the man's hips, sending it skittering across the floor. Hannibal Heyes's accomplice has the same quick-draw talent. When Wheat Carlson of Heyes and Curry's Devil's Hole Gang challenges Heyes during a bank robbery, Heyes refers Wheat to the loaded six-gun in the hand of Kid Curry. Wheat is immediately cowed.

Dismayed at modern technology that has made their "jobs" so much harder, both Butch Cassidy and Hannibal Heyes lament the improvements. When Butch inspects a refurbished bank, he is overwhelmed by the new bars, bolts, alarms, and safes. He asks the guard what happened to the beautiful old one. "People kept robbing it," the guard responds laconically. Butch muses that it was "a small price to pay for beauty." Heyes, unable to open the Brooker 202 safe in the train they've stopped, is doubly confounded by the Brooker 404 newly installed in the Porterville Bank. His nimble fingers are stymied by the locks built into the newer models. He concedes that "the banks they're building today are unrobbable."

There is dissension in Cassidy's gang, the Wild Bunch. With him and Sundance frequently absent, Harvey Logan takes charge and defies Butch for supremacy. In his own mind, Butch is, and always will be, leader. "I don't mean to be a sore loser," he whispers to Sundance as he's about to engage in a knife fight with Logan, "but when it's done, if I'm dead, kill him." Similarly, Wheat Carlson challenges Heyes for leadership. When Heyes's brilliant scheme to escape with the unopenable safe goes awry, Wheat insists that he could have done it better. When pushed further to detail how he would do it, he cryptically remarks, "Smarter." Heyes doesn't worry about a physical confrontation with his subordinate; Wheat's ideas usually fizzle out long before they come to fruition.

Despite the challenges aimed at the leaders of the Hole-in-the-Wall and Devil's Hole Gangs, their partners respect their brains, however sarcastically they may express it. Sundance laughs at Butch Cassidy's latest ideas. "You just keep thinkin', Butch, that's what you're good at." Curry depends on Heyes's wider vocabulary and wisdom, asking him to define "amnesty," and defers to him as leader of their gang.

In a way, they are all still boys at heart. Butch is fascinated with the newly-invented bicycle, tooling around a pasture with Etta Place to the tune of "Raindrops Keep Fallin' on My Head." Heyes, invited to the back room of the saloon by Deputy Harker, is entranced by the music emitted by a band organ, a gaudy, calliope-sounding music box.

When things get too hot for them, Butch and Sundance visit a lawman they know to find out about enlisting in the Spanish war, hoping to clear their names.

Visions of becoming officers dance in their heads. However, their crimes are too severe. The sheriff they've approached recognizes the futility of their doing anything but giving up. Similarly Heyes and Curry select as their mediator a reformed outlaw, now duly-elected Sheriff Lom Trevors whose town they've previously avoided out of respect for their old friend and his new position. This is where Heyes and Curry and Butch and Sundance part company. Our boys fare better because the governor agrees to offer amnesty, although with conditions attached.

With new, albeit temporary, jobs as bank teller and bank guard, Heyes and Curry are still after the pardon despite setbacks. Butch and Sundance found trading in old habits for new was not so easily accomplished and after an attempt at payroll-guarding jobs in the Bolivian mountains that soured, they were back to doing what they did best, robbing banks.

To Glen Larson's credit, he took a small concept from *Butch Cassidy and the Sundance Kid* and built it into a series that was among the last TV westerns to survive for more than a single season in prime time.[7] *Alias Smith and Jones,* unique in its own right with its theme of two outlaws seeking amnesty, was nevertheless one of the myriad of television westerns whose plots were, of necessity, fast-paced and repetitive, restricted to action and simple comedy.

The western craze on television had more or less begun with *The Life and Legend of Wyatt Earp* which debuted in 1955 and initiated a wave of adult westerns on television. It was followed by the longest running western in television history – *Gunsmoke. Wagon Train,* at one point number one in the Nielsen ratings, debuted in 1957. The enormous scope and variety of plot and cast derived from its contingent of regular players offset by individuals on the train played by guest stars. In *Alias Smith and Jones,* the concept varied only slightly. Heyes and Curry traveled from town to town encountering citizens played by the guests. Rated number three behind *Gunsmoke* and *Wagon Train* was *Have Gun, Will Travel.* An unconventional western, its antihero was Paladin, a debonair gentleman gunfighter, a good guy who defied convention by dressing all in black.

After a history of westerns in which the hero is always a good guy, stalwart, brave and honest, along came Bret Maverick, a creation of Roy Huggins. Breaking the rules of the already established western hero, in *Maverick* Huggins created a tongue-in-cheek comedy. Bret Maverick had no courage, no attributes of the typical western hero. Though tall, dark and handsome, the southern con man and his brother Bart tended to sneak out the back door if trouble appeared, more interested in money than honor.[8]

By the end of the 1950s, more than thirty regularly scheduled westerns were part of the television fare every week. Six of the top seven programs were oat-burners. ABC executive Fred Silverman realized that westerns had what people wanted – "a leading man with whom the audience can easily identify," possessing "an intangible quality which makes [him] real and believable, [and who was] involved in a larger than life enterprise."[9] He was right. At their height, westerns attracted more than sixty million viewers nightly.[10] For a genre that in its infancy had been attractive mostly to children, now only thirty percent of viewers were under eighteen years of age. As westerns proliferated and grew more adult-oriented, the characters matured, indulging in adult vices of drinking, smoking, and gambling. Violence became more prevalent. Handsome actors were chosen to play the leads. The western as an art form began to attract talented directors and producers.[11] Then a new type of western began to emerge in the 1960s when the genre turned to domestic situations.

The *Gunsmoke* characters evolved into a sort of family and *The Rifleman* offered the father-son duo of Lucas and Mark McCain beset with frontier family problems. *Bonanza* extended the father-son relationship to a father and three sons. If it did not feature a woman as a main character, it at least afforded the opportunity for female viewers to have their choice of beefcake in main characters of varied sizes, ages and personalities. Three years into *Bonanza*, NBC re-introduced the lone hero in *The Virginian*. Based on Owen Wister's novel, the theme centered on the Old West that was being destroyed by progress from the east.

Women became important characters on television when networks realized it is generally women who purchase the products advertised. *The Big Valley* was introduced in 1965 almost as a female *Bonanza*. Victoria Barkley, the elegant but gutsy matriarch of the Barkley clan, dealt with the contemporary problems of racism and civil rights as well as those of aging and prison reform.

But by the end of the 1960s, the popularity of all westerns declined. From an all-time high of thirty series during the 1959-60 season, by 1970 that number had fallen to four. After the moon walk in 1969, Americans looked forward to the future, not back to the past. Technology sent the cowboy riding off into the sunset. Frank Price, head of Universal Television in the 1970s, believes that "westerns were at their most popular when cowboys were more real. . . . As we got further and further away from that time, it was more of an unreality [to have] somebody riding around on a horse than going around in a space suit."[12] Indeed, as early as 1929, western stars faced aviation heroes like Charles Lindbergh as competitors for the public's adulation. After his transatlantic flight, *Photoplay* magazine declared, "Lindbergh has put the cowboy into the discard heap . . . the Western novel and motion picture heroes have slunk away into the brush, never to return. . . ."[13]

Never say never. Two decades later, the stories of western heroes became a staple of television fare. However, when the country became embroiled in the Vietnam War, violence that had been so much a part of western mythology wearied Americans already tired of the too real violence in the daily news. The clear-cut image of good guy versus bad and the trusting rural society of the television western were not reflected in real-life America. New methods of audience research determined that westerns remained popular with children and those less affluent than with the general population. However, since television relied on the income produced by advertising time, it had to appeal to the segments of the population more likely to part with their money. Familiar western heroes began riding off into the sunset.

Despite the moribund popularity of Westerns, *Alias Smith and Jones* took its place among the leading programs of its genre. In many respects, it resembled its predecessors. Their recurring characters met folks in towns that dotted the Old West. Guest stars supplied new faces. Instead of the singular hero (who was never really alone, the Lone Ranger had Tonto, Wild Bill Hickok had Jingles, Gene Autry had Pat Buttram), Hannibal Heyes and Kid Curry traveled together, sharing their unique talents, each acting as confidante and alter ego of the other. As partners, they reflected true frontier history when the physical or psychological hardships of being alone were eased by a companion. In the family sense, they are matched as cousins. To appeal to women, they are handsome and amiable; to men, they are free-spirited, poker-playing cowboy drifters living by their wits. Their peaceful, non-violent nature – "We never killed anyone" – and their desire to reform their outlaw ways made them excellent role models for children.

Nevertheless, after the suicide of actor Peter Duel mid-way through the second season – and despite Roger Davis's admirable continuation of the Heyes character – the demise of the program seemed inevitable. Fierce competition with Flip Wilson kept the ratings modest. When at last ABC grudgingly granted them a new Saturday night timeslot, *All in the Family* proved to be an even more formidable challenger in the ratings war. Those stunning blows, coupled with the network's vision of a non-western season, signaled its end.

However, life still beat in the heart of the television western. In 1974, *Little House on the Prairie,* based on the stories by Laura Ingalls Wilder and created by Michael Landon of *Bonanza* fame, rated as NBC's highest from 1977 to 1981. In 1989, *Lonesome Dove,* a miniseries based on the novel by Larry McMurtry, signaled the hoped-for revitalization of the western on television. Critics raved as it scored the biggest miniseries ratings in five television seasons. Over forty-four million viewers, no doubt including many who had never heard of the epic-length book, watched the first two-hour segment. Less than a year later, ABC introduced a new western series, *The Young Riders.* Though based on the historical Pony Express, the program explored contemporary society. Its shortcoming was that it was set in one location, costing the show what the Pony Express was all about – getting the mail from one point to another.

The 1990s saw the resurgence of interest in cowboys. The Arts & Entertainment network offered *The Real West* hosted by Kenny Rogers. It chronicled the lives of men and women and events that shaped the frontier. CBS was one of the last networks to believe in the promise of the Old West as entertainment. *Dr. Quinn, Medicine Woman* in the late 1990s was one of the few revisionist westerns with a focus on a woman in a role traditionally that of a man. Mid-season 1998, *The Magnificent Seven* was introduced, based on the 1960 movie that was itself a remake of the 1954 film *The Seven Samurai.*

Shortly after the turn of the twenty-first century, westerns began a tentative comeback. *Peacemakers,* a show integrating forensic techniques into a marshal's murder investigations, premiered on USA scoring the network's second highest rating. A series about 1876 life in Deadwood, Dakota Territory, aired on HBO and *The Legend of Butch and Sundance* is in development at NBC. Tom Selleck is adapting another of Louis L'Amour's novels for the TNT network. A mini-series based on *Little House on the Prairie* is also in the works. All this increased activity on the western front is most welcome and long overdue.

In 1967, Larry McMurtry wrote "The appeal cannot last forever . . . since the West definitely has been won, the cowboy must someday fade."[14] What McMurtry failed to take into account is the human desire to go back to one's roots, to learn one's history. As Selleck noted, "There's a bit of the frontier in all of us . . . . That's why Westerns are so much a part of the American spirit."[15] As a country, America is relatively young. Though our boundaries have been reached, explored and, some would say, exploited, the stories of how we got to where we are and the characters who peopled those stories will forever remain popular. This tale of two pretty good bad men is no exception.

CHAPTER 1

INTO THE WEST CAME MANY MEN

Into the West came many men, the first of whom was screenwriter William Goldman. For years he had been fascinated by the story of Butch Cassidy and the Sundance Kid and eventually wrote a screenplay about them. The script sparked a bidding war among the studios which Twentieth Century Fox won, acquiring the screenplay for a then record-shattering sum of $400,000. When *Butch Cassidy and the Sundance Kid* opened in theaters on September 23, 1969, audiences immediately fell in love with the wise-cracking outlaws on the run. They rewarded the studio with a box office take of $96 million,[1] making the film the most successful Western ever. The Academy of Motion Picture Arts & Sciences was also captivated by this film and awarded it four Oscars – Best Original Screenplay, Best Cinematography, Best Song and Best Original Score.

The popularity of *Butch Cassidy and the Sundance Kid* caught the attention of a young television writer-producer at Universal named Glen A. Larson. Larson was a Western history buff who was also familiar with Butch and Sundance. Convinced by the success of the film that there was an audience for a lighthearted comedy western series, Larson turned to another part of Butch Cassidy's story, one that William Goldman also found intriguing but had been unable to fit in his screenplay – amnesty.

Around the turn of the century, Butch Cassidy decided it might be safer to either retire or head to South America. Heber Wells, governor of Utah, and E.H. Harriman, president of the Union Pacific Railroad, were eager to put Butch Cassidy out of business, so they offered him a deal – amnesty and a job as a guard on the Union Pacific. A meeting was arranged, but a storm delayed Harriman and the governor on their way to the rendezvous with Butch. Butch waited long past the appointed hour, but eventually decided he'd been betrayed and left. With the amnesty deal now off, Butch headed for South America with Sundance and Etta Place.[2]

This historical incident was the springboard Larson needed to create a weekly television series. He believes, "Television is always very influenced by motion pictures and by the media . . . you generally can sell what they want to buy." [3]

With *Butch Cassidy and the Sundance Kid* setting records at the box office, it was obvious the television networks would want to buy a series that tapped into that audience. Of course, Larson couldn't just recreate *Butch Cassidy and the Sundance Kid*. He instead turned to his history books and latched on to the amnesty premise, a unique concept nonetheless based on fact. "I might not have made something like that up," Larson remembers, "because I wouldn't have thought it was too believable that they're going to give amnesty to a nationally known outlaw who stuck up all those trains." Intrigued by the possibilities, he set to work molding it into a premise suitable for network television. He wanted a pair of protagonists à la Butch and Sundance, but of course, using them was out of the question. "Maybe we could have because it's based on a true incident, so it's really historical, but I think [there] would have been a lot of legal problems if we had," Larson explains. Instead he took the historical Hole-In-The-Wall Gang member Kid Curry and matched him with the wholly imaginary Hannibal Heyes, a name he chose for its alliteration and because "it just sort of rolled off the tongue." He made Heyes and Curry outlaws on a par with Butch and Sundance – personable and intelligent – then added the amnesty deal along with a twist. In his show, amnesty would be the goal, won only after they've proved themselves worthy of it. After all, it seemed likely to Larson that pardoning two outlaws, no matter how well-liked by the populace, would be a matter of political delicacy. With the concept fleshed out, Larson was ready to pitch the idea and, following in William Goldman's footsteps, he became the second man to come into the West.

Frank Price was an experienced television producer at Universal in 1970. Reassessing his career goals, he realized he wanted to move out of the trenches and up into Universal's famous Black Tower as a television executive. Price approached Lew Wasserman, chairman of Universal Studios, and Sid Sheinberg, president of MCA, and made a proposal. While Universal was the number one program supplier to the networks, most of those shows were going to CBS and NBC. Price wanted to develop a relationship with ABC and to increase the amount of programming sold to them. Wasserman and Sheinberg agreed to his plan and Price began the transition from producer to studio executive.

It was at this time that Glen Larson made his pitch for *Alias Smith and Jones*. "Glen came to me and told me the idea that he had that was clearly a hit idea," Price recalls. "From that point on, it was a matter of 'Well, how do we get it done?'"[4] Price took the idea to Jerry Isenberg, Executive in Charge of Production at ABC. Isenberg liked it and, as was the procedure at ABC, set up a concept test.

Bringing a television series to life is a risky and expensive venture. ABC tried to mitigate the risks by asking focus groups what they thought of the various projects the network was considering buying. They would gather an audience of the right demographic mix and hand out written summaries presenting the concepts of potential series. The focus group would read the summaries, then answer questions designed to determine how well they liked each concept and how likely they would be to watch the series if it became a reality.

A week or so after the concept test was done, Isenberg relayed the bad news. *Alias Smith and Jones* failed. ABC's interest was wavering. The very low score it received from the focus group indicated that no one would be interested in watching two outlaws trying to earn an amnesty. Price was amazed. He began his Hollywood career as a script reader and story analyst and he knew a good concept when he saw it. Unable to believe *Alias Smith and Jones* fared so poorly, he asked Isenberg if he could read the summary they used in the test. "I read what they had and I said, 'This isn't what the show is, so you're testing something that we don't plan to do.'" Price asked if he could submit a summary of his own and have the concept retested. Isenberg agreed. "So I wrote a paragraph and gave it to them. They tested it and it came back with the highest concept [score] they had tested. You just had to tell it right." ABC gave the greenlight to proceed with the pilot. Frank Price, still with one foot in the production end of the business, would serve as the executive producer of the film, wielding creative control over the project. The third man had come into the West.

By the early summer of 1970, ABC had given Universal the order for fourteen episodes to begin airing at mid-season. Glen Larson began writing the pilot script. *Alias Smith and Jones* was Larson's first foray into the world of series creator, so a collaborator was brought in to help fine-tune the script. The collaborator was Douglas Heyes, a writer known for his deft touch with humorous Westerns, a skill developed during his stint writing and directing for *Maverick*.[5] While Heyes was perfectly happy to collaborate on the script, he had a policy of not putting his name on anything where he did not get sole writing credit; for *Alias Smith and Jones* he used the pseudonym Matthew Howard.

Larson was pleased to be working with a man who was one of his favorite writers, as well as something of a mentor. In 1959, Douglas Heyes was one of the core group of writers working with Roy Huggins on *Maverick*. Larson was a musician who decided to try his hand at writing a television script. He wrote a spec script for *Maverick* and, hoping to sell it, submitted it to Heyes, who read it and was impressed enough to give it a table reading with James Garner, Heyes and his wife all playing parts, much to the delight of the fledgling writer. Unfortunately, there was a writers' strike going on at the time which made it impossible for Heyes to buy Larson's script. Larson missed out on making his first sale, but was encouraged enough by Heyes's response to stick with writing.

Larson continued to write spec scripts while touring with his musical group The Four Preps. The group had been discovered at a high school talent contest in 1956 and signed to a long-term contract with Capitol Records. They enjoyed a long string of hits including "26 Miles," a song celebrating the island of Santa Catalina, located twenty-six miles off the coast of Southern California, and written by Larson and fellow group member Bruce Belland. That song set the tone for the West Coast beach sound of the sixties. "I wish we'd been as smart as Brian Wilson and the Beach Boys," Larson muses, "because we figured one song and that's over, you got to find something else." The Four Preps traveled the world, performing for students at college campuses and for the troops in Vietnam. Larson made his first sale as a writer to the series *12 O'Clock High* and saw his first screen credit – "Story by Glen A. Larson" – flash by on television just before he went on stage for a concert at the University of Arizona campus.

By this point Larson was tired of traveling and of being one of four with "all the disadvantages of a marriage without any of the advantages." He was ready to try a solo career as a television writer. His big break came with a spec script for *It Takes A Thief*. The series was a mid-season replacement show and was short on scripts, providing a welcome opportunity for a newcomer. Larson pitched a story to producer Gene Coon, who told him that if he could have the script on his desk by Monday, he'd buy it. Larson returned with the script on Monday. "They liked it so much they make me the story editor," Larson remembers. He continued writing for *It Takes A Thief*, eventually becoming a producer. He also worked on *McCloud* and *The Virginian* before getting the opportunity to create his own show with *Alias Smith and Jones*.[6]

For eight weeks Douglas Heyes and Glen Larson worked on the pilot script and finally at the end of September 1970, it was time to cast the roles. Into the West came two more men – Peter Duel and Ben Murphy.

(Sagala/Bagwell collection)

The Penfield, New York, house in which Peter Duel grew up. It is now home to several businesses.

Peter Ellstrom Deuel was born on February 24, 1940, the eldest child of Dr. Ellsworth and Lillian Deuel. He grew up in the small town of Penfield, New York, in a one hundred year old house that served as both the family home and his father's medical office. Behind the house were woods that Peter and siblings Geoff and Pam used as their own private playground. "We had a wonderful childhood," Peter once told an interviewer.[7]

Bright but not academically motivated, Peter skated through school, preferring a confrontation with the principal to the boredom of the classroom.[8] School was something that got in the way of his preferred outdoor activities. "I resented the way the school was ruining my day, making me waste time hanging around between classes."[9] His lackadaisical attitude extended even to the drama department where he participated in school plays, but abstained from learning his lines, a habit he occasionally indulged in even after becoming a professional actor.

Despite a happy childhood and a loving family, Peter became suicidal as a teen. His view of the world around him was bleak and he personally felt useless. "I didn't know what was going to happen to me if I died, but it seemed the only sensible thing to do."[10] He resisted the urge to kill himself at age sixteen, but never really recovered from the depression that drove the urge.

Peter's love of aviation had given him the ambition to be an Air Force pilot, but he was rejected when his vision tested at 20/30 rather than the required 20/20. However, in 1967 a journalist noted in her article, "Ironically, at the present – nearly nine years later – Pete has 20/20 vision. The only explanation for the previous reading would seem to have been fatigue . . ."[11] While it's possible Peter's eye test was influenced by fatigue, there is another explanation for his rejection. Peter had epilepsy. "He would have petit mal seizures," former girlfriend Kim Darby confides, "You couldn't really recognize them, but he would just go out for a minute and then come back."[12] While this could be dealt with in day-to-day life, it would not be acceptable in an Air Force pilot. As an actor, though, it didn't slow him down. As Jo Swerling recalls, "He never used [the epilepsy] as an excuse and it never affected his work."[13]

With the Air Force plan foiled, he attended St. Lawrence University in Canton, New York, more because it was a family tradition than from a real desire for higher education. Officially, Peter majored in English, Drama and Psychology, a pretty full load for someone who disliked school. Unofficially, he "majored in drinking and girls."[14] He moved in to Lee Hall, the freshman residence, and met a kindred spirit, Jack Jobes. The two became good friends. "We were *always* in trouble," Jobes remembers, "because we just didn't go with the mainstream." Their early days at St. Lawrence were spent making sure they didn't run out of beer and avoiding upperclassmen who delighted in hazing freshmen.

One night Jobes and Peter, along with other friends, staged a panty raid, a very daring escapade at the conservative school. Someone hissed, "The Dean's coming!" Peter put his head down and *ran*. Straight into a tree. The Dean of Men picked him up and commanded, "Mr. Deuel, I'll see you in my office!" Jobes laughs as he recalls, "And that was it, he was busted again."[15]

In his sophomore year, Peter was cast in *The Rose Tattoo*. His father came to see the performance and afterward encouraged Peter to leave St. Lawrence and enroll in drama school instead. "Why don't you go to New York now and stop wasting your time and my money?"[16] he asked his son. This advice coincided with the Dean's announcement that Peter Deuel was now *persona non grata* at St.

Lawrence, so Peter left the university and auditioned for The American Theatre Wing. He was accepted and spent two years there learning his craft and gaining practical experience. He returned to St. Lawrence as a visiting actor in what would have been his senior year, starring in *Born Yesterday* with Jack Jobes and Connie Ming.

His first television role came in 1961 when he appeared in an episode of *Armstrong Circle Theater,* one of the major dramatic anthology shows from television's "Golden Age." A part in the theatrical film *Wounded In Action* followed, which in turn led to a co-starring role in the national company of *Take Her, She's Mine.* The six-month tour provided Peter with his first glimpse of Los Angeles and after the tour ended he made up his mind to give up New York and the pursuit of Broadway in exchange for Hollywood and the pursuit of film and television.

In 1963 Peter made the move across country in a trip he described as an adventure wherein he scorned hotels and simply pitched a tent when he was ready to stop. He complained about a rainy spell in the Rocky Mountains, but the overall impression is that the journey was one long camping trip for this solitary young man.[17] However, he didn't make the trip alone. "His mother came out with him. They made the drive from New York. 'Come on, Petey, I'll get you going.' Isn't that neat?" friend Dennis Fimple recalled, still finding her devotion to her son charming after all these years.[18]

Once settled in Southern California, Peter made the rounds of auditions, where he won parts in series such as *Combat!, Gomer Pyle USMC, 12 O'Clock High* and *The Fugitive.* While these early roles were small, he was consistently employed and was becoming known in the industry. He developed a plan for his career – five years in Hollywood to establish his name, then back to New York and the Broadway stage. He also began playing with the spelling of his name, being variously credited as Peter E. Deuel, Peter Deuel, and Pete Deuel, before finally settling on the short and snappy Pete Duel. In 1965 he got his first real break when he became a regular on *Gidget,* playing stuffy brother-in-law John Cooper opposite Sally Field's free-spirited Gidget. The series lasted only one season, and Peter did not appear in every episode, but he was already being noticed by the teen magazines.

In 1966 Peter won the role of David Willis in *Love on a Rooftop,* where he co-starred with Judy Carne and moved into the ranks of full-fledged Hollywood heartthrobs. Suddenly every aspect of his life was fodder for movie magazines and his status as a handsome, eligible bachelor was of the utmost importance to teenage girls across the nation. *Love on a Rooftop* was a new breed of sitcom that found humor in realistic situations rather than in the fantasy worlds offered by *Bewitched* and *I Dream of Jeannie* or the improbable rural antics of *Green Acres* and *The Beverly Hillbillies.* Julie and Dave Willis were average people faced with average problems, inhabiting the same world the audience did. This realism contributed to its demise, because "it delivered very human, very funny characters in mildly realistic situations that many young adults could identify with. In doing so, the program was years ahead of its time – and it was totally destroyed by the more familiar competition of NBC's movies and CBS's *Petticoat Junction*."[19]

After *Love on a Rooftop's* cancellation, Peter signed a seven year contract with Universal and interspersed television guest spots with movie roles, appearing in feature films *The Hell with Heroes* in 1968, *Generation* in 1969 and *Cannon for Cordoba* in 1970, as well as in two failed television pilots – *The Scavengers* (a.k.a. *Only One Day Left before Tomorrow* and *How to Steal an Airplane*) in 1968 and *The Young Country* in 1970. During this time, Peter also became involved in politics, campaigning for Senator Eugene McCarthy during the 1968 presidential election. As a celebrity worker he was invited to the Democratic Convention in Chicago where he found himself facing a National Guardsman's bayonet in the midst of the riot. Jo Swerling recalls, "He witnessed all of this stuff and came back having nightmares about it. . . . It affected him very, very deeply, that whole experience."[20]

(Sagala collection)

Peter Duel as Hannibal Heyes.

Peter was enjoying the variety and the challenge that came with his guest star roles and wasn't particularly interested in starring in another series when *Alias Smith and Jones* came along in late 1970. But he was still under contract to Universal and they wanted him for Hannibal Heyes. Price explains, "Clearly we wanted Ben. The hard one to get was Peter, because he was a little mercurial, very talented. If we could get him, it was 'Lock him in.'" Somewhat to Price's surprise they were able to lock him in. Peter later complained that he was forced into accepting the role, saying, "I had no choice . . . As a player under contract, I had to do what Universal told me."[21] However, this claim might have been an attempt by Peter to justify his unhappiness, because Frank Price had been by no means certain they would be able to convince him to take the role. Forcing Peter to accept it just because he was under contract was not a tactic Price would consider using. "It never did any good to hold [a contract] over anyone's head," Price recalls. "You had to persuade them it was the right role because you didn't want an unhappy actor in there. Going in you know they're going to be unhappy ultimately because it's very difficult to do a series week in and week out." So while Peter might have felt he was obligated to take the part being offered to him, from Price's perspective it wasn't a sure thing. "I look back on it and say it was sort of fluke time. I was pleased to have him. He was in the right mood."[22]

During *Alias Smith and Jones's* too short run, journalists referred to Ben Murphy as television's Robert Redford.[23] Kid Curry, who remarkably resembled the other half of the Butch/Sundance duo, Paul Newman, had become the small screen's answer to the Sundance Kid.

(Courtesy of Chris Fimple)

Peter Duel as Hannibal Heyes.

(Courtesy of Ben Murphy)

Peter Duel.

Benjamin Edward Lesse Castleberry was born in Jonesboro, Arkansas, on March 6, 1942. His parents, Ben, Sr. and Nadine, divorced when he was two years old and Ben lived with his grandparents in Memphis. While his mother worked as an accountant, Ben spent his early years on the Tennessee farm. After his father died in 1956, his mother re-married and Patrick Henry Murphy officially adopted Nadine's young son and gave him his own surname.

As an only child, his early years accustomed Ben to seclusion. Eventually though, life on the farm grew too quiet and he was glad when, during his elementary school years, his parents moved to a house on Indian Head Drive in the Chicago suburb of Clarendon Hills. When his stepfather's business, wholesale produce, was hit by a recession, he and Ben's mother opened a women's clothing store. It was a profitable business venture. Mrs. Murphy, who also owned the land and the building, became a successful entrepreneur.

Teenage Ben Murphy with younger brother, Timothy Patrick.

Ben was fifteen years old when a baby brother was born. Because of the difference in ages, Ben was not particularly close to his brother but took care of little Timothy Patrick while his parents worked and admits to doing his share of "diaper duty." By the time Tim was past babyhood, Ben was out on his own, working and pursuing higher education and then investing in his acting career. When Tim grew up he studied law and passed the bar exam, eventually clerking for a California Supreme Court judge. Sadly, he was killed in a rock-climbing accident in 1984.[24]

As a college student, Ben was hardly typical. Over the course of acquiring his degree, he attended several universities for the education, of course, but also to avoid being drafted. He began his studies at Loras College, a Catholic school for men in Dubuque, Iowa. Sophomore year was spent at Loyola in New Orleans. For the next two years, Ben studied International Relations at the University of the Americas in Mexico City. During that time he began a serious romance with an American girl who was a fellow student. They were young, in a foreign country, and the magic of his first love remains strong in his memory.

After their breakup, Ben headed back to the States to Chicago's Loyola University and then to the University of Illinois at Champaign-Urbana where his interest in world affairs and his accrued credits led him to major in political science and history. He remains a lover of history and an observer of politics. In his senior year, Ben joined the university drama group. Though he had only a small part in the class's production of *Julius Caesar,* he found that he enjoyed acting. Because he had decided it was something he really wanted to do, he worked hard at it. As he does with most things that require his concentration, Ben centered all his attention on his new interest.

After graduation in 1964, he set out for Hollywood and attended the Pasadena Playhouse, graduating two years later with a second Bachelor of Arts degree, this one in Theater. In succeeding years, he also did some graduate work at the University of Southern California and spent only one day at San Fernando Valley State College. "I was so used to going to college that I just wanted to go to college [for] anything! It didn't make any difference. I signed up and then I realized . . . I could be just as busy with private classes and workouts and working that I didn't necessarily need to be in school any more. But it was almost like a security blanket, I didn't want to let it go."[25]

During the time he was at Pasadena Playhouse, he performed in all kinds of stage plays, some in very minor roles evidenced by his name listed with twenty-five others under "Soldiers, Townsfolk, etc." in *The Devil's Disciple.* As stage manager of *Always with Love,* he learned the importance of behind-the-scenes supervision. "It was the most work I had ever done in my life, but I felt I had found myself, that finally this was the real me." Bob Thompson, a talent executive at Universal, saw him in the role of the eldest son during the production of *Life with Father* and signed him to a seven year contract in 1967, promising him he was headed for the top, not just on television, but in the movies. It was a good contract but, of course, it was also in the best interest of Universal. It was regularly reported that actors who signed eventually came to regret the decision, feeling indentured, but Ben cites that as a common complaint of the time and not necessarily true. Under the old studio system, as many as fifty contract players were kept on payroll. Then Lew Wasserman launched a new talent program headed by Monique James. Since studios no longer had time or money to teach the craft of acting, actors were expected to come prepared to work. James said that actors might "get a script one day and be in front of the camera the next."[26]

It was that way with Ben. Shortly after he was signed, his first appearance was in the 1967 film *The Graduate* but it's hard to spot him. His face is lathered with shaving cream and his only line is "Save a piece for me," referring to the party

cake. It wasn't much, but it got him into *Yours, Mine and Ours* the next year with Henry Fonda and Lucille Ball in which he played the hippie boyfriend of one of their daughters. After that he spent two years as Robert Stack's sidekick Joe Sample in *The Name of the Game*.[27]

In the fall of 1970 when Glen Larson and Frank Price held auditions for the roles of Hannibal Heyes and Kid Curry, Ben was brought in. "I had such little chance for the *Alias Smith and Jones* co-lead that they didn't call me until the night before the auditions were going to be held," he remembers. "I was strictly from left field. Another young prospect was getting all the attention . . . I remember there were five chairs and six actors and I was the only one who didn't get a chair that day, so I sort of thought maybe I didn't have a good chance . . ." The studio spent the whole day testing and Ben was fortunate enough to be tested with Peter Duel. He clicked with the dark-haired young actor, the casting director liked what he saw, and he got the role.[28] Jo Swerling, associate executive producer on the show, believed that while Peter was a more accomplished actor and comedian than Ben was at the time, Ben had that inexplicable something called charisma.[29]

Before the series could begin production, one more man needed to come into the West. From the beginning Frank Price realized that, although Glen Larson had some producer credits under his belt, he was not experienced enough to be a showrunner. He needed a mentor. Price turned to a man with a wealth of experience; a man who was talented, who was available and who was, incidentally, his father-in-law – Roy Huggins.

Huggins became a writer accidentally during World War II. A bad knee kept him out of the military; instead he ended up in a government job and became the Special Representative in Charge of Recruitment, National War Agencies (West Coast). By late 1943, his work was essentially finished and, with the war in its final stages, personnel turnover had become a serious problem which the government addressed by freezing people in their jobs. No government employee was allowed to quit. Huggins was one of those who found himself going to his office every day, but not having anything to do once he got there. To pass the time, he decided to write a novel. Having read and enjoyed Raymond Chandler's *Farewell, My Lovely,* Huggins decided to, in his words, "shamelessly [write] a Chandler novel of my own."[30]

When the manuscript was finished, he sent it off to Howard Browne, editor of *Mammoth Detective* magazine. Browne responded with a rejection letter and a long list of notes on how to improve the story. Huggins revised the book and sent it back to Browne, who bought it instantly. Following that sale, Huggins wrote eight hours every day, "just as if I knew what I was doing." He wrote two novelettes which were published in the *Saturday Evening Post* and a second novel that went nowhere. By this time the war was over and Huggins decided to go to graduate school as he originally intended. He was making arrangements to return to UCLA and begin working toward a Ph.D. in political science when he got a call from Hollywood agent Ray Stark.

Within a few days of that phone call, Huggins had been hired to write a screenplay adaptation of his novel *The Double Take.* This deal led to his being hired as a screenwriter at Columbia, a position from which he was summarily fired and rehired twice before moving on to Warner Bros., where he first became involved in television. In 1955 he was summoned to a meeting by William T. Orr, Executive Producer of Warner Bros. Television. *Warner Bros Presents,* the umbrella title for three rotating series based on the films *King's Row, Casablanca* and *Cheyenne,* was that studio's first venture into television. Orr was in desperate need of a new producer for *Cheyenne,* the western portion of the series, which was in danger of losing its sponsor because of the poor quality of its scripts. He offered control of the show to Huggins, who worked on many westerns during his time at Columbia. Huggins agreed and so began his lengthy career in television.

Roy Huggins knew instinctively what made a good television series and the audience usually agreed with him. *Maverick, 77 Sunset Strip, The Fugitive, The Rockford Files* – these are just a few of his creations that enjoyed enormous popular and critical success. He was perhaps best known for *Maverick,* a show that turned all the conventions of the traditional Western upside down. Huggins left that show after only two years due to ill health, long before he had a chance to get tired of it. Looking at the concept of *Alias Smith and Jones,* he realized it had wonderful possibilities. "I took it over because I saw a chance to revive *Maverick* but with the two guys playing together all the time," Huggins recalled. "And I thought, 'Hey, that's great, I can do some more.'... I would never have taken it if it hadn't been for the idea of being able to resurrect *Maverick* with a different kind of background and a slightly different pair of heroes."[31]

On November 16, 1970, Huggins and Price screened a rough cut of the pilot. Huggins was not impressed. He felt the pilot was dreadful, a non-story. He knew that Larson used *Butch Cassidy and the Sundance Kid* as the basis for the show and

"A new-fangled invention." This publicity photo was taken before Roy Huggins set the series back to the 1880s.

felt that "as an imitator [Larson] had no understanding of what was good about what he was imitating and what was bad about it. He just imitated." Huggins added two conditions that would have to be met before he would agree to take over the show. First, the outlaw gang had to be changed from integral characters appearing in every episode to recurring characters appearing only occasionally. Second, the time period had to be switched from 1900, where Larson had set it, back two decades. "A western must not go beyond 1880," Huggins explained. "As soon as it gets into telephones and the earliest versions of automobiles you have a different world." Larson disagreed with this assessment; he thought the turn-of-the-century western was unexplored territory and would make an interesting backdrop. Frank Price had the final say, however, and decided to go with Huggins's instincts. "I agreed because that wasn't going to make or break the series and it would be confusing . . . better to keep it simple. If it added a great deal that was another thing, but it wouldn't. This was going to be based on the appeal of these two guys as these characters."[32] Price rewrote the opening narration of the pilot, changing Larson's references to the end of the Wild West and early twentieth century technology into an introduction of Hannibal Heyes and Kid Curry as "two pretty good bad men . . . and in all the trains and banks they robbed they never shot anyone." With his conditions met, Roy Huggins officially became the executive producer of *Alias Smith and Jones,* the final man to come into the West.

Roy Huggins had a somewhat unusual method of working, a habit that grew in part out of a dispute he'd had with Warner Bros during his *Maverick* days. Warner Bros was a company known for what is politely termed its thriftiness. In violation of a new rule that was part of the Writers Guild of America's Basic Agreement, Jack Warner had been successful in keeping Huggins from receiving a creator's credit on *Maverick* which would have given him a royalty for every episode produced. Warner followed that with another blow. He refused to pay Huggins for scripts he wrote for a show he was producing, despite a clause in Huggins's contract requiring such payment. Huggins had no choice but to go along if he wanted to get *Maverick* on the air, but he fought back in a subtle way. His "don't get mad, get even" scheme was to give his stories to other writers. Those writers turned them into scripts, which Warner then had to pay for. Huggins wasn't being paid for his stories, but Warner wasn't getting them for free, either.[33]

(Bagwell collection)

UL: **Livery stable on Universal's backlot** UR: **Hotel on Universal's backlot**
LL: **Train Station on Universal's backlot** LR: **Porterville bank on Universal's backlot**

On *Alias Smith and Jones,* Huggins again gave his stories to other writers, but he did retain full story credit under the pseudonym John Thomas James.[34] The prolific John Thomas James receives story credit on forty-three of the fifty episodes of the series, a sign of the total control Huggins wielded over the story-telling process.

Huggins's favorite method of story development was to go on long "story drives." With a tape recorder on the seat beside him, he would talk out the story while driving aimlessly, often ending up in Oregon, Arizona or New Mexico. This unlocked his creativity, but often worried his staff. According to Jo Swerling, "He was a perfectly terrible driver, and we used to worry about whether we would ever see him again when he would take off." His trips usually lasted about a week and he would return home with six or seven fully worked out stories. Swerling says, "All of us who worked with Roy were in awe of his ability to do this."[35] Huggins's story tapes would be transcribed, then a writer would be called in. Huggins would tell the writer the story and the two of them would refine it, tossing ideas back and forth, working out rough spots. After the meeting, the writer would go off to write the teleplay armed with a lengthy outline, often twenty to twenty-five pages of detailed notes and sample dialogue. The collaboration between Huggins and the writer would continue through numerous story conferences as the script was rewritten and polished.

(Jerry Ohlinger's Movie Materials Store)

It was now the middle of November 1970. The pilot film was in post-production, on schedule to be completed and delivered to ABC for its January 5, 1971, broadcast. Eleven scripts were in varying stages of development, but after reviewing them, Huggins threw out nine. During his first week on the show, in between meetings with ABC executives and his production staff, Huggins developed four totally new stories. With only two months to go before *Alias Smith and Jones* would have its series premiere, there was no time to waste. The final two weeks of November were filled with story conferences, with scripts being written and rewritten at great speed. "The McCreedy Bust" was selected to be the first episode to air and the work required to meet the network deadline called for a grueling pace. Huggins told the story to writer Sy Salkowitz at a story conference on November 24, received Salkowitz's first draft on November 29, and after reading it, decided to completely rewrite the script himself, finishing his own draft on December 1. He revised the script between December 1 and 3, then held a production meeting on Friday, December 4. On Monday, December 7, shooting began. In just two weeks "The McCreedy Bust" had gone from a story in Roy Huggins's head to a final shooting script.

Alias Smith and Jones was already behind and they had only just started. Huggins knew from experience it was going to take eight calendar days to shoot each episode of a show that aired every seven days. To solve this mathematical problem on *Maverick,* Huggins had introduced Brother Bart and was able to shoot two episodes simultaneously. On *Alias Smith and Jones* he already had two characters, so the only solution was to split them up. Huggins developed stories that separated Heyes and Curry so production could be expedited, but kept these episodes to the absolute minimum number necessary to solve his production issues. For the next four months, the cast and crew worked non-stop. Production was so tight that the schedule didn't allow for days lost to illness, weather or any other delay to shooting.

It was an exhausting time for all concerned, but the result was a program that held its own against the fierce competition of *The Flip Wilson Show,* a modicum of success for which third-ranked ABC was extremely grateful.

Chapter 2

Two Latter-Day Robin Hoods

As the super-posse pursues Butch Cassidy and his cohort the Sundance Kid over scrub, across rivers and up mountains, Butch frequently turns back to observe the unflagging pursuit. "Who are those guys?" he·wonders, that they can hold to the trail with nary a misstep or wrong turn. Television viewers might wonder the same thing about outlaw partners Hannibal Heyes and Kid Curry. However, in trying to determine the wheres and whens of Heyes and Curry, alias Smith and Jones, subtle, frequent missteps and obvious, ubiquitous wrong turns are not only required study but also unavoidable.

Wise writers, whether they pen stories for fiction tomes or television series, create a canon or backstory for their characters. Having a history and a list of characteristics guarantees consistency throughout the work. When different writers submit story ideas for a TV series, it is especially important to have such a written bible. Roy Huggins admitted *Alias Smith and Jones* did not. Given his genius and experience in westerns, Huggins knew his characters, what they would do and how they would act in any situation and often literally sent writers back to their typewriters with notes about how his people would behave. In one set of notes, Huggins told the teleplay writer: "In their own rough way, they should be a lot more sophisticated than they are in the present draft. They are more worldly. Curry is just as knowing as Heyes. The writer should go through the script and upgrade the level of sophistication. Our boys should be sharper, smoother. When they're with women, they're much more apt to say things like Cary Grant than like John Wayne."[1]

Occasionally a story line allowed Huggins to insert his own philosophy, humor or love of history into a script and if it made a good story, it didn't much matter that it didn't jibe with tenets already established. Viewers of *Alias Smith and Jones* in the 1970s had no access to video recorders which would allow them to record the program at 8 p.m. and view it later, repeatedly, or in slow motion. Inconsistencies were hard to spot unless one had a perfect memory. In the pilot, Kid Curry doesn't know what "amnesty" means. A few episodes later, he refers to their newfound friend Michelle as a *chanteuse,* yet when they encounter

Georgette on her way to Tombstone for her audition as a *chanteuse,* he doesn't know what that means. Another time, he cautions the Jordan girls to use "finesse" when pulling a con on a gullible stranger. Was he, or was he not, an educated man?

An attempt to create a canon or a timeline from the "facts" supplied by the characters leads to frustration. Because creator Glen Larson and producer Roy Huggins were history buffs, occasionally they used a verifiable date as a story tack as in "The Strange Fate of Conrad Meyer Zulick," when in 1885, Zulick became governor of Arizona with a little help from Heyes and Curry. In other instances, some dates are verifiably wrong. According to Huggins, the 1880s is *the* decade for westerns, so how does Hannibal Heyes know about Denver's Brown Palace Hotel which wasn't built until 1892? In one instance Wheat Carlson, wannabe leader of the Devil's Hole Gang, cites the excitement at Black Jack Ketchum's hanging that wouldn't take place until 1901. It is mental exercise to figure out just who those two lovable rogues were who gave up their outlaw identities, Hannibal Heyes and Kid Curry, to become the less infamous Joshua Smith and Thaddeus Jones. We must deal with the unwritten canon so far as we can deduce it from what the characters reveal in conversations or situations and from the few dates provided. With a little fudging, it almost makes sense.

(Courtesy of Chris Fimple)

The Devil's Hole Gang.

The narrator calls them Kansas cousins but, since Kansas did not open for settlement until 1854, it is more likely that they were born elsewhere. Hannibal Heyes may have been named for the Missouri town. Glen Larson named him and liked the alliteration. It didn't much matter what his first name was, as only one person, Big Jim Santana, ever referred to Heyes by his Christian name. Jedediah Curry may have become "the Kid" out of several options. "Jed" sounds similar to "Kid." Michelle Monet guessed in "Journey from San Juan" that he was called "Kid," because "there's still a lot of little boy" in him. It may have been simply Larson's fascination with the historical Kid Curry of Cassidy's Hole-in-the-Wall Gang.

Initially identified in the narration as latter-day Robin Hoods who "robbed from the rich and kept the money," Heyes's and Curry's names are already familiar to the train conductor when viewers meet them in the pilot. Up to that date, they had never been caught, probably because, as Wyoming Governor Baxter noticed, they "don't look like outlaws." But they are also already wanted dead or alive and worth $10,000 each, according to the posters circulated to lawmen about them. Though the posters may have been printed mid-way through, or nearer the end, of their outlawry, Curry is listed as being twenty-seven and Heyes twenty-nine years of age. Other posted details are more reliable. They are both five feet eleven inches in height. Curry, at 165, outweighs Heyes by five pounds. Curry's blond hair and blue eyes contrast nicely with Heyes's brown hair and brown eyes.

Of Irish and English ancestry, Hannibal Heyes and Kid Curry share a common grandfather, making them cousins. Historically, it was not unusual for family members to run in the same outlaw gang. Frank and Jesse James; Emmett, Grat and Bob Dalton; and Billy and Ike Clanton are a few of the well-known familial desperadoes. Even Huggins's earlier creations – the Maverick boys – were related. Though the idea of Heyes and Curry being related was not specified until well into the second season, Roy Huggins knew all along that they were. It wasn't until he had gotten used to working with them that he decided he needed to know a little bit more about how they got together in the first place. Because they were so close, and in many ways much alike, he made them cousins.[2] However, in the beginning of the third season, he inexplicably decided to abandon that relationship in favor of their simply growing up together.[3]

The Devil's Hole Gang visits the set of *Planet of the Apes*.

The boys reveal their folks were killed in the border wars, and they were about ten years old when the war started. Here their birth dates can be judiciously manipulated to account for ambiguous discrepancies. Did that mean the Civil War in general or the war when it reached their corner of Kansas two years later or even the border skirmishes that preceded the war? Unlike other men they encounter in the episode "The Bounty Hunter," it is clear from their lack of prejudice toward Joe Sims, the black bounty hunter, that they would have fought for the Union had they been old enough. During his impressionable pre-teen years, though, both the Rebs' and the Unionists' arguments made sense to Heyes. For his part, Curry dismissed both as wrong.

After the death of their parents, they were sent to the Valparaiso School for Waywards, implying that, not only were they orphans, but perhaps had already gotten into mischief. There they attended church services every Sunday, accounting for their many references to religion in later years. Curry quotes the Bible as though he is very familiar with it. In San Juan, he tells Michelle that Blanche will believe what she says as though it were "carved in stone and handed down from a mountain." He advises evangelist Sister Grace in Apache Springs that she has to have faith, just like it says in the book she carries, even though she is incapable of spewing hellfire and damnation. Evidently Curry has heard enough good preachers who made his blood run cold that he recognizes an inferior one. He has enough faith to believe that Heyes can pull off a miracle in Santa Marta and he even suspects the amnesty brochure Miss Birdie hands him in the pilot may be some sort of religious tract. Heyes too has his religious moments, reminding the sheriff in Red Rock, Montana, that "he who lives by the sword has got to expect to die by the sword." It may have been at a Sunday service where he learned the Shaker hymn "Simple Gifts" with which he entertains the Jordan family. Borrowing an adage from the good book, he pleads with the Kid to "turn the other cheek" at Joe Briggs's bullying in "McCreedy Bust: Going, Going, Gone." But perhaps the most fervent we see Heyes is when he hollers a "thank you" heavenward at finding water in the desert after Danny Bilson steals their horses and canteens.

Maybe Valparaiso was not the Vale of Paradise its name implies. Around 1867, after being there about five years, they ran away and, at age fifteen, pulled their first job, "which didn't seem all that different from everything [they'd] seen going on the past five years," while the Civil War raged around them. Many soldiers home from the war, jobless and unable to adapt to civilian life, turned to crime as a way to make a living. Curry, who learned to shoot before he could shave, may have already put his marksmanship talents to use. A year later, when Curry was about sixteen, Artie Gorman took the ruffians under his wing. By then they had been in enough trouble that, had he not, they wouldn't have made it to seventeen.

After Artie set them on the straight and narrow, or at least taught them self-preservation if they would decide to follow a life of crime, they turned to honest work. Driving cattle on the Chisholm Trail in 1873-74, they would have started the herd in Texas where they met Joe Horner, later known as Frank Canton. Horner had his cattle rustling career going in 1874. The boys made some money at trail driving but spent hard days in the saddle and no doubt caroused in the Kansas cowtowns at trail's end, a typical cowboy experience for twenty-two-year-olds. When asked in later years what they do for a living, the answer frequently is "as little as possible." It's likely that the hard days on the trail were enough to convince them of the comparative ease of an outlaw's life, except when he was running for it. Train and bank robbing beckoned with lucrative rewards, not to mention the "glamour and glory" of being an outlaw.

It is here that we need to separate the cousins in order to make sense of Heyes's story of the first gang he rode with. It was led by Jim Plummer, as Heyes informs Curry (and the viewers) when they meet his former leader using an alias in Wickenburg. Heyes also tells Curry that he was the "champeen tracker" in southern Utah, something Curry evidently didn't know and has trouble believing, given Heyes's lack of talent in a hunt for wild cats.

While separated, Curry, at least, traveled extensively. He had been as far as Philadelphia though he didn't remember it fondly, recalling not much about the city except it was "kinda dusty." When the two encounter a loud-mouthed drover in a Porterville saloon, the bully didn't know Heyes, but recognized Curry who was "one jump ahead of a posse" when he saw him near Fort Griffin, due west of Fort Worth, Texas. Because speculation is the only way to make sense of some traits or "facts," we shall assume that Curry learned to fast draw and practiced it frequently during the separation. In Wickenburg he continues to practice just to keep his skills up. His weapon serves them both well and in a third of the episodes he faces another man's gun. He rarely draws first and even announces that fact to his opponent. He never shoots to kill but the sight of Curry's gun cocked and ready to fire deters a man reaching for his own. Only the demand for justice for Seth provokes Curry enough to pull the trigger against Danny, the smiler with a gun.

As for Heyes's movements, he has never been east of the Mississippi river, but he may have stood on its banks wondering what went wrong after a failed attempt to rob the Mercantile Bank in St. Louis. In his rejection of Mrs. Fielding's claim that he represents the average western man, he implies a love for the west and a sense that he's seen quite a bit of it.

Heyes mentions that he grew up on a farm, but presumably he was sent to school and probably did quite well, given his intelligence, cunning, and inventive mind. He skipped the Latin courses, evidenced by his stumbling over *incommunicado* in the pilot episode and daydreamed through grammar class, not learning the difference of usage between *don't* and *doesn't*. Perhaps he learned his manners at his mother's knee or at school as well. In several instances, with a gentle nudge, he reminds Curry of his. It's proper form to remove one's hat in church and to stand when greeting a lady for dinner. The etiquette and gentility served him well in cons where he needed to act as a gentleman from Baltimore or a wealthy silver mine owner. He obviously loves to read and is the first of the two to pick up a stray newspaper. In devouring Mark Twain's *Life on the Mississippi,* Heyes discovers a valuable detection tool and uses the knowledge to save a friend from a murder charge.

If Heyes had been a twenty-first century student, he would have excelled on the debate team. Curry recognizes, and generally accedes to, Heyes's silver tongue. This gift for being able to "talk himself out of a tiger's belly" comes in handy when he needs to convince Harry Wagoner there's a bomb in the money bag; when he convinces Ribs to make a deal with Curt Clitterhouse; and when he talks Sarah Henderson into returning to her husband. As Curry is equally fond of pointing out, however, sometimes Heyes's tongue is not so silver. He fails to get Fred Philpotts to recant his lie about being Kid Curry and his long-winded diatribe to bounty hunter Joe Sims fails to create any doubt in Sims that he's got the wrong men.

(Sagala collection)

Nevertheless, Curry frequently turns over the thinking and planning to his partner. When the Kid does attempt to come up with a solution to their current dilemma, Heyes reminds him that they've had a pretty good arrangement wherein he does all the mental work. Curry does not appear to be as well-read as his cousin, wondering who the man behind the alias "Mark Twain" might be. Heyes does give Curry credit for having read *Tom Sawyer* three or four times but diminishes the praise with an observation that, as far as being able

Ben Murphy as Kid Curry.

to spout a philosophy, Curry is "somewhat inarticulate – you might even say stupid." Because of the circumstances, Curry does not deck his partner, but if looks could kill . . . even though Curry himself admits, "I'm not much of a talker. More of a man for action than words."

Giving up any semblance of being law-abiding, Heyes, in his early twenties, became leader of the Devil's Hole Gang, a position he held for seven years, taking over from Big Jim Santana. A year into his leadership, the cousins re-unite, Curry joins the gang and becomes Heyes's right hand man. Presumably with the gang, they emptied the latest model safe, a Pierce & Hamilton 1878, in Denver's Merchants' Bank and in the bank in Wichita but couldn't do it by manipulating the tumblers. They are sadly familiar with the workings and "un-robbable-ness" of Brooker 202 safes in St. Louis, in the Farmer's Bank in Fort Worth and the one in the train car. Heyes had to invent a new way to open them and came up with the dangerous but effective method of using nitroglycerin and a Bryant pump to create a vacuum to blow the doors open. This method worked fine for stationary safes in banks. Dynamite was the method of execution for those hauled in railroad cars. The train in the pilot was not the first they had stopped. On one occasion, they hit a train at Emeryville, and twice stopped the gold train headed to and from the Denver mint.

After the failed attempt to open the safe in the pilot and tired of being chased by posses, Heyes and Curry express interest in Miss Birdie's flyer on amnesty. Deciding to "get outta this business," they consult former outlaw-turned-sheriff Lom Trevors. They ask for and receive his help in convincing the Wyoming governor of their good intentions. Lom introduces them to Miss Porter as Mr. Smith and Mr. Jones, conferring on them their aliases by which he will know them in the future.

For having performed with such excellence throughout their criminal career, enough to make them "the two most successful outlaws in the history of the West," it is peculiar that only the law in Wyoming wants them. This may be simply because that's where the Union Pacific Railroad, Wells Fargo, and Western Cattlemen's Association filed their charges or where the court convened to try them *in absentia* for their crimes. Wyoming, unlike other states and territories, had no statute of limitations at that time, so they are quite sure if they are captured and extradited to Wyoming, a twenty-year jail sentence awaits them. Viewers never learn whether this was the customary sentence handed down in

Wyoming to robbers, or if they *had* been legally tried and convicted and managed to escape prison. The latter seems less likely because they are still on the loose, even after speaking directly with the governor.

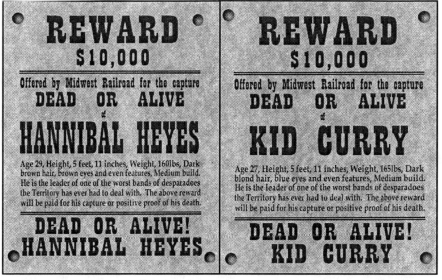

REWARD
$10,000
Offered by Midwest Railroad for the capture
DEAD   OR   ALIVE
of
HANNIBAL HEYES
Age 29, Height, 5 feet, 11 inches, Weight, 160lbs, Dark brown hair, brown eyes and even features, Medium build. He is the leader of one of the worst bands of desparadoes the Territory has ever had to deal with. The above reward will be paid for his capture or positive proof of his death.
DEAD OR ALIVE!
HANNIBAL HEYES

REWARD
$10,000
Offered by Midwest Railroad for the capture
DEAD   OR   ALIVE
of
KID CURRY
Age 27, Height, 5 feet, 11 inches, Weight, 165lbs, Dark blond hair, blue eyes and even features, Medium build. He is the leader of one of the worst bands of desparadoes the Territory has ever had to deal with. The above reward will be paid for his capture or positive proof of his death.
DEAD OR ALIVE!
KID CURRY

Hannibal Heyes's & Kid Curry's Wanted Posters.

The governor required that they stay out of trouble for one year in order to be considered for amnesty. The first year was about 1880 because in "How to Rob a Bank in One Hard Lesson," Heyes is forced to nitro a Pierce & Hamilton '78, the latest model, something he had also done "a year and a half ago" while still outlawing. Their probation stretched to three or four years as evidenced by their spending a winter in the cabin in "Night of the Red Dog," several weeks mining with Danny Bilson and Seth, and two Fourth of July celebrations over the course of the series. During that time, they encountered some historically familiar men. Wyatt Earp and Doc Holliday were well-known names in Tombstone, Arizona, from 1879 to 1881 during which time the boys accompanied their friend Georgette there for her debut as a *chanteuse* and regrettably attracted the attention of the famous marshal. After Doc Holliday left Tombstone because of "the shooting trouble," undeniably a reference to the OK Corral gunfight in October 1881, the boys run into him again in "The Ten Days That Shook Kid Curry." Joe Horner put his rustling career behind him, served some prison time, escaped, and fled to Wyoming. There he changed his name to Frank Canton and became, not only a respectable citizen, but sheriff of Johnson County, an office he holds when the boys wander into town. Curry is "pushing thirty," in 1885, when they retrieve Zulick from Mexico in time for his inauguration as Arizona governor. 1885 is also the year when Francis Warren served his first short term as territorial governor of Wyoming.

After meeting with Governor George W. Baxter in hopes of furthering their amnesty chances, they agree to do a favor for him which takes them to the Red Sash Gang's hideout. Because it's so remote, they don't learn the news until they return that President Cleveland replaced Baxter with Thomas Moonlight. That happened on January 24, 1887, specifically dating "The Day the Amnesty Came Through" and making it clear that the boys had been, and would continue to be, trying to stay out of trouble for a very long time. In fact, when devising how best to abscond with Zulick from the Mexican mining camp, Heyes studies the layout but can't come up with a plan. Curry encourages him to pretend that Zulick is like money in a bank, what's the best way to get him out? It had been so long since he had to use his bank-robbing talents that Heyes is stumped.

To paraphrase a Biblical quote Curry may have known, "by their acts shall you know them." Despite having dabbled in outlawry for many years before deciding to go straight, they were not all bad. The only thing we really know about their character in the early years is that they never killed anyone.

They are not always carefree and affable, however. Hannibal Heyes has a definite dark side. Shortly after they've committed themselves to seeking amnesty, they are confronted with the dilemma of what to do about members of their former gang. Do they let their past associates be slaughtered by a force of Bannerman men in lieu of revealing their own connection to them? Curry is sure the amnesty is not worth that big a price, but Heyes really has to think about it for awhile. If dealing with friends proved to be a catch-22, seeking revenge for Seth's death in "Smiler with a Gun," was a no-brainer for him. Though Heyes liked to think "there's a little bad in everybody," he saw full-blown evil in Danny Bilson. Since nothing would bring Seth back, Heyes wanted to take Danny for everything he had stolen from them. It can be argued that he goaded Danny into a gunfight with Curry, secure in the knowledge the Kid could beat him.

On the other hand, friendship is important to Heyes. Their investigation into the Touchstone bank robbery becomes as much an effort to learn what happened to Billy and Caleb as it is an attempt to clear their own names. The knowledge will offer some peace of mind to Billy's mother, their old friend Jenny. Heyes's concern and loyalty for his partner goes without saying. His despair at seeing

(Courtesy of Ben Murphy)

Curry falsely accused of murder by the Santa Marta alcalde prompts him to come up with a miracle to clear him. And as much as it pains him to do it, he resorts to robbery and deceit to rescue Curry from kidnappers Lorraine and Janet, and Amy Martin and Willard Riley. While Doc Beauregard is engrossed in playing poker, it is Heyes who nurses Curry when he falls sick. More than once Heyes takes Curry under his wing. At least three times he attempts to stop Curry from violence. He warns him in the Porterville saloon not to get involved because he can't back up his smart-aleck retorts. In Big Bend, he's willing to start a fistfight with the Kid, even before breakfast, to prevent him from instigating another encounter with bully Joe Briggs. In "The Girl in Boxcar #3," he stops Curry from delivering a punch, this time to Attorney Greer. However, because Greer so deserves it, he delivers it himself.

Heyes – the devious and more thorough schemer of the two – has faith in his own talents. Once he puts his mind to something it usually happens. He *will* succeed in getting the amnesty, a fact Curry acknowledges. More than once Curry suggests they separate, recognizing Heyes's forthright approach to his less sure one. But, as Heyes points out to banker Chester Powers, Curry has one solid virtue – he listens to Heyes. Heyes has a talent for being able to judge a person's character. His instinct tells him that trusting Sheriff Clitterhouse may not be the wisest course of action and, to his dismay, he's proven right. Luckily his judgment of Judge Hanley is equally sound, reinforcing his conviction that "trust is something people have to earn."

Kid Curry's single-mindedness and care for his friend is similarly evident when Heyes is in danger. Coming up behind the mountain man who shot and wounded Heyes, Curry would have killed the man if he made a wrong move. Similarly, believing Heyes dead of a gunshot wound to the head, Curry fanatically pursues the enforcers of the Wyoming Cattlemen's Association and, frustrated at their being out of range, fires into the air in a flamboyant show of anger. The other drover watches Curry with awe. Only wounded, Heyes remarks to Cress, "You ought to see him when he really gets mad."

Curry too is concerned for others. Even after Joe Sims, the self-proclaimed professional bounty hunter, captured them, tied them up and gave every evidence that he was serious about turning them in for the reward, Curry talks Heyes into shooting into the lynching party to free Sims. When they're forced to walk through the desert with Seth, it's Curry who takes the lead in keeping the old man upright and walking.

For being a confirmed fast draw, Curry is a different man when the weapon is not in his hand. He's insecure about their chances for amnesty, positive he will slip back into old habits and that Heyes has a much better chance at it. When things do go well, he's nervous, assuming it's only a temporary silver lining in a thundercloud. This puts him more on alert, a trait Heyes appreciates, knowing that, with senses sharpened, Curry will watch out for both of them. Curry would argue it is Heyes who sets the mood. "I know you, Heyes, you can't take it when things are going good. It makes you nervous and your being nervous makes me nervous." Perhaps because he is still a Kid, even if in name only, in each of the episodes where Heyes and Curry encounter children, Curry has the most interaction. While Heyes would rather ease into the morning, Curry joins Beth and Bridget Jordan for some fancy shooting. He appreciates their rifle shooting talents while agreeing with their mother that girls shouldn't play with handguns. Little Tommy Cunningham in Wickenburg would like to learn pistol proficiency but Curry wisely refuses to teach him, believing that, by the time the child grows up, people won't be wearing guns on their hips any more. Tommy Tapscott, charged by his mother to hold a rifle on the boys in the wagon, drops it when the wagon wheel hits a bump in the road. Curry stomps on the downed rifle and, for an instant, sees a way to escape. At the sight of

Tommy's frightened face, however, he removes his foot from the gun so the boy can retrieve it.

The boys are about equal in luck, both good and bad, with women. Over the course of the series, Curry charms Grace Turner and Michelle Monet, Margaret Chapman and Charlotte Austin, to name a few. Heyes beguiles Grace but also has romantic moments with Amy Martin, Julia Finney and Beegee. They have deep-rooted, though not always amiable, connections with Clementine Hale and Georgette Sinclair, whose own past stories suggest they've known Heyes and Curry a long time and consider them more long-lost family than paramours. More often than not, women feature in one of their scams.

When it comes to relationships, talents, and foibles, in the end Hannibal Heyes and Kid Curry represent Everyman. They exhibit anger, fear, intelligence, insecurity, faith, sophistication and naiveté, concern and peacefulness to varying degrees in disparate situations. During a fishing trip, they have time to relax. Pondering their situation, they wonder how their upbringing led them to where they are now – wanted dead or alive with a $20,000 bounty on their heads. If things had been different, instead of being bank and train robbers, they might be earning honest money as bank guards or train conductors. But then viewers would hardly tune in to watch. In one script Heyes tells Curry, "You know, Kid, I'm beginning to really admire you. You got depths I never expected."[4] Viewers might echo his sentiments about the whole of *Alias Smith and Jones*.

CHAPTER 3

AMNESTY? FOR YOU TWO?
THE FIRST SEASON

January 5, 1971 – April 22, 1971
First Season Credits (1970–71)

Director:	Gene Levitt, Jeannot Swarc, Jeffrey Hayden, Leslie H. Martinson, Richard Benedict, Bruce Kessler, Barry Shear, Fernando Lamas, Douglas Heyes
Casting:	Ralph Winters, Burt Metcalfe
Production Manager:	Dick Birnie
Unit Manager:	Joseph E. Kenny, Ben Bishop
Assistant Director:	Ralph Ferrin, Jack Doran, Richard Bennett, Dennis Donnelly
2nd Assistant Director:	Warren Smith, David Hamberger (trainee), Don White, Tom Blank
Art Director:	George Webb, Robert E. Smith, William Tuntke, Alex Mayer
Set Decorator:	Mickey S. Michaels, Joseph Stone, Perry Murdock, Hal Gausman
Props:	Dean O'Connor, Matt McCullen, Phil Haley
Script Supervisor:	Sandy Nelson, Al Pagonis, Hope McLaughlin
Camera:	John M. Stephens, Gene Polito
Sound:	Melvin M. Metcalfe, Sr., Edwin S. Hall, Robert Bertrand, David H. Moriarty
Costumes:	Grady Hunt
Costumes Supervision:	Vincent Dee
Wardrobe – Men:	Harry Pasen, Hugh McFarland, Jack Takeuchi, Pete Saldutti, Lorry Richter
Wardrobe – Women:	Pamela Wise, Helen Kolvig, Betty Griffin, Louise Clark, Grace Kuhn

MAKEUP:	BUD WESTMORE
HAIR STYLIST:	LARRY GERMAIN
PUBLICITY:	ROY GUIVER, ALLAN CAHAN
EDITORIAL SUPERVISION:	RICHARD BELDING
EDITOR:	BOB KAGEY, RICHARD BRACKEN, JOHN DUMAS, GLORYETTE CLARK, ALBERT ZUNIGA
ASSISTANT EDITOR:	JOE DiVITALE, RICHARD DODGE, DAVE SCHOENLEBER, JERRY LUDWIG

ALIAS SMITH AND JONES PILOT

"Please, please don't tell me anything about what happened here tonight."
— Sheriff Lom Trevors

STORY:	GLEN A. LARSON
TELEPLAY:	GLEN A. LARSON AND MATTHEW HOWARD
DIRECTOR:	GENE LEVITT
SHOOTING DATES:	OCTOBER 8, 9, 12, 13, 14, 15, 16, 19, 20, 21, 22, 23, 26, 27, 28, 1970
ORIGINAL US AIR DATE:	JANUARY 5, 1971
ORIGINAL UK AIR DATE:	APRIL 19, 1971

Into the West came many men. Some were good men and some were bad men. Some were good men with some bad in them. And some were bad men with some good in them. This is the story of two pretty good bad men: Hannibal Heyes and Kid Curry.

Together these gentlemen substantially altered the course of America's frontier. They did a lot to change railroad schedules, too. And in all the trains and banks they robbed they never shot anyone. This made our two latter-day Robin Hoods very popular with everyone but the railroads and the banks. Because, unlike Robin Hood, Hannibal Heyes and Kid Curry robbed from the rich and kept the money for themselves. It was a good life.

But times were changing. Safes were getting better, posses were getting bigger, sheriffs were getting smarter. And modern communications made it only a matter of time until they would be captured and maybe even killed.

So begins the adventure. It is 1880 and the West is still wild. The Devil's Hole Gang, led by Hannibal Heyes and Kid Curry, are at the top of their game and considered to be the most successful outlaws in the history of the West. On this particular day they stop a train carrying a safe containing $50,000. The gang hustles the passengers out of harm's way as Kyle Murtry sets dynamite to blow up the safe. Everyone hunkers down under cover, tensely waiting for the explosion. They wait. And wait. Finally a little old lady from Boston, Miss Birdie Pickett,

Heyes and Curry in a horseless carriage?

Glen Larson's original concept placed the show at the turn of the twentieth century where our amiable outlaws had to learn to cope with changing technology.

The opening montage was supposed to include examples of such new-fangled gadgets as telephones and motor cars. On October 16, 1970, Peter Duel, Ben Murphy and Pat Danova posed for this picture.

The series time frame was subsequently changed and the photo was not used in the montage, but it survives as a baffling publicity photo.

questions the delay. Ever polite, Heyes answers, "I'm sure I don't know, ma'am." He orders Kyle to check his fuse and is taken aback when Kyle refuses and lays the responsibility back on him. "What makes you such a great leader, Heyes, is that you never tell no man to do a thing you wouldn't do yourself," Kyle points out. Stuck by this logic, Heyes goes to check the dynamite himself.

He gingerly approaches the train, peeks cautiously into the car, and finds the fuse has sputtered out. Kid Curry and Wheat Carlson join him at the safe, where Heyes tells them Kyle got the fuse wet. Wheat immediately points out it's Heyes's fault for fording a river he warned him not to, and the situation is not improved when Kyle reports the passengers are questioning their reputation.

Heyes turns to Plan B – cracking the safe by manipulating the tumblers. As he starts to work, Miss Birdie investigates. When Curry asks her to be quiet so Heyes can hear, Miss Birdie offers her opinion that they don't seem to be cut out for this line of work and hands him a pamphlet, urging him to read it.

Heyes gives up in frustration as he realizes there isn't enough time for him to get the Brooker 202 safe open before the law arrives. He moves on to Plan C – taking the safe with them. The gang rides off, dragging the safe, leaving a trail even the blindest posse can follow. As Kyle

Devil's Hole Gang.

and Wheat gaze at the deep ruts, Wheat comments dryly, "When I said 'let's make tracks,' that ain't exactly what I had in mind." Kyle wants to know how Wheat would have handled the situation, but Wheat refuses to give details, just saying he would do it smarter.

The gang drags the safe to the edge of a cliff and pushes it off. At the bottom, they have trouble finding it, beating through the brush while Heyes calls out encouragement. Finally Kyle spots it buried in the mud. The gang has tired of Heyes's plans and turns to Wheat, who, put on the spot, orders them to dig it up. They return to the cliff where Wheat also plans to push off the safe, but this time on to "mean, hard, pointed rocks." Wheat brushes off Heyes's attempts to point out a problem, and once again the gang watches as the safe bounces down. This time it lands in a lake with a resounding splash. Heyes sighs and says it could have been worse. It could have been his idea.

The posse is on the way, wondering why the Devil's Hole Gang left such an obvious trail.

With time running out, Wheat dives for the safe, surfacing with a thumbs up. The gang hauls on the rope only to find out that what Wheat has found is an old stove. Heyes decides the time has come to give up all together. Wheat tells them if they leave now, they won't get any part of the loot, but Heyes and Curry would rather give up the money than face the posse, so they wish the boys luck and leave. For the first time Curry looks at the paper Miss Birdie gave him. It's an amnesty offer from the governor but Curry is unfamiliar with the word. Heyes explains, "Well, what it means is there's more chicken thieves, land-grabbers and rag-picking penny stealers around than there is lawmen, so if a man wants to turn

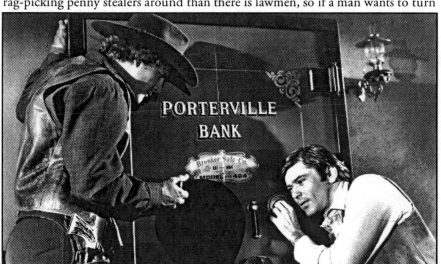

Smith and Jones test the Brooker 404 for Miss Porter.

hisself in, the governor might see fit to wipe his slate clean." Curry is a bit disappointed, figuring such a deal would never apply to them. With a final goodbye to the gang, Heyes and Curry ride off. In seconds they gallop past in the opposite direction, racing to outrun the posse chasing them with guns blazing. It's time to get out of the outlaw business.

Heyes and Curry ride to Porterville to have a chat with their old friend Sheriff Lom Trevors. He's surprised to see them and suspicious of their motives, especially after Miss Porter, who's running the local bank, stops to talk about extra security for a big payroll shipment the bank will soon be receiving. Lom is stunned when they explain they want him to be their spokesman with the governor in an attempt to gain amnesty. He can't believe they think the governor would give amnesty to the two biggest outlaws in the West. But Heyes points out that Lom, as a former outlaw himself, is the perfect one to plead their case. After some persuasion, Lom agrees to help them. The next morning he heads off to visit the governor while Heyes and Curry, having been introduced to Miss Porter as Mr. Smith and Mr. Jones, banking and security experts, help test the security of her brand new Brooker 404 safe. Heyes can't crack it, but points out a good dynamiter could blow it. As they leave the bank, Deputy Harker Wilkins stops them, escorts them into the sheriff's office and relieves them of their guns per Lom's orders. Harker explains Lom's new rule regarding transients, a rule made especially for them. Outside the sheriff's office, Miss Porter approaches and offers them jobs in her bank. Curry would accept immediately, but Heyes wants to discuss it first.

The Porterville Saloon shown in the pilot.

They retire to the saloon and debate the wisdom of taking bank jobs. Two drovers, Kane and Shields, are seated at a table watching them. Kane recognizes Curry and, noticing he's not wearing a gun, challenges him. Curry responds with a calculated insult, calling him a "walk-off." Kane doesn't know what that means, so Curry kindly explains. "You see, when the good Lord was making men, he got a whole bunch of them all whomped up together and then He decided to knock off for the rest of the day, thinking He'd put the brains in later. Guess what happened? A whole bunch of them critters just up and walked off before He ever got back. And that's what we've got here. Walk-off."

Heyes tries to defuse the tension, apologizing for Curry and pointing out he's not wearing a gun. Kane slides a gun down the bar toward Curry. He is about to pick it up, but Heyes pleads with him to back down and not ruin their chance for amnesty. Curry accedes to Heyes's wishes and apologizes. Kane and Shields swagger off.

The bartender pours Heyes and Curry a drink and assures them that if they keep out of sight the next morning, Kane and Shields will be gone with their herd, and nobody will get hurt. Heyes is pleased everything has worked out, but Curry is adamant. "It's decided. We're taking those bank jobs, because I'm not going naked one more day."

They start working at the bank, Heyes as teller, Curry as guard. The first day goes well, although Heyes suffers vertigo, surrounded by all the money he can't steal. That evening Curry, in possession of his gun once again, visits Kane and his buddy. With a demonstration of keen marksmanship, he convinces them it's *their*

(Courtesy of Ben Murphy)

faces that shouldn't be seen in town in the morning. His honor and pride satisfied, Curry returns to Porterville and informs Heyes all their troubles are over.

In the morning it becomes apparent their troubles are not all over as Wheat, Kyle and the rest of the Devil's Hole Gang have come to town to rob the bank. Wheat slips a note to the teller, demanding cash, his eyes widening as he recognizes Heyes. Heyes tells him about the amnesty plan and Wheat seems to approve, but when he rejoins the gang outside, he says Heyes and Curry are planning to rob the bank without them. The gang rides out of town, but soon returns.

That night Harker drags Heyes to the saloon and

Heyes and Curry with Miss Porter, played by Susan St. James

demands to know why this new group of transients has been hanging out there for fourteen hours playing nickel and dime poker. Curry, having just finished dinner with Miss Porter, leaves her flat to go to Heyes's aid. Harker confronts the gang, demanding their guns. After the deputy leaves, Wheat tells Heyes a sob story about the gang's lack of funds, saying the saloon offers them the only hope of having a roof over their heads. Heyes encourages them to stick it out until Lom returns. The gang agrees, but after Heyes and Curry leave, returns to their nefarious activity – digging a tunnel from the saloon to the bank.

Harker remains uncertain of the gang as they continue to play an unending game of poker with never more than $12 in the pot, but they seem to be staying out of trouble, so he leaves them alone. Heyes and Curry wait for Lom's return and are surprised when the gang suddenly visits the sheriff's office. They retrieve their guns, telling Harker they'll be leaving after just one more hand of poker. Heyes wants to know just what they have in mind. Wheat points out things could get nasty if Lom returns without the amnesty. Harker receives a telegram and, as if to prove Wheat's point, promptly arrests Heyes and Curry on Lom's orders. They don't stay in jail long, though, since Curry has lifted the keys to the cell from Harker's pocket. To get even with Lom for what they perceive as his treachery, they decide to rob the bank.

Heyes and Curry steal some dynamite and attack the bank from the roof. Unbeknownst to them, the gang has reached the safe from below. Each of them sets a generous amount of dynamite around the safe, because it is, after all, a Brooker 404. Harker meets Lom's train, assuring him everything is under control. At that instant, a tremendous explosion disintegrates the bank and money flies through the air. Heyes and Curry pick themselves up, wondering what happened. When Wheat and the boys stumble out of the saloon, all becomes clear. Angry at the gang's interference, Heyes and Curry order them to put down the money they're eagerly grabbing and get out of town. Miss Porter sees this and misunderstands, thinking Heyes and Curry are saving the money from the bandits. Lom and Harker race to the scene, where Miss Porter happily relates how the bank's money was saved by Mr. Smith and Mr. Jones. Lom isn't fooled, but doesn't press the issue. He takes the boys into his office and gives them the news from the governor. They have been granted a provisional amnesty, but they have to prove they deserve it by staying out of trouble for a year. In the meantime, the deal will remain a secret between them, Lom and the governor.

So for the following year the West's two most wanted men would lead model lives. Lives of temperance, moderation, tranquility. Hannibal Heyes and Kid Curry would cease to exist. In their places would ride two men of peace . . . alias Smith and Jones.

CAST

PETE DUEL	HANNIBAL HEYES
BEN MURPHY	KID CURRY
FORREST TUCKER	DEPUTY HARKER WILKINS

SUSAN ST. JAMES	MISS CAROLINE PORTER
JAMES DRURY	SHERIFF LOM TREVORS
JEANNETTE NOLAN	MISS BIRDIE PICKETT
EARL HOLLIMAN	WHEAT CARLSON
DENNIS FIMPLE	KYLE MURTRY
BILL FLETCHER	KANE
JOHN RUSSELL	MARSHALL
CHARLES DIERKOP	SHIELDS
BILL McKINNEY	LOBO
SID HAIG	OUTLAW
JOHN HARPER	OUTLAW
JON SHANK	OUTLAW
PETER BROCCO	PINCUS
HARRY HICKOX	BARTENDER
OWEN BUSH	ENGINEER
JULIE COBB	YOUNG GIRL

"If you're going to steal, and nothing comes from nothing, only steal from masters. . ." advises William Goldman in his book *Adventures in the Screen Trade*.[1] This is a tenet that Glen Larson has always embraced wholeheartedly. *Alias Smith and Jones* is the first series he created by "stealing from masters," in this case from Goldman himself and the highly successful film *Butch Cassidy and the Sundance Kid*. Hollywood is a place where imitation runs rampant, because it's much easier to sell an idea that is similar to one already proven successful than it is to sell something completely original. No studio executive ever lost his job going for the tried and true. Westerns had been a staple on television since its infancy, so a new series inspired by an Academy Award-winning film, taking full advantage of the lightheartedness that captivated movie audiences, was an easy sell.

The most obvious similarity between *Alias Smith and Jones* and *Butch Cassidy and the Sundance Kid* is the introduction of two good-natured outlaws who realize times are changing and they need to change with them. In Butch and Sundance's case this means fleeing to Bolivia; in Heyes and Curry's case it means going straight, a tactic more in keeping with the sensibilities of network television. Glen Larson hung his plot carefully on some of Goldman's most memorable moments – the amiable outlaws frustrated by a train robbery gone wrong, being chased by a determined posse, facing dissension within the gang, and blowing a safe to smithereens with too much dynamite – changing the details enough to ultimately have Twentieth Century Fox's lawsuit against Universal thrown out of court for a lack of distinct instances of plagiarism. But for all the creativity Larson showed in avoiding a lawsuit, he still didn't manage to create a good story.

The purpose of a pilot film is to introduce the characters and to set up the premise for what everyone involved hopes will be a long and successful run. In the case of *Alias Smith and Jones*, while the pilot is a fun, 75-minute romp through the Old West, it fails in certain critical ways. The characters of Hannibal Heyes and Kid Curry are introduced as successful outlaws through a montage of still photographs with a voice-over which does give the audience some necessary background, but is instantly contradicted by the train robbery where everything goes wrong. Kid Curry admits, "This ain't been our best day." However, to an audience who is just being introduced to the two characters, it appears that our amiable outlaws are suffering more from incompetence than from just a bad day. Nothing is offered to the audience to show that these men are indeed at the top of their profession and not the dolts they appear to be.

One of the major flaws in the pilot is the lack of explanation for the boys' change of heart regarding trying for the amnesty. In one scene they reluctantly decide such a deal would never be offered to them and in the next they're approaching Lom to ask for his help in obtaining it. Obviously something important happened between these two scenes, but what it was will forever remain a mystery to the audience. Numerous scenes present in the shooting script were edited out of the final film, including an entire Miss Birdie subplot. Miss Birdie's loss makes the story weaker, but does not do irreparable harm to it. The same cannot be said for the lack of a scene wherein Heyes and Curry make the momentous decision to try for an amnesty despite the odds against them. This is a pivotal point in the set-up of both the film and the series to follow. Its absence is inexplicable.

Heyes and Curry are introduced as the most successful outlaws in the history of the West, but in the pilot, Wheat is a worthy contender for the title. His plan to tunnel to the bank shows great style (not to mention top surveying and engineering skills), while Heyes's plan to come at the safe from above, with his unnecessarily complicated method of hauling dynamite across the street, roof to roof by pulley, seems overdone. The question that comes to mind is why didn't they just hoist it up from the back side of the bank, out of sight of any passerby who just might take it into his head to look up? Wheat is also the one who thinks ahead to what might happen if Lom returns without the amnesty, and shows himself to be a quick thinker and skilled liar when the gang retrieves their guns from Deputy Harker. Compared to Wheat, Heyes seems naive and one could be forgiven for wondering just how he became the leader of the Devil's Hole Gang.

Despite these holes, the pilot film succeeds in its most important duty – convincing the audience to return and watch the series. It accomplishes this because of the remarkable chemistry between Peter Duel and Ben Murphy. Despite the rush into production, the producers struck gold with the casting of these two actors in the lead roles. The connection is apparent from the moment they proudly introduce each other to the train engineer through the infamous "walk off" scene to the moment when Heyes carefully places Curry's hat back on his head after the explosion at the bank. It's apparent that these two men are close friends who would do anything for each other. The audience immediately recognized that this bond was something special and it's what kept them returning week after week to share the adventures of these two pretty good bad men.

THE McCREEDY BUST

"Grudges are for people with bad stomachs. Ours are in good shape."
— Hannibal Heyes

STORY:	JOHN THOMAS JAMES
TELEPLAY:	SY SALKOWITZ
DIRECTOR:	GENE LEVITT
SHOOTING DATES:	DECEMBER 7, 8, 9, 10, 11, 14, 1970
ORIGINAL US AIR DATE:	JANUARY 21, 1971
ORIGINAL UK AIR DATE:	MAY 10, 1971

The bartender of the Red Rock saloon serves wealthy rancher Patrick J. "Big Mac" McCreedy and his hired hand Blake, ignoring the thirsty Hannibal Heyes and Kid Curry. The two former outlaws have trouble dealing with this blatant favoritism. Goaded into a confrontation, Curry shoots the gun out of Blake's hand, ruining his holster, but impressing McCreedy with his fast draw and accurate aim.

> Given the time frame of the episode, it took the sheriff eighteen days to look through Wanted posters.

Humiliated, Blake complains about them to the sheriff who promises to look through his files. Meanwhile, Mac offers the boys a job. All they have to do is retrieve a bust of Caesar that, Mac maintains, was stolen by a Mexican named Armendariz. Mac will pay $10,000 but the deal sounds too good to be true.

Heyes and Curry waylay Blake and offer to have the holster repaired. They learn from him that Armendariz is the biggest landholder in Mexico and Mac has already offered many men the dangerous job, one of whom is still healing. Armendariz displays the statue during fiestas and keeps it in his safe at other times. Heyes is intrigued at the uncomplicated prospect of stealing it from the safe.

Armed with this additional information, Heyes and Curry tell Mac they'll do it for $20,000. He agrees, but only if they'll sit in on a poker game and give him a sporting chance to win it back.

After sneaking into Armendariz's hacienda, Heyes opens the safe by working the tumblers. The temptation to take the jewels and money they find inside is strong but they resist and only remove the bust. Armendariz's men, alerted to the intruders when Heyes accidentally knocks a flowerpot off the balcony, pursue them.

At the Saturday night poker game, Heyes fills a straight and bets a large amount on what he assumes will be a winning hand. McCreedy calls him on an obscure Hoyle rule that straights are not played in stud poker unless announced in the beginning. Big Mac, with only a pair of jacks, has won back the $20,000. The boys leave chagrined and penniless.

The next day, Heyes and Curry petition the banker, Mr. Peterson, to lend them $20,000. At the next poker game, Heyes requests a rematch with Mac, but there are already eight players in the game. Rather than leave, Heyes offers Mac a deal that he can make five pat hands from twenty-five cards with all $20,000 riding on the bet. Mac believes the odds would be a thousand to one, but Heyes does it. The banker laughs, saying the boys proved to him that it works nine times out of ten.

After celebrating their good fortune at the saloon, a drunken Heyes and Curry step out into the street where they are accosted, hauled out to Armendariz's ranch, and accused of stealing the Caesar bust. Señor Armendariz explains that the river that is the boundary between their two ranches changed course and Mac ended up with some of his land. When Mac sold the land to another Mexican, Armendariz had to pay $50,000 to get it back. Armendariz stole the bust in exchange. Under coercion, Heyes and Curry admit the crime but Armendariz mercifully frees them because when they opened the safe, they only stole the item they thought belonged to the man who hired them.

Meanwhile, the sheriff continues to flip through the wanted posters in his files.

As Heyes and Curry get ready to leave town, Mac grows suspicious of Jones's quick draw and Smith's ability to open a safe. Maybe they aren't who they say they are. He pressures them to stay with threats that he'll notify the sheriff. Mac wants one more chance to get even.

That Saturday, Mac bets he can cut the Ace of Spades on the first try. Heyes agrees to the proposition and shuffles the deck thoroughly. Mac stabs the deck with a knife, believing he has "cut" the ace, but Heyes has outwitted him and palmed the card. At that moment, Armendariz's men burst in to retrieve the sculpture. Señor Armendariz takes the $40,000 on the table as well and declares that he and Mac are now even.

Furious, Mac tries once again to hire the boys to steal it back. He offers them as much as $50,000 but they refuse and ride out of town in a stagecoach.

The sheriff has finally figured out that the men must be Hannibal Heyes and Kid Curry. Mac tucks this knowledge away. He informs the sheriff that no, Jones is his nephew, and then wonders aloud at the odds of building five pat hands from twenty-five cards randomly dealt as he and the sheriff head for the saloon.

GUEST CAST

BURL IVES	PATRICK J. "BIG MAC" MCCREEDY
CESAR ROMERO	SEÑOR ERNESTO ARMENDARIZ
EDWARD ANDREWS	PETERSON

DUANE GREY	———————	SHERIFF
MILLS WATSON	———————	BLAKE
CHARLES WAGENHEIM	———————	BARTENDER
ORVILLE SHERMAN	———————	HANK
MICIL MURPHY	———————	DELGADO
RUDY DIAZ	———————	GUARD

While the marble bust of Caesar is the immediately recognizable item related to the title, Heyes and Curry's pulling off the theft was a bust, i.e., a failure. Though Heyes and Curry temporarily procured it for Big Mac, Señor Armendariz ended up with the statue, signaling their inability to end the McCreedy and Armendariz enmity. The episode was the first one Roy Huggins had a hand in and, though as John Thomas James he wrote many of the episodes, this was his favorite.[2] Jo Swerling remembered it as "one of the best episodes of television that I think I ever had anything to do with, where they were getting one up on him all the time."[3]

Universal Studios put the episode to a test compiled by Audience Surveys, Inc. ASI employees gathered people of varying demographics, showed them the episode and recorded their reactions based on their turning a dial to indicate happiness or displeasure at what they were watching. "The McCreedy Bust" rated a huge score, helping to explain why McCreedy and Armendariz returned for two more episodes. But Swerling stated, "We would have done that with or without the ASI tests because we thought that they did such a good job."[4]

It also was one of the handful of scripts whose title remained unchanged from the initial story concept. In it, Huggins introduced "Big Mac" McCreedy, played by folksinger Burl Ives. Huggins was careful about his character's names and *McCreedy* may be a purposeful mispronunciation of McGreedy, which Mac

Señor Armendariz's villa as it now looks on Universal's backlot.

(Sagala/Bagwell collection)

certainly was. By his own admission, he owned most of the town, was a major railroad stockholder and had won the range war. His reluctance to allow the boys to walk away with their $20,000 winnings reinforces his tight-fistedness. His ego, echoed in size by his portly frame, would not allow two unknown cowboys to one-up him.

When Huggins told the story to writer Sy Salkowitz, he left the caper at the Armendariz ranch up to him, merely urging him to do research and check his facts. In the first draft, Salkowitz sends the boys to a small Mexican farm pretending to buy a guard dog. The animal who greets them is friendly enough, but when they try to leave, it becomes a snarling beast. The farmer explains that Armendariz likes to see his invited guests arrive but they cannot leave until he says so. In the next scene, Curry limps into a doctor's office and explains that his ankle is injured. He howls in pain as the doctor removes his boot, so Heyes asks for some ether to knock him out. When the doctor opens the cabinet to get it, Curry pulls his gun and they take the can of anesthetic, his ankle suddenly healed. Back at Armendariz's hacienda, they encounter the friendly dog and a not-so-friendly guard whom Heyes conks on the head. They drag the unconscious guard to a laundry room with the dog close at their heels. While Heyes heads to the safe in the main room, works the tumblers and retrieves the bust, Curry dresses in Armendariz's coat. When a second guard, alerted by the dog, approaches the laundry room, Curry brings his pistol down on the man's head.

As they attempt to leave, the scent on the coat Curry wears confuses the dog but not for long. Pretending to pet the dog, Curry instead grabs him by the scruff of the neck and holds a wadded cloth doused with ether over his nose. The dog goes down, but the ether is so strong, Curry's knees buckle. Heyes urges him to his feet and they escape. The next day, Mac, unaware of the lengths they've gone to, is happy to see the bust.[5]

When Huggins read the scenes with red pen in hand, he wrote a big NO on the descriptions of Curry knocking out the guards. Then, on second thought, Huggins X'ed out entire pages and re-wrote the bits about the boys getting into and out of Armendariz's home. Huggins noted, "Heyes and Curry didn't share misspent youths for nothing. They have come prepared." In his new version, Heyes uses a stiletto to open the door enough to allow the dog to poke his head through. Heyes quickly closes it and Curry holds a chloroform-soaked handkerchief over the dog's nose. Eventually these ideas, too, were scrapped.

Huggins also gave Heyes and Curry characteristics that would consistently define them throughout the series: Heyes was the skillful poker player with a "silvery" tongue whose talent for manipulating tumblers on a safe served him better at Armendariz's hacienda than it had in the pilot; Curry was the quick draw whose perfect but compassionate aim foiled an adversary without killing him. He could have seriously wounded McCreedy's peon Blake instead of merely shooting the gun from his hand but Huggins's philosophy was one of non-violence. "When there's action in one of my shows, it's because it had to be there. There is no other way for the story to go or to be resolved without that action. I don't ever put action in just to have action for the simple reason that I don't think I need it!"[6]

The card trick involving five pat hands randomly dealt from twenty-five cards was one Huggins learned as a boy in military school. He first introduced it to television viewers in a *Maverick* episode where it was known as Maverick Solitaire. Huggins was amazed to learn that the day after that particular *Maverick* episode aired, stores all over the country sold out of playing cards. Everyone who had watched the program wanted to try the trick.[7]

Similarly, the ruse in stud poker wherein a player waits for a competitor's winning hand featuring a straight, then announces that straights may not be played unless declared before the game begins was also featured first in *Maverick*. The beautiful con artist Samantha Crawford waits for Bret to declare a straight, then pulls out the Hoyle that she insists governs all plays. She triumphantly points to the rule in *Hoyle's Book of Games* and wins with a low pair.

It seems a recanting, Heyes and Curry's agreeing to rob a rich man's safe, when only in the previous episode they had promised to go straight in hopes of obtaining amnesty. That they did it for what they believed was fair play does not mitigate their guilt, nor would it hold up in a court of law. However, it is ironic that their honesty in admitting to Armendariz they were indeed the thieves saved them from life-long sentences in a Mexican prison.

Exit from Wickenburg

"You know, I really do like you fellows."
— *Sam Finrock*

STORY:	JOHN THOMAS JAMES
TELEPLAY:	ROBERT HAMNER
DIRECTOR:	JEANNOT SZWARC
SHOOTING DATES:	DECEMBER 16, 17, 18, 21, 22, 23, 1970
ORIGINAL US AIR DATE:	JANUARY 28, 1971
ORIGINAL UK AIR DATE:	APRIL 26, 1971

Hannibal Heyes and Kid Curry ride into the pleasant little town of Wickenburg, Arizona. Their first stop is the saloon where they settle down to play some poker. After losing to a pair of card sharps, Ben Morrison and Frank Johnson, who are using a trick called "the spread," Heyes and Curry search out the saloon's owner. Entering the office they find an attractive woman named Mary Cunningham, who wryly tells them, "I assure you, you're not half as surprised as I am" to find her owning and

As script development progressed, Sam Finrock's occupation changed from foreman of the Bar T Ranch to slightly shady lawyer to local businessman.

running such an establishment. They wonder if the card sharps they've been playing with are working for the house. Learning they're not, they return to the game, where Heyes exposes Morrison and Johnson's technique while Curry keeps tempers under control with his steady gun. Heyes reimburses the other players, including a grateful Sam Finrock, from the sharps' winnings.

Mary Cunningham inherited the Golconda saloon from her recently deceased husband and has not been doing well as a businesswoman. She hires Heyes and Curry to manage the place for the princely sum of $50 a month each. They rapidly settle in to the job, stopping Mary's employees from stealing her blind and bringing the saloon back to profitability in only a few days.

While Heyes goes through Mary's accounts, Curry practices his fast draw, just to keep his hand in. Mary and her two children, Tommy and Kate, stop by. Mary is pleased by how well the business is doing, but Tommy is more excited by Curry's shooting. "Can you teach me how to do that?" he asks. Curry could, but he won't because there's always someone faster out there. After Mary and the children leave, Heyes marvels at Curry's change of heart regarding gunplay.

That night in the saloon, Curry faces down another cheating card player, successfully and non-violently, prompting Heyes to confide, "All right, forget I said anything this afternoon." Things seem to be going well for the boys.

The next morning Mary interrupts their breakfast, obviously upset. She takes them into her office and fires them, saying she can manage on her own now and paying them for a month despite their having worked less than a week. Curry's chivalrous instincts are aroused and leaving town without finding out what's wrong is not in his nature. The boys find jobs in construction, a field in which they show no talent. The friendly and grateful Sam Finrock joins them at dinner where he politely but firmly tells them to leave town for their own welfare. But the boys decide to stick around.

The next day Finrock watches as they bash their thumbs with hammers on the building site. That night after supper Heyes and Curry are attacked by three men who take them out of town, leave them on the side of the road with their horses and gear, and urge them to move on to Gila City. The boys debate the wisdom of going to Gila City, but curiosity and stubbornness win out and they return to Wickenburg.

Mike, the bartender, gives them a name to put with the leader of the gang who beat them up – Al Gorman, foreman of the Bar T Ranch. Heyes and Curry have a little talk with Gorman. When he balks at answering their questions, insisting it was Finrock who hired him to move them along, Heyes loops a rope around Gorman's ankle while Curry attaches the other end to his saddlehorn. Curry picks up a branch, ready to bring it down on the horse's flank. At the threat, Gorman caves in with a frantic shout – Finrock hired him and Mary Cunningham hired Finrock.

Back in town, Heyes and Curry confront Mary. Heyes screams at her, all the pain and frustration of the situation bubbling to the surface. Mary becomes hysterical but still refuses to tell them anything. Heyes gives up.

Finrock visits them in their hotel room, wanting to know why they didn't ride on to Gila City. Heyes lies, saying Mary told them everything, but Finrock just laughs. He knows it's not true. This time Finrock is more blunt with his advice – if they don't get out of Wickenburg soon, someone will have them killed. And Finrock would hate to see people he likes get themselves killed.

Much to Heyes's dismay, Curry has been thinking and he's sure that Finrock and Gorman were not hired by Mary Cunningham. They decide to get a good night's sleep and ride on to Gila City in the morning.

Heyes spends the night pondering Curry's idea. As they load their gear on their horses, he comes up with a new thought – W.R. Sloane, the man who owns half the town. They've heard his name a lot since coming to Wickenburg, but they've never seen him and as Heyes says, "Now a man as important as this Mr. Sloane . . . all he'd have to do is come walking down the street and all the bowing and scraping would whip up a fair-sized dust storm." Since their curiosity is still unsatisfied, they go in search of Mr. Sloane.

After visiting several of his businesses, they finally come to his office. An accommodating secretary opens the door for them and they find an equally accommodating Sloane. Heyes decides his idea – that Sloane was behind the drive to get them out of town – wasn't one of his better ones. Stymied once again, the boys stop at the saloon before hitting the road. Mr. Sloane hurries past and Heyes comments on it. Mike is confused. The man hurrying past wasn't Sloane, it was Warren Epps, Sloane's bookkeeper.

Heyes and Curry sneak into Sloane's house that night, certain this time they're on the right track. Bursting into Sloane's study, Heyes discovers his idea was right after all. "Look who's calling himself Willard R. Sloane!" Curry still doesn't know Sloane, but Heyes recognizes him as Jim Plummer, leader of the first bunch Heyes rode with. He relates for Curry the story of how the gang robbed a train of a $30,000 payroll, but in the ensuing chase by the posse, Plummer disappeared along with the haul. Plummer is desperate to keep his whereabouts secret because he knows the remaining gang members would kill him if they ever found him. Heyes agrees to keep his secret if Sloane buys Mary Cunningham's saloon – for $30,000. Plummer is sorry to part with that kind of money but grateful to get off so easily.

The next morning Mary hurries to tell the boys about the wonderful and strange thing that happened – Mr. Sloane bought the saloon for $30,000. The boys agree that's wonderful, but not so strange. After all, the building alone is worth that much. "But I don't own the building," Mary reveals. "Mr. Sloane does."

GUEST CAST

SUSAN STRASBERG	MARY CUNNINGHAM
SLIM PICKENS	MIKE
MARK LENARD	WILLARD R. SLOANE/JIM PLUMMER
PERNELL ROBERTS	SAM FINROCK
FORD RAINEY	WARREN EPPS
MICHAEL BOW	YOUNG COWBOY
DAN KEMP	AL GORMAN
AMZIE STRICKLAND	GIRL
PAUL KENT	BEN MORRISON
LEW BROWN	FRANK JOHNSON
ROBERT GOODEN	1ST COWBOY
ROSS SHERMAN	2ND COWBOY
JOHNNY LEE	TOMMY CUNNINGHAM
JERRY HARPER	2ND PLAYER
DENNIS MCCARTHY	DEALER

Roy Huggins always developed his stories in meticulous detail, including not only plot points and sample dialogue, but also historical background and other tidbits of useful information before handing them off to the assigned writers. For "Exit from Wickenburg," the story outline given to writer Robert Hamner was nineteen pages long and included a lengthy description of how "the spread" is done.

In this episode we learn more about Heyes and Curry, who they are and who they want to be. They continue to move away from the two-dimensional caricatures of the pilot and are becoming well-rounded, slightly enigmatic characters capable of sustaining the audience's interest. Although Heyes was immediately established as the thinker, in this episode we see that while he jealously guards his status as the brains, he listens to Curry and gives serious consideration to his ideas even while teasing him about them. In the first draft script, it's Curry who does the thinking that ultimately reveals the truth, dragging a grumbling Heyes along with him as he searches for Mr. Sloane. While this scene worked fine, Huggins felt it could be improved, noting "we might play against the fact that Heyes is usually the one who does all the thinking."[8] So it was rewritten, adding the scene where Curry expresses his opinion that someone other than Mary is behind it all, but not having a clue as to who that someone might be. Heyes was given the task of coming up with a way to solve the riddle, cementing his role as the thinker and self-proclaimed genius.

Huggins, always most concerned with giving the audience a good story, wasn't averse to sneaking in a moral message now and again, as long as it didn't interfere with the entertainment. In this episode, eight-year-old Tommy wants to learn how to fast draw. In the outline, the original idea was to have Mary back Tommy up, saying it's important to know how to use a gun in the West, but Curry is hesitant. Huggins points out, "it would be wrong for him to be showing a small boy how to use a gun without making some concession toward the present attitude toward this kind of thing. Perhaps he extracts from the kid a promise that if he shows him how to use it, the kid will never actually use one." Hamner went one better and changed Mary's attitude, having Curry refuse because he realizes Mary does not want her son to learn to shoot. Huggins wanted to infuse Curry, the fastest gun in the West, with a philosophy of non-violence, an unexpected trait for a gunfighter.

In this early episode, the characters of Heyes and Curry are still being defined. Are they outlaws or law-abiding citizens? Will they be able to make a living without resorting to their outlaw ways? Jim Plummer is desperate to get them out of town, scared of what they might do if they discover him. When Al Gorman doesn't answer their questions to their satisfaction, Heyes and Curry turn to threats of great bodily harm. Gorman responds to this threat, but the audience is left wondering. Would Curry have hit the horse? At this point in the show, we can't be quite sure. We don't know them well enough, and with a criminal background, it's likely they have been violent in the past, even if they never shot anyone. This aura of danger, strangely enough, adds to the appeal of our two heroes. We know, or at least we hope, they're the good guys, but we can't be sure of what they'll do next. The only way to find out is to tune in next week and see if the boys can manage to stay out of trouble once again.

(Jerry Ohlinger's Movie Materials Store)

Wrong Train to Brimstone

"Want to tell me your names? Just for the gravestones?"
— Harry Briscoe

STORY:	STEPHEN KANDEL
TELEPLAY:	STEPHEN KANDEL
DIRECTOR:	JEFFREY HAYDEN
SHOOTING DATES:	DECEMBER 28, 29, 30, 31, 1970, JANUARY (1), 4, 5, 1971
ORIGINAL US AIR DATE:	FEBRUARY 4, 1971
ORIGINAL UK AIR DATE:	MAY 3, 1971

Briscoe, excited about the prospect of killing the "whole damned Devil's Hole Gang," then frustrated to learn the true identity of the dead outlaw, swears "Dammit!" His language was cleaned up by the network censors before the show aired.

Hal Needham, a stuntman and action film director, played the part of Wheat Carlson of the Devil's Hole Gang, the role introduced and played in the pilot by Earl Holliman.

In Bramberg, Hannibal Heyes and Kid Curry sell their horses for an $80 poker stake. Five minutes later, after spotting Deputy Wade Sawyer whom they know from Kingsburg, they turn around and attempt to undo the horse trade. The shrewd liveryman refuses to trade back their horses for even money. Their lack of success at horse-trading prompts them to inquire about transportation out of town. The last stagecoach has just left, they learn, and unfortunately, the next train is sold out.

Carl Grant and Fred Gaines arrive at the depot and are handed tickets because they had reservations. In the washroom, Heyes offers to buy their tickets from them. The men refuse and Gaines gets suspicious and pulls a gun. Heyes and Curry overpower them, tie them up, and board the train under their names. Shortly after departing the station, the "lady" passengers remove wigs and light cigars. Before Heyes and Curry can do more than wonder at the sight, Special Agent Harry Briscoe of the Bannerman Detective Agency calls for the attention of the passengers, every one of them also a Bannerman agent.

He informs them that the train they're on has picked up over a quarter of a million dollars in gold bars from the Wash Valley Consolidated Mining Company and is on its way to the Denver mint. The train and its cargo are bait for the Devil's Hole Gang and in particular, for Hannibal Heyes and Kid Curry.

Sara Blaine, the one real woman on board, alleges that she can identify Heyes and Curry. When the boys ask her how she knows them, she claims to have been a passenger on a train they robbed. Her cohort, agent Jeremiah Daley, is worried. He knows the two men who just boarded are not Grant and Gaines and confronts the boys as imposters. Heyes identifies himself and his partner as Heyes and Curry. Daley disregards the introduction as a jest as Heyes suspected he would, but Daley decides he won't tell Briscoe about them, whoever they are, so he can rely on their help later.

At the Brimstone station, Heyes and Curry intercept a telegram that the real Grant and Gaines have sent to Briscoe. Re-boarding, they're assigned guard duty over the gold shipment. They plot how, and if, to warn Wheat and the gang and face one of their first challenges in going straight – what to do about former gang-members. The dilemma is a difficult one for Hannibal Heyes. If they warn the gang about the ambush, they endanger their newly-declared bid for amnesty. Curry has no qualms. They cannot let friends die when they could prevent the slaughter that will surely be their fate. He would give up amnesty to spare the gang. Briscoe arrives in the storage car with rifles for them and holds the door for three men hauling a gatling gun. The sight of all the weaponry settles it for Heyes and he comes up with a plan to save both their amnesty and the Devil's Hole Gang, eliciting an enthusiastic acknowledgement from Curry. "You're the genius you think you are!"

In the morning, when the train stops for water, Heyes and Curry jump off and ride away to caution their former partners. The Devil's Hole Gang has already begun to tear up the tracks so the train has to stop. At warning shots from Heyes and Curry, the gang retreats with Bannerman agents firing on them, killing two.

Upon their return to the train, Heyes and Curry are held in the baggage car by a dispirited and angry Briscoe. One of the agents enters, hoping for some of the whiskey on board, a consolation for the letdown of losing Heyes and Curry. Briscoe sends him away with a tirade and proceeds to interrogate the boys. Heyes confesses they are not Bannerman detectives and identifies themselves as Smith and Jones. Meanwhile, Sara Blaine arrives to check out the bodies of the murdered gang members. Briscoe is thrilled when she identifies one corpse as Kid Curry and now allows the men to break out the whiskey in celebration. But Smith informs Briscoe that he knows Heyes and Curry from when he and Jones were wounded, in trouble and taken in by the Devil's Hole Gang. They got to know them real well, he says, and found Heyes and Curry to be "two of the kindest men on God's earth." That's why they got off the train to warn the gang. He also knows the dead gang member and identifies him as Henry Maxwell Jenkins, not Kid Curry. It can be proven by the initialed ring on Jenkins's finger.

Briscoe is deflated until Heyes tells him of their plan to make him a friend and a hero. Crooked Agent Daley and Sara Blaine, who arranged for the liquor to be on board, planned to have their gang rob the train when the detectives are drunk from celebrating. Briscoe allows Smith to confront Daley who implicates himself and Sara. Briscoe orders them tied up, so they can only watch helplessly as *their* gang attacks the train and are fired on by the now sober agents.

All's well that ends well. Before Smith and Jones go on their way, they happily supply Briscoe with updated descriptions of Heyes and Curry. Heyes, he learns, has a long scar on his chin and a gold tooth while Curry is skinny and holds his left shoulder low. The Bannerman Agency finally has really "accurate" descriptions of the outlaws.

The original title, "The Greater Train Robbery," leads to the conclusion that saving the gold from theft, the Devil's Hole Gang from slaughter, and their own hides from an angry Bannerman man credit Heyes and Curry with more success than they enjoyed in the pilot. Between Stephen Kandel's first story outline and the aired program, more changed than just the title. Kandel referred to Heyes and Curry's former partners as the Hole-in-the-Wall Gang, straight out of *Butch Cassidy and the Sundance Kid*. Huggins noted that it would be known as the Curry-Heyes Gang. In a later revision, it became the Devil's Gorge Gang until the name Devil's Hole Gang was finally settled on. Harry Briscoe began life as Ewart Briscoe. Deputy Wade Hollister became Wade Sawyer, Jeremiah Bronson turned into Jeremiah Bailey, then Daley. The more famous Pinkerton agency regressed to become the less historical, more fictional, Bannerman detectives.

Even Smith and Jones took on new aliases, pretending to be agents Grant and Gaines, but it so confused them they could not remember who was who. In *Life on the Mississippi*, Mark Twain proposes that his party of steamboatmen disguise themselves with fictitious names.

> *The idea was certainly good, but it bred infinite bother; for although Smith, Jones, and Johnson are easy names to remember when there is no occasion to remember them, it is next to impossible to recollect them when they are wanted. How do criminals manage to keep a brand-new* ALIAS *in mind? This is a great mystery. I was innocent; and yet was seldom able to lay my hand on my new name when it was needed; and it seemed to me that if I had had a crime on my conscience to further confuse me, I could never have kept the name by me at all.*[9]

Heyes and Curry managed to keep their original aliases straight, but taking on two more proved too much!

In the scene where the corpses of two Devil's Hole Gang members are slid into the baggage car, Heyes and Curry hop in after them. Ben Murphy and

Peter Duel stood with their backs to the open door of the railroad car and hoisted themselves in in perfect synchronicity. Such simultaneous actions occurred in other episodes as well. In "Jailbreak at Junction City," they dismount in exact harmony at the sheriff's offer of $100 pay. When Banker Binford in "A Fistful of Diamonds" meets them on the hotel porch, the boys raise their cigars in greeting, put them back in their mouths and rock forward, then backward in their chairs to allow Binford to pass. In Lom's office in the pilot, they begin to exit, then turn in unison. As they sit, they cross their legs, and remove their hats in exactly the same manner when introduced to Miss Porter. When asked if movements like these were rehearsed or spontaneous, Ben said he and Peter would probably try to do things differently, not alike, so the rare exception when they did things simultaneously was not planned. Their chemistry was such that they each knew how the other was going to act, so they almost never talked about what they were going to do.[10] The effect, however, was a visual representation of that harmony.

For this first appearance of Harry Briscoe, the Bannerman detective who, in later episodes, turns out to be somewhat inept, Roy Huggins expected the character to be "a smart, tough man." The Bannerman men were not "klutz heavies," but tough guys.[11] Huggins and Jo Swerling came up with the idea of hiring J.D. Cannon to play Briscoe. They had done a pilot called *Sam Hill* with Ernest Borgnine and had searched for an actor to play a Mississippi gambler as villain of the piece. They found it difficult to cast the role because it called for a humorous scoundrel. Director Fielder Cook suggested Cannon. Having their doubts but going with Cook's instincts, Huggins and Swerling hired him and he turned out to be hysterically funny in the part. At the time he came aboard *Alias Smith and Jones* to play the Bannerman man, Cannon was a regular on *McCloud,* playing a New York detective saddled with a southwestern cowboy cop. Cannon found the role boring, so he jumped at the chance to turn Briscoe into a sort of western Inspector Clouseau. Cannon told Swerling he always waited eagerly for the next *Alias Smith and Jones* job to come along because it was so much fun to play.

THE GIRL IN BOXCAR #3

"That's the only kind [of experience] to have – authentic."
– Kid Curry

STORY:	GENE RODDENBERRY
TELEPLAY:	HOWARD BROWNE
DIRECTOR:	LESLIE H. MARTINSON
SHOOTING DATES:	JANUARY 7, 8, 11, 12, 13, 14, 1971
ORIGINAL US AIR DATE:	FEBRUARY 11, 1971
ORIGINAL UK AIR DATE:	JUNE 28, 1971

Hannibal Heyes and Kid Curry ride into North Rim, a drab little town suffering from a depression. Under the watchful gaze of some local men, the boys visit Andrew Greer, Attorney at Law. Greer lets them into his office with a furtive air that Heyes and Curry find disconcerting. Greer demands proof they are the men that Colonel Harper sent. A letter of introduction coupled with a description of Harper suffices and Greer relaxes a bit. He tells them the job they're to do has gotten dangerous. Heyes and Curry aren't real happy about this, but still agree to transport $50,000 to Kingsburg.

The boys return to Greer's office in the wee hours to pick up the money. Greer, though nervous, is all business and he has them count the money, pack it in a saddlebag and sign a receipt.

Meanwhile, the local men – Griffin, Stacey, Briggs and Breen – notice the unusual activity in the office across the street and watch with renewed interest.

As Curry and Heyes leave with the money, the men follow. The boys split up, with Heyes leading the men out of town while Curry stays behind and waits for the arrival of a freight train.

The men catch up to Heyes. Griffin, angry at finding he doesn't have the money with him, backhands him in punctuation to his questions about Curry's whereabouts. Heyes stalls, first telling Griffin they had another horse stashed in an alley, then that they picked up a horse from a farmer named Johnson. Neither of these tales is believed and the truth soon comes wafting along in the form of a train whistle. Stacey immediately recognizes its significance and the men return to town, leaving Heyes sitting on the ground nursing his sore jaw.

Curry is ready when the train comes by and with the ease of long practice, jumps aboard the slowly passing boxcar. To his surprise it's already occupied.

The train travels through the night and by morning Curry's new companion, seventeen-year-old Annabelle, is eagerly telling him a rather improbable story of her life. She claims to be a rich girl, the daughter of a financier, running from marriage to Reginald Vandermeter of the Four Hundred, the premier families of New England. In her search for authentic experience, she's traveling by boxcar in order to meet the common people.

Griffin and his men are still in pursuit, trying to figure out where the train stops and for how long, while Heyes continues leisurely towards Kingsburg.

When the train stops to take on water and coal, Curry goes in search of food for the two of them while Annabelle stays behind with orders to open the door when she sees Curry return.

He is successful in his search for food, but not so successful at reboarding the train. The brakeman sees him running for the boxcar and kicks him off just as Curry gains hold. From his position in the dust at the side of the tracks, there's nothing he can do except watch the train steam away, taking Annabelle and the money-filled saddlebag with it.

Curry finds a farmer with a horse to sell – a swayback nag named Princess. He rides along the railroad tracks as dusk falls and eventually meets Annabelle walking toward him, carrying his saddlebag along with her own carpetbag. The first thing he does is check on the money. Annabelle is insulted that Curry seems to be more interested in the saddlebag than he is in her and her temper is not improved when she discovers he has already eaten all the food. Curry apologizes and Annabelle demands he find some more.

Griffin and his men catch up to the train and talk to the brakeman. No one has jumped off the train, but the brakeman did stop one fellow trying to jump on. Griffin and the others continue their pursuit.

Curry and Annabelle find themselves at the home of John and Minerva Lambert. The couple is suspicious at first, given the lateness of the hour, but when Annabelle spins a tale about a broken down buggy, adding that she and Curry are on their honeymoon, the Lamberts welcome them. Over a bowl of hot soup, Annabelle expands her story, sharing their plan for having three children. When Curry observes that the Lamberts' children must be all grown, John contradicts him saying they've been spared the heartache of having children.

John offers to let them spend the night in the barn and, as he and Curry fetch blankets, Curry notices his saddlebag is gone. John assures him it's safe in the hall closet and Curry apologizes for being nervous, blaming it on the honeymoon experience.

Curry and Annabelle retire to the barn, where he makes up two comfortable beds in the hay. Annabelle shivers under her blanket until she can't stand it anymore. She crawls over to Curry and admits she's freezing. He invites her and her blanket to join him. She's concerned about the proprieties and makes sure he understands it's only the cold that has her cuddling up to him.

Curry takes the opportunity their closeness has brought to point out that he knows Annabelle has been lying and asks what the truth is. Annabelle admits she exaggerated a bit, "for the sake of interesting conversation," and says she's on the way to Kingsburg to live with her father, who is not a financier, but is a gentleman. Warm at last, they fall asleep.

Heyes is still on Curry's trail, as are the angry men from North Rim.

The next morning Griffin and his friends finally catch up to Curry and Annabelle as they ride double on Princess. There's no chance of outrunning them, so Curry pulls up and faces the men. Griffin grabs the saddlebag, pulls out a packet of bills and opens it, revealing only newsprint between the real bills on top and bottom. Curry stares in disbelief. Griffin turns his attention to Annabelle's carpetbag but finds only clothing. In a rage, he pulls his gun and only Stacey's quick reaction in blocking his aim stops him from killing Curry. Griffin demands to know what's happened to the money, but Curry is as ignorant as to its whereabouts as the rest of them. Stacey convinces Griffin that the surprised look on Curry's face when the ruse was revealed proves he is telling the truth. Griffin cools down and explains that they're not a bunch of thieves, but simply men who lost money when the bank failed and they're just trying to recover what belongs to them.

After Griffin and the others leave, Curry turns to Annabelle, accusing her of stealing the money. She's deeply hurt. Faced with her tears, Curry relents, saying there's one other possibility – the Lamberts.

They return to the Lambert farm, where Curry explains the situation. Angry at the accusation, John Lambert grabs his rifle, determined not to let Curry search his property. Curry wrestles the gun away from him and a thorough search begins in every cupboard, every drawer, every closet. Faced with a locked door Curry insists, "Either you give me the key or I shoot the door open." When John refuses, Curry makes good on his threat. He shoots the lock off.

It's a child's bedroom. Draped in cobwebs and full of decaying toys, the room has obviously been untouched for many years. Curry, now ashamed of his aggression, quietly promises to repair the lock and make everything as it was.

Curry, Annabelle and the Lamberts continue the search in the barn. There they run into Griffin and his men, who figured they would return to the Lambert farm and have been waiting for them. This is the last straw for John, and he charges at Griffin in agonized rage. Curry takes on Stacey, while Annabelle grabs a shovel and prepares to bring it down on the nearest head. Into this melee enters Heyes, gun at the ready. Griffin and his men are defeated.

The train pulls into Kingsburg. Heyes, Curry and Annabelle alight and come face to face with Greer. Curry says they haven't got the money, something he's sure doesn't surprise the lawyer. Greer cheerfully explains he used them as a decoy, switching the saddlebag while they signed the receipt, and brought the money to Kingsburg himself. Curry starts to take a swing at Greer, but Heyes stops him. Heyes explains they'd have been in big trouble if they'd lost the money, but Greer just shrugs off their concern. "All's well that ends well," he says with a big smile. With a smile of his own, Heyes slugs him. Heyes and Curry share a moment of satisfaction before Annabelle extracts her own revenge on Curry with a sudden slap across his face. Under threat of another slap, Curry apologizes for thinking Annabelle was a thief.

At the hotel, Annabelle proudly asks after her father, DeCourcey Considine. The desk clerk is baffled for a moment, until he realizes she means Deke Considine. He tells her she'll find him in the saloon. If he's got money he plays poker for himself, and if he doesn't, he deals for the house. Right now he's dealing for the house. Annabelle is shattered.

She decides to leave Kingsburg. As she boards the train, she asks Heyes and Curry to tell her father that they've seen her, that she's all grown up and very happy. Curry wonders if she wouldn't rather tell him herself. "No," she replies. "I'm not that grown up." Heyes and Curry watch as the train pulls away, taking Annabelle back home.

ALAN HALE	ANDREW J. GREER
HEATHER MENZIES	ANNABELLE
JOHN LARCH	GRIFFIN
JACK GARNER	STACEY
CONLAN CARTER	BREEN
MICHAEL CARR	BRIGGS
ROYAL DANO	JOHN LAMBERT
CLAUDIA BRYAR	MINERVA LAMBERT
LIAM DUNN	TELEGRAPHER
SANDY WARD	BRAKEMAN
RAYMOND GUTH	FARMER
NORMAN LEAVITT	WAGON DRIVER
RAY BALLARD	HOTEL CLERK

This is the first of five episodes which separate Heyes and Curry for most of the story. The time crunch had already hit the production staff, so they considered any tactic which could speed things up. Short on scripts, in sheer desperation they turned to a 1963 episode of *The Virginian* which originally aired during Huggins's tenure as executive producer on that show. Because it was a Universal property, it was easy enough to dig out the script and go from there. Roy Huggins set about cutting the script, bringing it down from a ninety-minute show to sixty minutes and adapting it to fit *Alias Smith and Jones*. He tightened a story that dragged in spots, but also eliminated some exposition which should have been left in in the interests of clarity.

Heyes and Curry are given the task of transporting $50,000 from North Rim to Kingsburg for a mysterious Colonel Harper, who will put in a good word with the governor for them in return. Greer acts so furtively that the first impression is he's stolen the money. However, a reading of the source material, "Run Away Home," tells us that Greer (Moody in the original) is worried because his withdrawal of Colonel Harper's (Judge Garth's) $50,000 was the last straw for the failing bank. Griffin (Swenson) lost his life savings because of the large withdrawal and he's not about to take it lightly. This gives everyone a stronger motivation for their actions and is something that should have been made more clear in this episode.

While the lack of exposition makes the audience work harder to understand the story, Huggins also strengthened many areas, notably the poignant scene revealing the Lamberts' grief for their dead daughter. In a story conference on December 3, 1970, Huggins expressed concern about the Lamberts' secret. "The mystery about the family does not really pay off in the present script. We ought to be able to do better."[12] In *The Virginian* script, the Lamberts (Lewises), have a trunk full of their daughter's belongings, a trunk which hasn't been opened since the day they buried her. Huggins improved upon this, turning the trunk into a room and having Curry ruthlessly blow off the lock on the door, making this violation of their grief even more shocking.

Because this episode was adapted from a script from another show, it is not one of the best for showing off Heyes and Curry. However, some moments add to our increasing knowledge of the boys. Curry's appetite, already mentioned in "Exit from Wickenburg," is again shown to be a force greater than his common sense, leading him to leave the all-important saddlebag with Annabelle while he goes off for food. A dangerous temper, hinted at in the pilot, comes out here both in the scene where he forces his way into the Lamberts' locked bedroom and at the end where Heyes stops him from punching Greer, urging him to "cool down." In the end, though, this is a story not about two reformed outlaws, but about a young girl gaining new maturity.

Annabelle is seeking to make her fantasies real. Her desire to be part of Society, to have a father who is "a gentleman, an authentic aristocrat, a man of leisure and good manners and style" has led her to hop a freight train and flee from marriage to a wheat farmer. She gains the authentic experience she was after, but discovers that authentic experience also includes reality, the reality that her father is a gambler, not a gentleman. Suddenly, going home and facing marriage to a farmer doesn't seem so bad. Annabelle has grown up.

THE GREAT SHELL GAME

"I'm not much of a talker. More of a man for action than words."
– Kid Curry

STORY:	JOHN THOMAS JAMES
TELEPLAY:	GLEN A. LARSON
DIRECTOR:	RICHARD BENEDICT
SHOOTING DATES:	JANUARY 19, 20, 21, 22, 24, 25, 26, 1971
ORIGINAL US AIR DATE:	FEBRUARY 18, 1971
ORIGINAL UK AIR DATE:	JUNE 21, 1971

The original title of the episode was "The Big Store."

A major fault of the storyteller was in not letting the audience in on Curry's messenger job. If it were such an important document as to require hand-delivery, why was the address not there and why did Curry not worry about it after he met Grace?

At the Jennings County Fair, Hannibal Heyes inconspicuously removes the cotter pin from a wheel on Grace Turner's parked carriage. When the wheel falls off on the road to Mineral Springs as expected, Heyes coincidentally happens by. They introduce themselves and, at her request, he fixes the wheel.

That evening at dinner, Grace tells Heyes, whom she knows as Mr. Smith, that she is a well-invested widow from Philadelphia traveling on holiday. She discovers a wallet under their table containing a substantial amount of money and a card with strange markings on it that identify it as belonging to Dr. Michael Sylvester of the Gentlemen's Jockey Club. When they return the wallet to him, Sylvester, touched by their honesty, rewards them by inviting them to lunch at his club.

Seeing Grace to her room, Heyes discloses that he is owner of the Nevada Queen, a silver mine. Grace is suitably impressed and agrees to lunch with him and the doctor. Heyes returns to Sylvester's room and informs him that the date is set. Grace doesn't know that Dr. Sylvester is really "Soapy" Saunders, a former con man and good friend to Heyes.

(Sagala/Bagwell collection)

The Gentlemen's Jockey Club used in "The Great Shell Game."

During lunch, Dr. Sylvester places a bet for them on Carriepoise who wins the third race at Saratoga. Later that evening, Heyes and Grace help the doctor, now quite intoxicated, to his room. At her questioning, Dr. Sylvester informs her he had been personal physician to a prominent man in the racing world. The man shared the knowledge that the results of some races are known beforehand and the system allows the doctor to live comfortably in retirement. Grace is excited at the prospect of sharing in his easy winnings.

The next time the couple attends the club, Chuck Morgan, who had previously tried to ingratiate himself with Grace at the fair, introduces himself but she is not interested. When Heyes walks by, Morgan recognizes him and calls him by name. Heyes ignores the salutation and the club manager rebukes Morgan for his indiscretion.

Because of the doctor's system, Grace wins but while walking back to her hotel room, she confesses to Heyes that she is not as wealthy as she had led him to believe. She is intrigued by the doctor's system and would like to continue winning. To stop the talk, Heyes kisses her.

Later, Heyes stops by Soapy's room. Soapy wants to wrap up the scheme and return to San Francisco, but is amenable to Heyes's wishes. Watching his dejected friend, Soapy suspects something is wrong. Has he fallen in love with Grace? Should they carry on with the scam? Heyes, though worried that Grace may take the money they've invested in her so far and run, decides to give her "the full treatment."

While dining on their final evening together, Soapy toasts their friendship. Chuck Morgan approaches their table and Heyes has no choice but to introduce him to Grace. As Morgan leads her to the dance floor, Heyes tells Soapy that

Morgan was with Al Plummer when Heyes first started. Soapy knows him as an outside man for the club.

After dinner, Heyes escorts Grace back to her room and she worries that the doctor may be getting ready to clean out the Jockey Club and leave town. She wants another tip from his code book. As she unlocks her door, she spots a note on the floor. Dr. Sylvester has invited them to his room to tell them he has urgent business in San Francisco, but before he goes, will share a final wager. The odds may be as strong as five to one.

Because this will be their final opportunity to bet, Heyes wonders aloud about him and Grace each coming up with $12,500. She's leery, wanting to make a killing, "but I want to kill them, not me." Nevertheless, the doctor thinks that, on his say so, the club manager would take each of their personal checks for $10,000 plus $2,500 in cash. They agree to meet the next day.

Just before noon, the actors at the Jockey Club wait for Heyes and Grace to arrive. At the ringing of the bell over the door, they take their places and act the part of bettors. The club steward, Dr. Sylvester says, will accept their checks. They are to bet on the Isle of Erin in the third race; then he says goodbye.

The horse wins as expected and the steward counts out an even $125,000 but they cannot collect until their out-of-town checks clear. Because that could take a week, Heyes suggests they buy back their checks in cash and the manager okays the deal. Chuck Morgan watches closely as Heyes and Grace leave the club to raise $10,000 each.

Heyes discovers Morgan waiting in his hotel room, holding a gun on him and demanding to know how he could pull a sting on a lovely lady like Grace. The first rule of the Big Store, he says, is to find someone crooked who won't head off to the police when they're taken. He thinks Grace is fine and decent. Heyes proposes to set him straight.

(Sagala/Bagwell collection)

The Hidalgo church and fountain used in "The Great Shell Game."

He relates the story of Kid Curry who was hired to deliver a legal document to an address in Hidalgo, Mexico. After six days' ride, Curry arrives to discover that the building he is looking for doesn't exist. He encounters Grace who informs him that his horse has just been stolen but when he turns back to question her further, she is gone. Down on his luck with no food or money, he finds her in the cantina and asks her what she had seen of the horse thieves. "They were Mexican."

She offers to share her meal and, in return, asks if he would act as a bodyguard for her as she's carrying $20,000 worth of diamonds back to the States.

On the road, the stagecoach breaks down and Grace takes advantage of the unscheduled stop to cool off in a nearby stream. Climbing out of the water, she picks up her dress and finds a rattlesnake poised to strike. At her cry, Curry approaches carefully and kills it with one shot. Grace is weak with relief and embraces Curry, a caress he tenderly returns.

On the last evening before they reach Laredo, Curry admits he'll be glad to get rid of the bag of diamonds and Grace too because she has too many secrets. She hasn't asked about his secrets because she doesn't want to care about him any more than she already does.

As they pull into town and exit the stage, Marshall Slater approaches and arrests the Kid. Grace had sent him a telegram about Curry whom she recognized the first time she saw him. She was once a passenger on a train he'd stopped and now was set to collect the reward. Unfortunately, meantime, she's fallen in love with him.

Curry is sitting in jail when Grace passes him a note through the window advising him to seek cover. As soon as he squeezes under the cot, dynamite blows a hole in the cell wall and he escapes.

Heyes concludes his story to Morgan with the statement that everyone thinks Curry and Grace were in on the scheme together to collect the $10,000 reward on him. Now Heyes and Curry must return the money to get back in the governor's good graces for amnesty, hence $10,000 is the amount they must take Grace for.

At the Jockey Club, Heyes and Grace each present $10,000 cash and their checks are returned. As soon as the steward gets back from the bank, he'll hand over their winnings. Instructing her to order coffee while waiting, Heyes steps out. Grace looks up and finds Kid Curry standing in the corner, smiling at her. She rushes out to the teller's window, but the place is deserted. Realizing she's been duped, she says, "You must have needed it pretty bad." Curry admits they did and discloses that Mr. Smith fell as madly in love with her as he did.

GUEST CAST

DIANA MULDAUR	GRACE TURNER
PETER BRECK	CHUCK MORGAN
SAM JAFFE	DR. MICHAEL SYLVESTER/JONATHON J. "SOAPY" SAUNDERS
VINCENT BECK	CLUB STEWARD
KEN MAYER	MARSHALL SLATER
JIM MALANDA	HOTEL CLERK
PAUL MICALE	MAN

The production ploy of separating Ben Murphy and Peter Duel to film two episodes simultaneously was unfortunate because a primary *Alias Smith and Jones* quality was the chemistry between the characters. Even when the technique was employed, the two usually ended up with at least a few scenes together; there are none in "The Great Shell Game."

The connecting character between their stories is, of course, Grace Turner. Greed corrupted her morals to the point where she was willing to trade Kid Curry for the reward on him. Perhaps she told herself she was acting as a responsible citizen by turning in a notorious outlaw, but that was before she fell in love with him. She compromised her good citizenship by helping him escape, leaving Heyes and Curry no out except to get the reward money back through the elaborate scam.

If Hannibal Heyes and Kid Curry learned the concept of amnesty from *Butch Cassidy and the Sundance Kid*, then the favor was returned when Paul Newman and Robert Redford reprised their partnership as Henry Gondorf and Johnny Hooker and borrowed the Big Store scam, pulling it off in the 1973 film *The Sting*. Bogus bookie joints featured prominently, both in this episode and in the film, and were aimed not only at duping unsuspecting tourists, but could be a lucrative, if dangerous, method of conning a mark. The heyday of the American confidence man was between 1914 and 1923. Heyes, as usual, was ahead of his time, but exuded all of the traits usually associated with a con man: "charming good looks, smooth tongue, falsified and inconsistent background . . . and tailored clothes."[13]

Huggins knew about the Big Store con from having read the autobiography of Joseph R. Weil, known as the "Yellow Kid." In one of the early chapters, Weil tells about a con he pulled in which the results of a horse race were known beforehand and could be bet upon with that knowledge.[14] The prerequisites to any of these cons were that the mark have plenty of money, want to make more, and be willing to cheat. Set up with all its trappings, the fake bookie joint had betting windows, chalkboards for race results, a ticker-tape machine, smoke-filled rooms and up to several dozen actors, from the inside man running the show and the roper who brought the mark in to the bit players and extras, all doing their part for a percentage of the score. It was theater to everyone but the mark.[15]

In one version of the script, Heyes, seeing Grace's greed come to the fore, suggests that other things are more important than money, and their kisses outside of her hotel door suggest what those might be. Her rejection of further love-making makes him stand back and regroup. Finally, despite his growing feelings for her, a "determined" Heyes visits Soapy in his hotel room and insists unenthusiastically that they're going to give her "the works. She's got it coming."[16]

There is a propensity among the ladies of *Alias Smith and Jones* to need a swim to cool off when they're with the boys. Grace is the first one to enjoy a refreshing dip while she and Curry are waiting for the stagecoach wheel to be fixed. When she emerges from the creek, viewers only see her from the neck up. She may have modestly left on her nineteenth century undies and been semi-decent when faced with a rattlesnake curled up in the dress she'd left lying on the ground. However, a note in an early version of the script shows that she is to discover the snake when "she hasn't yet put on a thing. Naturally we are shooting this with discretion and have hired a director known for his stable family life."[17]

RETURN TO DEVIL'S HOLE

"Why did you become an outlaw?"
"As long as this trip is, ma'am, I wouldn't have time to explain that to you.
Or even me."
— Clara Phillips, Hannibal Heyes

STORY:	JOHN THOMAS JAMES
TELEPLAY:	KNUT SWENSON
DIRECTOR:	BRUCE KESSLER
SHOOTING DATES:	JANUARY 13, 14, 15, 18, 19, 20, 1971
ORIGINAL US AIR DATE:	FEBRUARY 25, 1971
ORIGINAL UK AIR DATE:	MAY 17, 1971

A chartered stagecoach speeds across the West. In Garden City, Mrs. Clara Phillips alights from the stage and heads for the hotel where she asks for Mr. Smith, bringing a delighted smile to the face of the unctuous clerk until he realizes she doesn't want Mr. Furnifold Smith, but Mr. Joshua Smith. He tells her with a sniff that Smith and Jones went west. Off goes the chartered stage once again.

Arcadia brings her better luck. Carlton, Mrs. Phillips's butler, brings a wary but intrigued Hannibal Heyes to meet with her. Mrs. Phillips tells him Sheriff Lom Trevors sent her to Heyes because he's the only one who can help her. Her husband, thinking he'd killed his business partner, fled and has taken refuge in Devil's Hole. But the partner didn't die after all and now she needs to find her husband and tell him all the charges have been dropped. As the former leader of the Devil's Hole Gang, Heyes can get her inside the hideout.

Heyes's first instinct is to refuse, but Mrs. Phillips waves a bundle of cash under his nose and he agrees. Kid Curry isn't happy about this and urges Heyes to let him come along. Heyes convinces him to stay behind and wait for Colonel Harper, who's promised them a high paying job. Heyes gives Curry the money Mrs. Phillips paid him, tacitly acknowledging the danger in going to Devil's Hole without his partner.

The original title for this episode was "Return to Devil's Gorge."

Knut Swenson is an alias for Marion Hargrove. In Douglas Heil's book *Prime-Time Authorship: Works About and By Three TV Dramatists*, Hargrove explains that he was unhappy with the way the script turned out and demanded his name be removed. The production office asked for a pseudonym and he chose Knut Swenson because he was fond of King Canute, a Danish king of England.

What's in a name? Black Jack Gibbons, Big Jim Hagenstad, Big Jim Hagen, Joaquin Jimenez Santana, Diego del Vaya Santana. At one time or another, these were all used for the character before settling on Big Jim Santana.

Heyes and Mrs. Phillips make the long trip to Devil's Hole. They pass Kyle at the checkpoint and he tells Heyes that Big Jim Santana is back and running things again. Heyes wasn't counting on this.

The tension mounts as the former and current leaders of the gang meet again, but Big Jim welcomes Heyes with a friendly hug and a slap on the back. Mrs. Phillips goes off with Lobo to get settled while Heyes and Jim talk.

The meeting begins with Jim marking his territory by punching Heyes in the jaw. Heyes reciprocates, just to let Jim know they are equals, and no longer leader and subordinate. With that settled, Mrs. Phillips returns and tells her story. From her description, Jim determines her husband must be Matt Hamilton. Kyle informs Hamilton his wife is here to see him, which he finds very surprising since he's not married, but he goes to see her nonetheless. Mrs. Phillips shocks everyone by pulling a gun and shooting Hamilton as he walks through the door. To justify her actions, she tells Heyes and Jim a new story. Hamilton is not her husband, but the man who seduced her teenage daughter, who subsequently took her own life.

Jim checks on Hamilton's injuries, leaving a disillusioned and disbelieving Heyes with Mrs. Phillips. He returns with word that Hamilton is still alive and soon they will be able to hear his side of the story.

Hamilton tells them Mrs. Phillips doesn't have a daughter and never did. He admits he spent time with her in San Francisco, but he tired of her and left. Jim doesn't believe him and threatens to let Mrs. Phillips have her gun back. Hamilton adds a little detail he hadn't mentioned before – he took $25,000 worth of her jewelry with him when he left.

Jim knows one of them is lying. "Oh, at least one," agrees Heyes. Jim demands proof from Mrs. Phillips that she does indeed have a daughter. A photograph in a locket is back at the Arcadia hotel. Heyes is elected to return for it, while she remains in Devil's Hole.

That evening Heyes tries to convince Jim to retire from the outlaw life. He's incredulous that Jim wants to risk his newly won freedom by pulling another job. But when Jim reveals that the job, the one he spent seven years planning while in prison, is to rob the Wells Fargo Clearing House in Denver, Heyes is impressed in spite of himself. He wards off temptation by arguing even more forcefully and finally stomps off, leaving Jim to think about what he's said.

The next day, after Heyes heads back to Arcadia, Mrs. Phillips breaks into Jim's desk and retrieves her gun with the idea of taking another shot at Hamilton. Jim catches her and puts an end to that plan.

In town, Heyes roots through her luggage and finds the locket. Meanwhile, she and Jim have been trading life stories and find themselves growing attracted to each other.

Heyes returns to Devil's Hole. Jim, Mrs. Phillips and Heyes come together for the unveiling of the photograph. Inside the locket is a photo, but only of Mr. Phillips, not a daughter. Mrs. Phillips now insists she has several photos of her daughter in a safe deposit box in San Francisco. The story of the locket was another ruse to buy time so she could try to kill Hamilton again.

Jim confides that he's thought about what Heyes said and he's decided to give up the outlaw life after the job. The gang would never let him back out now. Heyes agrees it might be tricky, but he talks to the gang about Jim's change of heart. They are not happy and it looks like things might get nasty, but Jim saves the day by telling them that Heyes misunderstood – his retirement will begin *after* the job is over. As they leave the bunkhouse, Jim admits to Heyes he's not going through with the job and they make plans to leave Devil's Hole immediately. The gang senses a double-cross and discovers Jim, Heyes and Mrs. Phillips riding away. They follow in angry pursuit, but the trio manages to escape.

In Arcadia, Mrs. Phillips is ready to board the stagecoach to San Francisco. When Jim asks her what really happened, she admits Hamilton's version is true. She invites Jim to come with her and he accepts. Heyes and Curry see them off, deciding they now have an important friend in San Francisco, if they ever need one.

GUEST CAST

FERNANDO LAMAS	BIG JIM SANTANA
DIANA HYLAND	CLARA PHILLIPS
BRETT HALSEY	MATT HAMILTON
DENNIS FIMPLE	KYLE MURTRY
WILLIAM McKINNEY	LOBO RIGGS
LEE DE BROUX	HARDCASE
SID HAIG	MERKLE
JON LORMER	2ND DESK CLERK
BOOTH COLMAN	CARLTON
CHARLIE BRIGGS	RED MATTSON
VAUGHN TAYLOR	1ST DESK CLERK
ROBERT B. WILLIAMS	STATION AGENT

Of the five episodes which split up Heyes and Curry to accommodate the production time crunch, "Return to Devil's Hole" is the least successful. This episode suffers not only from a lack of interaction between Heyes and Curry, but also from the missed opportunity to explore the conflict between Big Jim and Heyes as current and former leaders of the gang. Instead the story focuses on Heyes trying to convince Big Jim to quit while he's ahead and on the burgeoning romance between Big Jim and Clara Phillips. Taking the attention off the principal characters and placing it on the guest stars contributes greatly to the general dissatisfaction this episode leaves behind.

Several other elements contribute to its failure. Numerous flaws in logic begin with Clara Phillips's assertion that Lom Trevors pointed her toward Heyes. Aside from the fact that such a thing is extremely unlikely behavior on the part of the

SHOOTING DATES: JANUARY 27, 28, 29, FEBRUARY 1, 2, 3, 1971
ORIGINAL US AIR DATE: MARCH 4, 1971
ORIGINAL UK AIR DATE: JULY 26, 1971

Original title of the episode: The Great Western Diamond Hoax.

Skeptical businessman Binford needs re-assurance from a top name evaluator of the stones. The writers debated using Tiffany's and then decided they couldn't and chose a name that sounds like Tiffany's, T.F. Ayers.

August Binford may have been named for August Belmont, a wealthy financier of the 1800s, who had once been chairman of the National Democratic Committee. The Belmont Stakes was named for him in 1867.

It's after hours in Kingsburg and Charlie Wells, the bank manager, accuses president August Binford of speculating with the depositors' money. Threatened with a visit by the State Bank Examiner, Binford kills Wells, then removes all the money from the safe and leaves the bank. He returns shortly with a crowbar, conks himself on the head hard enough to draw blood and dynamites the safe.

Soapy Saunders, Hannibal Heyes and Kid Curry's old friend who helped out with the Big Store con on Grace Turner, is delighted to see them again. His opulent mansion is a wonderful place to visit but Heyes and Curry have come to ask him to teach them one of his scams. Binford has accused them of robbing his bank; the descriptions he gave of the thieves came straight from their inaccurate Wanted posters. Soapy is not surprised, he's never met a banker yet he could trust, but he maintains that cons don't work on bankers. However . . .

Heyes and Curry, dressed as scruffy miners, enter the Kingsburg bank, hoping to rent a lockbox. When Binford learns of their cache – ten fresh-out-of-the-ground diamonds worth a quarter of a million dollars – he's happy to hold them for safekeeping.

That evening they watch as Binford enters his paramour's hotel room. Betsy is a worldly woman who has heard Binford's promises of marriage and future wealth too many times before. But the sight of the uncut diamonds arouses her interest.

Binford steps out to find Heyes and Curry on the front porch of the hotel. He pleads his case to be their personal banker and financial advisor. They know he is untrustworthy because he took the stones to the local jeweler to be evaluated after promising to tell no one, but he retorts that it was necessary to determine their value in order to plot a course of action. They adjourn to Betsy's room to talk.

One man could not afford to pay them what the diamonds are worth, so Binford suggests they incorporate and sell stock to the public, or he could offer them $20,000. They had in mind $100,000 each with $50,000 up front in good faith money. Binford is flabbergasted but agrees only if a mining engineer surveys the diamond field and T.F. Ayers, the experts in New York, appraises the stones. Heyes and Curry cautiously agree.

The next day Heyes and Curry spot Betsy on the street and figure that Binford would tell her first the good, or bad, news from T.F. Ayers. Curry gallantly offers to woo Betsy and get in her good graces. But Betsy rebuffs him with the news that she and Binford are to be married.

Shortly afterwards, Curry spies a cowboy entering Betsy's room. Curry's knock on her door interrupts ardent kisses between Betsy and Ben, the cowboy. Quickly hiding Ben in the next room, Betsy opens the door. Over her protests, Curry enters and says he knows about the cowboy and he could tell Binford. Stepping out from the other room, Ben advises Curry to leave. When the Kid declines the advice, Ben goes for his gun but Curry is quicker. Ben hastily makes his farewells.

Betsy doesn't want to talk to Curry about the million dollar deal with Binford because, as she says, when it comes down to it, it's usually only $8.20. Curry offers her $10,000 if she will help keep Binford from chumping them. Betsy agrees to think about it.

The report from T.F. Ayers proves the diamonds to be top-grade but Binford still insists on seeing the field, accompanied by mining engineer Oliver Bristow. The boys lead blindfolded Binford, Bristow and Betsy to a grassy area they salted with more of Soapy's uncut diamonds. Bristow is knowledgeable in most ores, but not in diamonds, so the field looks authentic to him. Betsy and Binford hunt for the shiny stones as children would for Easter eggs, finding them hidden in the grass or under rocks. Their excitement mounts as they discover more and more. Heyes and Curry stand by smirking, barely containing their amusement.

Back in his office and satisfied with the reality of the field, Binford gives the boys the agreed-upon advance of $50,000. Heyes signs over the claim and a map to the field. On the way out, Heyes wonders about their timing in going straight. They're too good at cons like this.

Curry stops at Betsy's room to find out where Binford got the money. Now that the banker has the diamonds, Betsy sneers at the piddling $10,000 Curry promised her. He threatens to tell Binford about her cowboy friend, so Betsy admits Binford embezzled the money from his own bank.

The tri-colored stock certificates are a source of pride to Binford until Heyes announces there is no genuine diamond field and that rough, unpolished diamonds cannot be accurately evaluated. Heyes offers him a way out from being taken in their confidence game – all he has to do is rescind his claim about the men who robbed his bank. Binford doesn't understand. "I'm Hannibal Heyes and he's Kid Curry," explains Heyes. "We don't rob banks any more," Curry chimes in. "And when we were robbing banks, we didn't kill people. . . .We were trying our best to get an amnesty and you tore it all apart." If Binford retracts his statement to the sheriff about the bank robbers, they'll return the money. If not, they'll disappear, money and all. Binford is left with no choice.

Sheriff Lom Trevors arrives in Kingsburg to investigate the theft and the boys assure him they will be cleared in tomorrow's papers.

After reading the news story, Betsy confronts Curry about Binford's retraction, the diamond field and the money, angry that she can't ask Binford about it because he's home with his wife. Curry explains about the salted field and it suddenly dawns on Betsy why they pulled the elaborate scam. Thinking they still have the $50,000 and wanting her promised share, she offers the information that Binford confessed the murder and bank robbery to her on the night it happened. Curry thanks her for the knowledge but says they turned the money over to Sheriff Trevors and therefore can't pay her for the proof. She decides they can't be Heyes and Curry because outlaws wouldn't have turned money over to a sheriff. Heyes reveals they are really Hotchkiss and Rembacker, treasury agents who have been on the case from the beginning. Betsy leaves, smugly sure of nothing.

Returning Soapy's diamonds, Heyes and Curry listen as he reads aloud Binford's retraction in the Kingsburg *Gazette*. As they leave, Soapy begins to count the stones.

GUEST CAST

JOHN MCGIVER	AUGUST BINFORD
SAM JAFFE	SOAPY SAUNDERS
MICHELE CAREY	BETSY JAMISON
MIKE ROAD	SHERIFF LOM TREVORS
PAUL SORENSON	OLIVER BRISTOW
KEN SCOTT	BEN MORGAN
CLARKE GORDON	CHARLIE WELLS
LOU WAGNER	BUTLER

The character of Soapy Saunders is based on a man named Jefferson Randall Smith. The nickname "Soapy" came from a con Smith pulled. He would wrap hundreds of pieces of soap in full view of an unsuspecting audience while making a show of placing a $50 or $100 bill in about ten percent of the packages. He pocketed the large bill through sleight of hand before selling the nickel bars of soap for $1. Smith plied his trade in gambling halls and mining camps throughout the west. In the first draft of the story, Heyes remembers watching Soapy work, "hustling those bars of soap for five dollars apiece, swearing with a straight face that one of them was wrapped inside with a hundred dollar bill."[22]

This time it's not only the money that concerns Heyes and Curry but the murder of the bank manager. Though it's a well-known fact that, in all their thieving days, Heyes and Curry never shot anyone, they don't want Sheriff Lom Trevors or the governor thinking they've started to. Soapy is afraid bankers cannot be conned because they're too cautious. Given their desperation, though, he shows them the salted diamond field con, one he's learned about but has never used. At least it's new, he tells them.

Apparently, Soapy had never heard that Philip Arnold and John Slack pulled the exact same con on San Francisco Bank of California president William Ralston in 1871. But Roy Huggins had and "A Fistful of Diamonds" duplicates that story right down to the president being blindfolded while being led to the salted field. Other similarities include having Tiffany's evaluate the stones as having great value; including a mining engineer's validation of the field; and enticing the investors (in the episode only Binford) to charter a corporation.

Soapy had learned the con from a friend in Holland who told him there was no one in the United States who could evaluate rough uncut stones because diamond cutters know nothing about the raw gems. If his friend is wrong, if T.F. Ayers' evaluations came in low, the boys would be in big trouble.

Betsy starts off in the rough story line as a singer, the star attraction in the town's saloon, a young and pretty kept woman. She comes across as a bit of ditz, greedy and not too particular about where money comes from. She cozies up to Binford even though he's married because she expects to live like royalty as a banker's wife. "She is the one who has made a crook out of Binford. He was a relatively honest guy until he met her. Now he's trying to get rich quick so they can go to Europe. Betsy is the brains – she's been pushing Binford."[23] But on the side she has a lover, a lowly cowboy whom Curry easily outdraws. She's suspicious of Heyes and Curry, but is willing to listen to their deal if it would net her substantial cash to be independently wealthy.

When Robert Hamner wrote the teleplay, his first draft contained a scene in which Heyes explains to Soapy that Lom helped arrange amnesty for them, but they don't have it all yet. They have to show the governor they can stay out of trouble for one year and then he'll sign the amnesty papers and make it official. Roy Huggins knew where he stood on the boys' amnesty. In re-write notes for Hamner, Huggins told him they hadn't got *any* kind of amnesty. If they behave themselves and stay out of trouble, in a year or so the governor will consider the possibility of giving them amnesty. They haven't got partial amnesty, all they have is a promise.[24]

STAGECOACH SEVEN

"The truth is you're both better fellas than you think you are."
– Charlie Utley

STORY:	JOHN THOMAS JAMES
TELEPLAY:	DICK NELSON
DIRECTOR:	RICHARD BENEDICT
SHOOTING DATES:	FEBRUARY 8, 9, 10, 11, 12, 15, 16, 1971
ORIGINAL US AIR DATE:	MARCH 11, 1971
ORIGINAL UK AIR DATE:	MAY 24, 1971

Stagecoach #7 pulls into Benton Pass. Inside the station, the passengers – Dan and Ellen Loomis and their baby, Benjamin and Winifred Bowers, and Hannibal Heyes and Kid Curry – wait with varying degrees of patience while the coach is readied. Harry Downs crosses from the hotel and buys his ticket. As everyone prepares to board, the driver, Joe, points out there's one passenger too many and someone will have to ride up on top with him. No one volunteers.

Downs decides that Dan Loomis, being the youngest man, will be the one to ride on top. Dan protests, saying he needs to be with his wife who adds that she needs Dan to help hold the baby. Downs snarls, "This is between your husband and me. Women ought to learn to keep their noses out of men's business."

This is too much for Curry. He steps forward, pointing out that as Downs bought the last ticket, he should ride up top. Downs turns his venom on Curry and orders him to get up on the seat or get out. Or he could draw. Curry draws. "Did I make the right choice, Mr. Downs?"

The stagecoach leaves town with Downs riding next to Joe. Heyes and Curry sit on either side of Winifred Bowers. Heyes asks if she wouldn't rather have her husband beside her but she prefers to ride backwards and her husband will only sit facing forward. Mr. Bowers rudely cuts off her cheerful explanation and Winifred falls silent.

On the road, they're stopped by a gang of robbers led by Clint Weaver who orders the passengers out of the coach. Joe insists they're not carrying anything valuable, which is borne out by a quick search. The gang is disappointed and makes do with the passengers' money and jewelry. Weaver focuses on Heyes and Curry. He's seen them somewhere before.

The gang takes off with their loot. Curry and Heyes have recognized Clint Weaver in return and worry about whether he's recognized them, but there's nothing to do except climb back into the stagecoach and hope for the best.

The thieves gallop off. Weaver is still wondering about those two familiar faces. Eventually it comes to him. "Boys, we just held up Kid Curry and Hannibal Heyes."

Stagecoach #7 arrives at a way station, welcomed by Charlie Utley and his wife Hannah. Heyes and Curry linger outside looking for any sign of the Weaver gang before heading into the adobe cabin. Bowers, irritated at being robbed, fills out a claim form, insisting the stage line reimburse him for his total loss.

Charlie, switching out the horses, enters the barn and is shoved against a wall with a gun to his neck. He's not impressed by Weaver's assertion that this is his lucky day. Weaver offers Charlie $2,000 in exchange for his handing over a couple passengers. Charlie refuses, so Weaver informs him the two men are Heyes and Curry. Charlie, now more amenable to the plan, isn't convinced that he'll ever see the $2,000. To show his good faith, Weaver hands over the loot from the robbery and Charlie agrees to bring the boys out.

With the rifle from the stagecoach, Charlie enters the cabin, closes the door and cocks the weapon, focusing everyone's attention on him. Heyes and Curry slowly turn around. "Begging your pardon, sir, but your rifle . . . it's pointing at us," Heyes says politely. Charlie agrees and tells Hannah to take their guns.

Outside, the Weaver gang is moving into position around the cabin.

Charlie orders Hannah to tie the boys up. She protests, wondering why. Charlie inquires, "Which one's Heyes and which one's Curry?" Then he opens the window and calls out he's going to turn in Heyes and Curry himself. Weaver is angry. He'll give him three minutes to bring out the outlaws or the gang will start shooting. Charlie is unconcerned. He has the passengers turn over the solid oak table and take refuge behind it. Harry Downs is unwilling to put himself in danger for two outlaws, but Charlie relieves Downs of his gun, so he isn't tempted to try anything.

When three minutes are up, the gang starts shooting as promised. As the passengers duck behind the table, Joe tries to convince Charlie to give up Heyes and Curry in the interests of keeping the passengers safe. Charlie won't hear of it. Heyes offers his own reason for staying with Charlie – while not admitting they're Heyes and Curry, he thinks Charlie will turn them in alive, unlike the Weaver gang, who will undoubtedly kill them. Charlie is pleased with this reasoning and even Joe has to admit Heyes has a point.

Charlie and Joe return fire. When things quiet down, Charlie checks the passengers. Weaver once again demands the boys. When Charlie refuses, the gang starts another barrage of gunfire.

Downs watches for an opportunity. When it comes, he hits Joe over the head and takes his rifle. Downs gets the drop on Charlie, forces him to untie the boys, then makes a deal with Weaver. Dan Loomis jumps Downs, knocking the rifle from his grasp. Heyes makes a move for it, but Charlie commands him not to try it. Heyes and Curry thank Dan as Hannah ties them up again. Downs is also tied and left behind the table. Charlie offers Dan ten percent of the reward, but Dan refuses, saying he wouldn't feel right taking it. Ellen looks at her husband with pride.

Charlie informs Weaver there's been a change of plans. Bowers is angry. If it weren't for Dan, they could all be on their way by now. Dan is chagrined and Mrs. Bowers stares at her husband.

The gang begins shooting again. During a lull, Ellen Loomis screams. Harry Downs has been killed. Charlie covers the body, observing, "Some fellas just don't have no luck at all." Weaver again demands Heyes and Curry, threatening to shoot until everyone is dead.

Bowers continues to complain, insisting he's had all he's going to take on account of two criminals. He callously suggests they send Heyes and Curry out to their deaths. "Now you push those two out that door and get those killers off our necks!" Bowers shouts at Charlie. "Or so help me, I'm going to sue your company for every nickel they've got." This is the last straw for Mrs. Bowers. She unleashes a tirade – saying she's stood by for fifteen long years through all his petty tantrums, but this time it's not about money, but about the lives of two men, and she won't stand by silently. She orders him to be still. Bowers is shocked and sits down quietly as everyone in the room gazes at the mousy Mrs. Bowers in awe.

Curry speaks up, pointing out that in one way Bowers was right. It isn't safe in that room. The next bullet might hit the women or the baby. Heyes and Curry offer to leave. Charlie unties them but as Curry unbolts the door, he levels his rifle on them, demanding they stop. He just wanted to see if they truly meant to leave. He'll return their guns if they help hold off the bandits and promise not to use them on anyone in the room. The boys agree. Dan Loomis also volunteers to help. They take places at the windows. Finally Bowers comes out of his sulk and also volunteers. Now there are seven people to hold off the seven gang members.

The final battle begins. A posse, looking for the overdue stagecoach, arrives and the gang retreats, the posse on their trail. Curry figures they've aced the Weaver gang out of the reward money, but Heyes wonders about Charlie. Will he still turn them in?

As the passengers climb on board the coach, Charlie pulls out the loot Clint had bribed him with and returns it to them. Bowers humbly thanks him. Curry and Heyes ask what Charlie plans to do. They don't want to go to jail. Charlie urges them to relax, he won't turn them in now that he's gotten to know them. With handshakes and thanks, the boys board the stagecoach and leave with the others

Joe pulls up a few miles later and tells Heyes and Curry that this is where they get off. A rancher nearby will sell them some horses. Heyes and Curry wish everyone luck and walk off in the direction of the friendly rancher.

GUEST CAST

KEENAN WYNN	CHARLIE UTLEY
STEVE IHNAT	HARRY DOWNS
L.Q. JONES	CLINT WEAVER
DANA ELCAR	BENJAMIN T. BOWERS
JOHN KELLOGG	JOE
MITZI HOAG	WINIFRED BOWERS
ANGELA CLARKE	HANNAH UTLEY
RANDOLPH MANTOOTH	DAN LOOMIS
SALLIE SHOCKLEY	ELLEN LOOMIS
GEOFFREY LEWIS	PATCH
NICK BENEDICT	PHIL
BERNARD GREENE	STATIONMASTER

What usually comes to mind when you think of a Western is action – gun-fights, stampedes, posses in pursuit of the bad guys. While this episode has plenty of gunplay, the real action is far more subtle, confined to the changes of heart made by the characters. This is the first of three episodes to explore the conflicts between people confined together against their will. A routine stage hold-up is the catalyst for forcing this disparate group into a situation that tests both their courage and their beliefs. Everyone at the way station has changed by the time the ordeal is over.

Women are often incidental to a western story. Even in *Alias Smith and Jones,* there are episodes in which not a single woman appears, but in "Stagecoach Seven" the women are more important than it would first appear. The three women, Winifred Bowers, Ellen Loomis and Hannah Utley, symbolize three stages in the quest for equality with men.

Winifred Bowers represents the traditional female. Quiet and submissive, she defers to her husband's wishes in everything from conversation to stagecoach seating. Her husband is firmly in charge, not allowing her even to engage in polite chitchat without his express approval. One can see that she is beginning to think about challenging her husband as the journey begins. Inside the coach, Winifred is seated between Heyes and Curry. Heyes offers to switch places with her, but Mr. Bowers squelches her explanation and Winifred falls silent. But in the first draft script, this is where she takes her first small step of rebellion, finishing her comment to Heyes, "But it was very nice of you to offer, young man. Thank you." This was deleted in subsequent drafts and was replaced by a flash of anger directed at Mr. Bowers before she lowers her eyes. After the robbery, she studiously avoids looking at her husband, keeping her gaze fixed firmly out the window. Her distancing herself from her husband continues when the Weaver gang begins shooting and the passengers take refuge behind the table. Winifred helps the Loomises protect their baby, rather than looking for her own protection from her husband. She is also the one to rush over to check on Joe after he's been knocked out by Downs. Throughout the shooting, her husband looks only to his own safety. When Mr. Bowers insists Charlie give up Heyes and Curry or he'll sue the company, Winifred lets loose with fifteen years of pent-up frustration and her husband is left in shock. However, her words change her husband, causing him to re-evaluate his actions. His newfound willingness to change is demonstrated when they resume their stagecoach journey. Mr. Bowers is sitting next to his wife, both of them facing backwards. Roy Huggins wanted to keep this change subtle, trusting the audience to notice for themselves. In a story conference on February 1, 1971, he noted: "Skip the business about Mrs. Bowers wanting [her husband] to sit with her. We should not try to tie that string – we should leave it dangling a little. In other words, he may be riding beside her this time. We say nothing about it. He's riding backwards."[25]

Ellen Loomis represents the middle of the journey to equality. As a young wife and mother, she defers to her husband, but is also willing to stand up for herself, showing more gumption than Dan does. Downs sneers and tells her to stay out of men's business, dismissing her as being unworthy of his further attention. She backs down, as befitting a modest woman, but she fully expects her husband to stand up for her. Dan's timidity disappoints her, but she accepts it calmly, as a dutiful wife. Her actions have affected her husband, though. Later on he pulls courage from his wife's expectations of him and he jumps Downs, saving Heyes and Curry. The Loomises are on their way toward a marriage of true partnership.

The Utleys have already reached this point. Hannah Utley represents the emancipated female. A staunch woman of the frontier, she's an equal partner with her husband, following his orders not because she's cowed but because she trusts him and is willing to follow his lead and wait for a better moment to ask questions. Charlie depends on her to help defend the passengers from the Weaver gang and Hannah is up to the task, wielding her rifle to great effect, rather than hiding behind the table with the other women. Her femininity is never in question, though, as her compassion for others is apparent. Just as Charlie trusts Hannah to back him up in the gun battle, Hannah trusts Charlie to give up the lure of $20,000 and do what's right. Sure enough, Charlie uses Heyes and Curry's willingness to give themselves over to the Weaver gang in order to keep the others from being hurt as justification for letting them go.

These three women have changed the men in their lives in significant ways. Charlie has overcome his moment of greed, Benjamin Bowers has gained respect for his wife, Dan Loomis has grown from a young man to a confident husband. Heyes and Curry have also been changed. They've discovered that underneath their larcenous hearts, they might just have a bit of nobility.

THE MAN WHO MURDERED HIMSELF

"A good lawman can generally feel when a fellow's tellin' the truth or when he's lyin' to him."
– Sheriff Benson

STORY:	JOHN THOMAS JAMES
TELEPLAY:	ROBERT HAMNER AND JOHN THOMAS JAMES
DIRECTOR:	JEFFREY HAYDEN
SHOOTING DATES:	FEBRUARY 17, 18, 19, 22, 23, 24, 1971
ORIGINAL US AIR DATE:	MARCH 18, 1971
ORIGINAL UK AIR DATE:	JUNE 14, 1971

Gingerly, Hannibal Heyes and Kid Curry hoist a box of TNT onto a wagon. Curry has found them a job hauling mining supplies that pays $200. On the way out of town, he finds another job listed in the newspaper. An archy-ologist seeks a guide familiar with the Devil's Hole area and he's paying $30 per day plus bonus. Since each job only requires one man, they flip a coin to determine who takes which one.

Curry heads for the mountains with the wagon while Heyes meets Mr.

Alexander in the hotel lobby. Alexander questions Mr. Smith's knowledge of Devil's Hole country and asks him to draw a map of it, which he compares to a map drawn on a piece of rawhide. He finds them remarkably similar. He also insists that Smith demonstrate his shooting ability. Satisfied, Alexander introduces Smith to the other members of the archeological party – Mr. Parker and Mr. and Mrs. Finney. Alexander expounds on his theory that tall, red-headed Indians once lived in the Devil's Hole region and he hopes to find proof.

While packing for the excursion, Heyes is summoned to the sheriff's office and enters to find the sheriff studying his and Curry's Wanted posters. The sheriff wants to know how Mr. Smith knows the Devil's Hole area and how he got in there without being killed by Heyes and Curry. Heyes explains that he and a friend went gold prospecting in the region. They had seen the gang off in the distance but weren't bothered by them. The sheriff is surprised because they are "two of the orneriest critters that the good Lord ever set amongst us," but is satisfied with Smith's answers. Doc Wilson enters and tells Heyes that the Finneys were on their way to Boston when they

The original title was "Hunt for a Lost Tribe."

Curry's unfamiliarity with the occupation of archeologist prompts him to not only wonder what it is but to mispronounce it as "archy-ologist." Huggins had the mispronunciation in mind when he originally wrote the story. Curry finally settles on a definition as someone who is paying $30 a day plus bonus.

Heyes's drawing of Devil's Hole area showing mountains, lake, river and forest.

got off the train because Mrs. Finney was ill. The doctor could find nothing wrong and when Alexander invited Mr. Finney to go on the trip, Mrs. Finney suddenly got better. It's all very strange. Also, Doc knows something about archeologists and Alexander isn't one. The sheriff sends Heyes off with a warning about what he's getting into.

Despite the danger, Curry urges his team of horses hauling the wagonload of TNT up a hill. It's easier and faster, and even more dangerous, going down the other side.

As Heyes and the archeological party are riding along, the Devil's Hole Gang appears above them on a far ridge. Heyes volunteers to ride up and assure them they mean no harm. He tells Kyle and the boys the reason for the intrusion and Hank verifies the rumor about the seven-foot tall red-headed Indians. The gang, astonished to learn Heyes is earning $30 a day, decides to keep an eye on the group anyway.

Kid Curry urges his horses up another grade. This one is too steep and when the wagon begins to slide backwards, he jumps for cover, sheltering his head from the dynamite blast he is sure will come.

That evening, Mrs. Finney decides a nice way to cool off would be to wet her hands and feet in the river. With permission from her husband, she invites Mr. Smith to escort her. She slips when wading into the water and grabs Heyes's hand for help getting back onshore. They end up in a near-embrace.

MILLS WATSON	————————	SQUINT SIMPSON
DICK CROCKETT	————————	LEFTY GOOCH
WALT DAVIS	————————	SHERIFF BREWSTER
JEROME COWAN	————————	WALDO HENNESSY
CHUCK ROBERSON	————————	STAGE DRIVER
C. ELLIOTT MONTGOMERY	–	JENSON
FRANK ARNO	————————	PHIL LAUDERMILK
READ MORGAN	————————	CONDUCTOR

This episode was one of two stories already in development which Roy Huggins kept when he took over as executive producer, making this one of the few first season scripts not rushed. The treatment was turned in on November 2, 1970, followed by the first draft script on November 20. It was discussed and further developed in two story conferences and rewritten four more times between then and the end of February 1971. While the storyline itself went through only modest changes, the most important thing accomplished during the rewrites was developing the characters of Heyes and Curry.

Although this episode became the tenth one aired, it was the subject of the first story conference after Huggins came on board, thus many of the tenets of the series were decided during the development of this story. When Lom Trevors gave Heyes and Curry the aliases Smith and Jones, he didn't provide first names. They were still without first names in Howard Browne's initial script. Huggins wanted to add plausibility to the series and noted that "we must do something about those names. Perhaps we can use Dudley Jones and Ambrose Smith."[29] There followed a discussion about "Smith" and "Jones" and instead of Ambrose and Dudley the boys became Joshua and Thaddeus, names of the period that Huggins liked. Another change was made regarding the reward offered for the notorious pair. The first draft script opened with a close shot of Heyes and Curry's Wanted poster – which included photos of the boys, albeit "hairy and unkempt," and announced the reward of $500 for the pair. Huggins eliminated the photos and upped the reward to $10,000 a piece, a more fitting amount for the two most successful outlaws in the West.

Another first draft scene showed the boys considering keeping the $20,000 they've taken away from Squint's gang. Curry suggests using the money to head to South America where they could live the good life. Heyes reminds him they'd never get an amnesty if they did that. Curry responds, "I been thinkin' about that. Say we do keep outta trouble for a year and the Governor gives us amnesty. Whatta we do then? You see us workin' for day wages on a ranch? Clerkin' in a grocery store?"[30] Heyes is deep in thought and doesn't answer right away. Curry decides he's tired of running, so he's willing to stay on the straight and narrow. Heyes, though, now thinks keeping the money would be a good idea. They could go to Paris, open up an American saloon and get rich. Finally they decide to return the money because there is sure to be a reward, and that way they will still get a substantial sum, yet be able to continue to seek amnesty. Huggins didn't like this scene because it dealt with the ethical basis of the series in a way he found "unnerving." He wanted their attempts to earn an amnesty to be a sincere effort, based on their inherent humanity. He first thought the scene would work if handled right, but at the second story conference he cut it out, saying, "the audience won't be interested in two guys who are thieves, but who aren't stealing just because it isn't practical to do so."[31]

When it comes to ethics, Huggins wasn't overly resolute. He didn't want Heyes and Curry to be incorrigible, but since they were outlaws he didn't want them to be too noble, either. Another early scene that was ultimately abandoned concerned the letter. Heyes and Curry go after it because Leslie promised them $500. In Huggins's opinion it would be natural for the boys to open the letter to see why it was worth so much to her.

> Their temptation to open the letter and not opening it exposes a weakness in the story. There's nothing illegal or even terribly immoral about opening that letter. Far more realistically than their thinking about keeping the twenty grand would be their thinking about opening the letter . . . What makes this letter worth five hundred dollars? [I] would not be offended if they opened it.[32]

Maintaining the balance putting Heyes and Curry in the realm of "pretty good bad guys" was very important in the early days of the series. This was an era where the audience still expected the protagonists to be the good guys, so the writers had to be careful to make sure they were good enough to be worth rooting for while remaining larcenous enough to make them interesting and believable as ex-outlaws. "The Root of It All" strikes that balance perfectly.

THE 5TH VICTIM

"You worry about stayin' on your horse and I'll worry about stayin' on mine."
— Hannibal Heyes

STORY:	JOHN THOMAS JAMES
TELEPLAY:	GLEN A. LARSON
DIRECTOR:	FERNANDO LAMAS
SHOOTING DATES:	FEBRUARY 22, 23, 24, 25, 26, MARCH 1, 1971
ORIGINAL US AIR DATE:	APRIL 1, 1971
ORIGINAL UK AIR DATE:	MAY 31, 1971

Hannibal Heyes and Kid Curry gallop through beautiful country tracking a mountain lion. There's no hurry, Heyes insists, the tracks they're following are two days old. Curry disagrees, they're "two hours fresh." Heyes argues that he should know because he was the "champeen tracker in all southern Utah," a fact

The sheriff and deputy approach the house, having come to the same conclusion as Curry. Jake escapes out the back, hoping Rachel will stall them so he can get away. She successfully puts them off but when Curry rides up, she implores him to go after Jake. She will stick by her husband after all. Curry can't interfere in Jake's problem with the law, he tells her, and Rachel knows why. When Heyes was delirious, he let slip their true identities. She threatens to tell the sheriff who they really are if Curry won't go after Jake.

Curry worries Jake will shoot him in desperation. He tracks him over the course of a day and a night and gets close enough to call out Rachel's pleas for his return. It takes a lot of convincing; Curry argues he'll testify in Jake's behalf that Harvey was going to kill him. Jake finally agrees to return.

Next day, Heyes carefully climbs on his horse to leave for the stage depot. Rachel promises never to tell anyone that he is Hannibal Heyes and Curry is the Kid. How did she know? "You got a big mouth when you got a bullet in your head," Curry tells him.

GUEST CAST

JOSEPH CAMPANELLA	JAKE CARLSON
FREDERIC DOWNS	JUDGE PETERS
SHARON ACKER	RACHEL CARLSON
SEAN GARRISON	HARVEY BISHOP
RAMON BIERI	SHERIFF MOODY
BOYD RED MORGAN	AUGIE HELMS
WOODROW PARFREY	SAM WINTERS
LINDSAY WORKMAN	MINISTER
BILL QUINN	DOCTOR
DENNIS ROBERTSON	DEPUTY
BARBARA RHOADES	HELEN
GEORGE CHANDLER	BARTENDER

"The 5th Victim" claims a prestigious ancestor in Agatha Christie's *The A.B.C. Murders,* in which one killing is concealed within a series of murders committed to look like the work of a homicidal maniac. The sheriff fills the role of red herring à la Christie. Is he left because he's the murderer or because he needs to be the one to figure out who is?

Roy Huggins's original storyline called for Kid Curry to be shot and to spend the remainder of the show recuperating in bed "and we kind of forget him."[33] Heyes gets to figure out who is killing the poker players. In the first version of the story, Harvey was psychopathic; his aim was to murder Jake Carlson and win Rachel. Though she had said no to his advances, she didn't have him fired; perhaps he thought she was just strait-laced and needed convincing, taking her compassion as flirtation. Rewrite notes indicate it was Harvey who spread the rumors that he and Rachel were lovers. Rachel hadn't heard the rumors.[34] In the end, she does go as far as boarding the stagecoach to leave but changes her mind when she learns her husband turned himself in.

In this episode, the writers embellish the traits they had been developing for the two outlaws. Heyes's fingers, so adept at manipulating the tumblers of safes, are sensitive enough to detect one missing card in the deck. That one card was initially written as the Ace of Spades but Huggins found that too much of a cliché and changed it to the Ace of Hearts. Familial trust between the partners is confirmed when the sheriff escorts Curry to Heyes's bedside and Heyes corroborates that Curry was ahead of him when he was shot, despite the concussion which precludes any memory of exactly where Curry was at the time. Heyes claims to be a "champeen tracker," but Curry's tracking talent led them to the mountain lion and later to Jake.

Jake Carlson's name in the original story was changed from Ben Carlson in what appears to be a deliberate attempt to reflect the Biblical couple Jacob and Rachel. In Genesis 29, the couple first meets at a well. It usually required many men to shove aside the heavy stone that covers it, but Jacob is so taken with Rachel's beauty that he moves it by himself so her sheep can drink. Though wells were no doubt a significant part of nineteenth century life, no one in the series goes to draw water from a well but Rachel. Harvey's surname's transformation from the original Collins to Bishop also reflects an attempt to bring in a religious connotation.

Roy Huggins recalled that the director of "The 5th Victim," Fernando Lamas, hounded him for a directing job. Huggins had a theory which he believed was a Hollywood truism – anybody can direct. He was also sure that "every now and then you find someone who not only can direct but he can direct well. Fernando wasn't one of those people."[35] However, Lamas did create interesting camera angles in the scene in which Curry, the sheriff, and Jake question a bedridden Heyes. Instead of seeing the visitors through Heyes's eyes only, viewers see them through the rails of the headboard as though through the bars of a jail, giving the impression that the three are in a kind of cell, ignorant of who committed the murders. Heyes himself is confined by the bars at the head and foot of the bed, physically and mentally because of his injury.

In the scene in which Curry visits the sheriff's office but learns from the deputy that the lawman is out, the final shot is of a gun belt hanging on a coat rack. Viewers are left to ponder the implication. Huggins remembered another director who filmed something similar. Two people have conversed and get up to leave. The camera moved to a picture on the wall. "Now to the audience, this is intentional, this isn't just a dumb director who didn't know how to [end a scene], who said, 'Shoot the picture. The scene needs an end of some kind, so I'll move in on the picture.' He didn't have the brains to know . . . one of the fundamental principles of his profession."[36] The gun belt turns out to be equally insignificant.

However, Lamas was talented in his use of light and darkness to underscore the theme. It's a bright sunny day when the boys come in with a dead mountain lion and the scene is upbeat, they've done a good job. Both Heyes and Sam Winters are shot at night, the darkness hiding the killer from watchful eyes. It is also nighttime when Rachel is accosted by Harvey Bishop at the well. While questioning the saloon girl about Harvey, Curry repeatedly turns up the lamp in her room seeking illumination while Helen turns it down after each question to resume their love-making and to keep hidden her relationship with Harvey. An oil lamp on the sheriff's desk lights up his office but doesn't do much to shed light on who's committing the murders. It's another sunny day when Curry confronts Rachel in the meadow about his suspicions regarding her and Harvey Bishop. His threat to return if anything should happen to her husband casts a somber pall over Rachel's face. Sunset and sunrise show time passing when Curry chases after Jake to bring him back.

Curry is reluctant to go after Jake because he knows of his prowess with a rifle. Three times in the dialogue, Jake's marksmanship is established. His ranch hand Harvey was obviously also a good shot; he managed to hit all the men he took aim at. Heyes got lucky and recovered. So why did Jake need to hire Smith and Jones to track and kill the big cats on his ranch? Because, as Huggins, the great recycler of plots, story gimmicks, and stock footage, notes in the original story, "We have great stock of cougars being shot."[37]

JOURNEY FROM SAN JUAN

"Maybe I'll get over the way I feel about you, but I won't forget you."
– Michelle Monet

STORY:	JOHN THOMAS JAMES
TELEPLAY:	DICK NELSON
DIRECTOR:	JEFFREY HAYDEN
SHOOTING DATES:	MARCH 10, 11, 12, 15, 16, 17, 1971
ORIGINAL US AIR DATE:	APRIL 8, 1971
ORIGINAL UK AIR DATE:	JULY 19, 1971

Roy Huggins first used this story in an episode of *Maverick* titled "Escape to Tampico."

Hannibal Heyes and Kid Curry are rounding up maverick cattle under the suspicious eyes of two Mexican bandidos, Juan and Pedro. As the cows head down the trail, the two Mexicans approach wanting to know what the gringos are doing. Heyes cheerfully explains they're going to drive the cattle north and sell them in Arizona. Juan offers his opinion that such work could cause them to die before their time, but Heyes and Curry dismiss this notion. Juan and Pedro depart after one more subtle warning.

The boys return to their camp, complaining about the cowboy life as they herd the cattle into the corral. They are comforted by the thought that this job is just a cover to explain their presence in San Juan. A blood-curdling scream greets Heyes as he climbs into the chuck wagon. Curry pulls his gun, ready for whatever happens next. A young woman, Michelle Monet, pokes her head out of the wagon, spewing French invectives. Heyes shushes her and she calms down, somewhat abashed to learn they're the owners of the chuck wagon she's moved into. She tells them she doesn't have any money and is hiding from Captain McTavish, a man who promised her free passage home to New Orleans on his ship. Once at sea, she discovered her passage wasn't as free as she thought it would be and when they docked in San Juan she jumped ship.

In town, Curry pays for Michelle's hotel room while Heyes accompanies her to the casino to see if Captain McRavish is anywhere about. "McTavish, you mean," Michelle corrects. "Oh, you were making a small joke." Heyes gives a half-hearted chuckle. "Smaller than I figured." Curry joins them. While she freshens up for dinner, Heyes tells Curry to forget making a play for Michelle – has he forgotten why they're here?

Heyes and Curry exchange some of their American currency for pesos, meeting Blanche Graham, casino manager and hotel owner, in the process. After losing a bet on the roulette wheel, Curry says that's enough gambling for the night, but Heyes reminds him the whole trip is a gamble. He gazes significantly at Blanche.

Heyes invites her to join them for dinner. She normally doesn't socialize with hotel guests, but in his case she makes an exception. Blanche assures Michelle that Captain McTavish sailed two hours earlier and isn't surprised to learn he used the "free passage home" ploy on her. Michelle is an entertainer and wonders if Blanche can use a one-girl musicale in her casino. Curry and Heyes urge Blanche to let Michelle sing for tips and she agrees.

After dinner, Blanche and Heyes talk about his and Jones's plans to round up and sell the cattle. She warns him that El Clavo, the local bandit chief, thinks of the cattle as his and won't be pleased with their activities.

Meanwhile, Curry escorts Michelle to her room. Michelle kisses him, thanking him for restoring her faith in men. It's obvious feelings are growing on both sides.

The next day El Clavo and his men shoot at Curry and Heyes. The boys flee, but Curry is wounded.

At the hotel, Blanche brings brandy to the boys' room where Michelle is tending to Curry. Blanche admires their nerve, but laments their lack of good sense. Michelle is worried about them and wants nothing more to do with men who are trying to get themselves killed. After the women leave, Heyes and Curry congratulate themselves. Things are going according to plan so far, but Curry is still unsure that Blanche will succumb to Heyes's charm enough to cross the border into the US of her own free will, as their employer, Mr. McKendricks, wants.

Heyes and Curry venture into El Clavo's territory again the next day. This time they are met by his men and taken to see the bandido chief himself. Heyes offers him a deal – let them round up five hundred head of cattle, drive them north and sell them, and they'll split the money fifty-fifty. El Clavo isn't interested in a few gringo dollars since the cattle are food for his men. Heyes elaborates; the cattle will sell for thirty dollars a head. That's $7,500 for Heyes and Curry, $7,500 for him. Now El Clavo is interested.

Blanche is shocked they have managed to deal with El Clavo. Joshua's the kind of man she was beginning to think she'd never meet. They get close to a kiss, but Carlos, Blanche's majordomo, interrupts, telling her a business matter requires her attention. Blanche goes off and Heyes joins Curry to watch Michelle's debut.

Michelle sings a tender ballad, her eyes locked on Curry's. He and Heyes give her their full attention, but the rest of the patrons are more interested in gambling. Even a more rousing tune fails to interest them.

In her office, Blanche listens to a man with information to sell. The two men calling themselves Smith and Jones aren't who they say they are. He met them in Denver as Barton and Slattery, and whatever they're doing, he's sure it isn't what they say they're doing.

Later that night, Blanche gives Michelle the opportunity to earn her passage home. All she has to do is find out who Joshua and Thaddeus really are and what they're doing in San Juan.

Curry finds a sad Michelle in the courtyard and asks what's wrong. She tells him about Blanche's offer. Curry apologizes for his inability to explain. She offers to tell Blanche she couldn't get anything out of him. Curry is touched that she'd give up her chance to go home. "New Orleans will always be there," she says. "I'm not so sure about you."

Curry reports Blanche's suspicions to Heyes. Their first thought is to pack up and leave, but Heyes comes up with another plan. They have to get Blanche across the border willingly if they want to collect the $5,000 they've been promised. So all they need to do now is change the bait – to themselves.

Curry asks for Michelle's help. Blanche killed her husband, the son of a man he and Joshua like very much. They're trying to get her to return to the US to stand trial. If Michelle will tell Blanche they are really Kid Curry and Hannibal Heyes, they will be able to get her to return. Michelle doesn't think Blanche will believe the ridiculous story that they are notorious outlaws, but Curry says she will, as long as Michelle tells it to Blanche just the way he's going to tell her.

Michelle reports to Blanche who scoffs, but Michelle continues, saying she didn't believe Thaddeus at first either. But it may be true because this morning he came to her looking scared and apologizing for getting drunk and lying. Blanche agrees this sounds different.

She hurries to the telegraph office, where she checks on the two outlaws and discovers there's a $20,000 reward on them.

In the cantina, Curry heads to the bar while Heyes sits down with Blanche. She hasn't seen them for awhile and wonders if they were mad at her. Heyes reassures her it's only the cows that have kept them away. She comments on Michelle missing Thaddeus and her suspicion is confirmed when Heyes says Michelle brings out the worst in him. She offers to give them enough men to finish their roundup before the rainy season, if they'll cut her in for a third and take her along on the drive to Arizona. Heyes thinks it's a good idea; he'll put it up to his partner.

Heyes, Curry, Michelle and Blanche, along with several drovers, start north with the cattle. El Clavo and his men follow at a discreet distance.

On the night before they cross the border, Curry and Michelle share a romantic kiss. She doesn't want to say goodbye. Curry thinks she'll soon forget about him, but Michelle disagrees. She'll get over him, but she'll never forget him.

The next day, El Clavo's scout returns from the border with news that cattle prices in Arizona aren't as high as Heyes claims, and they'll only get $8 a head instead of the promised $30. El Clavo gives the order – "Mátanlos!" ("Kill them!")

To save themselves, Curry orders the drovers to stampede the cattle. El Clavo and his gang flee from the wave of animals bearing down on them.

Now there's no herd and the drovers have gone back home. Curry suggests they do the same. Blanche is alarmed at the suggestion that they'll return to San Juan, but Heyes says home is where the heart is and that's in the USA.

At the border station, Blanche turns Heyes and Curry in to the marshal, who believes they *are* Smith and Jones, only posing as Heyes and Curry. Mr. McKendricks emerges and identifies Blanche as his son's murderer. As she's taken into custody, McKendricks pays the boys for their services.

Michelle and Curry say goodbye. Michelle knows for certain who he is now, because Thaddeus Jones could have asked her to stay with him, but Kid Curry can't, he has to say goodbye. Curry watches mournfully as the stage takes her away from him.

GUEST CAST

CLAUDINE LONGET	MICHELLE MONET
SUSAN OLIVER	BLANCHE GRAHAM
NICO MINARDOS	EL CLAVO
JOAQUIN MARTINEZ	CARLOS
DUB TAYLOR	JOHNSON
MED FLORY	MARSHAL
CURT CONWAY	MCKENDRICKS
GREGORY SIERRA	JUAN

Roy Huggins was very particular about the scripts for his shows. His standard method of working was to tell the story at a story conference, then let the writer go off and do the script. Oftentimes, though, Huggins was disappointed with the results. "I was giving long stories to others and they were coming in bad. And I would have to start rewriting to get back to what I'd written."[38] This episode is an example of a script coming in bad. Huggins first told the story to writer Norman Hudis on November 24, 1970. Just a week later, on December 2, Huggins told the story to writer Dick Nelson, commenting during the conference that "the only good line in the present draft is the line about 'ministering angel, nurse, etc.' – which the Kid has been calling Molly."[39] The Hudis script was completely thrown out and Dick Nelson went off to write his first draft. In the meantime, the girl Curry falls for had gone through three name changes – from Marie to Mary to Molly. Before the final shooting script was complete she changed names twice more, from Molly Morton to Molly Norton to Michelle Monet. This final change was due to the hiring of Claudine Longet, who brought a touch of French to the girl from New Orleans.

In Nelson's first draft, the lecherous Captain McTavish makes an appearance, allowing the boys an opportunity to impress Blanche with their prowess. McTavish has come to the cantina to take Molly (as she was known at that point) back to his ship. When Curry interferes, McTavish pulls a knife and advances on him. Heyes makes good use of a nearby ice bucket and empty champagne bottle, kicking them under the enraged Captain's feet. As McTavish struggles to maintain his balance, Curry disarms him and shoves him chin first into the table. "The whole thing has been as deft as a magician's card trick . . . anyone not watching closely might think the Captain simply tripped and knocked himself out accidentally. Molly is one of those who missed the details . . . she stares at McTavish incredulously."[40] Blanche, however, did not miss the details and their slick handling of McTavish piques her interest. She declined their first dinner invitation, but has changed her mind.

This episode is something of a change of pace for the show. Rather than be let in on it from the beginning, the audience is teased by the careful doling out of clues hinting at the true story. Why would Heyes and Curry, who always shy away from hard work, be rounding up cattle in Mexico? Why is Heyes making a play for a woman he obviously doesn't trust? Why must they trick her into returning to the US? The mystery adds dimension to this otherwise rather straightforward tale of Heyes and Curry's latest effort to make an honest living.

Humanity is what makes a television character a real person to the audience. Curry's falling in love with Michelle adds depth to this footloose ex-outlaw. For the first time it's suggested that Heyes and Curry's apparent lack of interest in things domestic may be more protection from wanting what they can't have than a true philosophy of life. Knowing it was a mistake, Curry nevertheless continued his relationship with Michelle as long as he could. The final goodbye scene is quite poignant, with Michelle sadly accepting Curry's rejection of her because of his outlaw status while Heyes watches sympathetically from the sidelines. This ending wasn't only painful for Curry; writer Dick Nelson also found it difficult. He wrote a note to Huggins in the margin of the fifth draft. Referring to Heyes and Curry, he said, "Could they head for the saloon with something a little brighter to go out on?"

NEVER TRUST AN HONEST MAN

"Heyes, something's happened to you since we went straight."
"That's what happened, we went straight."
– Kid Curry, Hannibal Heyes

STORY:	JOHN THOMAS JAMES
TELEPLAY:	PHIL DEGUERE
DIRECTOR;	DOUGLAS HEYES
SHOOTING DATES:	MARCH 18, 19, 22, 23, 24, 25, 1971
ORIGINAL US AIR DATE:	APRIL 15, 1971 EASTERN/CENTRAL;
	APRIL 29, 1971 MOUNTAIN/PACIFIC
ORIGINAL UK AIR DATE:	JULY 12, 1971

After traveling for a week, Hannibal Heyes and Kid Curry are back in the "good ole U.S. of A," a fact Heyes delights in announcing to his sleeping partner. Jolted awake, Curry is annoyed, but before he can comply with Heyes's advice to get some sleep, James Quirt invites them to a poker game in Oscar Harlingen's private car. Harlingen owns the railroad and the invitation is not to be ignored. Curry rouses himself; Heyes picks up his satchel and heads for the poker game.

As the train rolls on, the four men play cards. Christine McNeice, Harlingen's secretary, sits nearby doing needlework. Red, white and blue chips grow in high stacks in front of Harlingen.

When their destination of Bountiful is only eight minutes away, Harlingen declares it's time to settle up. Heyes owes Harlingen thirty-seven cents; Curry owes him eighty-five cents and Quirt fifty cents. Heyes wonders why Harlingen plays for one hundred chips per penny, but miserly Harlingen advises that to be wealthy one must know the value of a dollar, a concept his former partner never grasped. At that allusion, Christine rises to leave. When she's out of earshot, Harlingen confides she hates

When the East and West were joined by rails, railroad stock was much in demand. Unscrupulous railroad barons could afford to speculate and made their fortunes. Many settlers disliked these railroad men who had obtained the right of way through farmlands that drove off the homesteaders. For this reason, train robbers were cheered by much of the general public.

"The Carpella Collection" was the original title of this story.

That stingy, miserly Harlingen lived in the town of Bountiful reflects Huggins's satirical taste in humor. In early drafts, the town was named Harlingen Junction.

him. Her father was his former partner who gambled away their money. "Nothing worse than a gambler," Harlingen chortles, "except, of course, a train robber."

At their hotel, while Heyes snoozes, Curry shaves. Finding his razor dull, Curry asks to borrow his partner's. Watching Curry root through his satchel, Heyes is shocked when he pulls out a corset. Heyes denies it's his bag, even though it *looks* like his. Inspecting it himself, Heyes pulls out a Bible. Only then is Curry convinced it's not Heyes's bag.

Investigating further, Heyes finds an inscription in the Bible identifying it as belonging to Christine McNeice. Their bags must have gotten switched on the train. Flipping pages, Heyes discovers a compartment cut into the book. In the compartment is a bag and in the bag is a handful of jewels. Curry is excited at the fortune, but Heyes quickly reminds him of the consequences of stealing something that valuable. Plus, they've gone straight and must return them.

At his mansion, Harlingen prepares to empty a similar satchel while Christine, Quirt and Harlingen's son Allen watch. Allen is infatuated with the young secretary, but Christine intensely dislikes him because he so resembles his father. Instead of finding the secreted jewels, Harlingen pulls out Heyes's longjohns. He realizes Smith and Jones must have his bag and sends Quirt to find them.

Heyes and Curry, heading toward Harlingen's house, nearly encounter Quirt, Hank and Carl, Harlingen's men, headed in the other direction. They veer off the trail to pass unseen.

Approaching the mansion at night, Heyes logically deduces which of the lighted windows belongs to Christine. He's wrong, as he finds out when she appears at a different one. They climb up and Heyes's face framed at her window startles Christine as she emerges from her dressing room. She faints and Heyes, rubbing her hands, instructs Curry to find something with which to revive her. Perfume ought to do it.

In the meantime, Quirt returns and informs Harlingen he has followed Smith and Jones's trail right back to the house.

Recovered, Christine starts to scream, but the sight of the Bible silences her. She's glad to have the jewels but wonders why the men felt they had to creep through her window. They want an explanation before talking to a federal marshal about her smuggling jewels across the border. Unwilling to explain, she escorts the duo downstairs to see Harlingen.

Harlingen is surprised, but also delighted to have the jewels back. He offers Smith and Jones his profound respect and gratitude and a reward of $100 each. They are aghast at the pittance offered for returning millions of dollars in rare gems. When Heyes casually mentions they have to see the marshal about calling off the men who must be looking for them, Harlingen says they are his men and admits the marshal knows nothing about the alleged theft.

Considering, he then offers them another $200, which Heyes quickly ups to $2,000, to keep his secret. Harlingen is a member of an international association. One of the members is near bankruptcy and Harlingen has loaned him $5 million. The jewels are collateral. Harlingen admits he would have paid as much as $20,000 for their silence. Too bad they agreed on only $2,000.

The next day, Harlingen finds his son Allen studying the jewels. To his unpracticed eye, they look like colored glass, so Harlingen, Sr. attempts to teach him the rudiments of gem identification. To his horror, he finds they *are* only colored glass. A jeweler confirms he has fine specimens of quartz, worth over $50!

Harlingen suspects Smith and Jones have the real jewels and instructs Quirt to bring them back alive. Christine witnesses their conversation and is startled by Allen who says it wasn't her fault. To show he holds no hard feelings, he attempts to kiss her, an attempt she evades.

James Quirt hires a man named Logan to kill Smith and Jones. Logan, in turn, hires a down-and-out drunk, the Preacher, to help him. Quirt, Hank, and Carl surprise Heyes and Curry at their campsite and tell them Harlingen wants to see them. All five head back through the canyon single-file. Heyes figures Harlingen thinks they crossed him somehow.

Atop a high ridge, Logan and the Preacher wait for the procession. When they come into view, Logan urges him to shoot the two in the middle, but Preacher recognizes Heyes and Curry and won't kill them. He used to ride with them and they're friends. Logan has no such compunction, so Preacher bashes him with his rifle, knocking him unconscious. An errant shot from Logan's rifle spurs on Quirt, the riders, and their prisoners.

In a narrow canyon, they stop to water their horses. Quirt takes Heyes and Curry aside and says it seems to him they are getting a rotten deal from Harlingen, seeing as how they returned the jewels. He'll let them escape, shooting over their heads. They know exactly what he's up to and spur their horses right into him. Quirt follows on horseback but the Preacher shoots at him from above. The horse falls, throwing Quirt off and breaking his neck. Inadvertently killing the man who hired Logan and him to kill his friends proves to Preacher that "the Lord moves in mysterious ways."

Heyes is eager to learn why Harlingen sent Quirt to bring them back, but first they hide Quirt's body in a ravine. In the darkest hour of the night, they enter Harlingen's room through a window, waking him up. Startled and angry, he informs them he had the jewels checked and knows they had to be the ones who switched them. "Who else could it be?"

Heyes tells Harlingen that Quirt hired two men to kill them. When the ambush failed, Quirt attempted to murder them himself, so he must know where the real jewels are but, unfortunately, he's dead. Heyes proposes Harlingen tell everyone Smith and Jones are not suspects and that Quirt has only disappeared.

Next day, Christine heads for a rundown house far from Harlingen's manse. Heyes and Curry quietly follow her into the kitchen where she removes the jewels secreted in the pump handle. At the sound of their footsteps, she turns, thinking it's her father. They accuse her of stealing the gems. When she pulls a small derringer, Curry draws his own pistol. Her father enters the room rifle in hand and orders the boys to drop their guns. When Heyes tells him Christine stole $5 million from her employer, she justifies it because Harlingen cheated her father. The old man is shattered to hear she believed the lies he told her. Harlingen's version was the truth.

A few weeks later, Heyes and Curry return to Harlingen's mansion where a grand party is in progress. Christine and Allen are to be married. Harlingen mournfully ponders the goings-on (and the expense). Heyes and Curry hope for remuneration for returning the $5 million collateral in light of the secret deal that would have been breached. Instead, Harlingen went to see the Preacher and, for a few dollars, learned they have a secret too. He'll keep theirs, if they'll keep his.

GUEST CAST

SEVERN DARDEN	OSCAR/ALLEN HARLINGEN
MARJ DUSAY	CHRISTINE MCNEICE
RICHARD ANDERSON	JAMES QUIRT
ROBERT DONNER	PREACHER
BILL FLETCHER	LOGAN
BURT MUSTIN	JEWELER
GLENN DIXON	BUTLER
FORD RAINEY	MR. MCNEICE
MICHAEL CARR	HANK
ROBERT BRUCE LANG	CARL

Phil DeGuere wrote the story outline in mid-December 1970. At that time, there was still worry about having enough episodes to air on time and thus, each character was made the sole protagonist in an episode. "Never Trust an Honest Man" began as a Heyes-only episode, but DeGeure's original treatment was vastly improved by Huggins's addition of Kid Curry to the action. Initially, Heyes plays poker with a Texas railroad man on the train from Mexico. Oscar Harlingen is one of the wealthiest men in the southwest. In his Brownsville, Texas, hotel, Heyes discovers gems in his satchel. Returning them to Harlingen, he learns the story of a Mexican cartel and of the jewels being used as collateral. Quirt and Christine schemed to steal the jewels and substitute replicas, but Harlingen suspects Heyes when the jewels turn out to be fakes. Quirt follows Heyes, confronts him and Heyes kills him. When Heyes returns with Quirt's body, Harlingen accuses him of planning to use the fake jewels to destroy the cartel. On his way to jail, Heyes escapes by wrapping his handcuffed wrists around a deputy's throat, strangling him and throwing him out of the wagon. Making his way back to Harlingen's mansion, Heyes finds the fakes in the study. He tricks Christine into revealing she hid the genuine jewels in a secret drawer of her jewel box. At that moment Harlingen enters and Heyes turns the real jewels and the thief Christine over to him. When Harlingen asks what he could do for honest Mr. Smith, Heyes replies that he could put in a good word with Governor Harrison in a nearby state.

Huggins's belief that violence for its own sake was unnecessary in a program and his insistence that the boys never killed anyone led to changes in the first draft. Huggins crossed out the scene in which Heyes strangled a deputy. It was also his idea to introduce Harlingen's son as a new character in order to take the romance away from Christine and Quirt. However, looks that pass between Quirt and Christine in the aired episode confirm that something is still going on between them. Yet, in the end, it appears that Christine stole the jewels strictly to avenge her father.

Reflecting *Butch Cassidy and the Sundance Kid*, DeGuere in his teleplay (or Huggins in the rewrites) imitated screenwriter William Goldman's technique of having what he calls "smart-ass lines." For instance, Butch and Sundance debate about the posse still pursuing them.

"I think we lost 'em. Do you think we lost 'em?"
"No."
"Neither do I."[41]

Heyes and Curry wonder about the unfamiliar contents of the satchel.
"Kid, this isn't my bag."
"Sure looks like your bag." (Heyes pulls out a Bible.)
"I'm convinced. It isn't your bag."

"Heyes, you've done it again." (Curry, excited at Heyes's figuring out which window is Christine's.)
"Heyes, you've done it again." (Curry, deflated at discovering the window they thought was Christine's was not.)

"I think it's gettin' to her." (Heyes waves the vial of perfume under Christine's nose to revive her.)
"I think it's gettin' to me too." (Curry turns away, his eyes watering.)

More than once in the series, Heyes's brilliant, deductive mind uses the process of elimination to narrow a list of choices. In "21 Days to Tenstrike," he limits the murder suspects to seven after eliminating Curry and himself. In "The McCreedy Feud," he needs to find Señorita Armendariz's room in the hacienda. His technique requires honing, because he gets it wrong there too, having not much improved since his error in locating Christine McNeice's room by logical deduction.

Another tenet of the *Alias Smith and Jones* canon was that Heyes and Curry must never end up with enough money to head for South America, because, at least in the beginning, they would have, much like Butch and Sundance. They can drive a hard bargain to return the jewels, but they cannot end up with the money.

THE LEGACY OF CHARLIE O'ROURKE

"The next time we meet a girl like her, we ought to flip a coin."
– Kid Curry

STORY: ROBERT GUY BARROWS
TELEPLAY: DICK NELSON

DIRECTOR:	JEFFREY HAYDEN
SHOOTING DATES:	MARCH 29, 30, 31, APRIL 1, 2, 5, 1971
ORIGINAL US AIR DATE:	APRIL 22, 1971
ORIGINAL UK AIR DATE:	JUNE 7, 1971

This was originally titled "The Golden Perch."

In the first draft script, when Alice Banion introduces herself the name "Banion" rings some bells for Heyes and Curry. She's the daughter of a prominent banking family. Curry says, "Banion Bank and Trust? Why we've hel— I mean, had business dealings with Banion Banks – twice." Heyes corrects him. "Three times – don't forget Denver."

Hannibal Heyes and Kid Curry ride into bustling Browntown, reacting with alarm when a voice calls out, "Kid!" A quick glance around reveals their old friend Charlie O'Rourke hailing them from the window of the local jail. Charlie is glad to see familiar faces and assumes the boys have come to Browntown because of him, just like all the other folks in town, but Heyes and Curry, who were just passing through, are appalled to find out Charlie has been sentenced to hang in the morning. They learn Charlie and a couple other fellows stole $100,000 in gold bars and killed several members of the posse. Charlie wants to tell the boys where he hid the gold, but Heyes doesn't want to hear. Charlie asks them to attend his hanging. The boys agree.

Heyes and Curry head to the saloon, sorry that Charlie spotted them, but even sorrier to run into Bannerman detective Harry Briscoe.

In the saloon, Vic, the bartender, is extremely friendly, anything they want is on the house since they're friends of Charlie. From a table nearby, saloon singer Alice Banion watches them with interest. Harry buys the boys a drink. He is curious to know why they visited Charlie, how they know him and, most importantly, if he sent for them. They admit Charlie is a friend, but he didn't send for them and he didn't tell them where he hid the gold. Harry tries threatening them, then points out, "When you go out after that gold, you're gonna think you're leading a parade." Heyes and Curry watch Harry as he leaves, lamenting the fact they're only $100,000 short of having enough money to leave town.

A note falls onto their table. Curry reads it and finds an invitation to visit Alice in her room. They settle back to enjoy her performance as she sings from her perch in a golden birdcage lowered from the ceiling. After the show the boys present themselves at her door. She offers them tea and a business proposition. She wants to open a saloon and dance hall in San Francisco, but she needs a stake. Since they'll soon be coming in to a large sum of money, perhaps they'd like to become her partners. Heyes and Curry set down their tea cups and leave.

Alice decides to take matters into her own hands. She visits Charlie and offers him the comfort of songs and companionship as he waits for dawn. Later she attends his funeral along with Heyes, Curry, Sheriff Carver and Vic.

Heyes and Curry return to town after the funeral and are grabbed by four men who hustle them into the livery stable. After a fierce battle, the boys exit, brushing themselves off. They stride into the saloon, then exit man-handling Harry

Briscoe between them. They shove his head into the water trough and hold him down long enough to subdue him. Pulling him out before he actually drowns, Heyes advises, "Mr. Briscoe, the next time you feel like sending men to beat Charlie O'Rourke's gold out of us – don't!" Harry struggles to breathe and gasps out one phrase guaranteed to interest the boys – "Five thousand dollars!"

Inside the saloon, Harry offers them a $5,000 reward for returning the gold. Heyes reiterates that Charlie didn't tell them where he hid it. Harry divulges that Alice spent the night singing to Charlie and undoubtedly now knows where the gold is. All Heyes and Curry have to do is get Alice to let them help her dig it up, then take it away from her and return it for the reward. The boys refuse, but Harry threatens to look at descriptions of outlaws in the sheriff's office. He's sure he'll find them there. Defeated, Heyes and Curry visit Alice.

She wonders why she should share her good fortune with them. Heyes and Curry spell it out – at $21 an ounce, $100,000 worth of gold bars weighs about three hundred pounds.

Heyes, Curry and Alice board the stagecoach, followed discreetly by a posse. At a relay station, when the driver is out of sight, Heyes hijacks the coach, whipping the horses into an all-out gallop. A few miles later, he pulls up, and Alice and Curry clamber out. Heyes slaps the horses. They take off again, pulling the empty coach. The boys and Alice take cover and watch as the posse gallops past them.

Alice doubts the wisdom of a plan that seems to have left them on foot in the middle of nowhere. Curry goes off to a pre-arranged spot where Harry is waiting with three horses. He brings them back and her faith in them is renewed.

The trio rides off into the desert. She notices someone behind them, so the boys check it out. It's Harry. Ordering him to leave them alone or the plan won't work, they return to Alice and spin a story about the fellow being an advance man for the railroad. Unfortunately for them, Alice had watched them through binoculars. "You two are the worst pair of liars that ever lived." They confess Harry promised them a reward which they planned to split with her. She's not convinced, so the boys try another tactic, telling her they did it for her own good because they didn't want her to steal the money and end up running for the rest of her life. "Running is something we know a little about," Heyes says. "You wouldn't like it." Alice agrees to settle for the reward.

Finally they reach the spot where Charlie buried the loot. Alice bubbles with excitement as they unearth the gold bars. They're rich and she's with two handsome men. Life isn't so bad, is it? She could fall in love with both of them, separately of course; she couldn't choose between them. Heyes suggests flipping a coin. Into this lighthearted moment enters Harry Briscoe, who attracts their attention by shooting at the ground near their feet. He takes the boys' guns as well as the horses and the gold, explaining that every man has his breaking point. For years he's been returning other people's money. Now he's going to take this gold and head for Mexico.

Heyes, Curry and Alice head for San Pancracio. It's tough going. Finally Alice complains she can't go on. The trio leans against a rock, eyes closed against the glare of the sun. Curry is sure Heyes has an idea and waits to hear it. "We're goners," Heyes offers glumly.

At that moment, a cheerful voice greets them. "Guten tag!" It's Kurt Schmitt, an immigrant who wonders what they're doing in the desert without horses. Over the hill in his camp, he serves them sausage and strudel. Heyes and Curry ask if they can borrow his draft horses to go after Briscoe. Kurt is a businessman, though, and offers to loan them in return for twenty-five percent of the reward. He'll throw in his two hunting rifles at no extra charge. Alice is impressed by Kurt's business acumen.

The boys track Harry, and find him taking a break, teaching himself Spanish. He shoots at them and tries to escape, but they circle around and wedge him between two rocks, Curry above him and Heyes beside him. Harry gives up.

They get ready to take Harry back and turn him in, but he thinks outlaws Hannibal Heyes and Kid Curry owe him a favor. He finally did check the Wanted posters and figured out who his friends Smith and Jones really are. He suggests they split the gold and go their own ways, but Heyes refuses. The reward is good enough for them. Harry is dumbfounded. "Mr. Briscoe, as you already know, an honest man will sometimes turn dishonest for a price. Well now, it works the other way around, too." Harry and the boys come to an agreement – they won't tell what he did if he doesn't tell who they are.

Back in Browntown, Heyes counts out Alice's share of the reward. She'll take Kurt's share, too, as she's the banker in their partnership. The Golden Perch Rathskellar will be San Francisco's finest restaurant. Alice bids goodbye to the boys, still wondering what would have happened if she'd met them one at a time. As she and Kurt leave, Curry remarks to Heyes they probably should have flipped that coin.

GUEST CAST

JOAN HACKETT	ALICE BANION
J.D. CANNON	HARRY BRISCOE
BILLY "GREEN" BUSH	CHARLIE O'ROURKE
GUY RAYMOND	SHERIFF CARVER
ERIK HOLLAND	KURT SCHMITT
HANK UNDERWOOD	VIC
STEVEN GRAVERS	PARSON
GARY VAN ORMAN	CLYDE

"The Legacy of Charlie O'Rourke" is one of the few episodes that did not begin as a story by Roy Huggins in his guise of John Thomas James. Huggins remembered, "It was very hard to come up with every story for that show. I was very pleased when I could find a story somewhere else or a writer would come in with a story."[42] Huggins liked the idea brought in by Robert Guy Barrows, but had Dick Nelson write the teleplay. At the story conference held on February 9, 1971, Huggins told the story to Nelson, making minor changes to the opening, then noting "until the end of the picture there are no big changes – except to have some fun with the story. The girl can be amusing – she should be attractive. The audience should feel warmly toward her. The girl likes *both* of our boys." Later in the conference, in the spirit of having fun with the story, they consider having Alice suggest the three of them move to Utah, but Heyes would point out that polygamy is "one guy with a lot of women – but not one woman with two guys."

In the original script, the detective is not Harry Briscoe of Bannerman Detectives, Inc. Instead he is Otis L. Johnson, a detective working for the Banker's Express Company, which Charlie and his companions robbed. Otis L. Johnson lasted through three drafts before being turned into Harry Briscoe. Huggins and Swerling were particularly fond of Harry Briscoe and of J.D. Cannon, the actor who portrayed him. Whenever possible, they'd work the fumbling detective into a story.

In this case, changing from the unknown Johnson to the known Briscoe caused some story problems. At the March 22, 1971, story conference, Huggins said, "We should pick up where we left off: Briscoe had bought their story – they're Smith and Jones, who once knew Hannibal Heyes and Kid Curry and gave him a helpful description . . . He's never found out that description was wrong." Later on, Briscoe goes looking for descriptions of Heyes and Curry at the sheriff's office. Given the events of "Wrong Train to Brimstone," this doesn't make a whole lot of sense. Huggins recognized this and brought it up at the conference. "This would be unbelievable if one saw the two shows back-to-back. But it will be believable, separated by several months." In 1971, before the advent of the consumer VCR, the writers could get away with this, but Huggins still wasn't quite comfortable with it. On March 25, at the next story conference, he said, "It doesn't work for us to hark back to the description the boys gave Briscoe, because then nothing that follows works. He can't say he went over and checked those descriptions. We have to actually accept a hole – when the two shows are put together. Forget that Briscoe ever read a description of Heyes and Curry."

At first glance, Charlie's legacy is the gold bars. More importantly, he left behind the love Heyes and Curry discovered for Alice, her newfound relationship with Kurt and Harry's recognition that he's not too good at being a bad guy. Charlie's legacy will affect all of them for a long time to come.

CHAPTER 4

LEADING MODEL LIVES OF TEMPERANCE, MODERATION, TRANQUILITY . . .

Though the last of the first season episodes, "The Legacy of Charlie O'Rourke," wouldn't air until April 22, 1971, the cast and crew were finished filming on April 5. They celebrated with a party in the saloon on the western set. There was reason to celebrate. ABC had renewed the show for another season, despite its finishing in the bottom third of the ratings.[1]

It had been Frank Price's job as an executive in charge of television at Universal to make the case to network officials to keep *Alias Smith and Jones* on the air. He emphasized its primary competition, comedian Flip Wilson, was "a phenomenon" and the show was doing as well as could be expected. He asked them for another time slot, believing that would improve its ratings. ABC turned a deaf ear and *Alias Smith and Jones* limped onto the ratings chart far behind Wilson. Then, after the show was pitted against *All in the Family* in the 1972-73 season, Price had to make the same argument. Even though his complaint about its scheduled slot was valid, network people were "getting suspicious" when Universal continually blamed the show's poor ratings on the timeslot.[2] Sid Sheinberg, then the head of Universal's television department, was concerned. Shortly after Roger Davis took over the role of Hannibal Heyes, he met Sheinberg in an elevator and asked him how he liked his new cowboy hat. Sheinberg observed, "[T]hat isn't what you need. You need a new timeslot. . . .It doesn't matter, you could do the greatest stuff in the world, you could have the greatest goddam show, Roger. You're dead. Unless we're able to move that timeslot, your days are numbered."[3] But when Wilson was pre-empted for a spring NCAA quarter-final basketball game and a large audience tuned in to *Alias Smith and Jones*, the show placed nineteenth in the Nielsens. That one break satisfied the network as to its continued viability.

Everything was about pleasing the network. Their approval was required on all of the scripts that aired. ABC had a hand in determining who was hired or even consulted. In any given episode, network executives, "who made up in power what they lacked in salary,"[4] might object to the story, to any scene or to the overall content. They might have criticism for how the characters reacted and they reserved the power of creative judgment. This angered Roy Huggins who believed that network people thought concept was the most important part of a show "because they can take credit for cast and concept," whereas he believed quality execution of the concept was the key. Huggins's reaction to network interference has always been, "'Hey, get lost. . . .You have no credentials, you're talking to someone who's had very few failures on the air, and I don't intend to listen to you.'"[5] Frank Price smiled while recollecting that Huggins "was brilliant [and] talented but not a diplomat when dealing with networks. Sometimes you just had to be more diplomatic because they could punish you finally by canceling the show. . . .You'd better keep that balance of getting the show you want to do plus not offend people at the network." And that's where Price excelled.[6]

ABC also pressed for star casting, that is, more recognizable names, but Price recalled, "we were always trying to do that anyway." The network was paying a fixed license fee yet hoped the studio would go out and pay millions of dollars to get stars like Paul Newman. This would never happen because the budget of any one episode was only about $190,000.[7] Newman would not be asked to guest star, but Universal did manage to include many big name stars as guests on the program. Actors such as Walter Brennan, Ann Sothern, Jim Backus, Chill Wills, Slim Pickens, Rory Calhoun, and Joe Flynn were old hands in film and television and familiar to viewers.

(Jerry Ohlinger's Movie Materials Store)

When *Alias Smith and Jones* premiered in January 1971, it aired on Thursdays in the 7:30-8:30 p.m. timeslot. The Prime Time Access Rule mandated by the Federal Communications Commission took effect in September 1971. After much discussion and dissension among the networks, the FCC eventually declared that Prime Time would be the three hours from 8:00 to 11:00 p.m. Even though ABC would do nothing to alter the time slot for *Alias Smith and Jones* except to move it one half hour to eight o'clock, executives bought Price's arguments for keeping the program on the air. Peter Duel explained it, "When you throw somebody to the wolves, and they don't get devoured, you keep them on. After all, it's cheaper. You save money by not trying with a new baby."[8]

Just because it was the end of the season did not mean that work would cease. Having signed a contract with ABC for a full season's offerings of more than twenty shows, behind-the-scenes people at Universal had much to do in order to be ready for season two in September. Throughout the summer, Huggins met with prospective directors, with promotion managers, and with Frank Price. For its part, over the summer ABC aired reruns and spent more money on publicity. Huggins was happy about that. His rule was "a show that succeeds in its first season will do even better in its second because it will pick up a new audience with the summer reruns."[9]

A month after first season wrap up, Edgar Penton of the *Muskegon Chronicle* interviewed Huggins about the show. He talked about Hannibal Heyes and Kid Curry's quest for amnesty. Because it was no easy task for them to stay out of trouble, "it gives us a gold mine of story ideas. . . .Occasionally [it] puts them in the awkward position of having to thwart a heist they previously might have engineered." The outlaws' succinct line when asked what they do to make a living – "as little as possible" – was Huggins's idea, knowing they weren't "trained for anything honest. Even when they get jobs they like, they can't keep them long because of pressure from bounty hunters. We aren't even limited to the West. Our boys really drift around [and] get into situations which are inherently funny." Unlike his previous creation, *Maverick,* in which Huggins tried to do something completely different with the western format and make his hero as unheroic as possible, in *Alias Smith and Jones,* "we did not aim for a spoof on the traditional Western [but] humor is a plus benefit in the show."[10] *The Los Angeles Times* sent columnist Cecil Smith to Huggins a few weeks later. His report ran on July 4 and in it, in reply to Smith's questioning, Huggins denied that the show was a spin-off of *Butch Cassidy and the Sundance Kid.* Instead of evolving from the movie, Huggins felt it was more accurately based on his two other television creations, *Maverick* and *The Fugitive.* He also argued that its themes go way back to the Elizabethans and the Greeks.[11]

For the second season, Huggins planned on introducing a recurring female character. Casting director Burt Metcalfe was involved with finding actresses whom Huggins would agree to for the role and he sent Huggins a memo of "name" and "non-name" actresses. Sally Field topped the list. Katherine

Crawford, Joey Heatherton, and Bonnie Bedelia were included. However, when Huggins reviewed the names, he crossed off women who, in his opinion, were not "names" or who, for whatever reason, he did not want to hire. The problem, director Alex Singer believed, was in trying to cast attractive young women. The reason is simple: "the combination of good performance and good looks is uncommon. So, the likelihood of both of them being in the same person is statistically small. The tendency of the production company was to favor looks over performance on the theory that the story would carry itself and the women were decorative."[12] Some ladies Huggins considered preferable to Field, who was eventually awarded the role, were Kim Darby, Tuesday Weld and Jackie Bisset. Among the "non-names" whom Metcalfe submitted were Brenda Scott, Joan VanArk, Linda Ronstadt and Shelley Fabares, many of whom eventually became "names."

Besides the scripts that would make it on the air next season, several other story lines were considered and abandoned. Titles included "The Wrecker," "Nester's Daughter" which Ben Murphy was to rewrite, "Standoff," "The Slick New Bank," "Girl of My Dreams," "The Miracle at Montoya," "Grubstake," "Harry Straight," "Young Man with a Dream" and "All That Glitters is Gold." In some cases, Huggins had already told the story to the writer and a first draft had come in before the title was scrapped. This was all day-to-day work for Huggins. After many years spent producing his westerns *Cheyenne* and *Maverick,* he knew what needed to be done and how to do it.

"I had a principle of how to do television," he said. "And that is, if you're lucky, what you like is going to appeal to a large number of people." Huggins didn't try to second-guess what any audience would like because he knew it was a losing game. Elaborate research tests and assessments of audience reaction were in place to gauge how viewers would react but most were fraught with error. "I gave all those up earlier and decided that I had to forget all that and hope that those things that I got a kick out of, that I enjoyed putting together and building, would have an audience."[13]

So, Huggins came up with stories appealing to him and assigned them to the screenwriters. Too often what they came back with was unsatisfactory. Huggins felt some young screenwriters thought as long as they knew the alphabet they could write a good show, but it wasn't that simple. "It just seems to be so easy. 'Anyone can do that.' And they had no idea that doing that is calculating hundreds of possibilities and going with the one that works."[14] Stephen Cannell, once a student of Huggins, now a television producer and author, learned from him that "a good screenplay is a series of the next-most-interesting-scene you can think of."[15]

Going with the circumstances that worked was a sign of Huggins's genius. Another was his ability to pick and choose among personality traits so as to create likeable characters. Dennis Fimple, who acted in the recurring role of Kyle Murtry, said, "Smith and Jones, they've gotta be likeable 'cause [if] the character's so thin that [with] one slip, you lose your audience. . . [well,] I think they both are really strong."[16] Fans of the program suspected Heyes and Curry weren't so much villainous as they were naughty. Huggins realized that's how it seemed. "But it would be a mistake to think that that would be the intent. The way it came out was kind of forced by the machinations of plot." However, some things happened that were "sheer accident. And as an editor, as a producer who really worked on editing, I loved that."

Roy Huggins's goal was to make the best film possible. His theory was that in order to make the film better, he couldn't go in to the editing room loving it, even if it was his script. Sitting in the projection room with Jo Swerling, the film editor, and other post-production crew, he watched the rough cut and "hated" it, looking for problems. Huggins would see a flaw and, ever the perfectionist, get irritated and order the projectionist to halt the film. Film editor Gloryette Clark recalls, "He expected his crew to always see what he saw and then to come up with ideas on how to fix it." Sometimes he would turn to Swerling or the editor, sometimes he would just yell out to the room in general. "How are we going to fix that?" The response was often dead silence as his crew struggled to figure out what was wrong. A general suggestion such as "we can always loop it" was a safe way to fish for clues as to what he saw. That would get Huggins to talk, giving the crew a reference point, and then they would bounce ideas off each other. "Sometimes he came up with an ingenious solution and we wondered why we didn't see it," Clark marvels. "[We] didn't have the same IQ, I guess."[17] Huggins didn't like to screen the answer prints, the final product that was delivered to the network for broadcast. He did, however, watch the show when it aired, and was known to call the editor and demand changes be made for the reruns.

Occasionally throughout the run of the series, social themes such as capital punishment, bigotry, or the plight of Native Americans would crop up. When it was present, the appearance was never an accident. Huggins wanted it there. "But," he said, "I also did not spend my time trying to do shows that had some social premise that would touch a current nerve. I didn't work at that. . . .I didn't feel that was my purpose in life – to sound the socially important note every chance I got." Instead his intent was to entertain as many people as he could. "And I think that show surprised everybody by having the kind of audience it had. It was popular. And the only reason it didn't do even better is that it came at the absolute tail end of the western cycle. Westerns were dead on television. And there was *Alias Smith and Jones* saying, 'Really?'"[18]

As influential and competent as Huggins was in creating and seeing each episode through, he couldn't do it all alone. Jo Swerling, Jr. was his right hand man. Huggins even created a special title for him and to this day, Swerling is so proud of the designation he keeps a large gold ruler on his desk engraved with *World's First Associate Executive Producer – Jo Swerling, Jr – Alias Smith and Jones*, a gift from his secretary.

In the early months, Glen Larson and Swerling had alternated as producers on the show. Larson would produce scripts he had developed while Swerling produced scripts Huggins developed. Swerling distributed the week's script to Universal's production office and a unit manager would break it down and put it on a schedule board. It was then Swerling's job to get started on the nuts and bolts of putting the production together.

After he had done research on which director was available and who would be best for a particular script, he and Huggins collaborated on hiring him after which Swerling would turn it over to Universal's Business Affairs department to finish the deal. When the director came in, Swerling sat down with him and answered any questions, then he and the director would cast the show. Though Huggins did not get involved in casting, Swerling would always consult with him about which actors they were considering and make recommendations. Huggins would either approve them or come up with other ideas, then Swerling had the final decision. Director Alex Singer worked with Swerling on eight episodes and found that he "was very good at settling problems and questions in all the details of filmmaking. Having a knowledgeable, shrewd producer who represents the executive producer as well as he represented Roy and who knows what your problems are is enormously valuable. Jo was very much that. It means you have a real support as opposed to somebody who is not knowledgeable or simply gets in the way, which also happens."[19] Swerling acknowledged the compliment. "I wasn't just in there to give directors trouble, you know, and say no to them. I wanted to give them the tools they needed to do the job, so if there was some way I could finagle it around so that I could say yes to them more than I said no to them, that was good. I tried to do that."[20]

With the script, director, and guest stars in place, another of Swerling's many jobs was to check the authenticity and readiness of the set. As itinerant outlaws, Heyes and Curry didn't need a permanent house or cabin, so the only standing sets were the saloon, the sheriff's office, and the western street on Universal's backlot. These could be dressed up or down to reflect any town into which Heyes and Curry rode. The sheriff's office set could be revamped for a lawman's office anywhere. Set crews could use two of the walls and install two new walls to make the appearance different. Because there were only a few permanent sets, the series was slightly more expensive. The more shooting done on standing sets, the more the studio saves money. The crew can prelight them and arrange them in other ways that save time in the shooting schedule. Swerling was very aware of costs because he was also in charge of enforcing the budget. Besides his head for numbers, Swerling's talent for the Spanish language also came in handy. Because the Universal sign shop was working so fast to keep up, they would often make horrendous mistakes. If an episode was taking place in Mexico, it seemed inevitable that the signs in Spanish would be wrong. Swerling was on hand to correct the spelling or idiomatic expressions before they got on the air.

When principal photography was done, Swerling worked with Huggins in the editing room where Huggins supervised the editing closely. "I work with the editors over their shoulders – drive them crazy – and do all kinds of things with [the]

(Courtesy of Ben Murphy)

film. . . If you want to write a book about how films are made, write about what you can do in editing, because that's where films can be remade – the whole story can be retold."[21] Huggins had definite opinions on how it should be done. On an occasion when he was stuck for an idea, he was very open to suggestions. But it rarely happened that Huggins was stuck, because he always had ways to fix a problem. "You can flop a film, you can blow it up, you can run it backward."[22] Since scenes were not shot in script order, the challenge might be to match colors from reel to reel or camera to camera or to make sure the sound quality was consistent throughout. If many takes had been required to get a scene on film, the actors' movements and objects on the set had to match from one scene to the next. Huggins also had to make sure that everything, including dialogue needed in the scene, had been filmed. Getting the story told was paramount to him but he was aware of all the errors that could occur on the set during filming. He also knew that "a bad editor will screw it up again even worse."[23]

When the show was finally locked down in terms of its film editing, it went to the composer who did the score. Huggins would usually be in the music room and he, Swerling, and the composer would run the show and share ideas about how and where the music should go. Once the music was recorded, the film would go on to the dubbing stage. Often, an actor's dialogue needed to be re-recorded because of technical problems on the set or unwelcome background noises, such a jet plane passing over. This is known as looping. Then the film ended up back in Swerling's court because he supervised the dubbing on all the shows. Finally, he would approve the answer print, that is, the finished product, at the lab. If problems arose with the answer print, he'd "make sure it was sent back through the soup again . . . "[24]

The timelessness of *Alias Smith and Jones* reflects the dedication of Huggins and Swerling. But Swerling remembered that, at the time, they were immersed in problems that come with every project. "None of them are easy, they're all difficult in one way or another starting with the fact that you never have enough time or money to do what you really want to do. . . .[We were] into just getting the shows out and making them as good as [we] can, trying to make them sort of the minimal level of quality."[25] If any one problem was bigger than the others, it was the rush into production and the continued harried pace to keep up with having a show to put on the air each week. The day before the pilot aired, the *Los Angeles Times* quoted Peter Duel, "This whole thing happened so fast I don't know [Heyes] very well yet. We have to kind of find him as we go along."[26]

(Jerry Ohlinger's Movie Materials Store)

Various interviews Peter gave to contemporary newspaper and magazine reporters are the only measure available to gauge his feelings about *Alias Smith and Jones*. In most, he is a paradigm of contradiction, proving that from the beginning he was of two minds regarding the show. Shortly after the series began, in a moment of frustration, he admitted to John Walker of the *Chicago Tribune* that he didn't want to do the series at first. "I was fighting with myself. I didn't want millions of people to see me do a poor job in a silly western. Then I accepted it and committed myself to it. And I've had a ball." Because he was under contract to Universal that he could only break by initiating a lawsuit, Peter felt put upon and for that reason considered it justifiable to criticize the show. He was especially angry when reporters compared *Alias Smith and Jones* to *Butch*

Cassidy and the Sundance Kid. "It's supposed to be humorous," he said, "but this is TV and any similarity to a class motion picture is purely coincidental."[27] But in another interview, he says about the comparison, "It was always the first question asked, and in my opinion a moot point. . . .It would be funny if the series runs a couple of years, then the film is re-released and a new audience that hasn't seen the movie will say *Butch Cassidy and the Sundance Kid* resembles *Alias Smith and Jones.* "[28]

Peter told a reporter for the *Los Angeles Herald-Examiner* that he regretted

being stuck in a western comedy after coming off acting in some pretty intense roles. He thought those easier and that "comedy takes more effort to get the juices going."[29] Yet previously he had expressed the opinion that "after the parts I'd had in recent years – from drug addicts to draft-dodgers – I was glad to have something with humor."[30] His co-star, Ben Murphy, felt the same way. "Comedy is a lot more fun to do. No question."[31]

Sometimes Peter found humor in the most mundane circumstances. One day Peter's friend from college, actor Jack Jobes, stopped by the set between shots. As they talked, Nature called, so they headed down to the end of Denver Street, took a turn and were out in the backlot's wilderness area. Although this area represented the wide open spaces of the Wild West, it was still a part of the bustling studio and a regular feature of the popular tram tour. "Oh God, we hated those tours," Jobes remembers. Outdoor shooting was challenging enough given Universal's proximity to the Burbank Airport; shuttling tourists through the sets was a nuisance the actors could do without. As the men stood there relieving themselves, a tram full of tourists from "East Nowhere, Iowa, or whatever . . ." moved slowly past. "Pete and I are there taking a wee-wee," Jobes laughs. "The tram drives by and the two of us just wave and say, 'Hi! Welcome to Hollywood!'"

Peter seemed resigned to being Hannibal Heyes, appearing to give up his self-imposed five-year plan for success. "Making a TV series is the same thing day after day, after day, after day. I confess to being a little restless. I was footloose and fancy free at Universal before this came along."[32] Then, with the hectic pace of production, his freedom was greatly curtailed. He complained, "Ben and I are in every damn shot. We don't have time for anything. I'm so tired I'm confused.

My ears are ringing. Ben is dingy. . . .It's been so cold and by 11 a.m. I start to drag. By 4 p.m., I can't do anything."[33] "Still," he contradicted himself, "if I have to make a TV series, I prefer being in the great outdoors and around horses than playing a lawyer, say, in a courtroom."[34] When reminded that the exposure in a weekly television series would be good for his career, Peter wondered why he needed the following of a television audience if independent Hollywood producers were willing to put him in movies. "I don't care if they know who I am in Ohio. I spent two years after *Love on a Rooftop* and *Gidget* trying to learn to act."[35]

(Jerry Ohlinger's Movie Materials Store)

Other reporters heard still more contrasting opinions from him. *The Chicago Tribune* reporter wrote later in the year that Peter said of the series, "I'm able to accept it and enjoy it. That's the only way to handle it, unless you want to become a recluse. Besides, it's only a passing phase. Five years from now, I don't want to look back and say, 'Why didn't I get into that?' Now I'll be able to look back and say, 'I enjoyed it and played the role to the hilt.'" Still others like Judy Stone of *TV Guide* found him to be a perfectionist who would pester the director with pertinent questions about character motivation. Producers could verify that he would protest if the script were inadequate or the acting not up to his standards. On the other hand, even if he didn't like a script page, he realized that the writers have a very difficult job so he tried to "often work around the situation and dialogue, trying to have fun."[36]

Despite his negative outbursts, in daily work, he was very cooperative with his fellow actors. Dennis Fimple remembered that Peter never said, "'You should do it this way' or, 'you should do it that way.' Maybe he did to some, but he never

[did] to me, he never said that. He was just supportive and he was a star, so it made you feel good and you felt strong enough to do what you wanted to do." Peter tried to make other actors feel at ease but "he'd get the giggles sometimes, . . ." Fimple said. "And you could see it coming, and you go, 'Oh no, no, no, no! Take seventeen!'"

But to Fimple, too, it was obvious that Peter and Ben were being worked hard. "I would come in and work a day or so and they would be working on another episode that they hadn't finished, kept falling behind on . . ." For awhile, it got to be so bad that Peter confided to him, "'I haven't had a chance to shower. I just do my armpits and private parts and that's it.' He said, 'I just don't have time.' And it was hard on him because he couldn't drive."[37]

On the evening of October 24, 1970, in the midst of shooting the pilot, Peter had been involved in an automobile accident. After work, the cast had gotten together at a restaurant. "Pete was getting pretty smashed, and . . . he said, 'Who wants to go with me? I'm going driving up in the mountains.'"[38] Only Jon Shank went along, the rest wished him well. The next day they learned that Peter's car had collided with a sportscar driven by Wayne H. Zitter, a 21-year-old cook at Los Angeles City College. Diana Lachman, Zitter's date, was with him. As a result of the collision, Zitter suffered minor injuries but Lachman was hospitalized in serious condition for several days with major head injuries, deep cuts and the loss of her front teeth. California Highway Patrolman Paul Lehner was first on the scene. In a preliminary hearing held in Beverly Hills Municipal Court three days later, Lehner testified that Peter Duel appeared drunk and "began to shake and tremble" when he was asked to perform a field sobriety test. After the test in which he rated a .17 on the breathalyzer, Peter became "very emotional, started crying, staggered and fell to the ground."[39]

His case was bound over for trial in Superior Court where he denied all the charges. Court and entertainment pundits guessed he would be able to continue his work at Universal. Ordinarily a jail sentence would not be indicated, though a possible probation might include the loss of his driver's license for a time and restrictions on where and when he might drink.[40]

In May 1971, while Peter was on hiatus after the first season, his drunk driving case came up in court. He wrote to the judge, Bernard S. Selber, "In recalling my feelings on that night, shame and terror were in my mind. Sitting here eight months later it is very difficult to re-create the events of the accident or even try to find justification for my conduct. But I do want Your Honor to know that I am a person basically interested in other people and I would not knowingly harm anyone."[41] Roy Huggins and a probation officer testified in his favor and the charges were not pursued. He was fined $1,000 for dangerous driving and put on probation for two years, during which time his license was suspended. If Duel had had trouble paying the fine, Universal might have advanced him the money against his salary. But Lew Wasserman would be more likely to tell him, "If you're getting into trouble, it's your expense."[42]

Fenton Bresler, a reporter for *Pageant* magazine, wrote in 1975 that Hal Frizzell, Peter's stand-in, became his chauffeur. Frizzell told Bresler, "I used to collect him in the morning, bring him to the studio, give him his script for that day – he said it was so much rubbish he couldn't read it except in small daily doses – then work with him all day, and collect him at the end and bring him back home."[43] No doubt the suspension of Peter's driver's license was a terrible hardship for him, as it was meant to be. He and his girlfriend Diane Ray enjoyed getting away from the city and heading into the mountains where he felt more at peace. However, he managed it, finding a degree of happiness in his relationship with Ray and in the comradeship and care of their canine pets. Ray would frequently join him on the Universal lot, bringing at least three dogs. Earl Holliman, outlaw Wheat Carlson in the pilot and second season premiere, remembered that "they always had dogs and they would be in Peter's trailer. . . .They were real dog people. They loved the animals."[44]

During the summer of 1971, even after five months of playing Heyes, Peter told another Los Angeles reporter, "I still haven't found my way in playing Hannibal Heyes. I know what Heyes should be, at least I did in the pilot. He favors sweet talking, card playing and safe cracking and needs situations to display those attributes."[45] The series seemed to grow on him as it did the audience. A few weeks into the second season, he said, "I'm not so sure I'd want it to fold. You develop an affection for the crew and the show. I have affection for the character of Hannibal Heyes. . . .I can sit on a porch with a horse tied up at the rail and relax and take a trip back to a time when it was dangerous, but there was a lot of peace."[46]

Peace was an important virtue to Peter, both in the world and in himself. Monty Laird, who was on the set every day as stand-in or stuntman, only saw him lose his temper one time. It was late at night. Assistant director Mike Kusley and Peter, "for some reason or another," clashed a lot. "Mike was trying to get everybody off the clock, you know, save the production money . . . and he was pushing Pete and Pete finally just had it up to here. He came up out of his seat and (hollered), 'Get this goddammned guy outta here.' I never saw Pete lose his temper before. . . .Then he apologized to the crew after that."[47]

Peter was already an experienced actor when he was hired to play Hannibal Heyes, but *Alias Smith and Jones* was Ben Murphy's first foray into a television series as star. "It took four shows before I knew where the camera was! Except of course for close-ups. You'd have to be pretty dense to miss the lights and lenses just two feet away from you. Otherwise, I was so concerned about where they were putting me and what I was supposed to do, that I literally had no idea from what angle they were shooting. All I did was relate to the other actors in the cast and do as I was told."[48]

One of the things Ben remembers vividly thirty years later was the daily routine. "I had a little one bedroom apartment with a mattress on the floor . . . and that was the greatest thing in the world to just roll out of bed and be at work. . . .I'd just drive three blocks and I was there. I was always barely awake, because it was always six in the morning or something like that. . . .You go through makeup, you go get a donut, you have your coffee. . . " Peter would have been going through the same morning routine but because he was so concerned with keeping the Earth ecologically pure and wanting everything healthy and natural, he tried to get rid of donuts and other unhealthy foods like that on the set. He wanted fruit and vegetables. "He put his foot down, and he got it." Peter's pet cause was ecology and he hated pollution. "He would not use plastic cups on the set – only glass ones. He would not use anything that would not dissolve and go back into the earth."[49] Yet, despite his complaints about the snacks, he smoked and drank, another indication of his contradictory nature.

Ben remembered that once he was on the set, "you hope you got your lines down for that day, if not, you kind of wing it the best you can . . . A lot of it's survival on television, especially doing an hour show. The grind is so hard that you just want to survive . . . and I was a young man then. . . .Eventually it grinds you down because the days are so long and by law, by SAG agreement, they're supposed to give you twelve hours off, but they can even give you less than twelve and just pay you double-time or double overtime. It doesn't amount to much; it's worth their while, so you can end up with ten hours off. That's ten hours to drive home – in my case it was a short trip – eat, sleep and then back the next day. But it's okay because you're either making a lot of money, or in my case you're starting your career, which is enjoyable. But what I remember mostly is it's a grind, it's not a lot of hijinks and fun."[50]

At 7 a.m. the clapperboard clapped and the cameras rolled for the first sequence which might require several takes to get right. Blocking out the scene took about ninety percent of the time while the other ten percent was the actors acting. "And that's why it's boring," Ben said. "There's very little acting, it's mostly just that technical part and that's why it's hard work."[51]

Finally the director would call for a break or the stand-ins would take over for a while as crews adjusted lighting or camera angles for the next scene. While waiting to do his next bit, Ben might be changing clothes or studying lines. Or, he remembers with a smile, "You might be just horsin' around with members of the crew, we certainly horsed around our fair share." During the down times, guest star Dennis Fimple recalled, "Ben was always off to himself, reading or something." The "or something"[52] often included Ben questioning the prop man. Heyes and Curry always traveled with saddlebags presumably carrying all their worldly goods including everything they needed in the way of clothes, shaving gear, etc. Besides their various vests and coats, during formal occasions, such as visits to governors or even bank presidents, the boys wore suits and derby hats. Ben had the same realistic question each time, "'Well, where's our stuff?' – because the saddlebags were always empty, they were just props." The prop man whispered, "Don't worry about it. It's on the back of the horse."

Aside from the exhaustion of always playing catch up, Ben was contented. Peter Duel was a good guy to work with and even if they often worked from early morning until late at night, Ben told a *Movieland* reporter that summer, "I've never been happier, thanks to the opportunity to act regularly."[53] Working with Peter was part of the fun because at the time Ben said, "Pete and I didn't really work as hard as we might have done . . . We never learned our lines properly or went through the usual system of rehearsal. . . .But the series seemed to gain rather than lose by this, because Pete and I could improvise together and it would always work . . ."[54]

Though in truth, the premise of *Alias Smith and Jones* was borrowed from *Butch Cassidy and the Sundance Kid,* Ben didn't base his Kid Curry character on anything particular in the movie or from his own life. There's a lot of Ben Murphy in his characterization of Curry but he puts himself into any part he plays because "for me that's the only way it's convincing and real. . . I just take out different bits of me for different roles." The role of Curry "was just based on fun, having a good time, if anything. An adventure."[55]

(Courtesy of Ben Murphy)

Playing a cowboy was new to Ben. He had done some horseback riding before he got the role of Kid Curry, but he wasn't very good. "I was never a horseman, never pretended to be. I didn't consider myself a very good actor on *Alias Smith and Jones* either. I was just a smart actor." For him, that meant making friends with the wranglers who would look after him. He was clever enough not to act like he knew more than he really did because "the wranglers are gonna show you

you don't eventually. So you make sure that they're your friends and I did that. . . .I was well-coached." His favorite wrangler was also the head stuntman, Monty Laird. Ben was an "excellent student," Laird remembered. "With props, he'[d] take any advice from anybody in order to be able to use that prop correctly." Laird wasn't Ben's only stunt double; Jimmy Nickerson and Chris Howell also stood in for him during dangerous scenes, such as fist fights and hopping freight cars.

Laird was a gunsmith who crafted the American-made Smith and Wesson Scofield pistols that Ben used on the show.[56] For Ben, who has kept one of the guns he used, "the most important thing for the Western actor is to be able to draw a gun convincingly. . . .If you're gonna see a picture of the whole guy, that's something that just can't be faked. The only way they could do it would be to take a close-up shot of some other guy's hand and flash it in. But most actors – including me even – manage to get as far as looking pretty dangerous on the draw!"[57] The speed and actual quick shooting could be later spliced in using film taken of a real professional fast draw, like Laird.

Besides coaching the main stars in horseback riding and marksmanship and filling in bit roles as telegrapher, posse member, or poker player, Laird was in charge of finding horses to suit the guest stars. Dennis Fimple recalled that he didn't want a horse that went fast – "I ain't no hero! . . . I just want one that I can talk to and we can get along." Laird found just the right animal for him and became Fimple's hero of horsemanship after that. Fimple would ask the stuntman how he looked. "Ya look good," Laird told him. "And tuck your legs in when you're tearing ass across here . . ." Fimple tried to remember all the tricks but he recalled one time when "Monty [and the other riders] were following us. I looked over and this guy falls off his horse right in the middle, and there's like thirty riders. It's Monty. Monty! My God, he's telling me how to do it. . . .The lines broke and he couldn't do anything about it. I thought, 'Boy, you're a good teacher, aren't ya? Do as I say, not as I do.'"[58]

Not only did the non-horsemen have to stay on their horses and look like they knew what they were doing with cowboy gear, but another thing Fimple and other guest stars, as well as Peter Duel and Ben Murphy, had to learn was to get the lines exactly right. To this day, Ben shakes his head, wondering how often he frustrated Roy Huggins by *not* getting the lines right. "I'm sure there were many times they wanted to tear their hair out," he says. After long hours on the set, Ben recalls that he goofed up more often than he uttered a gem of an ad lib. At times he didn't say what was written in the script, or he paraphrased it, or, "I forgot it quite frankly, and I was too tired to remember it that day on the fifth take or something. . . .Then the producer has to just start cutting like crazy and make it work or loop it in later." If that were the case, after some rest, Ben would head for the dubbing stage where he would recite his lines off-camera to get the information out the writers needed to tell the story. Fimple verified Ben's observation. "Sometimes they wouldn't let you get away with changing a 'that' to a 'but'. You gotta have it word for word for word."[59]

In this regard, director Alex Singer felt Huggins might have been a little more stringent than most producers. "The dialogue was kind of polished to a fare-thee-well and changes in it were generally changes in, he felt, changes in content, in substance. I think he was very sensitive to that. . . .They had to call in and say, 'Is it okay to say, "Thursday morning" instead of "Thursday afternoon"?' And the answer might be 'No, because we refer to Thursday afternoon in three other scenes.' There usually was a structural reason for a bit of dialogue, even the most casual thing, so . . . improvisation in dialogue was problematic."[60]

After nearly eleven weeks on hiatus from the show, Ben told Rochester, New York, reporter Tom Green that, in spite of the tensions, "I love *Smith and Jones.* I wouldn't want to be doing any other series. It pretends only to be entertainment, not social comment. . . .There's nothing phony about it." He was eager to demonstrate to the fall competition that the show could hold its own. "I've never been bothered by Flip Wilson. Having *Family Affair* on CBS was tough, too. I'm going to be glad to get up against a new show on CBS. I think they're going to be in trouble."[61] To get ready for the second season, Ben changed his hat and "tried to make it cool. . . .I went out and designed it."[62] Monty Laird gave him a hand and suggested he put buckles on it. Ben also changed the other clothing Kid Curry wore. Because the first season was done in a rush, everything was off the rack and it was scratchy wool, too hot for Southern California. Ben changed all his clothing to cottons for comfort.

By mid-June, everything was in place in order to begin the second season. Shooting started on June 23 with "Jailbreak at Junction City." The ninety-minute episode "The Day They Hanged Kid Curry," the second season premiere, took eleven days to film in July. After that, filming continued with hardly a break until Friday, September 3, when Peter and Ben left for a week-long promotional tour. Throughout that summer of 1971, except for four pre-emptions for Tom Jones specials, *Alias Smith and Jones* aired in re-runs. ABC hoped the continued exposure would help the show find its audience.[63]

On September 9, ABC aired the pilot as a way to re-introduce Hannibal Heyes, Kid Curry and their decision to seek amnesty. A week later, the second season officially premiered. Competition would be unrelenting from *The Flip Wilson Show* on NBC and *Bearcats* on CBS. The latter would fall victim to the Flip Wilson phenomenon, lasting only a half-season. The *Los Angeles Herald-Examiner* reported that as far as *Alias Smith and Jones* was concerned, "a fuss is being made, names are signed and brave words are bandied about yet nobody expects to give Wilson a serious run." That would remain to be seen.[64]

CHAPTER 5

So All We Gotta Do Is Stay Out of Trouble for One Year? The Second Season

SEPTEMBER 16, 1971 – JANUARY 27, 1972
Second Season Credits (1971-72)

DIRECTOR:	BARRY SHEAR, ALEXANDER SINGER, JEFFREY HAYDEN, FERNANDO LAMAS, HARRY FALK, JACK ARNOLD, NICHOLAS COLASANTO, RUSS MAYBERRY, VINCENT SHERMAN, MEL FERBER, RICHARD BENEDICT, JEFF COREY, BRUCE BILSON, JOHN DUMAS, RICHARD L. BARE
CASTING:	JOE REICH
PRODUCTION MANAGER:	DICK BIRNIE
UNIT MANAGER:	BUD BRILL, BURT ASTOR, CARL BERINGER
ASSISTANT DIRECTOR:	WARREN SMITH, JOHN GAUDIOSO
2ND ASSISTANT DIRECTOR:	MIKE KUSLEY, BOB GILMORE
ART DIRECTOR:	BOB LUTHARDT, PHIL BENNETT
SET DECORATOR:	BERT ALLEN
PROPS:	BOB BONE, DEAN O'CONNOR, BILL SMALLBACK, SOLLY MARTINO
SCRIPT SUPERVISOR:	AL PAGONIS
CAMERA:	JOHN M. STEPHENS, WILLIAM CRONJAGER, E. CHARLES STRAUMER
SOUND:	EARL N. CRAIN, JR.
WARDROBE – MEN:	HARRY PASEN, JACK TAKEUCHI, BERT HENRIKSON, FORREST (T-BONE) BUTLER
WARDROBE – WOMEN:	PAMELA WISE, NINA JOSEPH, CHUCK WALDO, LEAH RHODES
PUBLICITY:	ALLAN CAHAN
EDITORIAL SUPERVISION:	RICHARD BELDING
EDITOR:	JOHN DUMAS, ALBERT ZUNIGA, RICHARD BRACKEN, BUD HOFFMAN, BYRON BRANDT, TERRY WILLIAMS, GLORYETTE CLARK, HENRY BATISTA

THE DAY THEY HANGED KID CURRY

"There's only one thing in the world we're better at than breakin' into banks and that's breakin' out of jail."
– Kid Curry

STORY:	JOHN THOMAS JAMES
TELEPLAY:	GLEN A. LARSON
DIRECTOR:	BARRY SHEAR
SHOOTING DATES:	JULY 1, 2, 5, 6, 7, 8, 9, 12, 13, 14, 15, 1971
ORIGINAL US AIR DATE:	SEPTEMBER 16, 1971
ORIGINAL UK AIR DATE:	NOT AIRED

Hannibal Heyes arrives in a horse-drawn hansom at Silky O'Sullivan's San Francisco mansion. The fare is $1, but Heyes only has six bits and a $20 bill. He considers borrowing the dollar from Silky, but at that prospect, the driver is willing to settle for the six bits. When the driver wonders how Silky acquired his name, O'Sullivan screeches, "On account of my lyrical voice!–Now git!"

Heyes says he and the Kid ran into some trouble up north and had to split up. They planned to meet at Silky's but Silky informs him Curry is on trial for murder.

Heyes travels to Red Rock, Montana, and strides down the main street past carpenters busy building a gallows. He enters the courthouse in time to hear Mr. Hanson, the prosecutor, promising to prove Kid Curry murdered Warren Boggs. Curry is seated in the front row and, though he can only see his back, Heyes's shoulders slump at the sight.

Penelope Roach takes the stand and testifies that the defendant told her he was Kid Curry. When Hanson asks questions about Curry's past crimes, the judge rules them irrelevant and adjourns the court. As the gallery of onlookers rises to leave, Heyes hisses Curry's name. When the curly-headed man turns around, Heyes is surprised to see the face of a complete stranger. Befuddled, Heyes turns to leave and spots the Jed Curry he knows leaning against the doorframe, tipping his hat and smiling.

Curry is pleased with the good luck that has come his way. When the defendant

> This episode was not part of the original purchase when the BBC bought the series in the 1970s.
>
> All shots showing Fred at the gallows with the rope around his neck were deleted from the episode before it was shown on the BBC in the 1990s.
>
> Hangings often attracted large crowds. However, the mood was not so much a holiday spirit as a sense of excitement at seeing a famous outlaw die. Wheat says the crowd was as good as that of Black Jack Ketchum who died in Waco. Wheat was psychic; Ketchum wasn't hanged until April 26, 1901 and it was in Clayton, New Mexico.

is hanged in his name, he'll be a free man because lawmen will stop looking for him. Unfortunately, as Heyes points out, two men were involved in the murder, the other very much resembling himself. Curry wishes him good luck.

Over beers at the saloon, Heyes ponders how to get "the Kid" to change his story. Curry has an idea and Heyes is desperate enough to try it.

In the sheriff's office, Heyes identifies himself as "the Kid's" cousin from the honest side of the family. After being searched, Heyes is let into "the Kid's" cell and when questioned, the prisoner denies killing Boggs. Heyes doesn't believe him because he knows he's lying about being Kid Curry. "The Kid" knows he's going to be hanged and decides to go out in style. He was jailed once before for resembling the real outlaw, but was released after Sheriff Lom "Travers" said he wasn't Curry. The respect he got when people thought he was Kid Curry made him want to adopt the persona. He feels no remorse for further tainting the real Kid's reputation and scoffs at Heyes's suggestion that he might go the sheriff about "the Kid" not being who he says he is.

Curry bathes in bubbles as Heyes enters their hotel room and pours himself a drink. "He doesn't mind dying with his boots on," Heyes tells him, "as long as they're yours." Curry is charmed until Heyes reminds him of the possibility a lawman might see Curry after he's been legally hanged. Think of the consequences then! What would the governor of Wyoming say?

Curry suggests Lom identify "the Kid," but Lom is in Mexico and couldn't make it back in time. They have to ensure "the Kid" is acquitted because then he'll be sent back to Wyoming where proper identification will be made.

Curry meets "the Kid's" girlfriend Penny in the saloon where she works. She tells him that a Jack Brown came into town and got together with "Jed." She thinks they planned on robbing a poker game at a house outside of town. A ranch hand caught them sneaking around and Jack Brown killed him and escaped.

Testifying in court, "the Kid" said he and Jack Brown were headed out to participate in a poker game to which Jack had been invited. Rich ranchers played poorly but for big stakes. "The Kid" needed money and was a pretty good player, so he went along. As they were riding up, a ranch hand came out of nowhere. Jack shot him and rode off. The prosecutor questions "the Kid's" story, wondering why they snuck up surreptitiously on the house if not for criminal intent.

Hunched morosely over the saloon's bar, Heyes admits he believes "the Kid's" story. Nobody could make one up that bad.

Back in the courtroom, the jury finds "the Kid" guilty.

Meanwhile, in Devil's Hole, Wheat Carlson barges in on the gang's poker game. He's heard the news of Curry's arrest and conviction and proposes to bust him out of jail. His rousing speech fails to inspire the gang who has no intention of mingling in Curry's sad affair. Kyle, reticent at first, hikes up his britches and hustles to join Wheat on the ride to Red Rock.

The sheriff is prepared for anything the Devil's Hole Gang might contrive and hands out rifles to all his deputies with orders to keep alert.

Seeing the readiness as they ride into town, Kyle wonders if what they're doing is a good idea. They surprise Heyes in the saloon and are in turn astonished when Kid Curry joins them. Heyes and Curry fill in their former partners on the whole story and Wheat has to wonder why "the Kid" would do such a fool thing. (He plumb forgot about the "glamour and glory" of being a real outlaw.) Heyes has a plan but Wheat doubts it'll work if it doesn't involve dynamite. It involves having Penny talking him into telling the truth. It backfires when "the Kid" refuses to see her.

A carnival atmosphere prevails in Red Rock on the day of the hanging with balloons, calliope music and popcorn vendors. "The Kid" is led up to the gallows and allowed to make a final statement. He replies to the judge's questions that, yes, the man he was with the night of the murder was Hannibal Heyes.

(Courtesy of Earl Holliman)

Earl Holliman as Wheat Carlson.

Heyes stomps off and a few minutes later dashes up to the gallows on horseback with the news that his cousin's grandma is coming to say good-bye. Overriding the disappointed shouts of the crowd, the judge postpones the hanging.

A few minutes later, Heyes is let into "the Kid's" cell. As soon as the deputy departs, "Kid" grabs him by the lapels, angry because he was all ready to die. Heyes grabs "Kid" by *his* lapels and throws him onto the cot. "That makes one of us, because *I* wasn't." "Kid" realizes with horror that the man pretending to be his cousin is the real Hannibal Heyes. Though he's respectful of Heyes and sorry for the position he's put him in, he refuses to change his story.

Back at the saloon, Heyes is determined to save "the Kid" from hanging. Wheat insists the only way is to "bust him outta jail." Instead Heyes sends Wheat and Kyle back to Devil's Hole by way of Hillsdale. Their orders are to send a telegram to Silky O'Sullivan asking "Grandma Curry" to come to Red Rock. Wheat and Kyle dig deep for the $1.75 the telegram costs, then steal it back at gunpoint after the telegrapher sends the message.

Silky departs the train in Red Rock dressed in drag as Grandma Curry. At the sight of the boys, "Grandma" threatens to turn them both in if the situation is not a matter of life and death. He de-wigs at the hotel, telling them he had to come, no one else he knew would play "Grandma," not even 88-year-old Emma Holstem. Happy to see him, Heyes relates the plan. At the first mention that he must enter the jail with a gun strapped to his leg, Silky protests. In all his checkered

EARL HOLLIMAN	WHEAT CARLSON
MICKEY SHAUGHNESSY	DEPUTY HOLLIS
DENNIS FIMPLE	KYLE MURTRY
HENRY JONES	JUDGE CARTER
PAUL FIX	TOM HANSEN
FRANK MAXWELL	DEFENSE ATTORNEY
AMZIE STRICKLAND	MISS BUCKLEY
READ MORGAN	LOBO
BOOTH COLMAN	TELEGRAPHER
VAUGHN TAYLOR	DEPUTY WILLIS
C. ELLIOTT MONTGOMERY	DEPUTY COLLIE
SID HAIG	GRIFFIN

Roy Huggins was once asked what he would like his epitaph to say. He replied with a wish that he would be known as someone who consistently delivered a very high level of storytelling.[1] This episode is one example of his dedication to his art. Glen Larson and Huggins worked closely on the script to get it to the final aired version. The story was Huggins's, but Larson wrote some very funny lines which remained throughout multiple revisions. However, some story elements changed vastly from initial line to final cut.

In early drafts, instead of Heyes learning the news from Silky that Curry is in jail, the boys both learn about the young man calling himself Kid Curry from a newspaper headline. This approach of learning they're in trouble from a news story would also be used in "Everything Else You Can Steal" and "A Fistful of Diamonds." This time Curry is delighted he will be off the hook. Huggins loved the idea of Kid Curry sitting around crowing about his luck, supplying a reason for conflict between the characters. Heyes gets to remind Curry, whom he calls a "stupid sonofabitch" in the early stages of the script, that he'll be in trouble with the governor if it's later discovered the wrong man was hanged in his name. Heyes reasons it's not as if the governor was making them wait for the amnesty because he was mean but because he can only do what he can get away with politically. Huggins also loved Larson's line about Wheat's forgetting the glamour of being an outlaw. However, Kyle's remark about them not having been in a streak of glamour for a few days was cut so as not to carry the joke too far.

Fred Philpotts, whose name was to be learned from the outset, is a "Walter Mitty" type. Script notes reiterate that it is terribly important for the judge to clarify that he doesn't care what the young man's name is – Kid Curry or Fred Philpotts – because he's going to be punished for murder, regardless of who he is. Later, however, the writers decided that that approach wasn't logical and wouldn't work. And it wasn't until the fourth rewrite they realized Fred could not reveal his true identity in the beginning of the story. That Fred/"Kid" is perfectly willing to die as one of the biggest outlaws in the West is not an issue. He will be charged with the rancher's murder, but who he is must remain suspenseful.

When "the Kid" admits on the gallows that Ted Brown was really Hannibal Heyes, it becomes an issue for the real Heyes, so he concocts the grandmother story. In the initial drafts, Heyes and Curry, not Wheat and Kyle, ride into Hillsdale to send the telegram asking Silky to send "Grandma" Curry to Red Rock. A funny scene was cut in which the boys approach other little old ladies getting off the train because they don't know exactly who will arrive as Grandma. Emma Holstem, the lady who wouldn't play a grandmother though she's eighty-eight years old, was a woman Soapy used to work with in his con days.

In Huggins's original story, a deputy accompanies Curry to the saloon to find a girl to search "Grandma." When they get to an alley, Curry clobbers the deputy, pushes him into the alley and hits him again. Huggins later threw out this idea but "he doesn't remember why. Something was telling him there was something wrong with it."[2] Penny agrees to be the one to check "Grandma" for weapons because she likes Fred. She is then free to come with them or Curry will give her a couple hundred dollars to settle down somewhere else. But when the time comes, Penny's conscience bothers her and she can't do it, until Curry convinces her there is no other way.

As Heyes and "Grandma" walk to "the Kid's" cell, Curry pulls a gun on the deputies, gags them and ties them up. Heyes and Curry break Fred out and head for the livery stable. The plan is that they will stay in the mine shaft for four or five days (enough time for Fred and Penny to fall in love) then they'll walk ten miles to where the train stops for water and hop a boxcar. They arrive at the abandoned mine, let their horses go, then have to make their way to a ranch to steal more horses on the day they plan to escape. They're caught by the ranch owner and taken back to town. This plan was nonsensical and Huggins realized it would definitely not be up to Heyes's standards. He asked Larson, "Is it stupid that they don't have a better plan than that?"[3] Larson agreed and abandoned it, as well as the courtroom scene in which the judge, who has just locked up Ted Brown, proclaims Fred a pathological liar. However, Ted Brown's statement relieving Fred of guilt was kept.

In the first week of June, the writers were on the third rewrite attempting to make the above scenes fit. Details of names were tweaked for improvement as well. Red Rock, Oregon, where the murder occurred and the trial held, was changed to Red Rock, Montana; the prosecutor's first name, Fred, was changed to avoid having two Freds in the script; and Ted Brown metamorphosed into Jack Brown. Sam Jaffe, who had played Soapy Saunders – Heyes and Curry's gentleman conman friend – was filming Disney's *Bedknobs and Broomsticks* and was unavailable to reprise his role, so the character was changed to Silky O'Sullivan when veteran actor Walter Brennan was hired. During his scenes as Grandma Curry, Brennan was weighed down with twenty pounds of costume consisting of shawl, veil and long dress. The episode was filmed in 100-degree weather, so Brennan, who suffered from emphysema, occasionally had to retreat to his dressing room for oxygen to aid his breathing.[4]

Despite Huggins's misgivings about Larson as a writer, in several instances, script notes indicate that when Larson suggested a phrase or a *raison d'etre*, Huggins saw the wisdom and went along. For instance, it was Larson's idea for Heyes to remind Curry that, if Fred hangs, Curry will have to live in South America because if anyone ever saw him after he was supposed to be dead, it wouldn't bode well for him. Huggins also liked Larson's line when the judge tells them to get out of town, "whoever you are."

One line that Huggins did not approve of occurred in an early rewrite. Curry is championing his idea that living in South America wouldn't be too bad. No one would be looking for him there after had been hanged and buried. Heyes scorns him with "South America?! You wouldn't last two weeks down there. You can't even walk past a tamale stand without turning red." Wheat was to chime in, "Better to be red than dead" – a reference, perhaps, to Huggins's interest in the Communist party.

This ninety-minute episode opened the second season with a flourish. All the premises of the pilot were in evidence. Curry, already tired of chasing the elusive amnesty, was brought back to reality by Heyes's silver tongue. Devil's Hole Gang members Wheat and Kyle were on hand to support their former partners in crime. Heyes's plan saves the day, sort of, and by the end, both pretty good bad men are back on track. Thursday nights would find Heyes and Curry involved in more adventures and this was a rousing start to the season, further cementing Huggins's claim to fame as a master storyteller.

HOW TO ROB A BANK IN ONE HARD LESSON

"You're no fun at all, Harry."
– Hannibal Heyes

STORY:	JOHN THOMAS JAMES
TELEPLAY:	DAVID MOESSINGER
DIRECTOR:	ALEXANDER SINGER
SHOOTING DATES:	JULY 16, 19, 20, 21, 22, 23, 1971
ORIGINAL US AIR DATE:	SEPTEMBER 23, 1971
ORIGINAL UK AIR DATE:	NOVEMBER 29, 1971

Harry Wagoner pretends to fill out a deposit slip as he cases the First National Bank. His face falls when he discovers the bank's safe is a Pierce & Hamilton 1878. To add to Harry's woe, Deputy Lee Harper enters the bank, making his rounds. With one last disgusted look at the safe, Harry leaves, his plans spoiled. Outside, though, the answer to his problem rides up the street – Hannibal Heyes and Kid Curry.

Curry relaxes on the hotel porch while Heyes scopes out the town. Two undertaking parlors, a big bank with solid brick walls, five saloons full of poker players who don't know the odds against helping two pair and a sheriff who's a stranger to them along with a fat, lazy deputy make this a town they can really enjoy.

On the other side of the porch, Lester Wilkey harasses Janet Judson. Despite discouragement from Heyes, Curry goes to her rescue and a fight ensues. Lester, ready to shoot it out, has second thoughts when Heyes warns him with a shake of his head.

In the hotel restaurant, Janet explains she and her sister Lorraine have been fending off Lester's attempts to buy their ranch. With Lorraine's husband dead, they need help keeping Lester away until they can sell to a legitimate buyer. She offers Heyes and Curry foreman's wages if they'll stay and act as a deterrent. Janet tempts them further with the promise of good cooking and good company. Curry is willing to take the job right then, but Heyes wants to talk it over. He pulls Curry aside and says he'll take Janet and Curry can have the as-yet-unseen sister. Curry agrees easily. He can see the beautiful Lorraine over Heyes's shoulder as she joins Janet at the table.

"The Ransom of Kid Curry" and "The Imperfect Crime" were early titles for this episode.

"Note: the girls' mother was a saloon girl – or they wouldn't be behaving like this. The girls are interesting, in spite of their background."
– Story conference, May 14, 1971.

(Sagala collection)

Peter Duel and Jack Cassidy in "How to Rob a Bank in One Hard Lesson."

On the way out to the ranch, Janet and Lorraine are overcome by the heat and stop for a swim. Heyes and Curry sit on the bank, watching with great enjoyment as the ladies cavort in their skimpy underclothes until a voice behind them demands they raise their hands. Heyes and Curry recognize the voice, but can't quite put a name to it. They turn around and see Harry Wagoner.

The group resumes their journey as Harry relates his plans to the now restrained outlaws. Heyes will rob the First National Bank with Harry. Curry will stay with Janet and Lorraine. When the job is over, they'll release Curry, but if Heyes fails, they'll kill him. Heyes points out that a Pierce & Hamilton '78 is the latest technology and he can't open it. Harry just smiles. He knows they robbed the Merchants Bank in Denver a year and a half earlier, and it had a brand new P & H '78.

Heyes and Harry return to town while Lorraine and Janet continue on to their hiding place with Curry.

Heyes tries beating knowledge of Curry's whereabouts out of Harry and when that doesn't work, throws him into a pond and holds his head under water. Sputtering, Harry maintains he doesn't know where the women are taking Curry. That was part of the plan. No matter what Heyes does to him, Harry can't tell him anything. Heyes is forced to believe him.

The women and Curry arrive at the hideout. It's a ramshackle cabin with a grave to one side. "That your last victim?" Curry asks.

When Heyes and Harry settle in at the hotel, Heyes makes a list of everything they'll need for the job.

In the cabin, Curry needles Janet. He's sure Harry knows where they are, but Lorraine contradicts him. Then he asks if Harry doesn't know where they are, how is he going to find them after the job is done? Janet tells him not to worry about that. Curry tries once more, asking Lorraine to hit him over the head if he ever again goes to the aid of a woman in trouble. Janet snaps back that he wanted easy money and lonely women. He took her bait like a hungry coyote. With a sheepish grin, Curry acknowledges it's true.

That night, Heyes tiptoes to the door. Harry sits up in bed, gun drawn. Heyes explains he was just going to pipe the bank.

The next morning, Janet leaves. Curry, hands tied behind him, paces around the room while Lorraine keeps her shotgun trained on him and sweetly explains that the broken down cabin once belonged to her and her husband, before she killed him. She shot him as he put on his boots one day and she'll do the same to Curry if he does one thing out of the ordinary.

Harry has gone shopping and returns with quick-drying putty, safety fuse, an alarm clock and a canvas cabin bag. Heyes adds a bar spreader to Harry's list, but without a Bryant pump, the job's off.

That night, Harry creeps out of the hotel room when he thinks Heyes is asleep, but Heyes follows him. Heyes sees Janet waiting by the side of the road and takes off his boots in order to sneak up on her, but before he can get very close, Harry starts shooting at him. Janet quickly takes off. Heyes surrenders before Harry hits him by mistake.

In the morning, Heyes does a bit of sewing, modifying the canvas cabin bag. Harry is annoyed to find the door locked when he returns from his latest shopping expedition, but Heyes soothes him, saying it's a necessary precaution now that they've started gathering equipment. This time Harry has brought four ounces of nitro. Heyes also needs another alarm clock; he broke the one he had when he knocked it off the table.

While Janet is gone, Lorraine is feeding Curry beans. He wants to know how she came to be mixed up with Harry Wagoner. Lorraine spins another story for him. She didn't kill her husband; the man she ran off with did. That wasn't Harry, she clarifies; Harry's in love with Janet. Lorraine dishes up a second helping of beans as she continues her tale. She worked in a dance hall before she met Harry and the bank robbery was her idea. Lorraine is distracted and no longer holding the shotgun, so Curry takes a chance. He knocks her to the floor and throws himself on top of her, threatening to beat her with his head unless she unties him. Janet arrives and stymies Curry's opportunity for escape.

Heyes enters the hotel room and is met with a beaming Harry proudly showing off the new alarm clock, the bar spreader and, wrapped with a red ribbon, the indispensable Bryant pump. They'll do the job tonight.

Heyes and Harry use the bar spreader to get into the bank through one of the barred windows. The next step is to putty around the edges of the safe, making it airtight. Harry sets the alarm clock for forty minutes, after which the putty will be set and they can go to step two.

Back at the cabin, Curry, now gagged and tied, listens as Lorraine revises her story yet again. She didn't work in a dance hall, but in a saloon. Janet isn't her sister; she was her boss.

When the putty is dry, Harry pumps the air out of the safe. Exactly sixteen minutes later, Heyes pours the nitro into the tube leading into the safe. The vacuum will suck the nitro in, but it might blow up prematurely. Harry is appalled, but not willing to stop, and holds the tube with a shaking hand.

Lorraine decides to shock Curry one more time. "Janet's my mother," she says. "She had me when she was fifteen." Janet is doing this for her daughter and the bank robbery was Janet's idea. Curry, gagged as he is, can only sigh at this new version of her story.

The nitro has been harmlessly sucked into the safe. Heyes replaces the tube with a blasting cap and some fuse. He and Harry retreat to safety behind the tellers' counter and light the fuse. The muffled explosion doesn't bother the fat, lazy deputy at all.

The men ride out of town with the money tucked away in the canvas bag. Harry gives Heyes a note to give Janet, after which she'll take him to Curry. Heyes continues down the road as Harry rides off with the money.

As the sun rises, Heyes and Janet arrive at the cabin where Heyes releases Curry from his bonds, then turns to Janet and demands she tell him where Harry is. He made a bomb and if they don't find him soon, Harry and the money will blow up. Janet thinks Heyes is bluffing, but she can't be sure. Heyes explains he's the only one who can disarm the bomb.

Heyes, Curry, Janet and Lorraine ride to Harry's hideout. Harry doesn't believe the bomb story, either. Listen to the bag, Heyes suggests. He'll hear the clock he thought Heyes broke. Harry listens. Sure enough, the bag is ticking. Harry races out of the house, throwing the bag of money toward the well in an attempt to douse it. It falls short and everyone flings themselves to the ground. Instead of an explosion, there's only the sound of an alarm ringing. "You know, Kid," Heyes muses. "I guess I got to worrying so much about ruining all that money that I just forgot to stick in any blasting powder."

Heyes awakens Deputy Harper. He's going to make the deputy a hero by bringing in the bank robbers. "Deputy Smith" explains that he and his partner resemble a couple of outlaws and the prisoners are going to claim that he and Jones are really Hannibal Heyes and Kid Curry. Jones brings the chastened trio and the money into the jail. Harry whispers to Harper that the two men who brought them in are Heyes and Curry, but Harper ignores him. After thanking Smith and Jones, Harper turns back to the seething Harry. "I'm gonna ask you just one question. . . .Would Kid Curry and Hannibal Heyes hand over the loot from a bank robbery to a sheriff? Yes or no?" Harry sinks down on the bunk in defeat.

GUEST CAST

JACK CASSIDY	——————	HARRY WAGONER
JOANNA BARNES	——————	JANET JUDSON
KAREN MACHON	——————	LORRAINE
GREG MULLAVEY	——————	DEPUTY LEE HARPER
BOBBY BASS	——————	LESTER WILKEY

This is the first episode which shows the audience why Heyes and Curry were "the two most successful outlaws in history of the West." Instead of crudely blowing the safe open with an overabundance of dynamite, Heyes's technique for blowing a Pierce & Hamilton 1878 is sophisticated and makes use of advanced mathematics. As Heyes tells Harry, "There's a formula for everything." Just where Heyes learned the calculus necessary to figure out how long it takes to create a vacuum in a safe is left to the viewer's imagination. Fortunately, the writer didn't have to have a background in bank robbery to come up with the plan. During the story conference on May 14, 1971, he was told that he would "find the exact equipment in the research material Roy gave him."

The method Heyes uses to blow the P & H '78 was actually used by a highly successful bank robber by the name of David Cummings in 1873, when he and his accomplices robbed the First National Bank of Quincy, Illinois. They got away with $539,000 in cash, government bonds and other securities. The technique is detailed in *Our Rival the Rascal,* a book Roy Huggins turned to more than once for criminal inspiration:

> This successful burglary was further remarkable in marking the first intro-
> duction of the air-pump for the purpose of blowing powder into a safe. The

arrested for his complicity in the jailbreak.

Judge Hanley sits down with Heyes and Curry. He received the warning they sent through Brubaker, but he can't understand their motivation. They are Heyes and Curry, right? They affirm they are and admit to trying to clean up their record. Curry confesses being law-abiding gets to be a habit. Hanley suspects the governor offered them a secret amnesty deal.

Attorney Brubaker bursts in with the money from the robbery that was found in Clitterhouse's cabin. Hanley appoints him lawyer for Heyes and Curry and holds court. While he awaits their extradition papers and, because they're not wanted on a capital offense, he fines Heyes $8.12 and Curry $12.21 in bail. Often, he says, people put up bail and the court never expects to see them again. Heyes and Curry understand perfectly.

GUEST CAST

GEORGE MONTGOMERY ──────── SHERIFF CURT CLITTERHOUSE
JAMES WAINWRIGHT ──────── RIBS JOHNSON
JACK ALBERTSON ──────── JUDGE HANLEY
KENNETH TOBEY ──────── SHERIFF SLOCUM
ANGUS DUNCAN ──────── CHESTER BRUBAKER
THOMAS BELLIN ──────── SPRINGER
ALLEN EMERSON ──────── HANCOCK
WILLIAM BRYANT ──────── BARKER
HARRY HICKOX ──────── SAM BROCK
JON LORMER ──────── TELEGRAPHER
BRYAN MONTGOMERY ──────── DEPUTY JOHNNY
HARRY E. NORTHRUP ──────── POTTS

Several changes took place in the production credits on the way from the story to the aired version. Roy Huggins first told the story to writer Dick Nelson on May 11, 1971, who brought in a first draft on June 1, very closely resembling the story Huggins had told. Overnight, Huggins read it and wrote only six pages of rewrite comments. Two days after that, Nelson turned in a second draft. On June 8, Glen Larson replaced Jo Swerling as producer. Steve Heilpern, who would become associate producer twelve episodes later, received rewrite notes on June 10. On June 14 another revision was completed. On June 23 filming began on the script whose first page showed a crossed off Dick Nelson as teleplay writer and John Thomas James as story originator and gave the "written by" credit to John Thomas James.

In one of the early scenes, when Kid Curry faces Barker, the disgruntled poker player, the script calls for him to "face his antagonist with an expression of put-upon weariness. Although he's confident, Curry never faces a situation like this with boredom or smiling contempt, because he knows he could come up against someone some day who is better than he is." As script writer, who usually follows the protocol of not supplying directions for the director's shots, Huggins nevertheless added this note to show exactly what he had in mind: "We must see both men down to the holster in this and the following shot. We are using the draw that we use in all Smith and Jones shows in which we are on the antagonist for precisely twelve frames as he starts for his gun."[8]

According to Alex Singer, one of the directors of *Alias Smith and Jones* episodes, "this instruction is a familiar but always effective Editorial device. 12 frames is half a second of screen time. If the camera is on the antagonist for half a second while he's going for his gun and then you cut to our man with his gun already drawn, you in effect 'collapse' the time interval in which our hero has made his draw. Since you were watching the other guy draw first you believe the Kid allowed him a head start, confident that he would outdraw him in any case and also clearly establishing the first offender. Putting the instruction in the script is the Producer's way of making sure the Director gives the Editor the proper footage."[9]

Since Roy Huggins was a talented editor himself, he knew what he wanted and watched nearly all the dailies to make sure he got it. Very conscientious about the program, he said, "I never let somebody else edit the show. . . .One way in which I spent more money than other producers at Universal was in editing. And I probably spent times three times as much. You know, simply because I spent three times more hours with the editors in the editing room and tried to make every show have something, even if it was just a good story."[10]

As also delineated in the script, when deputies Smith and Jones lead the outlaws to jail, in order to maintain control of their small contingent, they fasten the horses together as in a pack train. The simplest method of doing this was by "tailing" them. This means the tail of the lead horse is doubled to form a knot of hair around which the end of the halter rope of the horse behind it is tied. This does not hurt the horse. We see Curry holding the halter of Ribs's horse and leading it, while Hancock's horse is "tailed" behind Ribs's horse.

The trick of standing an egg on its end appears at first very difficult to do and it can be, particularly with a smooth egg. This is because the albumen, or white, of the egg is a very thick liquid in which the yolk sits. Even when the egg is cooked, as the one in the saloon was, because the yolk is usually a bit off-center, it makes the egg difficult to balance. What helps is that, on some eggs, there are tiny bumps in the shell. Those irregularities are enough to help the egg stand, acting as tiny legs. Heyes's trick of salting his palm before resting the egg in it accomplishes the same end.

When the boys admit to Attorney Brubaker that they only have $8.12 and $12.21 in their pockets, they seem to be forgetting about the $100 each that Sheriff Slocum offered them to return the first two prisoners to Junction City. Did Slocum believe that they would come back to Big Bend to collect it or did

GUEST CAST

WILL GEER	SETH
ROGER DAVIS	DANNY BILSON
BARBARA STUART	LURENE
MILTON FROME	BARKER
LEO GORDON	EBENEZER
HARRY LAUTER	SHERIFF
DICK HAYNES	2ND BARTENDER
JAMES HOUGHTON	BARKER'S ASSISTANT
COLBY CHESTER	YOUNG COWBOY

Up to this time, Kid Curry has been portrayed as a non-violent gunfighter. He cows his opponents through sheer speed and rarely pulls the trigger. Working on this episode with Ben, Roger Davis realized he "really had something, a charm that was indefinable," and he complimented Ben on it. "I told him straight out that I thought he would rise very quickly and would become very popular."[13] However, in this episode Ben's charm as Curry is not so evident; he not only shoots his opponent, he shoots to kill. Curry's anger over Seth's death builds as it appears ever more likely Danny will get away with his crime. The last scene leading up to the final showdown is ambiguous, though. Did Curry truly mean to goad Danny into a gunfight in order to extract his own form of justice? Was Heyes's warning to Danny really a warning or was it a challenge? In the first draft script, Heyes goes to the saloon to give Danny a message.

HEYES

He told me to tell you he was going to kill you. Oh – not today . . . but he's coming back. He doesn't know *when*, but the minute he gets in town, he'll kill you. It may not be pretty, because he's mad. He may ambush you from a shed, or you might even be sleeping in your bed, but wherever – he'll probably shoot you from the back because he knows how fast you are on the draw. And . . . *that's* the message.[14]

Danny just laughs, figuring Thaddeus is trying to scare him. Heyes offers his opinion that Thaddeus is deadly serious. This dialogue is more direct than it became in the completed episode but is no less ambiguous. Given their creed and their history of never having killed anyone, Kid Curry would not shoot Danny in the back under cover of darkness. His desire to kill Danny is obvious throughout the episode, though, especially in the first draft script where Seth didn't die from exhaustion and dehydration, but instead shot himself because the boys wouldn't go on without him. The only logical response to expect from Danny after he gets this message is a showdown.

Even Heyes is unsure if Curry's intention was to push Danny into a gunfight.

He asks his partner if he knew Danny would challenge him. In the first draft, his answer is:

CURRY

No, I didn't. I wish he hadn't in a way. I'd have been just as happy if he spent the next few years of his life scared to death . . . waiting for me to show up.
(beat)
But then – when I think about [Seth] – [15]

However, Danny Bilson is a man who always wins. Curry knew Danny would never be satisfied letting them leave town without a decisive victory. Every move Curry made was calculated to make Danny pay for murdering Seth.

Roger remembers the scene in the saloon where Heyes and Curry confront Danny and demand the money. "[Peter] was bored as could be and he didn't know the lines. He had the script in his lap." Yet that didn't affect his performance. Peter, despite being unprepared, still managed to recite the dialogue perfectly and hit the emotional level the scene required, a feat Roger still recalls with some awe. "He was *very* good in the scene. He was very good." Because of the work they had done together on *The Young Country*, Peter also knew what Roger needed from him in order to give his own top performance.

The scene called for Danny Bilson to react to Heyes's threat with a lighthearted laugh. Roger explains, "He knew in the scene he was gonna go 'I want that money back!' But he knew that when he gave it to me in the [close-up] that I would have a much better reaction if he gave it to me sweetly, nicely." So on camera Peter was menacing. Off camera he fed the lines to Roger in a light, joking tone and ended with a big wink, allowing Roger to react to his silliness and imbue the ever-smiling Danny with an insufferable and provoking good humor. "[Peter] knew that that would take me to the thing . . . I was in the perfect place."[16]

THE POSSE THAT WOULDN'T QUIT

*"If you're going to skin somebody, you just don't bludgeon in.
Ya gotta try a little finesse."*
– Kid Curry

STORY:	JOHN THOMAS JAMES
TELEPLAY:	PAT FIELDER
DIRECTOR:	HARRY FALK
SHOOTING DATES:	AUGUST 4, 5, 6, 9, 10, 11, 1971
ORIGINAL US AIR DATE:	OCTOBER 14, 1971
ORIGINAL UK AIR DATE:	DECEMBER 6, 1971

Hannibal Heyes and Kid Curry spur their horses to top speed, outrunning a posse. Fording a river allows them to recover their breath but after wiping out the horses' tracks on the far shore, they resume full gallop.

From a vantage point they watch the posse cross the same river and Heyes concludes there must be an Apache tracker in the group. After three days they haven't been able to lose them. Curry considers that maybe it's the unlucky number of posse members – thirteen.

From atop a high ridge, the boys spot a lone woman, Belle Jordan, driving a wagon on the road below. Deciding to try a new transportation tack, they yank their saddlebags off the horses and drive them off before skidding down the steep slope. Belle Jordan greets the two strangers. After listening to their sad fib of how they lost their horses from poisoned water, she offers them a ride. Home is still a half day's ride away.

Curry takes the reins and they approach the Jordan homestead where Jesse Jordan is laid up with a broken leg. He allows that they can stay if they help with chores until Belle returns to town for supplies in two weeks. As the boys unload the wagon, Belle searches out her two young daughters, Beth and Bridget, who have found a hiding spot under the front porch. Belle introduces them to Mr. Joshua Smith and Mr. Thaddeus Jones and insists they act like ladies instead of the wild women she's afraid they're turning into.

The first night after supper, Heyes entertains them with a rendition of "Simple Gifts," accompanying himself on guitar. The Jordans share their dream to take the family back to Denver where Jesse hopes to find a teaching job. Belle fears that the girls are growing up wild, but the small herd they own doesn't provide much of an income nor the stake they need to start over.

The posse continues its unrelenting pursuit.

The next morning, rifle shots awaken Heyes and Curry. Fearing the posse has found them, they peer out the window but instead spot Beth and Bridget target shooting at cans set up along a fence. Curry ambles out to join them. The girls confess they're not good rifle shots and Curry admits the same. Bridget challenges him to a contest for ten cents a can. When Curry accepts, she efficiently hits ten cans out of ten. Duped, he digs deep in his pocket for one dollar, but advises them to try finesse if they're going to con someone.

When Beth asks about his skill with a handgun, Curry shrugs with self-deprecation. Believing his lack of confidence, they up the stakes to twenty cents a can. Curry whips out his revolver and fires off six quick shots. Six cans fly off the fence. Chagrined, the girls return his dollar and he reminds them that they owe him twenty cents. Heyes, watching from the bunkhouse door, simply chuckles.

The title morphed from "The Daughters of Belle Jordan" to "Hideout" before it was finalized.

The girls say they practice shooting when not "swampin' or bulldoggin'." According to wrangler Monty Laird that means cleaning or preparing the meat for meals.

At the picnic Bridget questions Heyes about Denver. He says it's beautiful and tells her about the Brown Palace Hotel where you can look up through the center and see the top floor. It was built in 1892, too late for the 1880s story!

The boys mend fences until Beth and Bridget bring them a picnic lunch. Both girls are clearly infatuated with the handsome cowboys.

The posse snakes through the hills and finally arrives at the Jordans' homestead. The next morning, the sheriff hides his men in strategic locations surrounding the cabin.

At breakfast, the Jordans and Heyes and Curry are startled at the sheriff's call. Belle goes out on the front porch and Sheriff Morrison of Diablo Wells informs her that he knows two outlaws are inside. Belle is confused as to which two outlaws and the sheriff identifies them as Heyes and Curry.

Hearing this, Jesse Jordan and the girls stare incredulously at their guests. Belle asks the sheriff to wait while she talks it over with her husband. Jesse sees no option but to turn them over to the lawmen. Heyes suggests that the Jordans turn them in at Buckton for the reward. After many protests, the Jordans reluctantly agree. When informed of the turn of events, the angry sheriff demands to enter the cabin to reassure himself that the outlaws are not holding the family hostage.

He finds Heyes and Curry bound to chairs. Heyes wants to know, and is gratified to learn, that there was indeed a good Apache tracker in the posse. Morrison insists on starting for Buckton immediately. He and his deputy will accompany them just for the pleasure of seeing Heyes and Curry locked up.

Belle sits on the buckboard alongside the deputy. Heyes and Curry ride in the back of the wagon, with the sheriff following on horseback. Along the road, gunfire startles the sheriff's horse, knocking him to the ground. Another shot sends the deputy's hat flying. Heyes and Curry escape while rifle shots pin down the lawmen. After untying each other's bonds, they run for the deputy's horse and escape. Sheriff Morrison, expecting to find the Devil's Hole Gang, circles around the shooters and discovers Beth and Bridget Jordan.

Safely ensconced in an empty railroad car, Heyes and Curry ponder the situation they've left behind. Curry wonders if they ought to return and do something about it. Heyes says no, they ought to hide out for a month, get a stake together, and then return. What could happen? They won't hang the little girls.

At a distant town, the partners play poker and rake in a sizable amount, then return to the Jordans' place. Though they arrive in the middle of the night, the family welcomes them back. Belle and the girls were arrested for aiding and abetting the fugitives, hindering the sheriff from doing his duty, and attempted murder. Despite the severity of the charges, Belle hopes to get only a few months jail time and believes the girls will be freed. She's willing to risk it to save the boys twenty years in prison.

At their trial, the prosecutor entreats the jury to convict Belle and her daughters of conspiracy against the lawmen. He walks along the prisoner's docket, pointing his finger at each in turn and proclaims them guilty – guilty – guilty. Then, relenting, he admits the impressionable young girls need not be dealt with as harshly as their mother.

While the jury deliberates, half the town awaits the decision in the saloon. In short order, the deputy announces that a verdict has been reached. At this, one drunken man shoots off his pistol in celebration and the deputy hauls him off to jail.

The jury foreman announces that Beth and Bridget are innocent because of their age but Mrs. Jordan is guilty. The judge sentences her to three years in prison. At this Kid Curry stands and Sheriff Morrison immediately identifies him. Having heard the sentence, Curry would like to testify and, though it's a bit unusual, the judge re-opens the case. Curry swears that Belle was unaware of what her daughters were planning. Given that Curry has turned in himself in, the judge believes him. Belle is set free and the Kid is led to jail to await extradition to Wyoming.

When the Jordans arrive home, they find a note signed by Joshua and Thaddeus. They've left nearly $1,000 hidden in the cookie jar, which they'd come by "fairly honestly," enough to get the family to Denver.

At the jail, Curry occupies the cell opposite that of the sleeping drunk. Deputies sit up with Curry and play checkers just outside his cell. They're aware that he'd like to pull a trick on them, but Curry says his partner does all the tricks. At that, the drunk rises, pointing a pistol at the lawmen. He peels off his mustache and smiles. Curry identifies him for them – "my partner, Hannibal Heyes, who does the tricks." They surrender the keys and Curry locks the deputies in the jail. As he mounts his horse, he wonders why Heyes looks so disgruntled. "I got rid of my mustache," Heyes tells him, "Why don't you get rid of yours?" Curry fingers his upper lip and promises to think about it.

GUEST CAST

VERA MILES	BELLE JORDAN
CHARLES H. GRAY	JESSE JORDAN
LISA EILBACHER	BRIDGET JORDAN
CINDY EILBACHER	BETH JORDAN
RICHARD X. SLATTERY	SHERIFF MORRISON
SIDNEY CLUTE	PROSECUTOR CLARK
BERT HOLLAND	D.A. LYONS
PETER BROCCO	JUDGE
RUSSELL GARLAND WIGGENS	HANK SMITHERS

When Belle Jordan introduces the girls and observes they're growing up like wild animals and not ladies, teleplay writer Pat Fielder, in her first draft of July 6, has Kid Curry saying he understands, he's got a kid sister who is also a tomboy. Roy Huggins wanted no misunderstanding on this point. Curry does not have a kid sister. "We are being very obscure about our boys' family background."[17] However, four episodes later, Huggins expounded on their background in "The Reformation of Harry Briscoe" with the revelation that they're orphans. Much later, he allows them to talk even more about growing up and about how their parents died.

In Huggins's original story, a condition which carries through all the rewrites is that the Jordan girls are very much taken with Heyes and Curry. Female viewers of the program were very much taken with Peter Duel and Ben Murphy as well. Photos and interviews with them were staples in teen magazines. Such photos showed a clean-shaven Ben; the mustache to which the amusing tag refers was a fake. Ben remembers his own "tended to be long and wispy and it took awhile to grow."[18] The show, however, was not targeted for any specific demographics and this episode was not written to take advantage of teenage girls' fondness for the show. Roy Huggins believed in creating a program he would enjoy watching and he "never gave any thought to the audience," hoping instead that what he produced would appeal to a large number of people. He knew it was fruitless to speculate on what an audience would like because "most of the time you'll be wrong."[19]

When the girls "persuade Curry – or shame him" into demonstrating how good he is with his revolver, Huggins notes that neither of the boys "have really used rifles much in their lives" so they are not as good with a rifle as they are with a revolver. But they recognize in Beth and Bridget a little bit of the con men that they are themselves. In the first draft, Heyes, awakened by gunfire, goes out to shoot with the girls. Huggins corrected that – it's Curry who has the talent of quick draw, not Heyes. It's also an unwritten tenet that Curry is most in tune with children in the episodes. When the girls have helped them escape from Sheriff Morrison, Curry considers that they ought to go back and see what kind of trouble the girls are in. Heyes doesn't think they ought to do anything about it. "That's a hell of an attitude to take," Curry replies in Huggins's story.[20]

When the posse arrives, the boys attempt to talk the Jordans into turning them in because they don't want the posse to split the reward money. The Jordans refuse so they consider making a run for freedom. Belle is horrified; they might be shot down. Fielder has Curry reply, "Well, I guess I'd rather not live if it means seeing them split up the money." Huggins took umbrage with this line. "Curry has suddenly become terribly noble – and he shouldn't be. Heyes is not noble either."[21] Huggins also wanted Fielder to add more "smart aleck" dialogue. Even when it's in ordinary conversation, he wanted it "oblique and witty" in keeping with their view of life. This view of life also would include their not feeling guilty over how their intrusion into the family's hospitality turned the Jordans' lives upside down. If the story had kept to true frontier justice, the girls would have been sent to reform school at the least.

The song "Simple Gifts" that Heyes sings to entertain the Jordans was a work song written by Shaker Elder Joseph Brackett, Jr. in 1848.

> 'Tis the gift to be simple,
> 'Tis the gift to be free,
> 'Tis the gift to come down where you ought to be,

And when we find ourselves in the place just right,
It will be in the valley of love and delight.
Refrain: When true simplicity is gained,
To bow and to bend we shan't be ashamed.
To turn, turn will be our delight,
'Til by turning, turning we come round right[22]

The copyright of the song is over one hundred years old and has expired. Therefore it is in the public domain and can be used for free. Otherwise, the network would have had to pay royalties.

(Courtesy of Ben Murphy)

Peter Duel with his dogs.

Peter Duel's own dogs, Shoshone and Carroll, have a guest appearance in this episode. They bark and follow the scruffy drunk who celebrates the jury's return. Apparently they weren't too happy with the deputy's rough handling of their master!

SOMETHING TO GET HUNG ABOUT

"I thought everyone played according to Hoyle."
– Kid Curry

STORY:	JOHN THOMAS JAMES
TELEPLAY:	NICHOLAS E. BAEHR AND JOHN THOMAS JAMES
DIRECTOR:	JACK ARNOLD
SHOOTING DATES:	AUGUST 26, 27, 30, 31, SEPTEMBER 1, 2, 1971
ORIGINAL US AIR DATE:	OCTOBER 21, 1971
ORIGINAL UK AIR DATE:	JANUARY 3, 1972

As the boys leave the sheriff's office, Sarah enters and asks to see Stokely. She urges him to tell the truth and if he doesn't, she will.

Heyes and Curry go to see the only lawyer in town, R.M Foster. Foster was Henderson's lawyer and his friend, so he's not interested in defending Stokely in court; he'd rather be prosecuting.

Once again Heyes reads while Curry theorizes aloud that Mrs. Henderson killed her husband so she could be a rich widow, free to marry Stokely. Heyes doesn't think much of this idea, but his book has provided him with a plan to free Stokely. First they'll go to see the friendly sheriff and steal the evidence . . .

Sheriff Lindstrom berates his deputy for allowing the murder weapon to be stolen and orders him to spread the word that the gun is missing. If it's returned, no questions will be asked.

Heyes and Curry visit Foster again. Confirming that, if they retained Foster as their lawyer, anything they tell him will be privileged communication, Heyes and Curry admit they stole the rifle. They want to prove Stokely's innocence through the new technology of fingerprints. Foster has never heard of fingerprints so Heyes enlightens him with information he's learned from *Life on the Mississippi*. Their friend Harry Briscoe of the Bannerman Detective Agency is an expert in fingerprints and they've already telegraphed him to come to Amity City. Foster is intrigued, but wants to know why they're telling him all this. If they can prove that Sarah, or someone else, killed Hank Henderson, then there'd be no reason why Foster couldn't represent Stokely in court.

Leaving the lawyer's office, Curry wonders whether anyone at the BDI really knows anything about fingerprints. "Not if they're all like Harry Briscoe, they don't," Heyes laughs.

They aren't sure their plan will work but they don't have any other ideas, so they ride out of town until Foster overtakes them and orders them to drop their guns. He's fascinated by their theories and, as their attorney, advises them to tell him where they hid the shotgun. The boys will take him there. Foster ties them up as Heyes wonders aloud if the fingerprints on the gun belong to Foster. Did Henderson catch him stealing from him?

When they arrive at the cabin where the gun is hidden, Foster is surprised to find Sheriff Lindstrom waiting for him. A brief gun battle ensues and the sheriff kills Foster. Lindstrom unties the boys and confirms that Foster was stealing from his best client.

Freed, Stokely is ready to ride out of town, but Curry is confused. Why not stay with Sarah now that the field is clear? Stokely explains his real name isn't Stokely. He got into trouble and spent some time in jail, but at least it was under the alias. "I didn't want to embarrass my family. I had a very proud father and mother. And a very lovely sister named Sarah."

GUEST CAST
MONTE MARKHAM ———————— JIM STOKELY

MEREDITH MAC RAE	SARAH HENDERSON
KEN LYNCH	SHERIFF GAINES
ROGER PERRY	R. M. FOSTER
NOAH BEERY	SHERIFF LINDSTROM
PAUL CARR	HANK HENDERSON
DICK VALENTINE	MESSENGER
GARY VAN ORMAN	DEPUTY
RALPH MONTGOMERY	POKER PLAYER #1
HARPER FLAHERTY	POKER PLAYER #2
JON LOCKE	MARSH
BOB ORRISON	MAN
JIMMY NICKERSON	STUNT DOUBLE – CURRY
HOWARD CURTIS	STUNT DOUBLE – STOKELY

Viewers could complain that this episode doesn't flow, that it seems to be two unrelated stories put together instead of one cohesive whole. The beginning is full of wry humor, but suddenly the story turns much darker and suffers from a couple of significant plot holes. According to the original story notes, dated June 6, 1971, the viewers would be right. Roy Huggins created the story in his usual meticulous detail until the scene where Sheriff Lindstrom introduces himself to the boys and welcomes them to town. That is followed by "Note: that's as far as we have gone in the story." The last page of the outline gives some possibilities about where the story should go from there, along with an explanation of the relationship between Sarah and Stokely, but nothing specific is determined.

In the story notes from June 8, Huggins continues to develop the story, adding the murder of Hank Henderson and the arrest of Jim Stokely. He also adds *Life on the Mississippi* into the mix, but at this point, remains mute on the reasons why. Huggins takes the story through to Foster's capture of the boys and the confrontation with the sheriff, but acknowledges that "we have to work out a whole new way of ending this story, so there's some excitement in it."

The next set of story notes, dated June 9, incorporates a new detail. The showdown in the saloon over the Hoyle rule is introduced in order to improve the relationship between Stokely and Curry. Huggins initially lamented that the relationship between Stokely and the boys was strictly adversarial. He wanted Heyes and Curry, as well as the audience, to like Stokely. Also, strengthening the friendship between them gives Heyes and Curry a stronger reason to help Stokely prove his innocence later on.

One issue Huggins struggled with was exactly when to reveal the relationship between Sarah Henderson and Jim Stokely. Choosing the proper moment was very important for the story and he tried it in several different places. The story notes of June 9 put this revelation during Sarah's visit to Stokely in jail. She explains to Sheriff Lindstrom that she asked Stokely to help her leave her husband and he agreed because he's her brother. Heyes and Curry are present during this scene and this information becomes motivation for them to go to Foster on his behalf. When Foster refuses to represent Stokely in court, Heyes and Curry return to Sarah and ask about Foster's relationship with her husband. Huggins eliminated this sequence before telling the story to the writer, which unfortunately led to a major plot hole. Without this discussion of Foster and Henderson's relationship, Heyes and Curry have no reason to suspect the lawyer killed his client.

These three sets of story notes were as far as Huggins went until he told the story to writer Nick Baehr on July 8. Huggins had finally decided on the story structure as it appears in the final episode, with the revelation that Sarah and Stokely are siblings being used as the tag. However, it seems that his concern about that revelation blinded him to the true problem with the story – the fact that there is no hint given to the audience that Heyes and Curry suspect Foster and enlist the help of Sheriff Lindstrom to trap him. The July 8 story notes also describe the theft of the evidence:

> Sheriff's house. Night. Our boys are creeping in. They're looking around by matchlight (or whatever) – and they finally find the sawed-off shotgun in a drawer. They take it. They start out – and they make a noise. The Sheriff comes out shooting – and our boys barely get away. They ride off; with the Sheriff firing at them. (He doesn't see who they are.)[23]

This doesn't sound like the boys are sharing any theories with the sheriff or asking for his help. In the aired episode, this scene has been eliminated entirely, replaced by a short scene with the sheriff berating his deputy for the loss of the gun, still offering the audience no clue he was in on the theft.

Heyes and Curry next go to see Foster and tell him they've stolen the gun. Heyes explains that, if Stokely can be proved innocent through fingerprints, then Foster shouldn't object to representing him. According to the story notes, though, "our boys, of course, are lying. They know damned well it's Foster." Having deleted the scene in which they discuss Foster with Sarah Henderson, there's no reason given to the audience to explain this knowledge and, in fact, it is not clear from the scene as written and played that Heyes and Curry do suspect Foster, although the audience might on the basis of his being the only other character in the story. But that's poor storytelling, a complaint one can rarely level at Roy Huggins.

Nick Baehr took the outline and wrote the first draft. On August 12, another story conference was held to discuss rewrites. Huggins notes one of Heyes's speeches "tells our audience it's Foster they're after, and it should be rewritten. . . .The longer we can hold back on revealing it's Foster, the better." Keeping the audience guessing is always a good thing, but the payoff has to have an element of inevitability to it. The audience should be left wondering how come they didn't see the solution for themselves, not wondering what they missed along the way. Huggins and Baehr worked hard to keep the identity of Hank Henderson's murderer a surprise as long as possible and, in the process, completely overlooked the problem of Sheriff Lindstrom. His presence in the cabin, obviously planned beforehand, is a surprise to the audience, but one which leaves them confused rather than satisfied because at no point in the story has it even been hinted that Heyes and Curry went to the sheriff with a plan.

This confusing ending adds to the sense that this is really two separate stories – the story of Sarah and Jim and the story of Hank Henderson's murder. Huggins had a great respect for his audience and always gave them credit for being able to get the point without it having to be spelled out for them step by step. In the August 12 rewrite notes he says regarding Lindstrom, "Cut 'I had somebody check the books. He was stealin' from Hank for years.' The writer threw in a line earlier, wherein one of our boys was speculating that maybe Foster was stealing from Hank – and that's enough. We do not have to tell the audience everything." In this case, he didn't tell his audience enough, rendering what could have been an excellent episode into one which is ultimately disappointing.

SIX STRANGERS AT APACHE SPRINGS

"Be a little frivolous, life will get grim soon enough without any help from you."
– Kid Curry

STORY:	JOHN THOMAS JAMES
TELEPLAY:	ARNOLD SOMKIN AND JOHN THOMAS JAMES
DIRECTOR:	NICHOLAS COLASANTO
SHOOTING DATES:	AUGUST 16, 17, 18, 19, 20, 21, 23, 1971
ORIGINAL US AIR DATE:	OCTOBER 28, 1971
ORIGINAL UK AIR DATE:	DECEMBER 13, 1971

At a leisurely trot, Hannibal Heyes and Kid Curry ride into peaceful Apache Springs. Checking into the hotel, they glance around the nearly deserted lobby and inquire about rooms and the likelihood of catching a poker game.

Caroline Rangely, a feisty middle-aged woman with upturned hat brim and suspenders supporting her trousers, approaches them. The sight of the good-looking men has aroused her curiosity. What do they do for a living? "As little as possible," Curry is quick to point out. Nevertheless, she'd like to talk to them when they're settled. Caroline confides to Smithers, the desk clerk, she believes she's found just what she's looking for – two men who are young, healthy, and not too smart.

A stagecoach pulls up outside the hotel with passengers Edward and Lucy Fielding. He appears happy to be there but his wife heaves an aggravated sigh. Before her husband even signs them in, she complains about the dust and heat.

Caroline hails the boys as they descend the stairs and wonders if they're available for some work. Over a beer, she explains that two years ago she and Barney, her dear husband, dug for gold up in the hills. They buried it where they found it in twelve different spots. Fifty or sixty scrawny Chiricahua Apaches broke out of their reservation and attacked them. Barney was killed. Now she wants the two men to retrieve it. After careful consideration, she offers twenty percent of it as pay and Heyes promises they'll think it over. "If we split it three ways," counters Curry. Caroline gasps, how dare they take advantage of a helpless woman? As she stomps away, Heyes and Curry lift their beers in a toast to her, a woman who seems anything but helpless.

The next stagecoach through town brings a serious young lady, demurely outfitted in a gray dress and black bonnet. At the desk, she inquires about room and board. The problem is she has no money, but she's an evangelist and on Sunday, she'll hold a service, take up a collection and pay her bill then. Smithers scoffs. Only sixty people are in town on a Sunday and half of those are cowboys hungover from Saturday night carousing. However, she could take on his job of cook for $8 a week, that'll cover the $4 for a room and $4 for food. She accepts and introduces herself as Sister Grace.

In the meantime, Caroline interrupts Heyes's bubble bath to counter-offer a fifty-fifty split. Heyes agrees and slides down deeper into the tub, declining to stand up and shake her hand to seal the deal.

At supper that evening, conversation centers on getting to know the new people in town. Caroline learns their names when they introduce themselves to the Fieldings. "Smith and Jones?" Caroline wonders if she's made a wise decision to throw in with them.

Mr. Fielding has come as a representative of the Indian Affairs Bureau. Unscrupulous agents have sold over half the meat that was supposed to go to the Indians. That's the reason they left the reservation. He hopes to get them into a more reasonable mood and to settle grievances. Curry wonders how unreasonable the Chiricahua are. As for Lucy Fielding, this is her first trip out west and, from what she's seen so far, she would simply like to leave.

The next day, Caroline retrieves her map of the buried gold sites from the hotel safe and cuts off a corner showing two of the twelve sites, not trusting her new partners with the entire map. The three women watch as the three men head for the hills.

After riding together for a while, each leading a pack mule, Heyes and Curry split from Fielding and head toward the first site. An Indian on a high ridge observes their progress. Comparing the map to the land, Heyes counts off steps and determines that they've reached the right place. They commence digging all the while being watched by the Indian. Several feet down, Heyes's shovel uncovers the first bag of gold dust. Curry raises his head and spots five Indians not too distant. Whistling nonchalantly, they head for their horses and the second site.

Mr. Fielding, too, finds himself observed by a handful of Indians as he plods on.

Heyes and Curry easily locate the other site marked by a boulder. Just as they find the bag of gold dust, shots ring out. Indians pursue them but are appeased when Heyes and Curry surrender the mule. Still fleeing for their lives, the boys see a band of Indians pursuing Fielding. They shout at him to let the mule go. Triumphant at capturing the animal, the Indians turn away. Dejected, Fielding heads back to town with Heyes and Curry.

At the general store, Mr. Evans weighs Caroline's gold dust. She hustles out the door with it trailed by her partners. Reluctantly handing over their share, she urges them to return for more, but they're pondering the wisdom of that. After all, they were shot at!

Curry shares supper with Sister Grace and learns her story. She was doing missionary work in the West. Her sponsor, meanwhile, had set up gambling and dishonest games of chance outside the tent. When she learned of it, she fled and is on her way back to Boston but her money ran out by Apache Springs.

It's Saturday night and the quiet town has come alive with gambling, drinking and fighting cowboys. Heyes and Curry watch from the sidelines as chairs, glasses, and men fly through the air all about them.

Next morning, Sister Grace stands on a crate preaching the gospel as the hungover cowboys get ready to head back to their ranches. After listening for a bit, Curry takes her aside and tells her she is too gentle to breathe the hellfire and brimstone expected from a good preacher. Meanwhile, Lucy Fielding joins Heyes, who surveys the scene from the hotel porch. She hopes that he and Mr. Jones won't return to the hills because then her husband, who thinks of them as typical western men, might not either. Heyes smirks at the idea that they are "typical western men." They are anything but – they travel a lot, pick up odd jobs, have no family or wives. He disagrees on another point, too – though she's known her husband for eight years and Heyes has only known him for eight days, he knows Fielding would return to talk to the Indians whether he and Mr. Jones go or not. Lucy apologizes for thinking she doesn't know her husband better, but whines that, with his job, they could be living in Paris or Rome! Heyes observes that Fielding doesn't know her too well either.

That evening, Curry visits Sister Grace in her room. He and Smith will be heading out for more of Caroline's gold and he offers her money for a stagecoach ticket east. She's been thinking about what he said and he urges her to let some fun into her life.

Heyes and Curry ride out with Fielding. The boys wonder if he shouldn't wait awhile. There's no time, the agent explains, the army wants to ride in and kill all the Indians. Splitting off from him, the partners lie on their bellies watching a band of Indians snake through the hills.

Caroline and Barney buried their third cache amidst the roots of a dead tree. An Indian shoots at the boys as they ride away from the site. They leave their mule again, hoping it will satisfy. Further on, when another shot brings down Heyes's horse, he jumps onto Curry's. A third Indian knocks them off it. After punching him senseless, the partners turn around to find themselves surrounded by the rest of the tribe.

Tied back-to-back in a tepee, Heyes and Curry commiserate, hoping the stories about Indians they heard as kids are not true. Curry doesn't have a gun and in Apache or Spanish, Heyes's tongue isn't silver. Relief floods over them when Fielding enters the tent, a free man. He says the Indians will keep their horses and gold but will let them go. He'll be remaining to talk more with the tribal leaders.

Next day, back in Apache Springs, Heyes and Curry relate the news about her husband to Lucy. Caroline doesn't believe the boys' story. She thinks they double-crossed her and are keeping her gold. Curry finds Grace waiting for him; she couldn't leave without knowing he got back safely. She tells him she's decided she can live life a little frivolously.

Before Heyes and Curry board the stage going west, Heyes says goodbye to Mrs. Fielding, expressing hope that both of them find out who they married. Just then Mr. Fielding rides wearily into town. Promised more and better land, food and blankets, the Chiricahua will be returning to their reservation. Caroline, thrilled, can retrieve her own gold.

On the stage, Heyes supposes they ought to do something restful next, like going down the Colorado River in a barrel!

GUEST CAST

CARMEN MATHEWS	CAROLINE RANGELY
PATRICIA HARTY	LUCY FIELDING
SIAN BARBARA ALLEN	SISTER GRACE
JOHN RAGIN	EDWARD FIELDING
LOGAN RAMSEY	SMITHERS
WALLACE CHADWELL	MR. EVANS
D. GALE THOMPSON	COWBOY

Occasionally Roy Huggins revised his writers' scripts so dramatically that, as John Thomas James, he was also given writer credit. That's what occurred during the preparation of this episode's script. Writer Arnold Somkin needed hand-on-the-shoulder guidance from the master. Huggins dictated the story on June 3 and three weeks later Somkin delivered the first draft. During a conference Huggins stressed the importance of character development and made it clear that any action or behind-the-scenes dialogue not shared by

Heyes and Curry were to be avoided. He urged Somkin to research evangelism to get Grace's sermon correct and gave the writer some geographical and historical information about the Indians. Somkin submitted a second draft on July 9. Another conference followed with eleven pages of rewrite notes, including an assignment to research the Chiricahuas' grievances and the weight price of gold in 1880. Somkin was getting close to the ideal. Huggins called the script "excellent" except that the writer failed in the mechanical part of the job, for instance, he had the characters announce that they were going upstairs in the hotel instead of merely doing it. A third draft came in. A short run of the script was printed on August 2, and on August 6, a yet-again-revised full run.

Once again, three diverse women share leading roles with Heyes and Curry. Huggins wanted Caroline Rangeley "not dressed in any ordinary way . . . she should not be dressed like Calamity Jane either . . . or perhaps she is." He wanted her to be a "female Andy Devine." Down to earth and bossy, Caroline exemplifies "gold digger" in character and fact. Only two strong-willed men like Heyes and Curry are able to stand up to her demands and that just barely. The promise of a substantial share of her gold is the only thing that keeps them interested.[24]

Sister Grace "should be a very sweet, gentle, warm girl" in her twenties. The audience should realize very quickly that she's shy; she's never had an experience with a man. Huggins told Somkin how he wanted the characters to relate. "Curry finds her very attractive. He'd like to go to bed with her, but he realizes that that probably would put her in absolute shock."[25] Instead of Curry worrying Grace about her preaching technique, Curry would like to "teach her how to kiss – although he doesn't want to seduce her. . . he shouldn't treat her like a nun. She's not."[26] As Mr. Fielding deals with the material needs of his charges, Sister Grace applies herself to saving souls. She conveys the admirable impression of total dedication and belief in her work, though personality-wise, she'd probably do better to serve hot meals in a soup kitchen.

Lucy Fielding is the one sexy woman of the three. She "has class – but she's also got sex." In the first telling of the story, Mrs. Fielding finds Heyes "rather attractive. She's not trying to go to bed with him, but she just feels that Heyes is the kind of guy her husband isn't. We realize that she's really an unhappy and disenchanted woman. In a very subtle way, she's being a bit seductive."[27] Peripheral as she is to her husband's career, Mrs. Fielding would be happier staying at home or shopping in New York or Boston. The West is as foreign to her as Paris or Rome would be, but she's positive she'd like it better there. At her insinuation that all western men are like Heyes and Curry, Heyes is supposed to get angry with her. "If I'm gonna judge the East by you, I'm not gonna like the East any better than you like the West . . ."[28]

Heyes has no trouble dealing with ladies, but Lucy Fielding puts him off because he respects her husband. However, he questions Fielding's assessment that the Chiricahuas may be reasonable. According to Huggins, this attitude was authentic but he wanted it avoided. "Our series is really not an accurate Western anyway. It's kind of a fairytale Western – and we should avoid this truth, which is that all cowboys were anti-Indian."[29] Heyes also wonders about the Chiricahuas' penchant for continued fighting after they took on both the United States and Mexico and gave up only after running out of food and bullets. Given that knowledge, the *Alias Smith and Jones* timeline, hardly an exact reference, nevertheless dates this episode after September 1886.

In May 1885, Apache warrior Geronimo and his followers fled the Arizona reservation in an attempt to regain the freedom they had known before the government instituted the reservation system. He and his warriors slipped into Mexico's Sierra Madre. General George Crook and the 6th Cavalry were sent to return them. In January 1886, the Chiricahuas, badly demoralized, agreed to negotiations for surrender. In a tragically confused incident, Mexican troops arrived and, mistaking the Apache scouts for hostiles, opened fire and mortally wounded a cavalry officer. After the Mexican departure, the Apaches agreed to meet with Crook who told Geronimo that unless he surrendered he would be hunted down and killed. Geronimo accepted a two-year imprisonment at Florida's Fort Marion. While being led there, Geronimo and a handful of his followers broke free again. The army replaced Crook with General Nelson Miles, who committed five thousand troops to the recapture of the Indians. Even when confronted by a force of this magnitude, Geronimo's band eluded their pursuers for six months. When Apache scouts finally talked Geronimo into laying down his guns in September 1886, the surrender was bloodless and strangely anticlimactic. Miles sent the Apaches east on a train under heavy guard. With their departure, the Indian Wars of the Southwest came to an end.

In the mid-nineteenth century, the appointment of Indian agents was often patronage from politicians and major scandals erupted involving corruption among them. As middlemen with few checks on them, they could confiscate supplies meant for the Indians and sell them for profit. In December 1868, the *Missouri Democrat* published an article in which the reporter wrote that he knew of persons who got rich – accumulating from $75,000 to $100,000 each – in three or four years from salaries of $1,500 per annum. The rich persons he's referring to were Indian agents.

Heyes admired Fielding's courage in facing the Chiricahua and his plan to simply put up his hands and try to talk. In his private life, Peter Duel felt saddened by the racial prejudices and injustices he saw. Jo Swerling knew him well. He remembers that Peter brooded about bad things going on in the world and that not enough was being done to correct them. "[H]e was a really . . . essentially very decent, very nice man. A good person."[30]

Night of the Red Dog

"Jones and me are pretty cowardly. When it comes to gambling anyway."
– Hannibal Heyes

Story:	John Thomas James
Teleplay:	Dick Nelson and John Thomas James
Director:	Russ Mayberry
Shooting Dates:	September 13, 14, 15, 16, 17, 20, 1971
Original US Air Date:	November 4, 1971
Original UK Air Date:	January 31, 1972

Hannibal Heyes and Kid Curry are in Wilksburg. An old man, Clarence Boles, collapses in the street and they rush to his aid. Leaning over him, Heyes realizes he isn't drunk, so he must be sick. Billy Boggs and Jason Holloway join them and, because there is no doctor's office, Jason suggests they take him to the undertaker's. Heyes and Curry try to lift Clarence up. They give a mighty heave and almost collapse with the effort, clutching each other to keep from falling. "He can't be that heavy," protests Curry. They try again and only succeed in lifting Clarence's shoulders an inch off the ground. With Jason's and Billy's help, the four men manage to lift Clarence enough to carry him into the undertaker's parlor.

When Roy Huggins told this story to writer Dick Nelson on July 16, 1971, he called it "The Long Cold Winter," but noted "the present title could be changed, if we can find one that tips off to the audience the fact that there's going to be something in this story about an early version of the lie detector." They were unsuccessful at working a lie detector into the title, so they contented themselves with referring to the card game that plays a pivotal role in the plot

Ralph Marsden, the undertaker, points them to his back room. Heyes tells Ralph that Clarence is still alive as Billy goes in search of the doctor. Opening Clarence's coat, the men discover the old man is carrying enough gold dust to open his own private mint.

With the town's doctor out on a call, Billy returns with Dr. Chauncey Beauregard, who was waiting for the stage. Dr. Beauregard cheerfully asks which of them is the patient. The one lying down with his eyes closed, Heyes points out, while Curry explains that Clarence may just be exhausted from carrying two hundred pounds of gold in his pockets. The doctor examines Clarence and determines he's near death.

Clarence has no family so, hearing he's about to die, he tells the men about his gold mine. Hating to see the gold go to waste, he gives them a map, then falls silent. The men remove their hats as a sign of respect for his passing, then sheepishly put them back on when Clarence gives a gentle snore.

Doc Beauregard declares the map is a clear case of a deathbed gift and all of them agree they'd like to do some gold mining. Loaded with supplies, the group heads to the mountains.

Upon arriving, they draw cards to decide who will get what section of the river. Doc draws first, proclaiming, "As they said in medical school in Atlanta, character is fate." He gets high card and first choice of sections.

For the next few weeks, each man works his site, collecting and carefully hiding their gold dust. Heyes and Curry believe they have at least $15,000.

Back in the cabin, Ralph announces it's time to be heading back to town. Winter is coming. Ralph figures he has $30,000 and he's satisfied. Jason has only $20,000 and wants to stay until the end of the week. Billy is happy with his $7,000. Doc hasn't mentioned a number, but says he's done much better than the rest of them, which brings to mind a young lad he knew at medical school in Baltimore. Curry points out the last time he talked about medical school it was in Atlanta. Doc testily informs him that doctors often attend more than one school.

The next day, as the men return from working, Curry notices new animals in the corral. Clarence throws open the cabin door and points an accusing finger at Doc. Clarence wasn't even a little bit dead; he had a hernia from carrying all that gold. Now he's back with a legal claim and they're all claim jumpers. He did give them the map, so he'll let them keep all the gold they've panned so far, but they have to leave in the morning.

Heyes and Curry head for their secret cache, but, though Heyes digs frantically, their gold is gone.

In the cabin, Clarence is weighing everyone's gold. Doc has $65,000; Ralph $30,000; Jason $20,000; Billy $11,000. Heyes figures he and Curry have $400 today. Yesterday they had about $25,000, which has been stolen. Everyone offers reasons for their innocence. Heyes decides to forget it for now and chalk it up to bad luck. There's nothing they can do.

The next morning Curry comments on the nip in the air as he dresses. When he opens the cabin door, it starts a small avalanche of snow. Clarence laughs uproariously; the greenhorns waited too long to leave – now they're snowed in.

The men sit glumly around the cabin. They're trapped for the winter in a one room cabin and one of them is a thief. There's enough food that no one will starve, but what are they going to do for the next few months? Jason pulls out his deck of cards and suggests a game of poker.

A marathon game ensues as winter passes. Curry develops a cough and a fever, but insists he'll be fine. He's not fine, though, and during one hand simply keels over. Heyes rushes to his side and with Billy's help he moves Curry into the store-room and covers him with blankets. Doc examines him, listening to his heart with a stethoscope, remarking it's beating much too fast. Heyes rips the stethoscope out of Doc's ears and listens for himself. It seems okay to him. Doc places it over his own heart to show Heyes how a normal heartbeat sounds. Heyes grudgingly admits there's some difference, but he doesn't know why he's listening to him, because he doesn't think he's a real doctor. At that, Doc's heartbeat speeds up. Heyes is intrigued and apologizes for upsetting him. Doc denies he's upset, so Heyes listens to his heart once more. It's back to a normal rhythm. Heyes asks him where he studied surgery and finds that Doc's heart speeds up when he answers. Heyes tests his discovery once more and finds that a question about Doc's credentials causes his heart to beat faster. Heyes explains his finding, but Doc claims he's not angry and he's not lying. Doc believes Jones has pneumonia and, unfortunately, there's nothing he can do.

Three days later, Curry awakens feeling better and is ready to play some more poker. Heyes shares his discovery about the stethoscope and his suspicion that Doc Beauregard is the one who stole their dust. There's no way to prove he has it, but Doc Beauregard is a very bad gambler. He'd be the perfect mark for Montana Red Dog.

Curry rejoins the poker game. When it's his deal he suggests a change – Montana Red Dog. Billy agrees eagerly. Jason and Ralph don't mind either, but Doc is unfamiliar with the game. Curry explains it to him. The players are dealt five cards. When it's their turn, they bet on whether they can beat the next card turned over, in the same suit. The minimum bet is $100, the maximum is the size of the pot. Doc agrees to play and Heyes's plan to recover their gold dust is put in motion.

The game begins. Doc bets heavily, while Heyes and Curry bet the minimum every time. The pot grows to $5,000, most of it Doc's money and he decides to bet the size of the pot when Clarence speaks up. Red Dog is a game for suckers, he tells Doc. You'll keep betting the size of the pot, no matter how bad a hand you have. Doc changes his bet to just what he has in front of him in chips. He wins. "I knew I should have bet the size of that pot!" Doc exclaims and orders Clarence to keep his mouth shut.

As the game continues, Doc bets the size of the pot each time, afraid someone will win the pot away from him. Finally he reaches the point where he can only bet $5,000 of the $51,000 pot. He loses and is broke. Curry asks Heyes about the loan he made him in Denver. Heyes quickly catches on and feigns irritation, claiming the loan was for $12,000 and will knock him out of the game if he pays it back now. Curry insists because he wants to bet the size of the pot. Heyes hands over his chips and Curry bets $56,000. Tension grows as Ralph turns over the next card: the queen of clubs. The men watch intently as Curry pulls out the king of clubs and wins the pot. Curry announces he's finished with gambling until spring.

The next morning, Jason heads for the door, but Curry stops him. He and Heyes went out to hide their gold and they don't want anyone to go outside until it snows enough to cover their tracks. Jason acquiesces.

Spring arrives. When Heyes and Curry are ready to leave, they ask the others to stay behind for a few days. They still don't trust one of them and don't want to be bushwhacked on the trail. Everyone agrees. The boys go out to retrieve their gold only to discover they've been robbed once again.

They return to the cabin and announce whoever did it, did it again. Clarence knows anyone familiar with snow country would have been able to follow their tracks even after a new snowfall. Heyes comes up with a plan. He wants to ask each man to his face if they stole the gold, but he wants to listen to their hearts with Doc's stethoscope as he does. The men agree. He questions everyone, including Curry who thinks fair is fair and takes the stethoscope from Heyes to ask him in turn. They retreat to the stockroom to discuss their findings. If Heyes's theory is right, it wasn't Doc Beauregard as he suspected, but Jason.

Back in Wilksburg, Heyes and Curry keep an eye on Jason. A saloon girl relays the information that he is getting ready to leave town. They follow him to his hiding place in the mountains, where Jason discovers his gold is gone. Heyes calls out, "Jason, don't tell us it happened to you, too." Jason denies knowing what they're talking about, but admits it happened to him, too.

The three of them visit Clarence. As they eat, Heyes wonders who ended up with the $112,000. Clarence says Doc Beauregard didn't sleep a wink after losing at Red Dog. He figures Doc saw Heyes and Curry go out to hide their dust, then later saw Jason go out. Doc is the one they need to find if they want their gold back.

Heyes and Curry track Doc Beauregard to San Francisco. They learn from his secretary that he passed on to his final reward a week ago. He met his demise trying to teach people a game called Montana Red Dog. But surely they'll take comfort in knowing he left $100,000 to build a wing onto the hospital.

The boys watch the construction. Curry points out the bright spot in all this. Their lives won't be a complete waste – the Chauncey Beauregard Hospital Wing wouldn't be there if it wasn't for them.

GUEST CAST

PAUL FIX	CLARENCE BOLES
JACK KELLY	DR. CHAUNCEY BEAUREGARD
ROBERT PRATT	BILLY BOGGS
RORY CALHOUN	JASON HOLLOWAY
JOE FLYNN	RALPH MARSDEN
SHANNON CHRISTIE	FLORENCE
PATRICIA CHANDLER	SECRETARY

Roy Huggins proclaimed that his favorite episodes of *Alias Smith and Jones* were those which were about nothing. "Night of the Red Dog" certainly falls into that category.[31] Unlike episodes which insert a subtle message into the story, such as "Everything Else You Can Steal" and its stand on capital punishment or "The Bounty Hunter" and its take on racism, "Night·of the Red Dog" is about nothing more serious than a months-long poker game. The writers keep it interesting by having Heyes and Curry use their card-playing skills to outwit the thief who stole their gold.

This episode is the second to feature a group stranded in one room with no way out. In contrast to "Stagecoach Seven" and "Shootout at Diablo Station," the other one-room stories, this episode does not put anyone in physical danger. The snow has them trapped in the cabin, but they have plenty of food, so there's no doubt they will survive until spring. Instead the dramatic tension comes through the interplay of the characters around the table – Doc getting ever more desperate as he loses one pot after another, Clarence throwing a monkey wrench in Heyes's plan by telling Doc that Montana Red Dog is a game for suckers, and finally the moment when Curry announces he's going to bet $56,000 on the next card. Usually Heyes is portrayed as the expert with cards, but this episode gives Curry the skill to win the game while Heyes watches and hopes Curry knows what he's doing. In the first draft, though, writer Dick Nelson followed the precedent and gave Heyes the unbeatable hand.

Having their gold stolen first by Doc, then by Jason, adds complexity to this simple story. The audience already knows the boys are good at cards, but now they are given another glimpse of why Heyes is the brains when he discovers that a stethoscope can be used as a lie detector, then turns the knowledge into a Hannibal Heyes Plan. Despite his initial suspicion of Doc Beauregard, he's confident enough that his theory is correct to follow Jason when he rides out of town to retrieve the gold. In the first draft script, Curry is not so trusting. Hearing Heyes's heartbeat speed up when he asks about the stolen gold, Curry decides Heyes's discovery isn't so useful after all, unless, of course, Heyes stole it. Huggins decided Heyes should not get nervous when his partner asks the question, so the scene was changed.

Huggins wanted the series to be infused with the kind of humor that comes from the character and not from the situation. The first draft of the scene where Curry collapses is a prime example. While the situation isn't funny – Curry is seriously ill – Dick Nelson had fun with Billy, giving him some great lines. After helping Heyes carry Curry into the storeroom, Billy peers worriedly at him and says, "Sure hope he ain't gonna die . . . ground froze like it is, be a chore to bury him." Heyes replies sardonically, "What we could do is let him freeze solid and then stand him in a corner till spring." Billy's comment was not made maliciously, but only practically, and he's appalled by Heyes's attitude. Thinking he's serious, Billy protests, "Golly, Josh – I thought he was your friend."[32] Huggins loved this exchange, saying in the rewrite notes from August 18, 1971:

> Here we have a very funny conversation about what they're going to do with Curry if he dies. It would be even funnier if it involved the undertaker. Ralph could be looking at Curry – and we give Ralph this speech.

In the second draft, Ralph was duly given this speech, Curry's fate being a matter of professional interest to him, but the exchange was eliminated in the final rewrite.

This episode isn't complicated or thought-provoking, but it provides an hour's entertainment with charm and style, and that's all Huggins ever wanted for his audience.

THE REFORMATION OF HARRY BRISCOE

"Reformed thieves – they're the worst kind."
– Molly Cusack

STORY: JOHN THOMAS JAMES
TELEPLAY: B. W. SANDEFUR
DIRECTOR: BARRY SHEAR
SHOOTING DATES: SEPTEMBER 22, 23, 24, 27, 28, 29, 1971
ORIGINAL US AIR DATE: NOVEMBER 11, 1971
ORIGINAL UK AIR DATE: DECEMBER 20, 1971

> Molly/Sister Isabel was first named Daisy.
>
> When begging to be untied from her wrist bindings, Molly calls Heyes Mr. Jones. He corrects her by saying, "The name's Smith, Sweetheart." This may have been an instance in which the actress made a mistake and Peter covered by adlibbing. The line isn't in the script. The part where Heyes and Curry deride Jim's cooking also is missing from the script.

Hannibal Heyes and Kid Curry, along with their wagon driver Jim, attempt to keep a herd of cows together on a drive when they happen upon two nuns. The sisters' wagon has suffered a broken axle. The best solution is for the sisters to drive the boys' wagon while Jim rides one of the horses.

When they stop to make camp, Sister Julia, inviting the boys to evening prayer, wonders if they're Catholic. No, we're "Kansans, Ma'am," Curry replies. Chuckling, Heyes explains that there aren't too many Catholics in Kansas. Curry expounds that they did go to church every Sunday at the Valparaiso School for Waywards where they grew up.

Next day, leaving Jim to watch the herd, Heyes and Curry escort the sisters into Pearlman. The nuns hope to sell their horses and then take a stagecoach to the convent. The partners head for the saloon and, watching poor poker being played for high stakes, mourn the lack of empty chairs. A young boy enters, calling for Smith or Jones.

Outside, Sister Julia tells them Sister Isabel has gone missing. They ask around town, talking to merchants and bystanders. Finally one man tells them, same as he told the other fella who was asking about a lost nun, that he saw her headed down that way. Heyes asks him to describe the "other fella." The description of the snake face, eyes set too close and citified clothes doesn't ring any bells for the boys, though it ought to.

Sister Julia decides to talk to the sheriff.

Meanwhile, in the girl's dressing room of the saloon, Madame Madge tightens the laces on the new girl's dress. A wig makes her almost unidentifiable as the former Sister Isabel. But Madge isn't finished; she adds some eye makeup and a beauty mark on Isabel's cheek. She also dispenses advice on how to deal with the men downstairs.

On the street, Heyes and Curry encounter their old friend Harry Briscoe, who's once more working for the Bannerman Detective Agency. His job is confidential but Curry tells Harry they know he's looking for a nun. With the secret out, Harry confides that the woman's name is not Isabel, but Molly Cusack and she's not a nun, she's a typewriter. She used to work a typewriting machine in an Independence, Missouri, bank before she stole $30,000. Harry is on her trail. The boys wonder why she hid when she recognized Harry on the street. How did she know him? Caught in a lie, Harry stammers that she must have seen him when he almost caught her in Lawrence, Kansas. Heyes and Curry see through the deception.

Sister Julia comes up with news that the sheriff is deputizing all the men in town to hunt for Sister Isabel. The boys warn Harry not to tell the good sister what the bad sister may have done. Excusing themselves with herding duties, they escort Harry away from her.

Still regretting the lack of empty seats at the poker table, Heyes and Curry sit with Harry in the saloon. Though Molly/Isabel serves them drinks, none of them recognize her. Harry suspects she somehow got out of town and may be hiding at the boys' campsite.

While they help themselves to Jim's coffee, Harry searches their wagon. Satisfied Molly isn't there, Harry leaves the boys to their supper of bad beans and coffee that, according to Jim, "ain't bad too."

The next day the drive continues. At Jim's insistence that he's hearing strange noises in the wagon, Heyes checks and finds Molly. She left town the previous night after the search had been called off and hid in a buckboard going in the direction of their camp. "He's a terrible man," she says of her pursuer; she had to get away from him. She admits she's not a nun, in fact, she was married to him. Asked his name, Molly is flustered but identifies him as George Beaudine. He was only a bookkeeper, though he told her he was an investment banker.

Heyes compliments her on her story but lets her know that he and Curry don't believe it because they've known her pursuer, Harry Briscoe, a long time. They tell her what they know, about her working as a typewriter and robbing the bank. That much is true, she concedes, but Harry courted her because he needed a partner to help him steal the money. It was easy to do but then she realized what a terrible person he was, so she hid the money and ran away, planning to keep it all for herself.

The boys wonder how Molly managed to convince Sister Julia she was a nun. It wasn't hard, Molly says, she was born Catholic, her parents came from Kilkenny and her sister is a nun. Her father, after years of suffering just for being Irish, taught her not to get mad, but to get even. Curry almost blows his alias, protesting that he's Irish too; Molly wonders that "Jones" is Irish? His grandparents came from Londonderry, which Molly dismisses as being in Ulster. Ulstermen are the Orangemen who dropped the o's and mac's from their names, so in America they'd be considered proper Englishmen. A true Irishman in America is supposed to stand quiet and know his place. When everyone thinks a man like her father died of drink, it's not proper for her to say it was from shame and hunger.

Heyes thinks maybe she grew up too angry and there are other ways to get even. It's a shame, but they will have to turn her in when they get to a town. They can't be associated in any way with a bank robber. Despite Molly's pleadings and promise to share the money, they stand firm. "Smith and Jones?" Molly begins to suspect why they can't help her and regrets that she's thrown in with reformed thieves.

Next morning, Harry startles the sleeping Heyes, Curry, Molly and Jim. While Harry ties them up, his cohort Sam keeps them covered at gunpoint. Harry never did go back to the Bannerman Detective Agency after Heyes and Curry saw him last, and now he's after the stolen money. Sam, frustrated at Harry's slowness, grabs Molly and rips off her veil. Slitting it open, he finds the money sewn inside. Harry grabs a handful of dollars and then, leaving them tied up, he and Sam ride away.

Working loose their bonds, Heyes unties Jim's hands too, then he and Curry mount their horses to go after the men and money. They leave Molly tied up with instructions to Jim to keep an eye on her. As they follow the horses' tracks, they hear cries for help. A short distance away they find Harry tied to a joshua tree. Despite receiving his promised share of twenty-five percent, Sam took it all and headed west. Harry begs to be untied, but Heyes and Curry ignore him and ride after Sam.

They follow his tracks to a deserted barn where he has holed up in order to let his horse rest. They call to him but get no response. Suddenly Sam bursts through the doors on horseback, shooting at them. The gunfire frightens his horse, which rears and throws Sam to the ground, breaking his neck.

Heyes and Curry return to Harry and untie him. Harry has pondered his plight and decided he could never be a crook. Too bad it's too late, Curry tells him.

That evening in camp, with Jim guarding Harry and Molly, Heyes and Curry kill time playing blackjack. Harry argues that they can't turn him in because he knows they are Hannibal Heyes and Kid Curry. That is a problem, so Jim will have to take Harry and Molly into town. Harry insists he's really reformed and if they will only let him turn the money over to the sheriff, his record will be clean. Wouldn't it be wonderful to have a grateful friend in the Bannerman agency, he argues. They could also let Molly go, truly a noble gesture.

While they're distracted with the conversation, Molly has been working at the bindings on her hands. She escapes and, though Jim could shoot her off the horse, because she's a woman, he can't bring himself to do it.

With one of their problems gone, Heyes and Curry ride with Harry into Kettle Drum. They've decided to let him take the credit for returning the money. As he talks with the sheriff, Heyes and Curry wait around the corner, wondering if they've done the right thing. What if Harry turns them in? What if he is in the sheriff's office merely asking for an escort to the bank? For some unfathomable reason, Heyes trusts him.

Harry returns, showing them the bank receipt and a telegram he'll send to Mr. Bannerman about the stolen money. Shortly, a return telegram arrives reinstating Harry as a detective.

On the street, Heyes and Curry spot Sister Julia alighting from the stagecoach. She never did learn what happened to Sister Isabel. Curry explains about Molly being an imposter and her wanting to get even with the world. Sister Julia finds it hard to believe, but accepts it if they say it's true.

They offer her a ride to the convent in their chuck wagon. Upon arriving, they are amazed to find Molly back in the habit as Sister Isabel. Sister Julia tells them they shouldn't be so surprised.

GUEST CAST

J.D. CANNON	HARRY BRISCOE
JANE MERROW	MOLLY/SISTER ISABEL
JANE WYATT	SISTER JULIA
DUB TAYLOR	JIM
JOYCE JAMESON	MADGE
READ MORGAN	CHARLEY
ALAN BAXTER	SAM
BEVERLY CARTER	LAURA
C. ELLIOTT MONTGOMERY	GROCERY CLERK

Producer Roy Huggins used events in his own history as part of the story line. Interviewed for this book, he recalled that either Curry or Heyes said he's Irish and the nun, who was supposed to come from the south of Ireland, said, "if he wasn't Catholic, he wasn't Irish, he was an Ulsterman or an Orangeman." Huggins still felt very strongly about that because "I have the misfortune of having a name that is Irish but is also English . . . It comes from a very weird Gaelic spelling pronounced 'O'Hugan', spelled 'O'Haogain' as pronounced in Ireland. When I was young, with an attitude, and I would find that people thought I was English, I'd say, 'I'm not English, for God's sake. Where'd you get that idea? It's an Irish name.' But I found out later that Huggins is, well, it's not a common name anywhere, but there are plenty of such names in Ireland . . . in England . . . . So I often ran into this very thing that I toyed with on the show because I was Catholic. And I was expressing myself here."

Given Huggins's Catholicism and the many religious references Heyes and Curry make, it was only a matter of time before a priest or nun showed up in the series. Teleplay writer B.W. Sandefur described Sister Julia as "an earthy sort in word and manner. Oh, she's reverent enough, absolutely devout. But she's uniquely perceptive to the needs of those who have chosen a more mundane path. Homely, penurious and sharp witted, she's hardly man's best friend, but is particularly well suited as God's." Huggins added that she should say something to Heyes and Curry about not having to be a churchgoer to be a good person.

"Thus we characterize her as not being a conventional Christian."[33]

Perhaps references to his own past gave Huggins the idea, because in his story notes for Sandefur, Huggins exposed an unusually large amount of Heyes and Curry's history. He wrote, their "families lived right next to each other in Kansas, and they grew up together. There were southern raiders in Kansas during the Civil War . . . their folks had farms next to each other. Their farms were raided – and both Heyes and Curry were suddenly orphans."[34] Curry gets carried away and elaborates on their background in reply to Sister Julia's questions. When the sisters have left to pray, Heyes believes that, if Curry had continued to talk, he'd have told the sister about the price on their heads. In his first draft, Sandefur continues Heyes's berating of Curry, ordering him to get carried away with cooking supper. Three weeks later, Huggins read the script and wanted that part cut. "Our boys are equals. Curry does not always defer to Heyes. Curry is just as sharp as Heyes – but he just doesn't scheme as thoroughly as Heyes. He is not as devious as Heyes."[35] Indeed, the devious one in this episode is Molly, the "typewriter."

In 1874, the Remington Model 1, the first commercial typewriter, was placed on the market. Less than five thousand were sold, so it was not considered a great success but it founded a worldwide industry and brought mechanization to dreary, time-consuming office work. Mark Twain bought one for $125 and became the first person to submit a novel in typed form to the publisher. The machine became popular and soon secretaries were trained to use them, creating a new career field. The operator was called a typewriter too until 1885 when the word "typist" was coined.[36]

DREADFUL SORRY, CLEMENTINE

"For an operation that's supposed to lean on trust, this one is off to a devious start."
– Hannibal Heyes

STORY:	JOHN THOMAS JAMES
TELEPLAY:	GLEN A. LARSON
DIRECTOR:	BARRY SHEAR
SHOOTING DATES:	SEPTEMBER 30, OCTOBER 1, 4, 5, 6, 7, 1971
ORIGINAL US AIR DATE:	NOVEMBER 18, 1971
ORIGINAL UK AIR DATE:	DECEMBER 27, 1971

Clementine Hale strides briskly towards the Boonville saloon, men scattering in disbelief as she pushes past them to enter the building. They watch in shock until she comes out again, still moving purposefully.

Hannibal Heyes and Kid Curry enter the hotel and ask for their room key. The desk clerk, Crawford, hands it over, surprised they're still hanging around such a slow town. They like it that way and plan to stay indefinitely. As they turn to climb the stairs, Crawford mentions that a stranger was looking for them. The boys abruptly about-face. "Fix us up a bill, Mr. Crawford," says Heyes.

Heyes and Curry duck out the back door just moments before Clementine reaches the hotel. Crawford offers her his opinion that Smith and Jones are heading to the livery stable.

Curry is the first to see her. He gives a glad shout and both boys run to greet Clem with hugs and kisses. Clem is as glad to see them as they are to see her until she mentions that she wants them to help her steal $50,000.

> Roy Huggins always liked women's names that could be shortened into a man's name. Clementine, shortened to Clem, was a favorite.
>
> In the 1880s photographs were tintypes which, of course, wouldn't burn. Huggins noted this in the margin of the final draft, but decided to leave the scene in.

Sally Field as Clementine Hale with Kid Curry.

(Jerry Ohlinger's Movie Materials Store)

Back at the hotel, Clem shows them a photo she has of the three of them. If they don't help her, she'll see to it that it is added to their Wanted posters.

That night Heyes sneaks down to the hotel safe and steals the photo.

The next day, Heyes, Curry and Clem take the stage to Silver Springs. Clem explains that she wants to steal the money from Winford Fletcher, a man who swindles helpless widows and steals money from people who trust him. With the photo now in their possession, Heyes and Curry are less amenable to Clem's plan. As she watches indignantly, Heyes sets fire to the only picture in the world of them . . . except for the one she has in a safe deposit box in Denver.

From the hotel balcony, Clem and the boys watch Fletcher leave the Silver Springs Land Office. Clem is impatient; she wants them to get the $50,000 right away, but Curry points out they can't stop him like they could a train. Knowing Fletcher won't have that kind of money in his pocket, they'll have to find a way for him to gather the cash and hand it over. The man to help them do that is Diamond Jim Guffy.

Diamond Jim arrives at the train station, intending to make only a brief stop. The boys are alarmed to learn of his short stay; they need his help. Clementine joins them with a brilliant smile for Diamond Jim. He takes one look at her and changes his plans. He'll stay.

The scheme begins as Heyes and Fletcher examine a derelict steamboat. Fletcher insists the boat is fundamentally sound, despite all evidence to the contrary, and is surprised when Mr. Smith offers $25,000 cash for the wreck. Fletcher quickly accepts it. As they return to town, Heyes asks about land ownership records, piquing Fletcher's interest with his mention of Golden Meadows. Fletcher tries to find out why Smith is interested, but Heyes simply says goodbye, being sure to leave his wallet behind as he climbs out of the carriage.

Curry and Clem watch from their hotel window. Clem can't see anything happening and is worried. Curry soothes her fears with a kiss. Heyes interrupts them and they watch from the window as Fletcher finds the wallet.

While Curry and Clem retreat to the adjoining room, Heyes sets the scene, placing a letter on the floor as if it's fallen out of the briefcase resting on a nearby chair. He opens the door a scant inch, a subtle invitation for Fletcher to come in and snoop. Satisfied with his work, Heyes joins the others in the adjoining room.

Fletcher knocks on the door. It swings open and he enters, calling for Mr. Smith. His eyes fall on the letter and he picks it up, reading enough about Golden Meadows land to be intrigued. As Smith enters the room, Fletcher drops the letter and holds out the wallet to explain his presence. Smith thanks him for being so honest and Fletcher leaves. Heyes, Curry and Clem are pleased. Fletcher is hooked.

Fletcher meets Smith outside the hotel, trying to find out if his business is related to Golden Meadows. Smith feigns irritation at Fletcher's snooping, but relents and allows Fletcher to accompany him to Kingsville. As soon as they are out of sight, Clem and Curry, suitcases in hand, jump into a carriage of their own.

Smith and Fletcher visit Mr. Brandon and his sister (Curry and Clem). Smith offers to buy their Golden Meadows land for $3 an acre. Mr. Brandon ponders that, then makes a counteroffer. He will sell for $8 dollars an acre. Fletcher sputters at the outrageous sum, but Smith agrees. Miss Brandon, though, declines to sell her acreage.

Fletcher berates Smith as they head back to town. The land isn't worth anything and could have been purchased for far less. Smith assures him his principals have guaranteed him a fixed price for Golden Meadows and he will make a profit even paying $8 an acre. Fletcher is skeptical, so Smith invites him to come along and see for himself, as long as he promises not to try and get in on the deal.

Smith and Fletcher go to the De Vega Land Development Company. Mr. De

Vega, a.k.a Diamond Jim Guffy, chastises Smith for breaching the confidentiality of the agreement, but pays him for the one thousand acres of land he's acquired so far at the agreed price of $20 an acre. Fletcher's eyes widen as he helps Smith count the money.

As soon as Fletcher and Smith leave, Diamond Jim packs the money that Heyes has slipped back to him and removes his props from the empty office. Diamond Jim's part is over.

Back in the Silver Springs hotel, Clem and the boys toast their success so far. There's a knock on the door.

Curry and Clem dash into the next room while Heyes faces an excited Fletcher. Smith won't have to pay Miss Brandon an inflated price for her land. He's found another owner right near by and he'll tell him who it is if Smith will let him have a share in the deal. They argue, but eventually Smith agrees to cut Fletcher in for fifteen percent.

Curry, Heyes and Clem consider the situation somberly. Fletcher's greed will cost him money, but it won't get them the $50,000 Clem wants. She wants both the money and to get even with Fletcher. So, all they have to do is get to Horace Wingate, the other holder of Golden Meadow deeds, and buy his land before Fletcher can. Great idea, but what will they use for money now that Diamond Jim is gone?

Heyes stalls Fletcher while Curry and Clem go to Horace Wingate and buy his land with a check. Wingate is loath to accept a check from strangers, so Clem offers to let him hold her pearl necklace until the check clears. Wingate relents. Curry and Clem leave just before Smith and Fletcher drive up.

Wingate is confused. The land is worthless, but today people keep coming by wanting to buy it. Fletcher asks how much he sold the land for. One dollar an acre, Wingate tells them proudly and asks how much they'd have paid. "As much as $5 an acre," admits Smith. Wingate stomps into his house for his shotgun. He's going to get that swindler who paid him only a dollar an acre!

Smith accuses Fletcher of leaking the news, creating a run on Golden Meadows land. Fletcher claims innocence, but admits he's been waiting for one big opportunity and this is it. He shoves Smith out of the carriage and whips the team, eager to get to Miss Brandon before anyone else does.

Curry returns to Wingate, ostensibly to have him sign the transfer of ownership papers. Wingate holds a rifle on him, accusing him of trying to fleece an old man and demands the deeds back. Curry reluctantly hands him the deeds, getting his bad check back in return.

Fletcher helps himself to $50,000 of his company's money, then buys Miss Brandon's land. Clem sighs with satisfaction as Fletcher leaves with his worthless deeds. As soon as he's gone, she dashes out of the rented mansion and whistles for the carriage she had waiting.

In Silver Springs, Heyes and Curry watch Fletcher's carriage race by. He seems to be in a hurry. "He wants to get to Diamond Jim's office before it closes. He'll be about two days late," Heyes observes. The boys take a seat at the train depot to wait for Clem.

Fletcher hurries to the De Vega Land Development office, but finds only an office for rent. He asks a janitor what happened to the company, but the janitor has never heard of them. That office has been empty for two months. Fletcher pales.

Many hours later Curry and Heyes are still waiting for Clem at the train depot, grudgingly accepting that she's taken the money and dumped them. They decide to track her down and save her from a life of crime. Since her father and her safe deposit box are both in Denver, that seems like the place to start.

Clem is not pleased to see them. She's expecting a Federal Marshal and a Deputy State Attorney General, men she's sure they won't want to meet. Heyes and Curry don't believe her, but do appreciate the imagination she's showing in trying to get rid of them. The argument is interrupted by a knock on the door. Clem urges them to hide in the closet, but they decline. With a shrug, she opens the door. Heyes and Curry leap to their feet in alarm as State Attorney General Hawkins and Federal Marshal Toomey enter.

Clem, Hawkins and Toomey discuss the next step in getting her father out of prison. The $50,000 represents full restitution of the money her father embezzled, but that doesn't automatically mean he will be released. But Clem has already arranged to have the firm audited, and she's sure there will be a substantial shortage found. Clem explains Fletcher is the embezzler; he blamed her father the first time, but won't be able to blame anyone else this time. Toomey and Hawkins depart. Now Heyes and Curry know the whole story.

They accompany Clem to the train station, but won't hand over her ticket until she relinquishes the photo of them which they know she's retrieved from the bank. Seeing they're adamant, she digs through her bag, then hands over an envelope. They wave goodbye as the train chugs away. Inside the envelope, they find only copies of their Wanted posters.

GUEST CAST

SALLY FIELD	CLEMENTINE HALE
DON AMECHE	DIAMOND JIM GUFFY
RUDY VALLEE	WINFORD FLETCHER
JACKIE COOGAN	CRAWFORD
BUDDY LESTER	DRUNK
KEN SCOTT	TOOMEY
STUART RANDALL	HAWKINS
WILLIAM BENEDICT	JANITOR

Roy Huggins was responsible for many popular television programs over the course of his career, but his favorite was always *Maverick,* both because it was totally his creation and because it had an enormous impact on Westerns that followed. He wanted to imbue *Alias Smith and Jones* with the same irreverence and sense of fun, so it isn't surprising that he resurrected what has been called "one of – if not *the* – most beloved episodes of *[Maverick]*"[37] – "Shady Deal at Sunny Acres."

Huggins told the story to writer Buck Houghton on May 13, 1971, noting "the writer will research crime in this period, reading the book *Our Rival the Rascal* specifically, in order to find the best caper for this particular story. We are also trying to locate another book, *Yellow Kid Weil*, which contains two great con games – one of which was used in 'Shady Deal at Sunny Acres.' The other con game did not deal in stocks but in something else, and it was almost as good as the Shady Deal caper. These con games are in public domain." Buck Houghton went off and wrote a first draft, which Huggins was disappointed with. His rewrite notes contain a completely new structure and significant changes to the caper. But Houghton's second draft was still disappointing, so Huggins gave the story to Glen Larson.

Huggins did not often give Larson writing assignments because he believed he "didn't know how to tell a story . . . I knew that the one thing he didn't have was the one thing I needed – someone to help me with story."[38] But after having received two poor drafts from Buck Houghton, he turned to Larson. The new rewrite notes, dated June 28, began with "Note: in the present draft Clementine's reasons for wanting to steal from Fletcher are rotten." They continued for eleven detailed pages and ended with "Note: the script needs a complete rewrite." Larson came through and "Dreadful Sorry, Clementine" became a worthy heir to "Shady Deal at Sunny Acres."

The one problem with this episode is Clem's approach in getting Heyes and Curry to help her steal the money. It doesn't seem logical that such a good friend would resort to blackmail without simply asking them for help first. While her reason for this tactic ultimately isn't explained to the audience, Huggins understood it and explained it to Larson during the story conference on June 28. "Clem didn't want to tell our boys the truth because she was afraid they wouldn't help her if they didn't think there was some money in it for them." As a long-time friend of Heyes and Curry, Clem is familiar with their larcenous and self-interested natures and she has no reason to suppose they've changed, despite their efforts to go straight. While her motive was not strictly larcenous, Clem thoroughly enjoys her foray into crime. She keeps the photo because she may want to use it to coerce them again, and while Huggins wanted her to remain honest in this story, he kept open the possibility that "in the next one, she may come to our boys and say, 'Fellows, I'm hooked.'"[39]

"Shady Deal at Sunny Acres" made use of every recurring character that had ever appeared in *Maverick* at that time. Huggins also wanted to make use of recurring characters in *Alias Smith and Jones*. Clementine Hale was introduced in this episode with the specific intention of her being such a character, although she ultimately appeared only twice in the series due to Sally Field's schedule.

Originally the boys go to their old friend Soapy Saunders for help with the scam, but when Sam Jaffe was unavailable, the character was changed to Diamond Jim Guffy, giving Heyes and Curry another friend and potentially even more opportunities for con games in the future.

SHOOTOUT AT DIABLO STATION

"This really sounds like this could be fun. We all sit around and think of places where nobody's coming from."
– Hannibal Heyes

STORY:	JOHN THOMAS JAMES
TELEPLAY:	WILLIAM D. GORDON
DIRECTOR:	JEFFREY HAYDEN
SHOOTING DATES:	OCTOBER 11, 12, 13, 14, 15, 18, 1971
ORIGINAL US AIR DATE:	DECEMBER 2, 1971
ORIGINAL UK AIR DATE:	JANUARY 10, 1972

The stagecoach driver, Ward Webster, started out as Wheat Webster.

Gravelly-voiced Neville Brand, who plays outlaw Chuck Gorman, was the 4th most decorated Army soldier in World War II.

The 38-star flag flying over Hayfoot's cabin was officially accepted in 1877, Colorado being the 38th state. In 1890, the 43-star flag became approved with the addition of North Dakota, South Dakota, Montana, Washington, and Idaho, dating this episode between 1877 and 1890.

Kid Curry walks into the Bridefoot telegraph office where Hannibal Heyes is composing a message to Sheriff Lom Trevors, informing him they're on their way to Porterville to see him about the latest amnesty news. Curry tells him that the stage will be leaving soon; they'll be safe as long as the sheriff doesn't see them together.

Horses pull the stagecoach at breakneck speed while inside, Heyes sits next to George Fendler opposite Curry and two women, sisters on their way to live with their uncle in Porterville now that their father, a judge, has died. It dawns on Fendler that he recognizes one lady from Yuma's Longhorn Saloon. She denies that this is possible. Fendler insists he's right until Curry strongly suggests he take the lady's word.

Long shadows fall as the stagecoach pulls into Diablo Station. Out of sight, four outlaws—Chuck Gorman, Bud, Harry and Hank – watch the passengers alight. Inside the station, Fendler complains about the price of whiskey and the rotten coffee. Before supper is finished, the outlaws barge in and tie up everyone but Hayfoot, the stationmaster, who insists upon lowering the US flag before sunset. Back inside, he tells the gang there is nothing worth stealing on the coach or in the station.

Heyes introduces himself as Joshua Smith and identifies one of the women as his wife, thinking it would be safer for them. Curry says he is Thaddeus Jones and identifies the other woman as *his* wife. At their queries, Gorman informs them that they're waiting for something to happen, probably about noon the next day. George Fendler offers a couple hundred dollars in an attempt to make a deal for his own release, saying he's got business in Porterville. He divulges to the outlaw leader that Smith and Jones cannot be married to the ladies because they boarded the stage at different times, and he knows one woman from the Longhorn. The women, Mary and Ellie, again deny they ever set foot in a saloon.

Mary asks for some whiskey, surprising all the men and her sister. At Fendler's query as to whether his information has earned his freedom, Gorman shoves him into his seat, believing Fendler would sell him out the same as he did the ladies.

When Bud, one of the outlaws, asks about food, Mary laughs at the thought of a man cooking supper, so Chuck assigns her the job. To prevent her escape after she's been untied, he demands her shoes and stockings. She willingly complies, foot propped up on the table as she seductively eases off her stocking and drops it over the outlaw's shoulder. Mary asks that her sister's hands be untied so she can eat more easily.

Heyes wonders what they're all waiting for and Chuck reveals that if the stage doesn't arrive in Porterville, the next morning the sheriff will come out looking for it. Curry asks if it's Lom Trevors he's talking about. Chuck says a man in Trevors's custody was shot in the back in cold blood, allegedly trying to escape. The man was Ambrose Gorman, Chuck's brother. Now Chuck is going to kill Trevors in revenge.

As the outlaws play cards to pass the time, Mary sits close to Chuck, her hand on his thigh. The subtle suggestion is not lost on Chuck and after the next round of cards, he and Mary head for the stationmaster's bedroom. With a knowing look, Fendler offers Heyes and Curry "Longhorn Saloon" as the succinct reason for her behavior.

While Hank stands guard at the window and Bud and Harry argue about the sin of playing cards, Hayfoot whispers to Ellie. Then, leaning toward Curry on her other side, she begins to untie his wrist bindings.

The station sits in darkness and all is quiet. Tiring of solitaire, Harry begins to pace, wondering why Chuck and Mary are so long in the bedroom. Bud and Hank, though curious, refuse to check on them and bother their boss. Harry's too worried and he slowly eases open the door. When he pokes his head in, Mary cocks a pistol and whispers for him to come in. Scared, she holds the gun on him and orders him facedown on the bed next to Chuck. The passengers and remaining two outlaws can only wonder what is going on behind the closed door.

Watching her prisoners, Mary's attention is diverted by the sound of the doorknob turning. Behind her Hank breaks the window and calls to her to drop the gun and to Harry and Chuck that they can get up. While the outlaws are occupied with Mary, Curry unties the rope binding his feet, leaving it loosely arranged around his ankles.

Angry now, Chuck orders the women tightly bound and then he strikes Mary several times. She's lucky he didn't kill her but Heyes points out that it could have been the other way around since she had the gun. Chuck reiterates his orders to stand guard and the passengers and Hayfoot drift off to sleep. Boredom entices the outlaws into a semblance of sleep as well.

Chuck rouses and relieves Bud at the window. As Bud ambles back to sit by the bedroom door, he notices that one of the passengers is missing. Heyes awakens and pretends to just notice that Mr. Jones is gone. The outlaws search frantically. Chuck pries up a floorboard, but there is no cellar he could be hiding in. Frustrated, Chuck turns to George Fendler for information, but he will not give it. Chuck then asks Hayfoot, the only one who would know of a hiding place, but Hayfoot also refuses to talk even when Chuck threatens him with a bullet to the forehead. At that point, Heyes says Mr. Jones wouldn't want him to die; he should tell where he is. Reluctantly, Hayfoot tells about a secret cupboard he built for his wife in case of an Indian attack. When the door is pried off, Curry uncurls himself from his hiding place.

In the light of morning, Chuck watches out the window. Heyes suddenly laughs aloud at the thought that Sheriff Trevors will know there's trouble inside when he doesn't see the flag flying. The prisoners berate him for thoughtlessly giving away their last chance. Harry is ready to go out to hoist up the flag, but Chuck sends Hayfoot out in case of an ambush.

Fendler apologizes to the women for the way he treated them. Their courage has put him to shame. The outlaws gag him and the other passengers so they can't call out a warning. They wait until a posse of three men arrives. Delighted at the small number, Chuck calls his men to cover the front of the cabin and is shocked at sudden gunfire. They are surrounded. Lom orders them out, but Chuck threatens to start killing passengers if the sheriff doesn't let the gang ride away. He pulls Jones to the window to verify that no one has been hurt so far. Lom agrees to let the gang go and calls them out one at a time to drop their weapons. Before they exit, Chuck and his men hide extra guns in their shirts.

Chuck is the last to step out and asks how Trevors knew there was something amiss. Lom recognized the flag flying upside down as a distress signal. As the gang rides away, Heyes pulls off Curry's gag and he shouts a warning. The outlaws turn and fire on Lom, hitting him in the shoulder. The posse pursues them.

As the passengers pack up to leave, Hayfoot says he realized what Heyes had in mind when he started in about the flag. Otherwise, Lom says, he would have blundered in and got shot and it wasn't even him who shot the prisoner. Ambrose Gorman had pulled a gun on his deputy, not him.

The stagecoach is ready and the posse returns with the outlaws. Fendler watches as the women talk to their Uncle Bart. Though they were coming to stay with him, they've learned they can take care of themselves and will head back to their home in Tucson.

Heyes and Curry ask about their amnesty but Lom knows it would be political suicide for the governor to issue it now. They just need to keep trying. The stagecoach, the posse and Heyes and Curry all ride away, leaving Hayfoot to right the flag.

their finances to the beauty of the day. Curry refuses to be swayed and stubbornly repeats "How much?" until Heyes admits they have $2.16 between them. With a sigh Curry wonders whatever happened to Heyes's nimble brain and silver tongue. A voice interrupts his grumbling, demanding they stop and raise their hands.

Heyes and Curry follow the unseen man's instructions, throwing away their guns, dismounting and lying on their bellies next to the trail. When they're properly subdued, a black man rides out from behind the rocks, his rifle aimed unwaveringly at them, and introduces himself as Joe Sims. He's a bounty hunter – professional – and they're under arrest.

Joe orders Heyes to tie Curry's hands behind his back, then ties Heyes's wrists together himself. Back on their horses, Joe announces his intention to turn them in at Carbondale. It's a long ride but Joe is hoping the sheriff there will be more cooperative about the reward than the sheriff in Hartsville, who doesn't like black folks.

The three men trek to Carbondale. All the while Heyes tries to convince Joe he's mistaken about them, but Joe is a professional. He's memorized the descriptions of all outlaws worth more than $2,000 and he compares descriptions from different sources. He knows they're Heyes and Curry.

As they travel, Heyes wonders how Joe came to be a bounty hunter. Joe was a slave before the Civil War; afterwards he drifted west. Facing the reality that no one would pay a black man more than room and board, if he could find work at all, Joe decided the best way to make money was to become a bounty hunter.

A rattlesnake strikes out. Joe's horse rears in fright, throwing him, and the boys don't waste the opportunity – they spur their horses and gallop off. Joe takes out after them. He carefully shoots over their heads, but his bullet hits a horse belonging to a passing rancher. Six angry ranch hands quickly surround him. Grayson, the spokesman of the group, doesn't believe Joe is a bounty hunter and isn't mollified by his apology for

(Courtesy of Ben Murphy)

accidentally killing the horse. The men decide to lynch him.

Heyes and Curry stop in the shelter of some trees and free themselves from their bonds. They spot the lynch party from the crest of the hill and Heyes offhandedly notes, "There's an end to a budding career." Curry doesn't answer and Heyes is dismayed to see him reloading his gun. Curry reminds him Joe could have killed them, so they should stop the lynching. Heyes reluctantly reloads his own gun, insisting that twelve quick shots had better be enough to scare off the lynchers because that's all they're going to do.

The men scatter when the shooting starts, leaving Joe behind. He struggles free of the rope, then rides off in a different direction.

Curry is pleased with himself. "You know what we just did, Heyes? A good deed." Heyes doesn't want to make it a habit.

They ride along and this time Curry waxes poetic over the beauty of the day. A familiar voice commands them to stop. "Joe, it's us," Heyes calls out. Curry points out that they were the ones who scared off the lynch mob, but Joe knew that and figured they were still nearby. They go through the now-familiar routine of being tied up, astonished by Joe's ingratitude. For his part, Joe is only puzzled by their actions. He doesn't know why they'd save his skin instead of their own. It seems kind of stupid to him.

The men ride single file, Heyes needling Curry about their good deed while Joe chuckles at their frustrated squabbling. Three men – Nate, Jesse and Hank – approach them on the trail and Nate asks what's going on. Joe explains, but Heyes offers a different version of events. Joe *thinks* they're outlaws, but he's mistaken. In reality, he's Joshua Smith, on his way home to his wife and baby boy, while his friend Thaddeus is going to get married next week. To Heyes's dismay, Nate wishes Joe luck, then he and his friends go on their way. Joe is still suspicious, though, and keeps a sharp eye out on the trail.

Nate, Jesse and Hank turn to watch Joe and his prisoners ride off. When they're out of sight, the men double back.

As Joe and the boys approach, Nate steps out from behind a tree and fires a warning shot. Joe told too good a story. If he really has got Curry and Heyes, Nate and his friends figure they'll turn them in. He relieves Joe of his horse and his gun, telling him to go back to where he came from. Heyes and Curry watch with mixed feelings as Joe trudges away through the trees.

As Nate's prisoner, Heyes expands upon his story about the wife, baby boy and forthcoming wedding in an attempt to convince him they're not outlaws. He throws in a complaint about being the victims of a terrible injustice, and wonders what the country is coming to when honest, hard-working American citizens can be manhandled by anyone who comes along. Nate is unmoved, so Heyes demonstrates their respectability by describing Curry's erstwhile fiancée as the daughter of the mayor of St. Louis, even inviting Nate and his buddies to come to the wedding. Nate takes it as long as he can, then finally blurts out, "Will you shut up?"

As the procession crosses a river, shots ring out. Joe has returned with a new horse and gun. He wounds Jesse and Hank, but Nate escapes. Heyes asks in awe, "How did you do that?" It was easy. Joe walked to a nearby ranch and bought what he needed. Heyes and Curry are once again Joe's prisoners, as are Jesse and Hank.

When they settle down for the night, Heyes reasons with Joe. Nate is sure to come back for his friends. Joe disagrees, saying Nate hasn't got the guts. Curry complains of hunger, but Joe brushes him off; they're no hungrier than he is. Jesse then speaks up, insisting he's in pain and needs a doctor. Joe points out that if he's able to complain, he's not too bad off. "I just love the way he gets rid of problems," Curry remarks to Heyes.

As Heyes argues with Joe, Curry focuses on freeing his hands, straining at the rawhide until his wrists are bloody. He's making progress when Nate reappears, gun in hand.

Nate orders Joe to throw away his gun and forces him to walk toward the river, where he plans to shoot him. Heyes and Curry work feverishly on their bonds. Wrenching his hands free, Curry grabs Joe's gun and shoots the pistol out of Nate's hand. Joe turns to stare at Curry in amazement. "My God, you didn't go and do it again?!" Curry grins and shrugs.

Joe kneels to check on Nate, ignoring the gun in Curry's hand. When Curry orders Joe to untie Heyes, he refuses. He knows Curry can't shoot him – he just used the last bullet. Curry pulls the trigger. Sure enough, the hammer clicks on an empty chamber. Joe's been so busy he just plumb forgot to reload.

Joe reties Curry. By now Heyes has freed himself, but the ever-watchful Joe orders him to put his hands on his head. Joe decides to leave the three wounded men tied up on the outskirts of town where someone will find them. Then he and the boys will ride south towards Briartown.

Joe leaves Heyes and Curry securely bound hand and foot, back to back. They struggle to get free, but finally concede it's hopeless. Curry still has faith in Heyes's ability to get them out of this predicament, but Heyes himself isn't so sure.

Joe returns and relates his real plan. They'll head north to Big Butte, a direction no one will expect. Heyes tries his silver tongue once more. Joe has thought of everything, but he's still mistaken about them being Curry and Heyes. Joe's taken Thaddeus's gun away from him twice and tied them up four times. They fired twelve shots at the lynching party and didn't hit anyone. The real Kid Curry would have left dead bodies strewn in his wake. Curry jumps in, pointing out that Heyes is supposed to be able to talk himself out of a tiger's belly, but Joshua hasn't been able to talk anybody out of anything. Joe listens thoughtfully, then admits he has been bothered by all this, but he finally figured it out. "Even Curry and Heyes can have an off day."

The next morning, on the way to Big Butte, they find themselves approaching a group of white men. Heyes urges Joe to untie them so they'll look like three friends riding together, but Joe decides to take a chance – white folks aren't all bad.

Max, the leader, listens to Joe's story, then to Heyes's rebuttal. He orders two of his men to untie the boys, then take them into town and turn them over to the sheriff. Joe is angry – Max just cost him $20,000. It's not your place to arrest white folks, Max informs him, and orders him back to where he came from – South. Joe gallops off, but before he's gone far Max shoots him in the back.

Heyes and Curry overthrow their latest captors and race to where Joe has fallen.

Blood bubbling from his lips, Joe asks what they're doing there. Heyes and Curry try to figure out how best to get Joe some help, but it's no use. Curry asks him if he would really have turned them in. "Sho' would," Joe gasps with a pained smile and dies.

The partners debate the wisdom of reporting Joe's murder to the sheriff. Taking one last look at Joe's grave, Curry asks Heyes if he thinks Joe meant it, that he would really have turned them in. With a rueful smile Heyes replies, "Sho' would."

GUEST CAST

LOU GOSSETT	JOE SIMS
ROBERT MIDDLETON	GRAYSON
ROBERT DONNER	NATE
R.G. ARMSTRONG	MAX
JAMES McCALLION	JESSE
GEOFFREY LEWIS	AL
ROBERT EASTON	HANK

As the Associate Executive Producer, Jo Swerling was in charge of many of the day-to-day details of the production, from making sure the sets were built on time to riding herd on the actors. Swerling faced a challenging issue during the "Bounty Hunter" shoot. The production was on location in Malibu Ranch and the first couple of days Ben, Peter and guest star Lou Gossett all had early calls. Peter kept coming in half an hour late, so Swerling had a chat with him. "He got a little bit defensive and he didn't have any particular excuse," Swerling recalls. "I said, 'Peter, you know, everybody else has to be here on time and when they're ready to go, and I'm including Lou Gossett, who's an actor of some stature, and your co-star, and the cameraman and the crew, it shouldn't be too difficult for you to figure out that they can come to resent the fact that they're here and you're not.'" Peter was surprised because actually it hadn't occurred to him he could be causing resentment. He agreed to be punctual from then on.

Swerling next found himself dealing with Ben, who also started coming in late, but this time his chat brought an unexpected response. "Well, I kind of have to do it," Ben told him. "Because Peter's going to come in late and if I come in on time I start resenting Peter." This was exactly what Swerling had warned Peter about, but Ben had more to say in his own defense. "If that begins to fester, I'm not a good enough actor to be able to turn that off when the camera rolls. And my fear is that if I'm mad at Peter, it's going to come across on screen and it's going to screw up this wonderful thing we have going and it'll hurt the show. So I figure out how late he's going to be and I'll come in ten minutes before he does, but I'll still be late."

Swerling was stopped dead in his tracks. Having already chastised Peter for the very issue Ben was now coping with in his own inventive way, he didn't have a response to Ben's excuse. Acknowledging Ben's point, Swerling told him nevertheless that he needed to come in on time and Swerling would see to it that Peter was on time as well. "But, you know, that was one of the smartest excuses I ever got," Swerling laughs. "I had nowhere to go."[42]

Serious social issues are not often dealt with in *Alias Smith and Jones*. This is mostly because Roy Huggins preferred to focus on strictly entertaining stories in westerns. "It's very difficult to have social overtones with a western . . . I never tried it because those were usually moralistic and dull. I like to make social comments that are very specific."[43] In "The Bounty Hunter," Huggins and Baehr managed to tackle a serious, and specific, social problem in a manner that is far from being moralistic and dull.

While the Civil War abolished slavery, it did not change the long-established racist attitudes among the population. Even ardent abolitionists, while abhorring slavery, did not always regard blacks as equal to whites. In 1971, as it still is today, racism was a hot topic offering Roy Huggins a rare chance to explore a contemporary social problem in a western.

He told the story to Nick Baehr on June 1, 1971, incorporating specific notes as to how the ex-outlaws respond to Joe. He noted "Heyes and Curry have no prejudice. They were both born and raised in Kansas – and Heyes should make a point of that." In Baehr's first draft script, Heyes points out that Joe would probably have an easier time in Oregon or Montana, areas that aren't full of former Confederates who dislike black folks. "That go for you, too?" Joe asks. Heyes responds, "Hell, we're from Kansas. If you run into people from Kansas it's a different story . . ." Heyes and Curry are the only men who accept Joe as an equal, and "in the course of our story, our boys and Joe [Sims] develop a grudging affection for each other." Indeed, it's obvious that if not for the $20,000 bounty, Joe and the boys could become good friends. But Joe is a bounty hunter – professional – and not about to let friendship get in the way of his bank account. In fact, Joe comes across as much more competent than Heyes and Curry in this story, which is demonstrated not only by his ability to continually outwit them, but also by his reappearance, fully outfitted, after being set afoot by Nate. While Heyes and Curry started out lamenting that they have just $2.16 between them, Joe is able to get $110 worth of equipment for only $221, a rip-off Joe accepts with only a wry comment about free American enterprise, but an indication of just how successful he is in his profession.

As Joe leads his prisoners to the sheriff, it becomes apparent that the white men they meet are more outraged by the idea of a black man arresting white men than they are about Heyes's and Curry's crimes. The first group of ranchers care only that a horse has been killed; Nate and his friends believe Joe's story, but decide that they should get the reward, not a black man; and Max, while willing to turn in Heyes and Curry, is really most interested in punishing this uppity black man for daring to arrest them.

Joe is a sympathetic, likeable character whom Heyes and Curry defend, despite the danger to themselves. He is smart and professional, and despite his past as a slave, holds no grudge against white people. He is easy to identify with and, as a result, the audience is asked to face their own attitudes toward other races. Huggins and Baehr manage to slip in a message about the evils of racism by using a fast paced story, a serious dilemma for our boys and clever dialogue. The combination results in a powerful story that is arguably the best in the series.

EVERYTHING ELSE YOU CAN STEAL

"Smith and Jones? Y'all couldn't do any better'n that?"
— Blackjack Jenny

STORY:	JOHN THOMAS JAMES
TELEPLAY:	JOHN THOMAS JAMES
DIRECTOR:	ALEXANDER SINGER
SHOOTING DATES:	OCTOBER 29, NOVEMBER 1, 2, 3, 4, 5, 1971
ORIGINAL US AIR DATE:	DECEMBER 16, 1971
ORIGINAL UK AIR DATE:	JANUARY 24, 1972

The original title was "Alias Black and White."

Heyes's quote for Blake's headstone was borrowed from *Maverick*. The Pappyism came from the episode "Passage to Fort Doom."

In the dead of night, a well-dressed man pries open the back door of the bank. By match light he deftly dials the combination on the safe, empties the cash into a satchel, and leaves by the same door. A few minutes later, he meets two young cowboys in a deserted area. They've done the job he's asked them to do and he kills them.

Hannibal Heyes and Kid Curry ride into town weary of life in the saddle. Maybe it wouldn't be too bad getting caught; they wouldn't have to ride a horse for twenty years. Easing himself onto a bench, Curry leans back to relax. Heyes picks up an abandoned newspaper and begins to read the front page. Resignedly he hands the paper to his partner who perks up at the headline. It means they have to climb back into the saddle and ride.

Reaching the little town of Touchstone, New Mexico, Curry would like a drink, but instead they barge into Sheriff W.D. Coffin's office, introducing themselves as Smith and Jones, bounty hunters. The sheriff has a low opinion of the profession but Smith jokes there was no other work after they got done killing all the buffalo. Jones tells the lawman they were three hundred miles north on the trail of Heyes and Curry when they heard that the two outlaws had robbed the Touchstone bank. The sheriff, ashamed for not recognizing the crooks whose Wanted posters hang on his wall, says they got drunk and identified themselves to someone in town. The bank is offering a $10,000 reward, making Heyes and Curry worth $30,000.

Outside, Curry is disgusted. There goes their amnesty and there's nothing they can do except admit to the sheriff that *they* are Heyes and Curry. They decide to head for South America, but first that drink . . .

Blackjack Jenny sits at a table in the saloon dealing cards. She spots the boys and hurries over. They are glad to see their old friend and before she can blow their cover, Heyes whispers their aliases into her ear.

That night, Jenny tells them her son Billy and his friend Caleb came to Touchstone a month ago. Billy wrote to his mother that they were into something good, then his frequent letters stopped. When the bank was robbed, the safe wasn't blown but opened by working the combination, something Billy and Caleb could never have done. Jenny thinks the boys are dead. So she deals blackjack and asks questions, trying to learn what happened to them. Heyes and Curry promise to help.

The next day, they approach Assistant Bank Manager Kenneth Blake and ask to talk to Mr. Blodgett, the bank's owner. The overweight, heavy-jowled Blodgett brusquely allows them five minutes of his time.

Heyes and Curry hold to their false identities of professional bounty hunters. It couldn't have been those notorious outlaws who robbed the safe because it's a Pierce & Hamilton '78. Heyes once spent a night in Denver trying to open one and failed; he finally had to use nitro to blow it. Given that the safe here was opened, with only Blodgett knowing the combination, perhaps he robbed his own bank? Outraged, Blodgett blusters that he is a deacon in the Baptist church, a faithful husband, father of three daughters and a very wealthy man. How dare they accuse him? Because he is all of those things, they know he knows who identified the two men in town as Heyes and Curry. It seems they sincerely want to help get the money back so he reveals that it was Louise Carson, a waitress at the café.

For supper, the boys order beef stew and when Louise serves them, they invite her to sit and talk. Jones tells her that they are on the trail of the vicious criminals Kid Curry "and that other fella." Can she tell them anything that could help them? No, she says, they were just nice, pleasant young men. Smith explodes. Hannibal Heyes and what's-his-name were nice, pleasant young men? Louise explains they were calling themselves Caleb White and Billy Black before they got drunk and admitted who they really were. Then a few nights later the bank was robbed and they left town. But, if Smith and Jones say the two men weren't Heyes and Curry, she believes them.

After she returns to her work in the kitchen, the boys figure she may be an innocent who got used but they'd better watch her round the clock until they can be sure.

Curry loses the coin toss and pulls the first night's watch. He spends it perched in a tree outside of Louise's room. Nodding off, he jerks awake at sounds of a cat fight and falls from the tree. In the morning, he limps into their hotel room and drops onto the bed mumbling his report of no action. Heyes stops shaving long enough to pull a quilt over his sleeping friend.

Sitting on the hotel's front porch, Heyes watches Louise enter the bank. He follows in the pretense of having bank business. Louise then heads for the café. Spotting the sheriff, Heyes detours in the opposite direction.

That night, Curry again takes his position in the tree.

Heyes meets Jenny and says if nothing turns up with Louise, they may borrow money from Soapy or Diamond Jim Guffy and head to South America. Jenny won't give up that easily.

Long after dark, Louise walks purposefully down the street. Curry climbs out of the tree and follows. Through the window of an abandoned house, Curry spies her and Ken Blake in an embrace. He hears Louise say she is worried about the two men who have asked her about the robbery, but Blake reassures her they probably are bounty hunters as they say. He silences further misgivings with a kiss.

When Louise and Blake leave, Curry heads back to his bed at the hotel, but he's awakened when his partner lights a lamp. Heyes has figured out what happened. Curry wonders why they have to talk about it in the middle of the night but Heyes says his best ideas come then and goes on. They know that Blake is married to Blodgett's oldest daughter, who probably looks like her father. So Blake falls in love with pretty Louise Carson, but he doesn't want to give up the Blodgett money, so he steals some from the bank and blames it on Heyes and "what's-his-name." Even though Blodgett is the only one who knew the combination, Blake could have easily picked up a number here, a number there. Then he shot and killed Billy and Caleb throwing the blame on them. This also means that Louise is party to cold-blooded murder.

Trying to piece out Louise's part, they invite her on a picnic.

That night at another midnight tryst, Heyes and Curry watch as Louise tells Blake about the proposed picnic. He advises her to go ahead with them, but he'll be watching. She should wear her shawl around her shoulders and, if she feels she's in danger, she should drop it as a signal to him. If worse comes to worst he'll get out and meet her in Vera Cruz. They end the evening with a kiss.

Through a rifle's telescopic lens, Ken Blake watches as the boys and Louise pick at the picnic food. He can't hear them inform her that they know about her and Ken. They figured he must have robbed the bank because Hannibal Heyes couldn't do it by manipulating the tumblers. Only Blodgett or his son-in-law could have stolen the money and it wasn't Blodgett.

Blake also killed Billy and Caleb, they insist. Her shocked expression proves that Louise was unaware of this. She didn't know Ken robbed the bank until he told her to tell the sheriff the story about Billy and Caleb getting drunk and saying they were Heyes and Curry. Ken said he'd given them money and sent them to Mexico.

Louise is convinced she should go to the sheriff.

In town, Heyes and Curry confirm Jenny's suspicions about Caleb and Billy being dead, but won't tell her who robbed the bank. Jenny guesses it was Blake.

Blodgett hails Heyes and Curry from the door of his bank. He has found a note under the door jamb signed by Billy and Caleb claiming that the money is in the abandoned house. Heyes and Curry, along with Blodgett and a deputy, search and find a money bag stuffed up the chimney. News of the found money spreads through Touchstone.

Heyes and Curry ask Louise to step outside the café to talk. She convinced Ken to return the money because she doesn't believe in killing. Even if Ken did kill Billy and Caleb, she won't help New Mexico execute him. Heyes threatens to go to the sheriff but Louise doesn't think he will. She has figured out why they were so desperate to clear the outlaws' names.

That afternoon, as the train pulls in, they say goodbye to Louise. She's going to Yuma to live with her sister and hopefully find a husband. Then Curry spots Jenny headed across the square. Dropping their gear, they race to the bank in time to hear two shots. Jenny has killed Kenneth Blake.

Heyes and Curry beg Louise to stay and testify on her behalf. No jury will convict her once they hear the story. Blake admitted to Louise that he killed Caleb and Billy and that makes her a firsthand witness.

On the train, Heyes wonders how much a headstone for Blake would cost. It would be engraved with the words, "The only thing you have to earn in life is love. Everything else you can steal." Curry is pleased with the original poetry. It's not his, Heyes confesses. He stole it.

GUEST CAST

PATRICK O'NEAL ———————— KENNETH BLAKE
ANN SOTHERN ———————— BLACKJACK JENNY
JESSICA WALTER ———————— LOUISE CARSON
DAVID CANARY ———————— SHERIFF W. D. COFFIN
KERMIT MURDOCK ———————— HENRY BLODGETT
DENNIS RUCKER ———————— BILLY BLACK
PARKER WEST ———————— CALEB WHITE
ALLEN JOSEPH ———————— OLD MAN
ROBERT GODDEN ———————— DEPUTY SHERIFF

Roy Huggins first told the story to Glen Larson on May 11, 1971. Two days later, he dictated addenda for Dick Baer, giving him an introduction to the whole seeking-amnesty history and a week later, Huggins wrote another story outline. Though Baer submitted a first draft three weeks later, nothing was done with the script until October 4 when Universal received another draft from Huggins who wrote it "over weekend."[44]

In Huggins's original story, the boys have been prospecting in the mountains. After three months, they've only got $18.30 worth of gold dust, which works out to their having worked for two cents an hour. While discussing whose "rotten" idea it had been,[45] they come face to face with Lom Trevors. He shows them a newspaper article reporting they're wanted for a robbery in Touchstone, Colorado. Allegedly Heyes and Curry came to town using the names Billy White and Jesse Black. Lom tells them they'd better do something about it because the governor is "really boiling." They know they can go to Touchstone because they *weren't* there previously and won't be recognized.

Heyes and Curry meet with the bank owner, Henry Murchison. His bank uses a "Davis and Newbound" safe but Huggins changed it to a Pierce & Hamilton because "in another story we're doing, Heyes knows how to open that particular model." They also contact Louise Baylor,[46] who owns the millinery shop in town. Her having this shop supplies a meeting place for her and Ken Blake. To contact her, Blake goes to the shop to pick up dress material for his wife. Huggins's idea was for Curry to offer to walk Louise home, then he suggested that Curry meet her at a dance. "Or would this be too expensive to shoot? (Some dance footage is available.)"[47] Louise claims she recognized Heyes because she was once on a stagecoach that was robbed by the Devil's Hole Gang. When they question her closely about the alleged stage robbery, she fudges and they know she's lying.

From this point, the teleplay pretty much follows the final version. However, at the end, Louise talks to Blake. He admits that he killed the two men but insists he did it for her. She says that he must return the money or she'll turn him in for murder unless he kills her too. The next day the money is found back in the bank's safe.

When Jenny kills Blake, many people, including the sheriff, run into the bank and find her standing over his dead body, still holding the gun. In the tag, as the train moves slowly out of town, Heyes and Curry spot a beautiful girl walking on the sidewalk. A man who boarded the train with them identifies her as the banker's oldest daughter. Huggins thought "the idea may be worth playing with, because it blasts the old cliché – that the banker's daughter a guy marries for money is always ugly."[48]

Opposites abound in this episode. The most obvious, of course, is the Black/White names of the young men who, when drunk, claim to be the notorious outlaws. Heyes and Curry identify themselves as bounty hunters when, in fact, they are the hunted. Louise Carson is portrayed as a sweet, simple woman who made the mistake of falling in love with a married man. Her naiveté belies her intelligence in figuring out why the "bounty hunters" so desperately needed to clear Heyes's and Curry's names. The man she loves, Kenneth Blake, is one of *Alias Smith and Jones's* most despicable villains, totally lacking in charm or redeeming qualities. Not only is he a cold-blooded murderer, but also an adulterer who robs the bank managed by his trusting father-in-law. In the end, vigilante justice is served instead of lawful retribution. Heyes and Curry planned to leave town with Blake untouched by the consequences of his crimes. Both they, who usually try to rectify wrongs by having the responsible party admit his guilt, and Louise, who forgives Blake because of her opposition to capital punishment, are frightfully lacking in judgment, leaving Jenny to hand down the sentence Blake deserves.

Jenny is the most uncomplicated of the characters. According to Huggins's backstory, she deals blackjack "in Montana where she's very famous and popular . . . one can always play blackjack with her and knows he's going to get a square deal . . . because she's honest."[49] Jenny was let down by her old friends, so she took the law into her own hands. Her straightforward motivation in killing Blake is that of a mother seeking justice for her son.

MIRACLE AT SANTA MARTA

"Here you are, trying to get framed for murder – or even killed – in his town. Nobody likes a nuisance."
– Hannibal Heyes

STORY:	JOHN THOMAS JAMES
TELEPLAY:	JOHN THOMAS JAMES AND DICK NELSON
DIRECTOR:	VINCENT SHERMAN
SHOOTING DATES:	NOVEMBER 9, 10, 11, 12, 15, 16, 1971
ORIGINAL US AIR DATE:	DECEMBER 30, 1971
ORIGINAL UK AIR DATE:	FEBRUARY 7, 1972

The annual horse race is about to begin when Hannibal Heyes and Kid Curry arrive in Yuma. Munching on popcorn, they observe the favorite being saddled by his owner, Sam Bleeker. A well-dressed man introduces himself as Rolf Hanley. If Bleeker doesn't mind, Hanley will enter his filly in the race. Bleeker agrees. Hanley's entrance fee will just increase the purse that he plans to win.

Heyes and Curry follow Hanley as he returns to tell his handler to saddle Hyperia. They've recognized the horse as a thoroughbred and place their bets on the filly.

The race begins. Bleeker's gray quarter horse takes an early lead, but is eventually passed by the filly, who wins by more than ten lengths. Heyes and Curry happily collect their winnings.

Accused by Bleeker of using a ringer, Hanley calmly points out that Hyperia is not a ringer, but she *is* a

> "Santa Marta is a beautiful little resort town on a small bay. It's perhaps 150 miles below Yuma. It's a very exclusive resort. People get there mostly by yacht, but they can also come from San Francisco or wherever by stage-coach or train. Every three or four days a stagecoach leaves Yuma, goes down to Santa Marta, and comes back."
>
> Story notes, Sep 16, 1971.

thoroughbred. Bleeker demands Hanley either get a gun or disqualify his horse from the race. Hanley refuses to do either. By this time Heyes and Curry have joined Hanley, interested in keeping the race results as they are. Curry stands up for Hanley and finds himself in a showdown with Bleeker. Curry wins.

Hanley offers them a job as bodyguards for his horse. He'll pay them $500 to accompany him to Mexico in a private coach. After giving it some thought, Heyes decides to stay in Yuma. He's found poker players who believe the laws of probability should only be obeyed when a sheriff is watching. Curry can do the job alone.

Curry and Hanley head for Mexico. The coach breaks an axle outside of the resort town of Santa Marta. Leaving Turner, the driver, to await a blacksmith, the two men ride in to town.

As they dine that evening, Señor Cordoba, the alcalde, stops by to introduce himself and welcome them to Santa Marta. As he leaves, Hanley comments on what a charming man he is, but Curry isn't fooled. "Mr. Hanley, he was checking us out. But charmingly."

The next evening Curry dines alone, having received a note from Hanley saying he wouldn't see him at dinner. The alcalde gives him a friendly nod from a neighboring table.

The next morning there's a knock on Curry's door. Expecting Hanley, he invites him to come in. Instead of Rolf Hanley, though, he's faced with two Mexican policemen giving him orders in Spanish. He responds, "No comprendo" and the policemen pull out their guns. *That* Curry understands.

Inspecting Curry's gun, the alcalde notes it has been recently cleaned. Insulted, Curry explains his gun has always been recently cleaned. The alcalde then questions Curry – where does he come from, who can provide references for him, how long has he known Mr. Hanley? Curry doesn't know what the alcalde is getting at, a claim the alcalde finds difficult to believe. "Mr. Hanley was shot last night and thrown off the Punta Piedras cliffs."

The alcalde explains his suspicions. Curry is the only one in Santa Marta who knew Hanley and could possibly have wished to harm him. The gun that killed him was a .45 caliber, just like Curry's. Hanley was not robbed and Hyperia is still in her stall. Before locking Curry up, the alcalde allows him to telegraph Heyes. "Am in Santa Marta in jail, charged with murder. Bring money."

On board the stagecoach for Santa Marta, Heyes finds his traveling companion is a lovely widow named Meg Parker. He's puzzled to find her traveling alone to Mexico, but she explains her husband left her some money and she likes doing the unusual.

Heyes visits Curry in jail, bringing the bad news that Bleeker, the likely suspect, was shot dead the day Curry and Hanley left Yuma. Heyes will have to come up with a miracle to save Curry.

Meanwhile, the alcalde has learned two new things in the case. First, Turner, Hanley's driver, has a criminal record and spent ten years in prison for murder.

Second, Hanley came from Lexington, Kentucky, and Santa Marta has a permanent resident, Margaret Carruthers, also from Lexington. Because Curry is no longer the only suspect, the alcalde is willing to let him out of jail. In return he'd like Curry to be his guest at dinner along with Miss Carruthers. If Curry will casually bring Lexington into the conversation, the alcalde can observe her reaction. Curry eagerly agrees.

Heyes and Curry confront Turner whose rage at being held in Mexico, not drawing wages, while the alcalde investigates the murder, convinces them of his innocence. Heyes sums up the situation – if it wasn't Curry and it wasn't Turner, then it has to be Margaret Carruthers.

The boys head out to pay Margaret a visit. As they admire her villa from a nearby hilltop, Heyes spies Meg Parker in a buggy on the road below. At the time, Heyes didn't think Meg's story of traveling around the world was peculiar, but now he does.

That evening at the alcalde's dinner party, Margaret Carruthers chats with Curry, who dutifully brings up Lexington. The alcalde watches Margaret closely. She seems surprised that Hanley was from her hometown, but denies knowing him.

Meanwhile, Heyes dines with Meg Parker in the hotel restaurant. Meg enthusiastically recounts her adventure of the day – watching the fisherman return with their catch. Heyes asks if she saw any of the countryside, but Meg claims she didn't have time.

Curry and Heyes are out for an evening stroll, comparing notes. Heyes is sure Meg is lying while Curry reluctantly believes Margaret is telling the truth. A gunshot interrupts their conversation. Heyes grabs Curry's arm and pulls him down to safety behind a log. A second shot takes off Curry's hat. Heyes shoots back at the unseen assailant. When the excitement is over, Curry wonders if being shot at is good or bad. "If you don't get killed," Heyes assures him, "I think it's good."

The boys wake up the alcalde to tell him of this latest event. They wait up until he returns with news: Turner was playing poker, Margaret Carruthers returned to her villa after the dinner party. When pressed, the alcalde admits she could have left again. Also, Mrs. Hanley arrived on the ten o'clock stage.

In the morning the boys visit Mrs. Hanley. She believes Curry killed her husband and is getting away with it. Shocked at his suggestion that she shot at him, her attitude softens when he tells her about Margaret Carruthers, whom Mrs. Hanley remembers she once met.

Curry and Mrs. Hanley call on Margaret. Margaret recalls meeting Mrs. Hanley years ago, but points out that she has changed. Mrs. Hanley feels Miss Carruthers has changed, too, so much so that she'd never have recognized her. Margaret now admits she was acquainted with Rolf Hanley, but didn't wish to become involved in the investigation. She hadn't seen him since she was eighteen and that's why she lied.

Meanwhile, Meg Parker, not feeling well, has breakfast in bed. Heyes sends flowers along with a note asking to see her. Meg is delighted to have his company.

Curry and Mrs. Hanley ride back to town discussing the mysterious Margaret Carruthers. Mrs. Hanley is not certain she's the same woman she met back in Lexington.

Heyes challenges Meg on the subject of her visiting Margaret Carruthers. Meg explains she heard there was an American woman living nearby, so she went to call on her, unannounced. Unfortunately, she wasn't home.

The police are waiting as Curry pulls the buggy to a stop in front of the stable, and he is again taken into custody.

Heyes storms into the jail, demanding to talk to the alcalde. Curry has been arrested because a witness saw him at the Punta Piedras cliffs the night Hanley was murdered. Curry's trial will be short and if he's convicted, a firing squad will shoot him.

Heyes bows his head in defeat. Curry exhorts him to do something, but Heyes is out of ideas. For what it's worth Curry offers Mrs. Hanley's doubts about Margaret Carruthers. Heyes brightens. He'd been wondering why Mrs. Parker suddenly became bedridden.

Heyes brings Mrs. Hanley to meet Meg Parker, whom Mrs. Hanley immediately recognizes as the Margaret Carruthers she met in Lexington ten years ago. Meg protests. She's never been to Kentucky, her maiden name is Stanfill and she grew up in Ohio. Heyes attempts to persuade Meg to tell the truth before Thaddeus is convicted of murder, but Meg still insists she's never seen Mrs. Hanley before in her life. Heyes leaves her with one last thought. "Whatever it is you're hiding, is it important enough to let a man die for it?"

Mrs. Hanley rides out to Margaret Carruthers's villa. To prove her identity, Margaret pulls out her birth certificate and passport, then agrees to accompany Mrs. Hanley to the alcalde's office, determined to meet this woman who claims to be her.

Heyes arrives at the villa and learns from the housekeeper that the two women are on their way to town. He hurries after them.

Mrs. Hanley is surprised when Margaret drives past the road to Santa Marta. She suspects they are going the wrong way and is proven correct when Margaret hits her with the butt of her whip and pushes her out of the buggy. Margaret is prevented from continuing her attack by Heyes's arrival.

In the alcalde's office, Margaret denies attacking Mrs. Hanley, suggesting that perhaps her grief over her husband's death has affected her mind and caused her to tell such lies. Heyes enters with Meg Parker in tow. She's finally ready to tell the whole story.

Meg read of Rolf Hanley's death in a Lexington newspaper. She was surprised to read that Margaret Carruthers, formerly of Lexington, was now living in Santa Marta because *she* is Margaret Carruthers. Recently widowed, she was free to come to see who was using her identity and why. Margaret angrily informs the alcalde that Meg tried to blackmail her, a charge Meg admits. Margaret is really Elizabeth Carter, an old schoolmate who ran off with outlaw Charles Morgan when she was eighteen. She killed Morgan's brother, stole a huge sum of money from the gang and disappeared. At this, Margaret jumps up in rage and tries to throttle Meg until Heyes and a policeman separate them.

Heyes goes to the jail and gives Curry the good news. He brought off a miracle.

That night Curry relaxes in a bathtub while Heyes mends the bullet hole in Curry's derby and finishes the story of Elizabeth Carter. She had a lot of stolen money and an angry outlaw gang on her tail. She decided to move to Mexico, which takes papers. She helped herself to her friend Margaret Carruthers's birth certificate and assumed her identity. Rolf Hanley, learning that his old friend lived in Santa Marta, paid her a surprise visit and instead found Elizabeth Carter, whom he also knew.

Mrs. Hanley, realizing that her husband never had a chance to pay Curry, offers the boys a job. She's taking the filly on to Rancho Verde for breeding and she needs both a bodyguard and a chaperone. The boys happily accept.

GUEST CAST

CRAIG STEVENS	ROLF HANLEY
NICO MINARDOS	ALCALDE (SEÑOR CORDOBA)
INA BALIN	MARGARET CARRUTHERS
PATRICIA CROWLEY	MEG PARKER
JOANNA BARNES	MRS. HANLEY
FERNANDO ESCANDON	CLERK
CHARLES TYNER	TURNER
STEVEN GRAVERS	BOOKIE
GREG WALCOTT	SAM BLEEKER
RUDY DIAZ	FIRST POLICEMAN
REF SANCHEZ	STABLEMAN
HENRY CARR	PORTER
QUETA DE ACUNA	MARGARET CARRUTHERS' SERVANT

It's no secret that Roy Huggins often recycled stories. Glen Larson recalls, "I didn't always know the genesis of some of the ideas he was spinning . . . I didn't have the historical warehouse that he did in his head."[50] Huggins did indeed have a phenomenal memory, not only for his own work, but also apparently for everything he ever read. The genesis of his stories could be anything from a con game learned in military school to a single chapter in the middle of a Mark Twain novel. It's amazing to see how different the end results could be when the same basic germ of an idea was used in different settings.

"Miracle at Santa Marta" is a story Huggins borrowed from himself. In this case, he went through that historical mental warehouse and pulled out the very first story he ever wrote – a novel called *The Double Take,* published in 1946. Author Max Allan Collins, who was instrumental in giving Huggins the Private Eye Writers of America Lifetime Achievement Award in 1991, once commented that *The Double Take* was "undoubtedly the most-filmed private eye novel ever." Besides the movie based on the novel, Huggins used it on almost every series he produced from *Maverick* to *City of Angels* to *The Rockford Files.*[51]

The novel is a contemporary Chandler-esque hard-boiled detective story, yet Huggins and writer Dick Nelson were able to turn the same basic story into a believable western. In the novel, detective Stuart Bailey is hired to look into the background of a woman whose husband has been approached by a blackmailer. What seems a simple case soon becomes a tangle of changing identities. When the story is finally resolved, Bailey has learned that Ellen, a gangster's wife, stole a large sum of money from him, then disappeared. She hid in plain sight as a student at UCLA, but to gain admittance to the school she needed a good high school transcript. She wrote to her school and requested, not her transcript, but that of classmate Margaret Bleeker, and assumed her identity. In "Miracle at Santa Marta," it's Elizabeth Carter assuming classmate Margaret Carruthers's identity to escape from the angry outlaws. Huggins gave a secret nod to his novel by keeping the name Margaret for the stolen identity and giving the sore loser of the horse race the name Bleeker.

The desire to change one's life is a common thread to both stories, one which fits well within the tenets of the amnesty deal so instrumental in changing Curry and Heyes from outlaws to law-abiding citizens. Because Huggins preferred to avoid violence whenever possible in *Alias Smith and Jones,* Elizabeth Carter came to a better end than Ellen, who was killed at the end of *The Double Take.*

21 Days to Tenstrike

"That's where the money was kept."
– Hannibal Heyes

STORY:	JOHN THOMAS JAMES
TELEPLAY:	IRVING PEARLBERG AND JOHN THOMAS JAMES
DIRECTOR:	MEL FERBER
SHOOTING DATES:	NOVEMBER 30, DECEMBER 1, 2, 3, 6, 7, 1971
ORIGINAL US AIR DATE:	JANUARY 6, 1972
ORIGINAL UK AIR DATE:	APRIL 2, 1973

Hannibal Heyes and Kid Curry meander through the countryside, stopping at a water hole to allow their horses to drink and nibble grass. Watching them, Curry wonders what kind of a meal he can afford and counts his money, coming up with sixty-eight cents. Heyes, without even looking, knows he only has forty-one cents.

Two men on horseback approach and ask what they're doing on private property. If the boys are on their way to Smoketree, they won't find jobs there because of the depression. The strangers ask whether they've done any ranch work or trail driving. Only when they couldn't avoid it, Heyes replies, although they have had experience on the Chisholm Trail in '73 and '74.

The men introduce themselves as trail boss Jake Halloran and Terence Tynan, owner of the property. Tynan is hiring hands to drive a herd of cattle north. Are they interested? When the boys learn that the herd is headed for Tenstrike, Colorado, and has to be there in twenty-one days, they decline but Tynan offers a bonus of $400 if they make it on time. Given the lucrative incentive, Heyes and Curry sign on.

A short while later, the drive begins. Two thousand head of cattle head across the plain, raising great clouds of dust.

The first evening, the drovers play poker around the campfire. With no money, Heyes and Curry sit out the game, but Heyes thinks he recognizes Ralph and Bud, two of the players. He worries he might have encountered them while robbing a train.

Next day, the drive continues. That evening in camp, Ralph approaches Jones with news that he'll be riding drag the next day. Curry understood his position was to be on flank and decides to verify the change with Jake, the boss. Ralph grabs his arm to stop him; he doesn't want the positions switched back. Curry turns, Ralph punches him. A fistfight ensues with Gantry the cook and the other drovers rooting for Ralph. Heyes grimaces at the beating Curry is taking. When swinging fists endanger the chuck wagon supplies, Jake stops the fight. He should have told Curry about the job switch. Ralph had never been on a drive and didn't realize how much dust he'd be eating as drag man, so when he asked to switch, Jake decided to rotate the men.

Curry sarcastically thanks Heyes for the support he didn't give. Heyes replies he wouldn't want him to back a loser, would he? Mrs. Tynan comes by with an offer of iodine and compliments Jones on his still handsome, though bruised, face. She's seen Ralph in other disputes and no one's been able to hold his own against him before.

When she leaves, Heyes shakes his head, incredulous. Only two days out and Curry's gotten beat up, made an enemy and the boss's wife "has got her big brown eyes pointed right at you. And only nineteen more days to go!"

Another day passes, running the herd. Curry, a bandanna covering his nose and mouth, rides drag.

At supper, Gantry, on Ralph's side in the fight, serves Curry less than a tablespoon of stew. Heyes, meanwhile, worries that, if they recognize Ralph and Bud, they may in turn have been recognized.

On November 14, 1971, the day after Huggins told Irving Pearlberg the story, Pearlberg screened *The Virginian* episode "50 Days to Moosejaw" to see about using the stock footage of a cattle drive.

Alias Smith and Jones producers usually took advantage of the stable Los Angeles weather to film all of the exterior scenes outdoors. However, the campfire scenes in this episode were obviously shot on a soundstage. Los Angeles newspapers for December 1971 indicate that the month was an extremely wet one; over five inches of rain fell. Rather than hold up production waiting for clear skies, the camera and crew were moved indoors.

Early on day four, Jake awakens the crew. When Ralph doesn't respond, Jake rolls him over and finds a stiletto-sized wound in his chest. Jake first suspects Jones killed him, but no one has seen him or anyone else with such a weapon. A search for it proves fruitless. With no time to lose, Tynan suggests they bury Ralph and go on, planning to tell the sheriff in Tenstrike. Because Jones is still the most likely suspect, Jake has him tied up in the chuck wagon.

That day, Curry is jostled about as the wagon bumps over rocks and into ruts. Heyes comes by to talk and Curry thinks he should run away when they untie him to eat. They can't go into Tenstrike or they'll be found out as Heyes and Curry. His partner reminds him that, if he runs, authorities will add a murder charge to his record. They have to figure out who killed Ralph.

Checking the map with Jake, Tynan is dismayed to see how much time they've lost with two men out of the drive. If he doesn't make the delivery date, he'll go bankrupt. But Jake figures that if Jones were not tied up, he'd be gone anyway.

Gantry bangs on a pan indicating that supper's ready. As they eat, Curry complains to Heyes about riding in the wagon and wishes he would come up with the name of the murderer. Heyes has seven suspects, the trick is to narrow it down to one.

For sleeping, Curry's leg is shackled to a wagon wheel. When Jake begins his wake-up call the next morning, he finds Bud dead of a similar stiletto wound. Over his grave, Gantry eulogizes Bud and Ralph and promises their killer won't be far behind.

The killer, Gantry suspects, is Mr. Tynan. He figures Tynan heard the rumors about Mrs. Tynan "carrying on" with Ralph and then Bud. Maybe the rumors weren't true, but people believed them anyway. Tynan admits he heard the rumors but considered them only "dirty bunkhouse stories." Even if he did believe them, he didn't kill the men because if they don't make Tenstrike on time, he loses everything. Jake will post a guard all night, each man having a two-hour shift.

Sitting with mugs of coffee, Curry wonders if Heyes knows who the killer is yet. Heyes is working on it, he's eliminated Curry – "I appreciate that, Heyes" – and himself "'cause I'm the one doing the eliminating." He figures the new hands didn't do it; that leaves the remaining three ranch hands, Mr. and Mrs. Tynan, Jake and Gantry. Curry feels that Gantry was too broken up; it wasn't him. Then Heyes eliminates Jake just because he has to believe in the trail boss.

Next morning, Jake awakens the sleeping guard and orders him to wake the others. As he rousts them, the guard finds Phil dead. The drovers gather around and Jake tells everyone that Gantry predicted Phil would be next because the bunkhouse rumors also included him. Jake told Phil he could leave the drive but the drover felt safe because the rumors weren't true.

As a precaution against another murder, Tynan posts two guards on duty each night and if no one gets enough sleep to get the herd to Tenstrike, he's resigned to the loss. Heyes suggests another search, this time in places they

Dick Cavett guest starred as the sheriff in "21 Days to Tenstrike."

didn't look before.

They overturn saddles, check rifle barrels and empty coffeepots. No stiletto.

The drive continues.

Another campfire, another supper. Heyes and Curry go for a walk so they can talk privately. Curry has found the stiletto hidden in the bushy tail of a horse in the remuda, but short of someone confessing, it doesn't solve their problem. They can't go into Tenstrike and be part of a trial where they swear their names are Smith and Jones. But if they ride off without collecting their pay, they'll also be suspected. Heyes has to come up with the killer, *then* they have to ride off without collecting their pay.

On the nineteenth evening, Jake and the Tynans check the map again. Despite the delays, they are fairly certain of making the deadline.

Gantry ambles over to Heyes and Curry with the coffeepot. He apologizes for the way he treated Jones in the beginning. Having earned his friendship, Curry asks Gant if anyone ever tempted him to the tune of $20,000. Heyes explains the killer knows they are worth that. Though they've mended their evil ways, banks and railroads would pay a reward for them.

Gant is surprised. Why did they rob banks? Because "that's where the money was kept," Heyes quips. They won't tell Gant who they really are, but admit they found the stiletto and suspect their trail boss Jake. They lay out how they figure it happened: Ralph and Bud recognized them, maybe from a train robbery, and told Jake. He didn't want to split the reward, so he murdered them. Then he killed Phil to prove Gantry right about the rumors involving Mrs. Tynan. Gantry is remorseful that it may be his fault Phil is dead, but Curry makes him promise not to use the stiletto on Jake except as evidence.

Jake calls Gant away from the confab, wondering what it's all about. Gant fibs that he thought he saw Jones show Smith the stiletto.

When morning dawns, Jake checks for the stiletto he hid in the pony's tail. Gantry approaches and accuses him of the murders. When Jake pulls out his gun, Gantry shoots him.

Mr. Tynan doesn't believe Gantry's story and assigns Jones the task of turning him over to the Tenstrike sheriff. As they ride together on the chuck wagon, Gantry says he wasn't sure of their story because he liked Jake. He had to prove it to himself. If the law can show that Jake owned a stiletto, then he won't be in trouble. Either way, Smith and Jones can collect their pay.

Heyes and Curry visit Gantry in the Tenstrike jail. They won't leave town until they know he's all right. The old cook's been reading the wanted posters and has figured out who they are. If they don't get out of town, he'll be tempted to collect the reward on them and he'll die a rich man.

Reluctantly, they lead their horses out of the livery, then spot the telegrapher heading for the sheriff's office. For a dollar, they learn that the stiletto did indeed belong to Jake.

With Gantry about to get a new lease on life, Heyes and Curry ride hell bent for leather out of town.

GUEST CAST

WALTER BRENNAN	"GANT" GANTRY
STEVE FORREST	JAKE HALLORAN
PERNELL ROBERTS	TERENCE TYNAN
LINDA MARSH	ELIZABETH TYNAN
ROBERT COLBERT	BUD
GLEN CORBETT	RALPH
DICK CAVETT	SHERIFF
HARRY HARVEY, SR.	TELEGRAPHER
RICHARD WRIGHT	HANK
JOE HAWORTH	STEVE
PAUL SCHOTT	PHIL

The famous Chisholm Trail that Heyes claimed they rode opened in 1867 and was named for Jesse Chisholm, a Scotch-Cherokee trader who traveled back and forth from Texas to Wichita, Kansas. Over a million head of cattle tramped over the trail in the first five years, cutting a swath as wide as four hundred yards. Bones of cattle and men attested to the harsh work of a cattle drive. For suffering through dust, thirst, blisters, cold, stampedes, quicksand and Indian danger, the drover might earn $100 in wages for three to four months of herding. If Tynan offered as much, plus a $400 bonus, the three weeks of driving cattle was a hard push but well worth it.

Probably the most important man on the drive was the cook. However, it's not likely he would bang away at an empty pot, as Gantry did, to alert the drovers it was time for supper. Stampedes were a hazard of the trail and the unpredictable longhorn might bolt at the slightest sudden noise. The cattle themselves were silent during a run; the only notice to the drovers would be the thundering of the earth. Once a herd had broken, it often suffered from chronic fright and the unlucky drovers would be saddled with the threat of continuing stampedes. With thousands of cattle running in frenzy, horses and riders could be overrun or a startled horse could throw its rider, who might then be trampled under the cattle's hooves. Most times the only way to stop a stampede was to get in front of the leaders and circle them around.

In the first story notes, Gantry was named Pike. Being seventy-five years old in 1880, Pike came from a culture "where if you decide a man committed a murder, you strung him up. You didn't wait for a trial." Huggins believed a jury would be satisfied if the stiletto could be proven to be Jake's. He has the sheriff tell Mr. Tynan that they'll probably find Pike guilty of nothing more than firing a gun within city limits and maybe accidental homicide.[52] Seventy-seven-year-old Walter Brennan, who had portrayed the Kid's grandmother in a previous episode, played the affable Gantry. On the last day of filming, Huggins presented him with the "Grandma Curry" award – a wig on a stick.[53]

When Heyes and Curry admit to Gantry that they are worth $20,000, he wonders why they robbed banks. Heyes's reply that that's where the money was kept was a famous quote attributed, mistakenly, to thief Willie Sutton. Sutton was raised near Brooklyn, New York, and started his criminal career by pilfering as a child, graduating to breaking and entering. Made-up and wearing a rented uniform, he cased a bank until he was familiar with its routine and its vulnerabilities. Sutton robbed nearly one hundred banks during his career which spanned the years from the late 1920s to his final arrest in 1952. Over the years, Sutton "withdrew" roughly $2 million. He died in 1980.

Why did he rob banks? "Because I enjoyed it. I loved it. I was more alive when I was inside a bank, robbing it, than at any other time in my life. I enjoyed everything about it so much that one or two weeks later I'd be out looking for the next job." It wasn't simply because "that's where the money was kept."[54]

After a long day's work, Peter Duel and Ben Murphy appeared on Merv Griffin's talk show. It was obvious to Griffin how tired the guys were. He asked them what scenes they'd been shooting all day and Ben replied, "A lot of cattle herding with no cattle." Griffin wondered how one did that. Ben replied, "They take stock footage that we did last year with all the cattle, just to save money, and then they have us riding the horse going 'whoopee' with the hat and shooting up in to the air." Griffin wanted to know if the cattle don't have a union. "Yeah," Ben answered, "but they don't do reruns."[55]

The McCreedy Bust: Going, Going, Gone

"I'm not much of a philosopher. I just kind of take things as they come."
– Kid Curry

STORY:	JOHN THOMAS JAMES
TELEPLAY:	NICHOLAS E. BAEHR
DIRECTOR:	ALEXANDER SINGER
SHOOTING DATES:	NOVEMBER 18, 19, 22, 23, 24, 25 (H), 26, 1971
ORIGINAL US AIR DATE:	JANUARY 13, 1972
ORIGINAL UK AIR DATE:	FEBRUARY 14, 1972

Kid Curry's speed with a gun was accomplished with the "twelve-frame draw," an editing trick. Briggs was also supposed to be pretty fast with a gun and Roy Huggins assigned him a "sixteen-frame draw," making him four frames, or 1/6th of a second, slower than Curry.

In the original story, Curry's shooting of Briggs resulted not only in cementing Spencer's faith, but also in a political change in West Bend. The waiter at the cafe gives the boys a free breakfast and comments, "I got a notion a lot of people are gonna be coming in to vote next Tuesday, when this gets out – and it will."

Kid Curry sulks as he and Hannibal Heyes ride toward Red Rock because he's sure the job Big Mac has for them is to get the bust of Caesar back again. Heyes disagrees. Why would he have them return only to offer them the same job they already turned down? Before the argument goes very far, a well-armed welcoming party meets them. Heyes and Curry question, "Does this have anything to do with the job Big Mac has for us?" "Well, sure!" is the surprised reply. Heyes and Curry about-face, but the cowboys stop them.

At the ranch, the boys confer with Big Mac. He wants them to steal back the bust of Caesar, as they suspected. At their resistance, Mac plays his ace – he knows who they really are. Heyes still refuses the job, but offers to teach one of Big Mac's men how to blow the safe. Mac agrees to the compromise and gives the boys a different job instead. They will go to West Bend, a town one hundred miles west of Red Rock, and wait. When Mac's men get the bust, they'll leave it in an abandoned well outside of town. Heyes and Curry will retrieve it and take it to San Francisco where Mac plans to put it up for auction, thus ending the feud with Armendariz.

The boys ride into West Bend expecting a quiet, peaceable town but instead find cowboys racing through the streets, shooting guns and terrorizing the populace. They wonder what all the ruckus is about and a man named Spencer explains that election day is nearing. Joe Briggs, foreman of the Running W ranch, is in charge of scaring the farmers. He and his men come to town and stare at the sodbusters, subtly implying something dreadful will happen to them if they dare to vote.

That evening Heyes suggests going to the saloon and making friends. Curry doesn't think the ranchers looked too friendly, but goes along with Heyes to play poker.

Joe Briggs takes note of the guns Heyes and Curry wear as they enter the saloon. The sheriff hadn't noticed them. Briggs coldly tells him to forget about it – he'll deal with them himself.

The next morning Heyes and Curry visit the abandoned well. It's empty.

They return to town and are met by Briggs demanding to know where they went. Curry explains they were just exercising their horses, but Briggs isn't convinced. The boys try to be conciliatory, but Briggs gives them an ultimatum – tomorrow they'd better not be wearing their guns. He'll be watching.

The next day the well is still empty.

Back at the hotel, the partners fight. They got up early to avoid being seen by Briggs, but Heyes forgot they'd have to go out to have breakfast. Curry won't leave the room without wearing his gun, despite Heyes's desperate attempts to convince him it will cause nothing but trouble. Heyes blocks the door, puts up his fists and threatens to flatten him. Curry looks at the raised fists with bewilderment. "Before breakfast?" Curry solemnly promises Heyes that no matter what Briggs says, he will not lose his temper, he will not draw on him and he will be as meek as a mouse, but he's going to wear his gun.

After breakfast, they enter the saloon and find themselves face to face with Briggs. The crowd quiets as Briggs orders Curry back to the hotel to take off his gun. Curry sheepishly explains he's worn the gun so long that without it he limps. Briggs offers him a crutch. Curry then admits he feels naked without his gun, almost as if he didn't have his pants on. Briggs isn't asking him to take off his pants, just his gun. Curry calmly explains he doesn't plan to use the gun, but he doesn't like being told he can't wear it. Briggs seems convinced and if Curry will do a jig, he'll let him wear it. Curry says he doesn't know how to jig and Heyes testifies to his clumsiness. When Curry and Heyes exchange a look, Briggs pulls his gun. Apologizing for his lack of skill, Curry does a half-hearted jig. Having humiliated his prey, Briggs holsters his gun as laughter fills the saloon.

The boys take a seat at a nearby table. If the bust isn't in the well tomorrow, Curry swears to give up on this job. Heyes points out they can't do that to Mac, but Curry is adamant. Before another quarrel can erupt between them, Spencer comes to their table. During the confrontation, he watched Curry's face. Not once did he see fear, yet Curry backed down. He turned the other cheek and Spencer is curious to know why. "I guess I'm just a peaceable man," Curry offers, causing Heyes to choke on his beer. Spencer persists, certain there's a philosophical reason for Curry's actions. Curry denies being a philosopher, but Heyes contradicts him, painting him as a people's philosopher, albeit inarticulate and a bit stupid. Spencer smiles and introduces himself as the town drunk.

The next morning, Seth Griffin, one of Briggs's men, follows the boys out to

Señor Armendariz, played by Cesar Romero.

the well. Heyes keeps Seth occupied with a card trick while Curry checks the well. It's empty. Heyes assures Seth they won't tell Briggs he got caught, then they return to town.

After stabling their horses, the boys run into Briggs again. He demands another jig from Curry, who's still wearing his gun. Curry complies, inwardly fuming.

At the saloon, Spencer joins them with a bottle to share. He admits that Curry's had a great impact on him. For the second time, Curry has turned the other cheek and shown himself to be a man who instinctively believes in the spirit of love and brotherhood. Both Curry and Heyes are stunned by this interpretation of events. Spencer reveals he is a minister, but the killing, stealing, and other abominations of his congregation in Taos caused him to lose his faith, so he left the church and took up drinking. But as of now he is taking his last drink. Curry has shown him that it is possible to live by the Christian creed. With quiet thanks, Spencer walks away, leaving Heyes and Curry humbled.

It's a new day and once more Heyes and Curry head for the well. Again Seth follows, explaining that Briggs doesn't believe they're just exercising their horses. Heyes shows Seth a new card trick as Curry checks the well. The bust is there! So Heyes shows Seth yet another trick – he pulls Curry's gun and holds it on Seth as Curry ties his hands. Seth protests as Heyes blindfolds him, but he promises they'll send someone out to untie him.

Back at the hotel, Heyes wants to wait in their room until the stagecoach comes, but Curry is hungry. Incredulous, Heyes tries to dissuade him from going to the cafe by reminding him Briggs will be waiting. Does he want to do the jig again? Curry doesn't want to jig, but he does want to eat. Maybe they can slip in and out of the café without being seen. Certain that Curry will do something stupid, Heyes nevertheless buckles his gunbelt, slams on his hat and heads out the door.

Briggs is waiting for them, wanting to know where Seth is. The boys claim ignorance, but he threatens to come after them if Seth doesn't return within an hour. Then he notices Heyes is also wearing a gun. There will be two jigs today. Curry and Heyes exchange looks, then Curry turns back to Briggs and refuses. Heyes notices Spencer watching and softly urges Curry to do the jig for Spencer's sake. Curry tries to placate Briggs by promising to stay off the street as soon as they finish eating, but Briggs isn't about to let him off that easy.

Curry has had all he can take. He pulls off his glove, preparing to draw his gun. Heyes desperately wants him to turn the other cheek, but this time Curry won't budge. The two men face each other tensely. Briggs goes for his gun, but Curry beats him to the draw and shoots him in the arm.

Curry turns to the disillusioned Spencer. What did he expect? Did he think Curry was a saint? Spencer remains silent, a sick look on his face. Curry angrily accuses Spencer of leaving his congregation because the people in Taos weren't saints either, then offers one last observation. "If we were all saints, we really wouldn't need you, now would we?"

Heyes and Curry cringe as the stagecoach driver flings the bag with the bust of Caesar on top of the coach, despite Heyes's pleas to be careful. Spencer is nowhere in sight. Curry apologizes for losing his temper, but Heyes understands. He'd be ashamed too if he couldn't do a better jig than Curry's. Spencer joins them after spending the past hour in the saloon, a drink in front of him, thinking about what Curry said, and deciding he is right. He's returning to his congregation.

Heyes and Curry meet Mac at the San Francisco auction. Only one man bids on the bust, a bid so low Mac bids against him. "That's your own property!" Heyes reminds him, stopping him from placing yet another bid. The bust sells for $1,200. As the buyer pays the auctioneer and carries off his prize, Señor Armendariz enters and greets him happily. The man hands over the bust. Armendariz smiles at Mac. "I think we can agree now, Señor McCreedy, that the bust is mine. Can we not?" Stunned, Mac opens his mouth to offer the boys another job, but they cut him off. The answer is no.

GUEST CAST

BURL IVES	PATRICK J. "BIG MAC" MCCREEDY
BRADFORD DILLMAN	SPENCER
LEE MAJORS	JOE BRIGGS
CESAR ROMERO	SEÑOR ERNESTO ARMENDARIZ
TED GEHRING	SETH GRIFFIN
PAUL MICALE	LITTLE MAN
NEIL RUSSELL	SHERIFF
ROBERT P. LIEB	AUCTIONEER
MITCH CARTER	LUKE
JOHN RAYNER	MAN
JERRY HARPER	POKER PLAYER #1
DANIEL FRANCIS MARTIN	DEALER
HAL NEEDHAM	DUKE

Hannibal Heyes and Kid Curry are somewhat unusual television heroes for the 1970s because they actually are crooks. They are the good guys of the series, but unlike Dr. Richard Kimble in *The Fugitive* or Jason McCord in *Branded*, Heyes and Curry are guilty of their crimes and mostly unrepentant, despite their decision to change their ways. This made them challenging characters to develop without alienating the audience. Roy Huggins recalled:

> I had the problem of how do you make them functioning human beings who don't rob banks and don't steal money from very rich men, but who actually live law-abiding lives? Well, they did, and they did because they had to, but they also had the inherent humanity to do so without its coming apart and having them go slightly berserk. Which, actually, in most cases would have happened. In most cases, within a year one or both would have gone absolutely berserk and gone out and committed robbery and murder and ended up the rest of their lives in jail.[56]

In this episode, Curry faces his ultimate test – can he handle Joe Briggs without going berserk?

Curry's adversary delights in humiliating him, yet he can't respond as he would like because of his promise to stay out of trouble. The writers pile on the stress, boxing Curry in with his duty to Big Mac, his promise to Heyes to keep Briggs placated, and his need to live up to Spencer's expectations of him as a man who turns the other cheek. The pressure builds and the audience waits breathlessly to see if Curry will break. He does. But by finally losing his temper and shooting Briggs, Curry actually has a much more significant impact on Spencer than he did by meek conciliation. Curry's forceful example of why ministers are needed provides Spencer with faith bolstered by the hard realities of life rather than the lofty idealism of the Christian creed.

The tension between Curry and Briggs is masterfully played. Real antagonism between Ben Murphy and Lee Majors helped it along. The two actors were continually trying to one-up each other. "If you didn't cry, you would break up laughing," director Alex Singer remembers. "Two leading men who are trying to outdo each other is either the funniest thing or the most tragic thing, depending on where you are. If you're an outsider, they're hilarious. If you're trying to make a film with them, you want to blow your brains out – after you shoot them."[57]

Singer found it difficult to be patient with Lee Majors, who saw himself as "the new Clark Gable or the new Something." He knew the actor was not a great performer and, when he was cast, Jo Swerling announced, "The good news is we got Lee Majors; the bad news is we got Lee Majors." To temper this, they also had Bradford Dillman. Singer felt it was worth putting up with Majors's overblown ego in order to work with Dillman. "Every time we had to get [Majors] on the set, there was a difficulty because his feet dragged. The message was: 'I am a star. I move at *my* pace. You'll not hurry me, I'm too important.'"

Singer remembers losing one battle with the recalcitrant actor. In the final confrontation between Curry and Briggs, Briggs says, "You've got exactly two seconds to start dancing, in which case life goes on. Or you can start walking across the street, in which case life doesn't go on." Majors consistently misread the line, missing the obvious emphasis in the second sentence. Singer tried to explain to him that the line should be read ". . . in which case, life *doesn't* go on." The actor simply looked at him and said, "Look, you're the director. Let me do the acting. Don't tell me how to read my lines." So Singer gave up and let him read the line in the flat, awkward way that appears on screen. Despite the difficulties with his actors, Singer felt the result was one of the better shows, an assessment with which most viewers would agree.

THE MAN WHO BROKE THE BANK AT RED GAP

"There goes our amnesty! Not to mention that we'll be hunted with a little more enthusiasm now that we're Number One."
– *Kid Curry*

STORY:	JOHN THOMAS JAMES
TELEPLAY:	BRONSON HOWITZER AND JOHN THOMAS JAMES
DIRECTOR:	RICHARD BENEDICT
SHOOTING DATES:	DECEMBER 9, 10, 13, 14, 15, 16, 1971
ORIGINAL US AIR DATE:	JANUARY 20, 1972
ORIGINAL UK AIR DATE:	APRIL 16, 1973

As a train carries them to Black River, Hannibal Heyes and Kid Curry play parlor poker with banker Chester Powers for fun, not money. Heyes inquires whether straights and flushes are allowed in the game. It once cost him $20,000 to learn they are not unless declared so at the beginning of play. Advising him not to go into the banking business, at which Heyes grins at Curry, Powers says knowledge like that can be exploited for gain; it's a basic business principle. Winford Fletcher, a passenger in the same train car, recognizes the boys from a previous encounter and observes the conversation from behind his newspaper.

When the train pulls into Colton, Fletcher makes his move. Holding a gun on them, he orders Heyes and Curry to get up; he's removing them from the train. They protest his calling them by those names, saying they are often mistaken for the two miserable outlaws, but they are *not* Hannibal Heyes and Kid Curry.

When Heyes and Curry first encounter Fletcher in one of Clementine's schemes, she's very precise in toasting his downfall. "To Win-ford Fletcher," she pronounces. It's too bad the set decorator did not consult the script for this episode. If he had, he would not have painted Fletcher's office door with his first name as Winfred.

No women appear in this episode.

Up to now, Roger Davis, in the opening narration, introduced Heyes and Curry as "two latter-day Robin Hoods." Beginning with this episode, they were known as "Kansas cousins."

Fletcher knows better.

Banker Powers argues with Fletcher that he should let the men stay on board, but Fletcher remembers not too long ago when their swindle cost him a small fortune. Powers insists he has a cocked two-barrel .60 caliber derringer pointed at Fletcher from under the table.

The threat convinces Fletcher to leave them be for now, but he will shoot if they try to get off before Black River. As Fletcher leaves the car, Curry congratulates Powers on his bluff – they don't make a .60 caliber derringer. Winford Fletcher's words had a ring of truth to them, however, and convinced Powers of their identity. Heyes, believing uncharacteristically that honesty is the best policy, wonders why a *banker* would help Heyes and Curry. Powers helped them out of the sticky situation because he sees a need and how they can help fill it, another basic business principle.

Powers needs someone with imagination, courage, and a little desperation. Curry explains that they've mended their desperate ways. Powers offers them $500 to do a job, but won't tell them what it is until they reach Red Gap. About seven miles outside of town, while the train is trudging up a steep grade, the boys should jump off and make their way to town. Powers will keep Fletcher busy by engaging him in conversation.

For some unfathomable reason or maybe the $500 each, the boys agree and start the long walk to town, the train disappearing into the distance.

Fletcher barges into the sleeping Powers's railroad car with news that Heyes and Curry are no longer on board. He is angry, having lost $20,000 in reward money, and threatens to sue the eyes out of Powers's head. The banker apologizes, then offers Fletcher $2,000 to settle out of court, plus a share of the reward when the posse catches them. His generous offer pleases Fletcher.

Heyes and Curry walk on in the dark, stopping occasionally to remove stones from their boots. Seven long miles later, they gingerly pick their way into town, trying not to let their blistered feet touch the ground. The two strangers interest Sheriff McWhirter. How did they get to Red Gap? They say they had to walk when their horses were stolen. His job, the sheriff explains patiently, is to take complaints from victims of horse thieves. Heyes offers their aching feet as an excuse. They need at least four or five whiskeys first to dull the pain.

Next day, as Curry inspects his tender feet, Heyes reports that Powers is in his office. They wonder why he's not contacting them. Maybe he's waiting for them to heal up.

After a day of playing poker, Heyes and Curry return to their room and find a note from the banker. "Meet me at the granary three miles out on River Road at ten o'clock. P.S. Burn this note." Curry is not sure he likes the sound of that.

At 10:30, after a no-show by Powers, they are even less sure they like the sound and sight of a posse headed their way. Back in town, they learn that the Red Gap bank has been robbed. Figuring they were set up, they hop a freight train conveniently headed out of town.

In Hillsboro, the *News Courier's* headline proclaims "Curry and Heyes in Record Robbery." According to the press, the outlaws got away with $80,000 and a half million dollars in securities and negotiable bonds – the largest robbery ever west of the Mississippi. Winford Fletcher came from Silver Springs to corroborate the bank president's testimony about seeing them on the train.

The news angers Heyes, so they return to Red Gap and break into Powers's house. To their surprise, he's waiting for them and offers them each a brandy and $10,000 for "robbing his bank." His generous offer exemplifies another basic business principle – everybody profits. He kept $60,000; the stocks and bonds he had speculated with and lost long ago. Now, all is well, confidence in his bank is restored and his credit is good.

Since he already knows their true identities, they tell Powers about their amnesty deal. He pooh-poohs the idea and counters with his better one that they take the money and move to South America. When Curry argues vociferously that they just want their amnesty, Heyes restrains his friend and feigns interest in Powers's plan. He stuffs the bundles of money under his arm and they set off for the train. On board, Heyes schemes.

In a broken down shack off a deserted street populated only by tumbleweeds, Heyes and Curry persuade two members of the Devil's Hole Gang who faintly resemble them to impersonate them. The men will need to create a commotion in Harristown on the night of the tenth making sure they identify themselves as Heyes and Curry. Kyle will go along.

Meanwhile, Heyes and Curry visit Fletcher and offer him the $20,000 that Powers gave them, the exact amount Powers stopped him from collecting on them. They ask him to return to Red Gap and testify that Powers robbed his own bank, but Fletcher is fearful of the powerful banker and refuses. The boys must resort to Plan B.

In the wee hours, they climb through a window into the bank. Curry hopes Kyle and the others are hurrahing Harristown as planned but, doubting Kyle can even read a calendar, Curry is worried. Heyes greets his old nemesis, a Pierce & Hamilton '78. Working quietly and carefully, they prepare the safe for a nitro treatment.

Some time later, they return to Fletcher's office, this time emptying their satchel onto his desk. Out drop bundles of the bank's money. With Fletcher's help, they hope to prove that Powers robbed his bank a second time. This time Heyes and Curry couldn't have done it because "they" were three hundred miles north in Harristown. Once more they offer him the $20,000 if he'll tell what he knows about Powers. Agreeing to this surefire plan, Fletcher greedily begins to count the bills.

That evening, with the money in a satchel, Heyes and Curry break into Powers's home. Noiselessly, they search for a place to hide the bag. They stuff it up the fireplace, but it falls down and creates such a clatter Powers is awakened. With candle and shotgun in hand, he investigates the noise and, just to be sure nothing's been disturbed, checks his wall safe hidden behind a painting. Heyes and Curry watch with interest from their hiding place outside under the window. Satisfied that all is secure, the banker heads back to bed. They debate their chances of getting back in to hide the money. Meanwhile a troop of lawmen gallops feverishly on their way to Powers's house.

Once more inside, Heyes presses his ear against the combination lock of the safe and begins to turn the dial. Anxious moments later, he opens the door, but the moneybag won't fit. A sudden loud banging on his door awakens Powers again, as Heyes and Curry scramble to cram the money into the already full safe.

Powers opens his door to Red Gap's Sheriff McWhirter, Assistant Territorial Attorney General Collins, his assistants, and Winford Fletcher. Just as Heyes slams the safe door and the two climb back out the window, Powers leads the lawmen into his study. They have a warrant to search his house on Fletcher's word that Powers conspired to use Heyes and Curry as a ruse while he robbed his own bank.

As the boys watch through the window, Powers lets them search anywhere, even his safe. No one is more surprised than he to see the moneybag in it. Dumping it out onto the desk, Collins assumes it's the loot from the second robbery. Powers blusters that it had to be Heyes and Curry who stole it and put it there. Collins's assistant notes that some came from the first robbery – $20,000 of it. Suddenly Fletcher is aghast.

He hastens back to his office, opens his safe and finds, not the $20,000 Heyes and Curry had given him, but a note from J. Smith advising him to get a better safe.

From a high ridge, the boys watch as the lawmen lead Powers away in handcuffs. There's one basic business principle Powers didn't know. "Crime doesn't pay," quotes Heyes. "Nope," Curry says, "Never get involved in another man's game."

GUEST CAST

BRODERICK CRAWFORD	CHESTER E. POWERS
RUDY VALLEE	WINFORD FLETCHER
FORD RAINEY	ASST. ATTORNEY GEN. COLLINS
DENNIS FIMPLE	KYLE MURTRY
CLARKE GORDON	SHERIFF MCWHIRTER
JERRY HARPER	TOWNSMAN
BILL TOOMEY	JENKINS
JOE SCHNEIDER	JESS
RICHARD WRIGHT	BILLY

Roy Huggins told the story to Ric Hardman and originally titled it "The Man Who Broke the Bank at Red *Rock*" because in it he brought back Ralph Peterson, the banker from "The McCreedy Bust." When they encounter him again on the train, Peterson is playing poker with Edgar Simpkins, an insurance man from San Francisco. Simpkins recognizes Heyes and Curry from a train he was on that they held up. Following the same story line, they enter Red Rock on foot and encounter the sheriff from "The McCreedy Bust" who welcomes them back to town. Later, when they're arguing with Peterson in his study, Heyes reveals that they're hoping the Governor of Wyoming will do for them what the Governor of Colorado did for Billy Brewster, i.e., give them amnesty someday. When they need to break into the bank's safe, Huggins wanted to "use the same technique we used in 'How to Rob a Bank in One Hard Lesson' . . . we can probably use a lot of the stock from that picture."[58] While they're robbing Peterson's bank, two strangers who vaguely look like Heyes and Curry will be hurrahing Charleytown. It's been real quiet in Charleytown and the town council is thinking of doing away with the sheriff's job. The sheriff happens to be Heyes's cousin Duke. No town would stand for firing the sheriff after Heyes and Curry had been seen there.[59]

Three weeks later, the first draft of the teleplay came in, written by Bronson Howitzer, an alias of Ric Hardman (?). Shortly thereafter, Chester Powers was substituted for Ralph Peterson and Edgar Simpkins, "a whey faced worried looking accountant in his forties"[60] became Winford Fletcher. "Followers of the restless lives of Curry and Heyes . . . will recognize Winford Fletcher instantly as the greedy victim of Clementine's virtuous vendetta."[61] Fletcher may have lost a fortune, but he apparently didn't do any jail time.

When Powers invites the boys to play poker, Heyes replies that Whist is his game. Unless betting heavily on the outcome, Whist seems much too tame for the risk-taker in Heyes. He merely used the old gambit to con the other players into believing he was a novice poker player. However, his remark about it once costing him $20,000 to learn a Hoyle rule disproves his original story. No amateur would deliberately find himself involved in a game with a $20,000 pot.

With the kind of money available to them from all of the safes they've robbed, Heyes and Curry could have taken off for South America as did Butch and Sundance. Laying low for a few years and then returning to find that the governor had granted the amnesty in their absence may have been a good plan. In several other episodes, the boys discussed it. In "Everything Else You Can Steal," Heyes tells Jenny they may head for South America. That they don't speak "South American" may be a deterrent, she says. When Heyes wins big in "The Biggest Game in the West," Curry suggests they take the money and go to China. Indeed, if Glen Larson had his way, the boys may have gone to London and had a run-in with Jack the Ripper.[62] But when the suggestion comes from Chester Powers, Curry strongly reiterates that, though they may have considered the idea, they like it right here, thank you, and want to stay. That Powers would have them abscond with stolen money plays a part in Curry's resistance. They have expended so much time and effort into striving for amnesty, Curry is not about to give it up, no matter how basic a business principle it is.

At the end of the story, the federal agents identify the money from the first robbery. Nowadays all US currency looks the same, but Huggins was aware that in the 1880s, each bank issued its own money. Bills from one bank could look quite different from any other and, therefore, would be easy to identify. The money from the first robbery was issued by the bank in St. Louis.[63]

THE MEN THAT CORRUPTED HADLEYBURG

"What made us go the way we went? How come you and I ended up with warrants for our arrest that could put us in jail for twenty years?"
– Kid Curry

STORY:	JOHN THOMAS JAMES
TELEPLAY:	DICK NELSON AND JOHN THOMAS JAMES
DIRECTOR:	JEFF COREY
SHOOTING DATES:	DECEMBER 17, 20, 21, 22, 23, 24, 1971
ORIGINAL US AIR DATE:	JANUARY 27, 1972
ORIGINAL UK AIR DATE:	APRIL 23, 1973

This episode, like "Something to Get Hung About," started off being called "The Tapscott Trial." In this case, the character's name remained Tapscott and there was a trial, but Roy Huggins instead chose to give a nod to Mark Twain, who provided the inspiration for Heyes's plan to save the family.

Hannibal Heyes and Kid Curry lurk anxiously outside the Denver office of Bannerman Detectives, Inc., waiting for their old friend Harry Briscoe. When he appears they each grab an elbow and steer him into the nearby saloon for a talk.

Harry hunches his collar up to his ears, not wanting to be seen with them. Heyes tells Harry they need a big favor. Harry reluctantly agrees he owes them something, so he listens to their story, even though he has a feeling he isn't going to like it.

Curry and Heyes were in Yuma when they spotted a sheriff who knew them. They barely escaped his notice and decided to head into the hills where they found a nice spot to camp and fish and reflect upon the course their lives have taken. Curry wonders why they ended up with a price on their heads. Heyes figures it's because they grew up in the middle of a brutal civil war and lost their parents at a young age. Curry is still skeptical and Heyes admits his theory is probably just a way of making himself feel better. Their musings are interrupted by a demand that they put their hands up.

Prospector Matt Tapscott, his wife Bess and young son Tommy have overheard every word. They're going to take the boys to Hadleyburg and turn them in.

Heyes and Curry ride in the back of the Tapscotts' wagon, securely tied and barely able to keep their balance as the wagon bounces over ruts. When Matt asks for a drink of water, Bess hands the rifle over to her son. The wagon hits a rock, sending Tommy and the rifle flying, and Curry promptly stomps on the gun, holding it down with his foot. "Why'd you do that?" the boy asks when Curry kicks it over to him. Curry explains, with his hands tied he can't pick up the gun. They'd have to knock him out, jump off the wagon and hope his parents didn't see them. "Knocking a tough kid like you out, now that's not easy," says Heyes. Tommy smiles.

That night over supper, the boys get to know the Tapscotts a little better. Matt tells them how he missed out on the biggest strike this side of Virginia City because he chose the wrong direction to take at a fork in the road, but the $20,000 he'll get for turning in the outlaws will suit him just fine. Heyes reveals the amnesty deal. Matt is sympathetic to their plight, but he's still going to turn them in.

In Hadleyburg, Matt does just that, to the delight of the sheriff. He confirms the amount of the reward and instructs Matt on how to collect it. The prospector has finally struck pay dirt.

That night the Tapscotts have a celebratory dinner, but the celebration falls flat. Matt tries to buoy his family's spirits with the prospect of all that money, but it's no use. They're all miserable.

Before Matt can visit the boys in jail, the sheriff searches him and finds the gun he's got stuck in the back of his pants. He explains that he always carries it there, because he's no gunfighter. Heyes and Curry watch this exchange, hiding their smiles. Matt tries to strike up a conversation, but there's not much to say. Learning the boys don't like the food, he offers to have Bess cook something for them. Matt leaves and a puzzled Heyes remarks, "I don't understand it, but I do appreciate it."

The next day the deputy brings over a blackberry pie that Bess baked. As he cuts into it, Curry indulges in a little wishful thinking. "Wouldn't it be funny if I started cutting into this pie and there's a file in it?" Heyes tells him he's been reading too many dime novels. Clink! Curry digs into the pie with his fingers and comes up with a gun. Heyes wraps it in a napkin and hides it. The boys wolf down the rest of the pie planning their escape.

When the sheriff relieves the deputy on watch, Heyes calls him over and points the gun at him. The lawman is dismayed at this turn of events, opening the cell door and asking the boys if they really think they're doing the right thing. Pretty sure, Curry assures him. They leave the sheriff bound and gagged in the cell and escape.

Another round of beers is delivered as Heyes finishes telling Harry what happened. The most fascinating thing, Harry thinks, is that it doesn't have anything to do with him. Curry reveals why it does. As a Bannerman detective he can wire Hadleyburg inquiring about the Tapscotts without raising suspicion. The boys want to make sure they're all right.

They wait outside the telegraph office while Harry sends the inquiry. The response is what they feared – the Tapscotts are about to go on trial for aiding and abetting the escape of two outlaws. Harry suggests they break the Tapscotts out of jail, but Curry points out that making fugitives of them isn't in the best interests of their son. Harry realizes there's nothing the boys can do for the Tapscotts, but they could do something to help him with his job in Colorado Springs. A wealthy Denver man lost $17,000 at the Silver Palace casino there and has now hired the BDI to prove the games are crooked. Heyes agrees to help Harry, because he's thought of a way it will help the Tapscotts too.

At the Silver Palace, Heyes introduces himself as Carleton Balfour and begins his first hand of blackjack. As soon as the hand is dealt, Heyes informs the manager, Mr. Phillips, that the house is using a marked deck. Phillips bristles and denies anyone could have introduced a marked deck into the casino. Heyes demonstrates, announcing the value of each card before turning it over. Harry steps up and confiscates the deck. Heyes apologizes to Phillips for not keeping the matter private, but he had no idea a Bannerman detective was lurking nearby. The manager takes a new deck from the bottom drawer in the table and the gambling begins.

Heyes wins consistently. Finally the dealer consults with Phillips, who's certain there can't be any system in blackjack, so sooner or later the percentages will switch back in the casino's favor. The game continues, and so does Heyes's winning streak.

Phillips finally figures out that Mr. Balfour is memorizing the cards as they're played, making large bets only when there are about twelve cards left in the deck and he can be fairly certain of what they are. This puts the odds way out in his favor. Phillips advises the dealer to reshuffle the deck when he reaches the middle from now on.

Heyes protests when the deck is reshuffled, but Phillips calmly explains there is no rule against it, either in Hoyle or in the house rules. Heyes is good-natured about being found out, content with the $32,000 he's won. But before he goes, he'd like to see what kind of cards they keep in the *top* drawer of the table. Curry's gun stops Phillips from objecting while Heyes and Harry check out the cards under the watchful eye of the local marshal. They're marked. "Show him your warrant, Marshal," Harry says. "I think the Silver Palace just went out of business."

In Hadleyburg, Attorney Brubaker arrives to represent the Tapscotts. He asks the judge for a delay while he prepares his defense. The surly judge isn't inclined to be helpful, but Brubaker insists and finally the judge agrees, not wanting his verdict to be overturned by an appeals court.

Hadleyburg, a shabby little town, is undergoing a flurry of civic improvements. Brubaker strolls along the main street, noting with satisfaction the large signs proclaiming the construction is compliments of Hannibal Heyes and Kid Curry. From their vantage point in a tree outside of town, Heyes and Curry watch the workers through binoculars, pleased at how well Brubaker is handling things. Curry is kind of choked up about it. "You mean, all the good we're doing for Hadleyburg?" Heyes asks. "No," Curry replies. "All the money it's costing us."

As the trial comes to an end, the prosecutor gives his summation, but he has difficulty whipping up any enthusiasm for his case and trails off, saying the prosecution rests. The judge is incensed. "Rests? If you want my opinion, it laid down and died." The judge takes over, pointing out that Hadleyburg is enjoying the benefits of Heyes and Curry's largesse, but the jury should realize that the two outlaws have spent at least $25,000 on the town. Where did they get that money? They got it by robbing banks and holding up trains! Mr. Brubaker objects. He has a witness who can disprove that prejudicial statement.

The judge re-opens the trial and Brubaker calls Harry Briscoe to the stand. Harry testifies that Heyes won over $32,000 exposing the crooked games at the Silver Palace. The judge sinks back in defeat and the jury wastes no time in acquitting the Tapscotts.

Harry leaves the courtroom and fires a rocket from the middle of the street in celebration. Heyes and Curry see the signal, happy to learn the Tapscotts are free.

GUEST CAST

J.D. CANNON	HARRY BRISCOE
ANDY DEVINE	SHERIFF PINTELL
SHEREE NORTH	BESS TAPSCOTT
WALLY COX	MATT TAPSCOTT
DAVE GARROWAY	JUDGE MARTIN
DANIEL FRANCIS MARTIN	JURY FOREMAN
ADAM WEST	MR. BRUBAKER
DAVID GRUNER	TOMMY TAPSCOTT
FREDERIC DOWNS	MR. HANSON
BILL ANDERSON	COBB
GENE EVANS	PHILLIPS
ROBERT GOODEN	DEPUTY

The title of this episode comes from a short story by Mark Twain. In that tale, the citizens of Hadleyburg had an unassailable reputation for honesty which they jealously guarded from all temptation. But faced with the opportunity to claim a fortune through lies and deceit, each of the leading citizens succumbs to the lure of corruption that would lead to riches rather than maintaining the integrity that would keep them poor. Heyes uses the same psychology to gain public sympathy for the Tapscotts and ensure their acquittal.

Roy Huggins was always concerned with the historical accuracy of the show, yet he would occasionally accept some stretching of dates. *Life on the Mississippi* was published in 1883, putting it within the acceptable range for Heyes and Curry to have knowledge of it, but "The Man That Corrupted Hadleyburg" wasn't published until 1899, so Heyes was allowed to come up with his plan for corrupting the citizens of Hadleyburg here without any help from Twain. In the early drafts of the script, when Curry hopes for a hidden file inside the blackberry pie, Heyes tells him he's read *The Prisoner of Zenda* too many times. Huggins made a note to check on the publication date of this novel and, finding it was published in 1894, deleted the reference and changed it to "too many dime novels" instead.

"The Men That Corrupted Hadleyburg" was the last episode to finish filming before Peter Duel's death. It typically took two to three weeks to finish post-production once principal photography was completed and this episode was no exception. By January 7, 1972, the show had been edited, with music and sound effects added. But there was a problem. Parts of the soundtrack were bad, not an uncommon occurrence, and Peter Duel's death forced the studio to make another tough decision. Having already decided to keep the show in production, they didn't want to lose an episode just because of the soundtrack issues. Paul Frees, a talented voice actor, was hired to imitate Peter's voice and replace the dialogue in the bad sections. Luckily only a few scenes needed to be looped: where Heyes and Curry are outside the Bannerman Detective Agency waiting for Harry Briscoe; where Heyes and Curry share a campfire supper with the Tapscotts; and where Harry tells them of the Tapscott's fate. Jo Swerling remembers the agony of that dubbing session. "It was awful . . . it was just one of the little shades of awfulness that [was] added when we had to replace those scenes with another actor, however good he was or hard he tried . . . [Paul Frees] came in and listened to the tracks and did a remarkable job. But I cringe when I think of how we all felt when we were doing it. We just wanted to quit."[64]

When the final day's shooting on this episode was over, no one knew that tragedy was soon to strike. It was Christmas Eve, 1971. After wrapping things up, the cast and crew attended a Christmas party where they cracked open a bottle of champagne Peter Duel had provided to celebrate the season. One more episode was in the can, and the holiday weekend was upon them. Spirits were high. A week later everything would change.

CHAPTER 6

DECEMBER 31, 1971

Friday, December 31, 1971, dawned bright and clear. The rain that had been pounding Los Angeles all month finally moved on, ensuring that the annual Tournament of Roses Parade on New Year's Day would once again enjoy dry, sunny weather. Director Alex Singer was on his way to the studio for another day of shooting on his current assignment – an episode of *Alias Smith and Jones*. He took a shortcut through Hollywood Hills, listening to the radio as he drove. The morning news came on and in stunned disbelief he listened as the reporter announced that Peter Duel was found dead in his house with a gunshot wound to his head. He pulled the car over to the side of the road and just sat there staring out the window. "I'd never heard that, I'd never heard of somebody that I knew killing themselves."[1]

Thursday, December 30, had been a normal day on the set. It was the fourth day of shooting "The Biggest Game in the West" and the schedule called for filming a big poker game. The complex scene involved several master shots and numerous two-shots as well as close-ups of Peter and all of the guest stars. Peter was in a good mood and had been throughout the shoot, turning in an excellent performance. Jo Swerling remembers, "They were the best dailies that any of us remember. There seemed to be something extra dynamic about his performance . . . his work was impressive in that episode, more so than in the others."[2]

When shooting wrapped for the day, Peter planned to go to the movies to see *A Clockwork Orange* with friend Dennis Fimple. But at the last minute, Peter was called back to do some looping for "The McCreedy Bust: Going, Going, Gone." Fimple had already seen the film and was only going to keep Peter company, so the delay caused Fimple to reconsider. "I don't want to go and sit while you do looping and then go to a movie," he told his friend. Peter was fine with that, saying, "We'll catch it next time."[3] The looping session didn't take too long, and Peter was home in time to tune in that night's broadcast of *Alias Smith and Jones* – "Miracle At Santa Marta." Peter, girlfriend Diane Ray and friend Hal Frizzell watched the show together. When it was over, Frizzell left and Peter switched over to the Lakers basketball game. The Lakers were trying for their thirtieth straight win, a feat no sports team had ever accomplished.[4] Throughout the evening, as he often did, Peter drank heavily. Diane went to bed before the game was over and was awakened when Peter came into the bedroom and retrieved his gun. Peter's last words to the half-asleep Diane were "I'll see you later." Shortly afterward, she heard a gunshot and went to the living room to find Peter dead.

No one will ever know exactly what went through his mind that night. Those who were around him can only offer observations, naturally tempered by their own perceptions. Did Peter finally reach the end of his rope and consciously decide to kill himself? Jo Swerling believes so. "He was very subject to massive mood changes. That was one of the sides to his personality and I suppose contributed to what happened." Peter had been upbeat the week before his death and, in hindsight, Swerling wonders if his exceptionally dynamic performance was the result of having made the decision to die. "That sort of fits into this thing one hears about suicidal people . . . when they make up their mind that they're going to do it, they all of a sudden for a brief period feel like the monkey's off their back and the albatross is not around their neck anymore and they seem happy. And then, boom, they're out the window." But while Swerling feels this psychology might apply to Peter, he admits that no one will ever know what really happened. "Why that night? . . . We'll never know."[5]

(Courtesy of Ben Murphy)

Monty Laird had a different theory. Despite Peter's depression, Laird believed that his actions were not deliberate, but accidental. Peter had a bad habit of playing around with the gun he wore as Hannibal Heyes, especially while sitting in makeup. He'd aim to the right, "bang," to the left, "bang," and at his head, "bang." This disturbed Laird, who told him on numerous occasions not to fool around and to treat guns with more respect. His admonitions made no impression on the actor. When Peter was on the set this game was harmless because the gun wasn't loaded, but it led to a dangerous habit. Was Peter's suicide the result of him fooling around with a gun that was loaded? There's no way to know, but Laird was convinced this was the answer.[6]

Dennis Fimple, never certain if Peter's death was suicide or accident, nevertheless always blamed himself. "If I'd stayed and gone with him [to the movies] maybe it wouldn't have happened," Fimple recalled sadly, still missing his friend decades later. He was familiar with Peter's problem with alcohol and felt it contributed to his death. "He would be fine, smoke grass or whatever, he would be *fine,* but he'd start drinking and it was like – oh no. He'd reach a point where, you know, he ain't coming back, he's gonna go on."[7] That night Peter did indeed go on, mixing large quantities of alcohol with a loaded gun.

Whether his death was a deliberate act or the result of drunken carelessness remains a mystery. What is undeniable is that Peter Duel suffered from depression.

Clinical depression is widely recognized today and is considered to be the common cold of psychiatric disorders,[8] however, it was not so widely known in 1971. Peter exhibited classic symptoms but they sounded no warning bells to those around him. Moodiness in an actor was nothing unusual – most people called it "artistic temperament." But depression is an illness, not a mood. It's a chemical imbalance in the brain that makes it almost physically impossible to feel happiness, to have fun, to put life's problems into proper perspective. Nowadays anti-depressant medications offer help to sufferers by restoring their brain chemistry to more normal levels. Recognition of the illness has led to advances in therapy and a lessening of the stigma attached to psychiatric disorders, leading more people to seek help.

Peter Duel gave many interviews during his years in Hollywood and as we look back at them, certain comments he made stand out starkly against the events of December 30/31. In March 1967, *Modern Screen* published an article in which Peter described his feelings at the age of sixteen. "I didn't see one thing in my future that I really wanted . . . I was down, terribly depressed. That's when I decided to commit suicide. I thought about it for a long time. I felt useless."[9] The author of the article passes this off as teenage angst and contrasts it with his new status as Hollywood heartthrob following his success in *Love on a Rooftop.* But these feelings were an early symptom of Peter's lifelong struggle with depression and not just a passing phase of adolescence. In another 1967 interview, Peter offered this viewpoint, "I don't believe that anyone is ever perfectly contented in any situation. That's a fact of life we have to accept."[10] To Peter, accustomed to the debilitating effects of depression on his ability to feel happiness, a lack of contentment seemed normal and he would probably not have believed that many people do feel perfectly contented in their lives, despite tribulations they face. As

Peter Duel as Hannibal Heyes.

family and friends struggled to understand Peter's suicide, his sister Pamela observed that Peter magnified his problems out of all proportion, "He couldn't cope."[11] Co-star Ben Murphy recalls that "he took everything to heart. If a whale died off the coast that bothered Peter. Social injustice bothered Peter. He was an idealist to the core."[12] Jo Swerling echoes this view. "The impression that I had of Peter was that he tended to assume the responsibility for the evils of the world. You know, as long as people were starving in India, he was frustrated because he couldn't do anything about it."[13] His inner sense of worthlessness, another common symptom of depression, was only exacerbated by his compassion for others, leading him to take upon himself the blame for social ills. Shortly before his death, Peter commented to an interviewer, "I can't help myself. I live with a constant feeling of futility and frustration." The reporter noted that Peter's "voice had a ring of doom."[14] To someone suffering from clinical depression, those feelings of worthlessness make every setback seem insurmountable and it is impossible to face problems with any sort of optimism that things will eventually improve. In Peter's case, his depression led to his feeling of being trapped in his Universal contract, forced to perform in a series that, on his bad days, he considered to be "trash." In a normal mental state, he'd have seen that *Alias Smith and Jones* was not trash, but instead a charming and witty western, that it entertained millions of people and, if that weren't enough, well, contracts can be broken or renegotiated.

So on that December night, fortified with alcohol, Peter Duel pulled the trigger of a loaded gun. He ended his own pain, but the pain only began for his family, his friends and his fans.

❧

News of Peter's death spread quickly. The coroner officially pronounced him dead at 1:33 a.m. and within two hours the media had latched on to the story. Local radio stations began broadcasting the news before dawn and, by the time the city woke to face the new day, the *Los Angeles Times* was alerting its readers with the banner headline "'Alias Smith' Shot to Death."

While the police located the Deuel family in New York, the Hollywood grapevine was operating in full force. Dorothy Bailey, Roy Huggins's secretary, was the first member of the *Alias Smith and Jones* production team to learn of Peter's death. She was awakened at 4:00 a.m. by a phone call from a relative who heard the news on the radio while working the swing shift. Bailey was a good friend of Peter's and had even dated him briefly. The tragic news devastated her. In hysterics, she called Jo Swerling.

Swerling raced over to Bailey's apartment and spent the next half hour calming her down. When she regained control of herself, together they called Roy Huggins, waking him up to break the news. Huggins recalled, "I immediately decided that the show was cancelled. That was it." He told Swerling to begin shutting down the production company. Neither man wanted Ben Murphy to learn of his co-star's death through the media so, before heading to Universal, Swerling and Bailey stopped at Ben's apartment.[15]

It was now a little before 6:00 a.m. Instead of his alarm clock, Ben was roused by them knocking on his door. He was shocked, but not surprised by Peter's suicide. Ben always looked up to Peter as a talented and experienced actor, but he'd had a premonition that one day Peter would screw things up for him. Now he'd done it, although not the way Ben expected. He thought Peter would break his contract or in some way sabotage the show, not end his life. "His psychology was set up to view it as a trap," Ben explains, "So, it was doomed. . . .The more success [the show] had, the more he would have felt trapped and undermined it." The two men had been amicable co-workers, but not close friends. Still, it seemed to Ben that Peter was spiraling downhill, abusing alcohol and growing more depressed. "Peter and I never talked about these things," Ben admits, "but it just seemed that he was despondent about his life, his situation, even being on the show, the work." Swerling advised Ben to stay away from the studio that day. Ben took the advice.[16]

By 7:00 a.m., the crew was on the set, silently milling around, unsure what to do. Huggins and Swerling arrived at the studio expecting to shut down the company. But ABC had different plans.

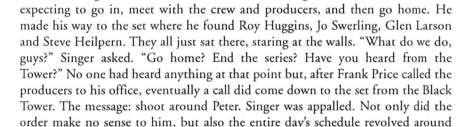

After sitting at the side of the road for awhile, Singer continued to the studio, expecting to go in, meet with the crew and producers, and then go home. He made his way to the set where he found Roy Huggins, Jo Swerling, Glen Larson and Steve Heilpern. They all just sat there, staring at the walls. "What do we do, guys?" Singer asked. "Go home? End the series? Have you heard from the Tower?" No one had heard anything at that point but, after Frank Price called the producers to his office, eventually a call did come down to the set from the Black Tower. The message: shoot around Peter. Singer was appalled. Not only did the order make no sense to him, but also the entire day's schedule revolved around Peter. How much material did they have that didn't involve him that they could possibly shoot? Singer remembers scrambling to find scenes to film. "You know, a horse riding up with some other guy on it, somebody getting off the horse and a close-up of the gun and a close-up of my foot and somehow [we] put together, not a day's work, but sort of a half day's work. It's the first time in my life that I watched a crew and, not only watched them, but cheered them on internally for working at a snail's pace. It was a way of saying 'You shouldn't do this to us.'"[17]

∞∞∞

Up in Universal's Black Tower, Frank Price was also in a state of shock. "It was devastating," Price remembers. "I liked [Peter] a lot. He was an interesting guy to talk to, troubled in some ways, but bright and thoughtful."[18] Besides facing the personal heartbreak of Peter's death, Price was also frustrated by what had happened. The series that he nurtured and fought for now had the potential to be as dead as its star. "Here's this series that we loved, that was hard to keep alive, to keep on the air. This could have been the blow that really got it cancelled." Price also found himself besieged by the press. Reporters were outside, clamoring for information, eager to get all the gory details in time to meet their deadlines, but Price had nothing of real value to tell them. At this point no one knew anything for certain beyond the fact that Peter was dead. Even the manner of his death was still a matter for the police, who hadn't yet made a final determination on whether it was accident, homicide or suicide.

As the head of television for Universal, Price had to look at the matter from several different perspectives. Personally, he spent the day operating in a state of shock. Professionally, he had a job to do, which was to deliver a series to ABC and fulfill the studio's contractual obligations. Artistically, he had to decide what was best for the show – recast the role or shut down the production. The studio's obligation to the network took precedence when ABC made it clear they wanted the series to continue. As Jo Swerling remembers, "The show was doing well for them. . . .They had sold the time to sponsors and didn't want to default to (them), so they expected us to keep delivering the show. And if we didn't, they would sue us. . . .They said, 'You've got a contract. We expect you to deliver, and if you don't, you're in breach of contract and we will pursue all legal remedies.'"[19] Peter Duel's death put ABC in a tough spot and they in turn put Universal in a tough spot.

In 1971, ABC was ranked third in a three-network television universe, a position they often found themselves in for a variety of reasons, not all of them relating to the quality of their programs. In the early days of radio, NBC had gotten a jump on the competition with CBS by creating two networks, which they called NBC Red and NBC Blue. The two networks offered different programming and had different affiliate stations but as the television race began, the Federal Communications Commission became concerned about a potential monopoly and created a regulation prohibiting anyone from operating two competing networks at the same time. As a result of the new law, NBC sold the smaller Blue network, whose new owner renamed it ABC.[20]

Because of its late start in the new field of television, ABC had been playing catch up from its very inception. FCC regulations limited network station ownership to five owned-and-operated stations. To further expand a network, local stations had to be signed up as affiliates. NBC and CBS had been going after television affiliates with gusto since the FCC declared commercial broadcasts could begin on July 1, 1941, although World War II and the subsequent focus on war-related technologies temporarily halted all work in television. An FCC freeze on the processing of new television licenses, enacted just as ABC was trying to get established, added to the network's problems. By the time ABC was able to enter the television race in earnest, most of the larger local stations had already become affiliates of the other two networks, leaving ABC to work with newer, smaller stations that reached a correspondingly smaller audience. Many areas of the country still lacked the capacity for broadcasting three channels, creating a further challenge for ABC, which often found itself shut out of the television market altogether.

Affiliate agreements between local stations and a national network are meant to be beneficial to both parties – the network gains a wider audience to sell to advertisers and the affiliate gets quality programming to fill the prime time hours, along with a certain number of minutes they can sell to advertisers themselves. However, affiliates are not required to broadcast the network's offerings, and in 1971 ABC found itself caught in a seemingly unending cycle of anarchy with its affiliates, who would often choose to air alternate programming rather than the network feed with disastrous results for ABC's ratings. Les Brown describes that situation in his book *Televi$ion: The Business Behind The Box:*

> Such was the spiral: ABC ventured a new show, too few stations carried it, advertisers buying the circulation therefore paid too little for it, the show failed in the ratings, and ABC was forced to cancel it and offer a new program in its place, which in turn would be passed over by the stations. Thus failure perpetuated failure.

Alias Smith and Jones was not a highly rated show when considered against the whole prime time schedule, but it was able to hold its own against the formidable competition of *The Flip Wilson Show* on NBC. Peter's death also came at a strategically bad time for the network. The number of completed episodes the studio would be able to deliver to them would take ABC through the month of January, but February is the most crucial of the sweeps months; ratings during this time set the advertising rates for the next year. Already struggling in the ratings race, this would not be the best time for them to be trying out a brand-new series, assuming they could get one on the air that quickly, nor did they have a library of specials that could air in its place. In fact, ABC had recently dumped millions of dollars worth of programming because of a new FCC regulation that had gone into effect changing the number of hours networks could program in prime time.[21] Programming executives at ABC were not willing to abandon *Alias Smith and Jones* because of this latest crisis and turned to Frank Price for a solution.

Price felt like the captain of the Titanic. "You've just struck an iceberg. What do you do?" he wondered. "Can the ship be saved or do you hit the lifeboats?" Under pressure from the network, Price decided to try and save the ship. He called a meeting with Roy Huggins, Jo Swerling and Glen Larson to discuss options. If anything were to be done to save the show, it had to be done immediately. "My first question was 'What do you think?'" Price recalls. "What should we do here?" Despite the circumstances, each of them wanted to keep the show alive and as Price points out, "If you're doing *Hamlet* and Hamlet dies one night, you don't say 'We retire this play.' You cast a new Hamlet and go on." The conversation turned to recasting the role. Huggins immediately suggested Roger Davis, an actor he knew and liked. Larson disagreed. Although he also liked Roger, he had reservations about using an actor who had recently guest starred on the show as a villain suddenly returning as a replacement for the star. But there was little else to do. Larson recalls, "It's not that there [was] that great a panoply of performers that you [could] call on, especially on short notice. Again, we were behind and we had to kind of keep moving." Jo Swerling believed Roger had a different comedy sense than Peter's, but Roger in his own way knew how to read the kind of wry lines that Huggins and Larson wrote. "It was his own distinctive way of doing it, but it worked. And Roy had been happy with Roger's work in the part that he did [in *The Young Country*]. He just popped into his mind and he said, 'Here's somebody I think can do it and he's available.'" There was no time to hold auditions or screen tests, so Price went with Huggins's suggestion. "I [knew] that Roger was good and it's hard to find people that are good."[22] Swerling contacted the network and got their approval to hire Roger Davis. Now all they had to do was find him and bring him in as quickly as possible.

∽

Unaware of the tragedy, Roger Davis was on his way from Houston, Texas, where he and his wife had spent Christmas with her parents, to Denver, Colorado, to record some voice-overs. With flight information provided by Roger's wife Ellen, better known as Jaclyn Smith, Huggins hoped to intercept Roger at the airport. Roger noticed two airline officials questioning the exiting passengers. As he got closer he realized they were asking, "Are you Roger Davis?" Replying in the affirmative, Roger was directed to a phone where Roy Huggins was holding for him. "Roger, something has happened and you've got to come straight back to California, no matter what you're doing." Surprised by this urgent summons, he asked Huggins what was going on. Huggins was reluctant to go into details over the phone and at first only offered the explanation that he was needed to replace Peter Duel in some shows because there had been an awful accident. But Roger's confusion eventually led Huggins to elaborate as far as he could. "Pete has shot himself . . . Roger, let's talk about this when you come back. Just come back, okay? Get on the next plane out of there." Not able to believe what he was hearing, Roger asked, "Roy, when's he gonna be back? I mean, how many shows?" And Huggins finally said what he'd been trying to avoid. "Roger, look, Pete has shot himself and he's dead . . . I really don't know any details. All I know is what we've got to deal with . . . either the show's going to go off or we've got to move very quickly. As sad as this is and as difficult as it is, if we don't it's going off." Roger silently absorbed that information before asking his next question. "Do I have a choice?" Huggins responded, "From my point of view, I hope you don't. I do want you to think about it, but I hope that you will do it."[23]

So Roger booked a seat on the next flight to Los Angeles. During the flight, a hundred questions raced through his mind. He had doubts about stepping into Peter's role. A few years earlier, against producer Jerry Davis's advice, Roger had taken the Montgomery Clift role in a remake of *From Here To Eternity*. The producer argued that Clift "owns that role. You'll only be compared, and never favorably . . . you're making a huge mistake . . ." Would it be the same stepping into the Heyes role that Peter owned? Roger thought about Edward G. Robinson's line from *The Cincinnati Kid* and that became part of his philosophy – "That's really what life's all about. Life's really about making the wrong move at the right moment. When you screw up is [when] you make the wrong move at the wrong moment." Despite his doubts, Roger was touched by the personal nature of Huggins's appeal to him. "And I'm gonna *refuse* Roy Huggins, who [was giving] me a great show?"

Roger was met at the airport by representatives of Universal and discovered that the local papers were already running the story of him being Pete Duel's replacement. He was whisked straight from the airport to Western Costume Company, where Jo Swerling was waiting for him. Together they assembled a wardrobe for the new Hannibal Heyes, picking out suitable attire and tailoring it to fit Roger.

That weekend Huggins held meetings at his house with Roger and Alex Singer, giving the actor and the director a chance to meet privately before facing cast and crew when shooting resumed. "It made it more comfortable for us to relate," Singer recalls, appreciating the grace Huggins showed in making the transition technically easier for him and more palatable for Roger. Although Roger still had reservations on the wisdom of accepting the offer, on Monday morning, January 3, 1972, the new year would begin with a new actor in the role of Hannibal Heyes.

Peter ended his pain with one bullet. While the world mourned the loss of this talented young man with tears, one friend raged. Jack Jobes confesses, "I wasn't thrown into fits of depression and sadness and all because I was so *annoyed* at him for doing it. I was so *angry*, I mean, I was just angry all the time." What truly broke Jobes's heart was that he knew Peter was getting his life back on track. The two friends had had a heart-to-heart talk in Peter's kitchen two weeks before his suicide, talking and laughing late into the night, drinking gallons of coffee, catching up on what was going on in their lives. "We talked about life, love, the pursuit of happiness, everything like that. But he was *really* getting it together. . . .He was so on the mend. He really was." Jobes thought Peter was on his way onward and upward, with a great series and a great future. "Then you get that kind of news . . . it was just awful." To add to Jobes's anger, Peter's manager, John Napier, was arranging for the funeral to be held at Forest Lawn, a place Jobes knew Peter would hate. "Usually I wouldn't even say anything and let them do what they want, but that [was] just so blatantly wrong," Jobes recalls. He went to Peter's sister Pam and suggested the Self-Realization Temple on Sunset Boulevard, a beautiful and peaceful reserve near the ocean. "That's the perfect spot. That's what he would like," Jobes told her. Pam agreed and Napier changed the arrangements.[24]

The memorial service drew a crowd of over one thousand mourners, among them Frank Price, Roy Huggins, Glen Larson, Alex Singer and the entire *Alias Smith and Jones* crew. Ben chose not to attend the service, feeling his presence would only create a distraction at a time when the focus should be on Peter and his family. Instead, he went to the funeral home the day before, slipping through the back door to avoid the media and keep his visit private. "I paid my respects, said good-bye, then that was it. It was over for me."[25]

Roger did attend the service, expressly against the wishes of Roy Huggins, who warned him it would be a mistake to go; that replacing Peter would be difficult enough without the added trauma of attending his funeral the day before taking over his role. But Roger felt it wouldn't be right not to show up, especially since he knew both Geoffrey and Pam. "It was the one thing to do that was completely right," Roger says, but admits Huggins was right about the emotional toll. "It made it much harder for me to do it."[26]

Jon Roger Davis was born in Bowling Green, Kentucky, on April 5, 1939, the middle son of Edwin and Virginia Davis. The family soon moved to Louisville, where Edwin Davis established a successful tire company, the profits from which allowed him to indulge his desire to own racehorses. Though the tire company no longer exists, Roger still owns the property, a corner of historic downtown Louisville. Roger remembers his dad as a colorful character who could have been an actor, a cross between Gary Cooper and Fred Astaire.

Roger, along with older brother Edwin and younger brother Brent, attended school in Louisville, where he enjoyed his first acting experience at the young age of nine, playing the Archbishop in a school production of *The Prince and the Pauper*. After graduating from Castle Heights Military Academy in Lebanon, Tennessee, he attended New York City's Columbia University, majoring in American and British literature, with a minor in architecture. The acting bug had bitten him so, along with keeping up his studies, he also appeared in summer stock at Woodstock, New York, and with the Repertory Theatre in New York City. To further his education, his father insisted he study law at Harvard, but Roger didn't care for his studies there and instead took a job teaching freshman English at the University of California at Los Angeles. He made the trip to California by bus with only $13 to his name. Once there, besides teaching, he pumped gas, washed dishes and waited tables to make money. While at UCLA, Roger completed his Master's degree.

Right out of college, Roger was signed to a contract at Warner Brothers. His professional acting debut came in 1962 on the ABC series *The Gallant Men*, a World War II drama about the American campaign in Italy. Robert Conrad befriended him while he was at Warners and helped him to get other jobs, to break out of the mold of the series. Dorothy Bailey, secretary to Hugh Benson who ran the day-to-day operations of Warner Brothers under Jack Warner, later became Roy Huggins's secretary. It was she who brought Roger to Huggins's attention.

When *The Gallant Men* was cancelled, Roger took the role of a ranch hand in *Empire*, an NBC western. The next year, he and Peter Duel vied for the role of a surfer in the beach movie *Ride the Wild Surf*. At that time, Peter told Roger, "You're going to get it. I'm not the surfer type." Roger believes Peter could do whatever he wanted, but Peter's prediction was on target. Roger got the role. Working in Hawaii for three months at the age of twenty-three, "Well, it was pretty great to be able to go do that," Roger remembers.

Roger continued acting, winning a role in the feature film *PT 109* and guest starring in shows such as *The Twilight Zone, Bonanza* and *The Big Valley*. Roger's and Peter's paths crossed once again when Roger turned down the lead in *Love on a Rooftop* in favor of the remake of *From Here to Eternity*. Producer Jerry Davis told him, "You know, you're turning down a role that is perfect for you, that will make you a star, that will . . . allow this gift for light humor that you have to come through . . . " Nevertheless, Roger took the ill-advised role of Pvt. Prewitt in *From Here to Eternity* and the role of David Willis in *Love on a Rooftop* went to Peter Duel. The pilot was filmed and Roger recalls the reaction, "I was compared to Montgomery Clift and, oh, what the hell . . . So I land back in New York doing off-Broadway shows."[27] He admits ruefully that Jerry Davis was absolutely right.

In 1967, he played the role of Bobby Kennedy in the drama *MacBird* in Boston and then in New York City. Because of his ability to mimic Kennedy's Boston accent, during the production, *MacBird* directors gave Roger his first voiceover job. He went in to do an aspirin commercial using Kennedy's voice and was so dead on the producers were afraid they would get sued, so they told Roger to read the words in his own voice. When he then sounded like Henry Fonda to them instead, they asked if he could he sound even more Fonda-esque. The commercial went on the air with "Fonda's" voice. "And a career in voiceovers, which made me millions of bucks, was born. So I had this great voiceover career, doing the play, and starting to do lots of commercials on-camera. I'd go in for off-camera and they would say, 'What the hell are you doing off-camera? You could be on-camera.'"

The next year, Roger was offered the role of lawyer Peter Bradford in ABC's afternoon gothic soap opera *Dark Shadows,* and met his future wife, Jaclyn, the former Ellen Smith of Houston, Texas, on an elevator in New York. Roger would go on to play several different roles on *Dark Shadows* for the next two years: Peter

Bradford, Jeff Clark, the ghost of Peter Bradford, Ned Stuart, Dirk Wilkins, and Charles Delaware Tate, appearing in 129 episodes. Roger and Jaclyn were married in 1968. His career as an announcer was thriving as well; he and Jaclyn appeared as announcer and actress in toothpaste commercials in the early 1970s. He also did guest shots on *Night Gallery, The Bold Ones* and *Medical Center* during this period, as well as a couple of ABC Movie of the Weeks.

Roger Davis in *The Young Country.*

Roger and Peter came together again when they were both cast in Roy Huggins's pilot *The Young Country.* Huggins had initially cast Peter as Stephen Foster Moody, the lead. After talking with Roger, Huggins decided he'd erred in that decision and switched their roles around, making Roger the lead. Roger was concerned that Peter would resent being demoted from star to supporting character, but Huggins brushed aside his protests. "No, no, no. You don't know Pete Duel. It won't bother him at all. First day of shooting, he'll understand completely." Huggins was right. Peter didn't mind and, in fact, phoned Roger to talk about it. Roger remembers Peter joking, "I followed you into *Love on a Rooftop* and now I'm going to follow you into *The Young Country.* What kind of a life is this?"

Huggins had a firm rule that his actors were not permitted to ad-lib dialogue, however, Roger could get away with it occasionally. One time Huggins told him, "One of the things I love, Roger, is that you don't ad-lib bromides . . . stuff that you hear constantly. You come up with some stuff that I never (could) . . . I couldn't write it." In *The Young Country,* Roger's character had Peter's character tied up and was ready to leave. Peter motions for Roger to remove his gag and he says, "Untie me!" Roger, however, secures the bandanna in his mouth and heads for the door. His line was supposed to be simply, "So long, H.J." Instead, he turns back and says, "You know the old saying, 'I love ya when your money's gone, but I can't be with ya! So long, H.J.'" Roger remembers, "That is something my old daddy used to say . . . Roy saw that and he called me up the next day on the set and he said, 'I love getting credit for that line . . . That was really a perfect moment and the perfect thing, and *I* didn't write it!" *The Young Country* did not go to series, but Roger developed a lasting friendship with Roy Huggins.[28]

In 1971, when his roles on *Dark Shadows* were finished, Roger was hired as the narrator on *Alias Smith and Jones* and also guest-starred in the episode "Smiler with a Gun." "I think it was Doug Heyes who liked me for [that episode], who went to Roy and said, 'You know, you're not going to believe this, but we should do this.' . . . I think Roy went along with it, but I don't think he would have thought of me because Roy had a way of pigeon-holing you. He had a way of thinking, 'This is what you do.' . . . This was a rather straight leading man . . . No humor to him at all. And I don't think Roy saw me that way." Ironically, in his role of Danny Bilson, Roger was the only man Kid Curry killed.

∽

Monday, January 3, 1972. The first day on the set was the toughest. Everyone had returned except the director of photography, William Cronjager. Cronjager, a very close friend of Peter's, had walked out on Friday and he just couldn't bring himself to return. A substitute was brought in to finish the camera work on "The Biggest Game in the West," although Cronjager later returned to finish out the season. Ben, although he also would have preferred to quit, returned to work without argument. "I could have been a thorn in their side and been petulant and said, 'No, I can't go on.' But that would have been bullshit. My job is to be an actor and do a job. I can't quit because someone else chooses to end their life."[29]

Director Alex Singer gave a speech to the cast and crew, then work began. Singer remembers, "I think that all I got to say to Roger was 'Good morning.' . . . There wasn't time to do that. . . .So, he's dumped into the middle of this thing."[30] The plan called for using all the footage already shot of the guest stars, which meant Roger had to duplicate Peter's performance so the reactions would match properly when the film was edited. A movieola was brought to the set and Singer and Roger studied every move Peter had made in every shot. Roger then gave his own performance, matching Peter's in every nuance. Singer was impressed with the results. "He [did] this with a level of professionalism and good will and good humor that I [found] really quite remarkable."

The work continued throughout the morning, going very well under the circumstances. "I'm thanking my lucky stars that we have another actor that's clearly a competent professional," Singer remembers. "He is, I think, going to be easy to work with." At lunchtime, Singer had cause to wonder if his first assessment was correct. On his way to the screening room to watch the dailies from the previous Thursday and Friday, Roger stopped him and asked if he could come along and see them on a big screen rather than the television-sized movieola. Singer normally refused to let actors watch dailies, but, under the circumstances, this time had no objections. He wanted Roger to feel as comfortable as he could. "I certainly didn't want him to feel he was getting the cold shoulder from me, so I said, 'Sure, come along.'"

They walked along in silence for a while. "I hear the sound of choking," Singer recalls, "and I look over and Roger is strangling with an effort to hold back tears." Singer put his arm around the actor. "I wasn't using my head. I'm a director on the job and my first thought is, 'My God, I have another nut and this is not

Roger Davis as Stephen Foster Moody in *The Young Country.*

Roger Davis.

going to be funny.'" He then asked Roger what was wrong. Roger knew that the opportunity to play a role as good as Hannibal Heyes was a lucky break for him, but Peter had been a friend, and he didn't like how he had gotten the part. Roger broke down and wept. The two men went into the screening room. "He sat through the dailies then and that was the worst moment," Singer remembers. "Whatever he felt after that he was able to keep pretty much to himself and [he] didn't tell people about this. It was kind of forbidden terrain."[31]

While Roger had the unenviable task of imitating Peter, Ben Murphy had his own problems to face. "It was like waking up in bed with a different wife," Ben recalls. "That's the way I best describe it. It was very jarring. It was emotionally just very, very difficult."[32] Ben found himself re-doing scenes he had done just days earlier with Peter, reciting the same lines "and now there's somebody else there." He recalls that everyone just did what they had to do and somehow managed to get through it. "[It] wasn't fun for Roger, wasn't fun for me, wasn't fun for anybody." While he managed to perform on camera, in between shots Ben retreated to his dressing room, not feeding lines to Roger for his close-ups. Roger did what was required of him and, in his own dazed state, didn't think too much about it, but guest star Jim Backus was furious. He said, "You can't do these close-ups without the other boy, what are you talking about?" He felt that Ben's behavior was unconscionable and lost no time in telling him so when Ben returned to the set for a three-shot. Roger recalls that Backus "turned and said, 'You know, I've been at this a long time and . . . I wouldn't put up with it. I guess this fella has to put up with it, 'cause he's stuck. But you'll get yours. You know, what goes around . . .' Oh, he was really angry."[33]

The cast and crew struggled through their grief and completed "The Biggest Game in the West." Singer notes that Peter's temperament had given the crew its share of trouble, but he was well liked and the crew was deeply affected by his loss. "Peter . . . was a good, good craftsman and a kind of charming guy. And for all the trouble that he gave people because his temperament did slow them down, they liked him and they cared about him . . . They were really affected by it." Singer was also affected. He had worked with Peter on *The Bold Ones* as well as previous episodes of *Alias Smith and Jones* and recalls, "For all the behavioral things that [were] troublesome or irritating about Peter, he was a beautiful young man and a *very* good actor." There was also lingering resentment over the Black Tower's actions. Already shocked by Peter's death and dismayed that they were asked to continue shooting, the crew expected Universal executives at least to come to the set and acknowledge Peter's death. No one did. More than thirty years later, Alex Singer is still angry about that. "The absence of human connection was chilling. It was bone-chilling."

The old show-biz adage "the show must go on" was followed with a stubbornness that left cast, crew and fans alike reeling. "I think there was shock in general and some anger at Peter that he'd done that to himself and to everybody. In situations like that, it's always something you can figure out [later]. Maybe you could have handled it better," Frank Price explains. "But, again, if you were present at the time, who knows?" Price made the decision to recast the show with the full agreement of the producers who were, as Jo Swerling recalls, "accused of being ghoulish at the time, because we barely skipped a beat. I think we lost half a day of production." The only thing making the decision bearable was that continuing production saved a lot of jobs. "Our rationale . . . I don't think it's a spurious rationale . . . was that there are 125 jobs on the line," Swerling explains. "And Peter wouldn't have wanted all those people out of work and that was sort of the bright spot in the clouds that kept us from feeling like complete ghouls."[34]

"The Biggest Game in the West" aired on February 3, 1972, with no explanation of why Hannibal Heyes was now played by Roger Davis. Although the reason was certainly common knowledge among the audience, many of Peter Duel's fans were dismayed that no acknowledgment of his death was made publicly; that Roger Davis simply appeared one Thursday night and the show continued as if nothing had happened. Today Frank Price admits that things probably should have been handled differently, but that's an easy call to make from the perspective of several decades later. It was not so easy in 1972. At the time, Price explains, "the fact of the matter was that we were casting another actor and wanted him to have his shot at showing the audience who he was and how this relationship worked." Neither the studio nor the network wanted to dwell on the tragedy to the possible detriment of the series they had just struggled to save, so the broadcast of Roger's first episode was made with as little fanfare as possible.

ABC was fairly confident the audience would accept the new actor. The studio had sent test tapes of the episode to several television stations around the country to gauge audience reaction before the national network broadcast. On January 29, 1972, these stations broadcast the show in their local markets, then surveyed viewers and sent the results back to ABC, who was anxious to see how well the show would stand up after the cast change. The results were favorable and the network felt the series could survive the death of Peter Duel. They watched the ratings closely and were pleased that they didn't significantly drop. The audience appeared to be willing to give Roger Davis a chance to give his own interpretation to the role of Hannibal Heyes. ABC renewed *Alias Smith and Jones* for a third season.

There were four more episodes to be filmed before the season ended. But the relationship between the actors was strained and Universal nearly lost Ben Murphy. When he was working with Peter, he was earning $450 a week, significantly less than his co-star. Roger was not under contract to Universal and came in as a replacement earning Peter's salary of $5,000 per show. The injustice angered Ben. "You're bringing in another actor, I should at least get what he gets and I shouldn't have to take second billing to a new person if we're going to do this." Ben held out despite threats from Lew Wasserman; he called in "sick" and refused to meet with anyone, letting his agents bargain for him. They eventually negotiated a deal that satisfied Ben. He graciously finished the season at his original pay, but got the parity he wanted for the next season. The crisis was over.

(Sagala/Bagwell collection)

Peter Duel's grave in Penfield, New York, cemetery. His mother lies next to him on the left.

(Courtesy of Ben Murphy)

Peter Duel.

CHAPTER 7

THE SHOW MUST GO ON
CONTINUATION OF THE SECOND SEASON

ROGER DAVIS TAKES OVER AS HANNIBAL HEYES
February 3, 1972 – March 2, 1972

THE BIGGEST GAME IN THE WEST

"You're all right, cousin, you're all right!"
– Hannibal Heyes

STORY:	JOHN THOMAS JAMES
TELEPLAY:	JOHN THOMAS JAMES
DIRECTOR:	ALEXANDER SINGER
SHOOTING DATES:	DECEMBER 27, 28, 29, 30, 31, 1971; JANUARY 3, 4, 5, 6, 7, 1972
ORIGINAL US AIR DATE:	FEBRUARY 3, 1972
ORIGINAL UK AIR DATE:	NOVEMBER 26, 1973

Hannibal Heyes and Kid Curry doze in a gully on a beautiful day. A satchel of money thrown from a passing stagecoach lands near their heads, disturbing the idyllic scene. A galloping posse pursues the coach.

Curry opens the satchel and finds stacks of money inside which Heyes recognizes as counterfeit. Since they can't spend it, they decide to build a $200,000 bonfire but, as they're about to set it alight, Heyes comes up with a way to use it.

Heyes exits the stagecoach in Lordstown dressed in suit and derby hat and heads for the hotel. He orders Curry, who rode on top with the driver, to bring in his bags. After signing in, they visit the Lordstown bank, managed by Joseph P. Sterling.

For the first time, Heyes gives his alias a middle initial – Joshua P. Smith – a reflection, perhaps, of banker Joseph P. Sterling's monogram. Two prominent bankers — John P. Morgan and John P. Getty — also share the middle initial.

The counterfeit bills worth $200,000 in 1880 would have been worth four times that amount by the early 1970s.

Introducing himself to Sterling, Heyes tells him he wants to put $200,000 in his bank, not deposited or collecting interest, but merely in the vault for safe-keeping. He plans on looking for cattle land with Jones to advise him. Over the next few days, they ride around ostensibly looking at land with rich ranchers who may be in the market to sell.

On Saturday, as Heyes shaves off his mustache because he's afraid it makes him look sinister, Curry worries that their real objective in coming to Lordstown is not working. An invitation to the poker game Heyes is hoping to get hasn't been forthcoming. Just then two wealthy ranchers, Bixby and Halberstam, arrive to extend an invitation for the biggest poker game west of the Mississippi. The game lasts from 3 p.m. on Saturday to 3 a.m. on Sunday and players can generally afford to lose as much as $200,000. For appearance, Heyes declines, then lets himself be talked into it.

(Courtesy of Ben Murphy)

At 3 p.m., the ranchers sit down and lay their money on the table. Heyes is chagrined to see the bundles; he figured they'd play with chips and settle with bank drafts later. Bixby apologizes for not telling him and lends him $5,000 to get started. The ante is $200. Thousands are raised and tossed in the pot.

Meanwhile, Curry plays poker in the saloon. He tosses in twenty-five cents and requests four cards. Between hands, he flirts with a pretty saloon girl. When one player raises $2, the others toss in their hands. The game has become too rich.

That night, Heyes returns to their hotel room with a handful of money – $14,800. The Kid sees the money as a stake toward a trip to China, while Heyes wants to stay and play poker again the next week.

The following Saturday, Kyle and Lobo of the Devil's Hole Gang watch with binoculars as the ranchers enter the hotel for the weekly game.

Curry plays poker in the saloon again, a whopping $3 in the pot. Heyes plays in the hotel, $30,000 in front of him. At that moment, the door to the private room is battered in by a telegraph pole in the hands of men disguised with flour sacks over their heads. It's the Devil's Hole Gang, come to rob the game.

Kyle spots Heyes in the midst of the players and calls, "Hey, Wheat, look!"

The thieves quickly scrape the money into sacks and skedaddle. Heyes directs the ranchers to figure out how much money they lost while he rouses the sheriff, first stopping to check on the gagged and bound hotel clerk.

Later, in their hotel room, Curry berates Heyes for wanting to stay for one more game. Then Heyes delivers the additional bad news about Kyle using Wheat's name. "Wheat" can only mean Wheat Carlson, a known member of the Devil's Hole Gang which is led by Heyes and Curry. Curry wants to leave town right then, but they can't leave the counterfeit money in the bank and they can't get it until Monday. After ruminating over alternatives, Heyes convinces Curry he has to get the money back from the gang. They can keep the $35,000 that was in front of Heyes, but they must return the rest. It will save them from having wealthy, angry ranchers after them. Curry is incredulous that Heyes is asking him to do this.

Nevertheless, Curry leaves on Sunday morning just as Sterling confronts Heyes. In the privacy of Smith's hotel room, Sterling says he was checking stock certificates and happened to look at the money Smith put in his bank and discovered it to be counterfeit. Heyes reminds Sterling he didn't deposit it so it would gather interest, nor did he use it – that would be illegal. No, replies Sterling, but he *did* have it, and still *does* have it, and *that's* illegal. Sterling offers to sell his silence for $15,000 and gives Heyes until Wednesday to come up with it. After that he'll call in the law.

Just then the law, in the person of Sheriff Grimly, pounds on Heyes's door. Grimly questions Heyes about the robbery. Did he hear the robber say "Weed" or "Wheat"? Heyes is pretty sure he heard "Weed" because he knew of an outlaw named Weed Bronson and assumed it was him.

Meanwhile, Curry has reached the Devil's Hole hideout and attempts to talk the gang into giving back the money. Do they want the $35,000 scot-free or the whole $235,000 with six angry, wealthy ranchers hiring bounty hunters coming after them? Kyle convinces the rest to give it back because they'd be doing it for their former partners.

A few days later, when Curry hasn't yet returned, Smith asks Sterling for more time. He refuses and notes that he removed the money from the vault and put it in a Pierce & Hamilton '73 safe where it's still secure. Sterling is going to send for a federal agent. If Smith meets his terms by the time the agent gets to town, Sterling will deal with him.

As Curry rides hell bent for leather back to Lordstown, the sheriff peruses a stack of Wanted posters in his office.

Outside the livery stable, a grim Curry greets the questioning Heyes. Heyes believes the gang wouldn't go for it, until Curry's face widens into a big grin and he tosses the saddlebag full of money at him.

That night, Heyes and Curry slip into the bank through the window. While Curry keeps watch, Heyes works the tumblers of the safe. It takes only two tries to open it. After opening the safe deposit box with his key and a bent hairpin,

Heyes loads Curry's arms with the stack of real bills from their satchel, before exchanging them for the counterfeit bills in the box.

The next morning, Sterling confronts Smith and Jones in the hotel lobby. Is he going through with the deal or not? Heyes and Curry feign ignorance of any deal. When the agent, Mr. Collins, arrives, he tells the banker he's been looking for the exact sum Sterling wired him about. Sterling accompanies him to Smith's hotel room. Heyes confirms for Collins that he put money in Sterling's vault for safe-keeping. "Goodness me," he says innocently, he hopes it's not counterfeit as Sterling alleges. At that, Collins appears confused and Sterling dumbfounded. All four men head to the bank.

Collins inspects the bundles of money with his magnifying glass and in no time pronounces it "good federal currency." Smith is vindicated and accuses Sterling of opening his deposit box without his consent or his key. Being big-hearted, though, Smith lets Sterling off the hook and the banker agrees to drop the matter. Collins, however, brought to town on a false alarm, will have a bath and dinner at Sterling's expense.

After Smith leaves with the satchel of money, Jones gives Sterling back his receipt. The banker can't help but ask "How did he do it?" Placidly Curry replies, "Do what, Mr. Sterling?"

Sheriff Grimly's search through Wanted posters has finally struck gold. He holds up those of Hannibal Heyes and Kid Curry. Looking from one to the other, he's sure he's identified his men.

Heyes enters his hotel room and tosses the empty satchel to Curry, explaining that he got in and out of "there" in a hurry. As they pack to leave, there's a knock on the door. The saloon girl whom Curry met warns them that the sheriff is rounding up his deputies.

The next moment, Grimly races through the hotel lobby. He throws open the door to Smith's room but finds it abandoned. While he and the deputies check Jones's room, the two partners ride out of town at top speed. As Collins boards his stagecoach, he wonders at the posse tearing around the corner in hot pursuit.

Once on his way, Collins opens his satchel and finds bundles of cash. Holding up one bill to inspect it closely, he pronounces it all counterfeit. His fellow-passengers – two middle-aged ladies – cling to each other in fear and fascination.

The posse tops a small hill just in time to hear the train whistle and see the last car disappearing in the distance. Crestfallen, Grimly suspects Heyes and Curry are on the train.

Saturday at 3 p.m., the poker game commences again. Before the ranchers enter the game room, Grimly announces it was Heyes and Curry who robbed the previous game. In fact, Heyes was the Joshua P. Smith with whom they played. Grimly has alerted sheriffs in the towns down the line and they'll soon be caught.

When the players see the poker table, they stop in their tracks. All the money has been replaced. After reading a note left on the table, Bixby sends for the sheriff.

Lounging in a boxcar, Heyes and Curry remember that they started off with

$12.70. At one point they had $200,719 in real money. Now they have eight cents, not counting the $100 bill that fell out when Heyes opened Sterling's safe. In the rush he didn't get a chance to return it.

When Sheriff Grimly returns to the hotel, Bixby says the men are rescinding their complaint. There wasn't any hold-up. Bixby insists Heyes and Curry weren't in town for two weeks, a fact which should relieve the sheriff. The other players are as confused as Grimly, so Bixby reads the note aloud:

"Gentlemen: I hope I divided the money accurately. Anyway, it's all here, except for what I had in front of me when the game was robbed, which I haven't got any more. If anyone ever tells you it was really Hannibal Heyes you were playing poker with, I hope you'll point out that, since none of you lost a nickel, either that person is wrong or Hannibal Heyes must be an awful honest man. Signed, Joshua Smith."

GUEST CAST

JIM BACKUS	JOSEPH P. STERLING
CHILL WILLS	BIXBY
ROD CAMERON	SHERIFF GRIMLY
JON LORMER	PARSONS
BILL MCKINNEY	LOBO RIGGS
FORD RAINEY	COLLINS
DONALD WOODS	HALBERSTAM
DENNIS FIMPLE	KYLE MURTRY
X. BRANDS	POKER PLAYER
STEVEN GRAVERS	MATTSON
JACKIE RUSSELL	SALLY

The episode began with a depiction of all the best elements of a lazy summer's day and deteriorated with one gunshot into a morass of grief, re-takes and resentment. Peter Duel had been in the middle of shooting this episode when he took his life.

When Roger Davis came on as a replacement, because the studio was on a tight schedule, filming resumed immediately. He remembers that he "just popped right in and did it, there was no building or how to do it or . . . talk about [it]. . .We just had to go on."[1]

His first scene was one that had been filmed on Thursday before Peter's suicide in which the boys are relaxing in a gully. Thirty years later, watching himself on video, Roger observes, "It was so stupid. It was a really bad, phony moment. . . .I don't react to the satchel being thrown off the stage. You know, I just sort of get up, because I was in a daze anyway, it was the first scene. . . .*Normally*, had that satchel come down and hit me on the head when I was sleeping, I would have gone, 'Whoa, wait a minute, whoa . . .' But I just languidly get up and start doing the scene, which was, I'm sure, just because it was that first scene. . . .It was just a very intense moment with everybody on the set."

Ben Murphy and Roger Davis.

Ben played it as well as any actor could under the circumstances, smiling in anticipation, as directed, of spending the money. But, by now in the series, the audience knows it's not going to work out for them. "They're kind of hard luck guys in a low-key way." Director Alex Singer praised Huggins the writer. "That's very skillful story-telling. You've established the milieu enough to know that . . . there's going to be a sharp turn of some kind . . . Even when you have set up the rules, and what I just described is nakedly commercial, it's hard to be *nakedly* commercial and effective. It's not under-stood by anybody who isn't a writer . . ."[2]

Roger needed to re-do the master shots and all of the close-ups to take Peter's place in them. Because the production crew already had close-ups of the six other poker players, they didn't want to waste them. They had been filmed from many different angles, so it was many more than just six shots. According to Singer, "It was probably a dozen shots and done with some difficulty and time-consuming hours and hours of work. . . .But Roger would have to, in effect, fit his performance into what Peter was doing."

Fortunately, several of the scenes with Peter were salvageable. For instance, when Heyes walks into the Lordstown Hotel after leaving the stagecoach, Roger remarked after he watched the episode, "I noticed . . . it's the back of Pete . . . I certainly know what Pete looked like and more than that, I know what *I* look like." Also, when Heyes explains to Curry why he has to ask the gang to return the money, close-ups of each of them show the partners in discussion. Studying the scene closely, Singer points to the differences in shadows and lighting from shot to shot, indicating it is more than likely the back of Heyes's head is Peter's. When Heyes's full face is seen, obviously it needed to be re-shot of Roger.

Several lines were added to accommodate Roger that were not in the earlier scripts. Curry enters Heyes's room and laments that, despite their having looked at land with several ranchers, none has invited Heyes to join the poker game. In the Duel/Heyes script of December 23, 1971, "Heyes is shaving" is the only stage direction. However, the scene was revised on January 4, 1972, to include a line in which Curry notices Heyes has shaved off his mustache. The line about Heyes thinking it makes him look sinister was also added to complement the scene. The peculiarity of these lines leads one to wonder why, if Roger appeared on the set with the mustache, it was necessary to include his removing it as part of the episode.

Roger explains. "I was coming off the show I'd done and I had the mustache." When Huggins saw the dailies of the first few scenes, he called immediately, "You got to get rid of that mustache, Roger, . . . everyone in the Tower thinks it makes you look sinister." So Huggins expanded the shaving scene, including the "in" joke about the sinister-looking facial hair. It was an easy solution to avoid shooting Roger's already completed scenes over again.[3]

(Courtesy of Chris Fimple)

One trivial difference occurs in the way the two Heyeses open a safe. When Peter as Heyes manipulated the tumblers, he put his ear to the combination lock as if to hear them falling into place. Roger/Heyes relied more on his sensitive fingertips to feel the tumblers. Tapping first to get the feel of the metal, he then lightly held the dial in his fingertips as he rotated it. The insert, however, was probably a stand-in's hands because Roger was busy filming more important bits and keeping him overtime would have added to production costs.

As for the secondary characters, according to the script, Wheat Carlson allegedly is part of the robbery, but he "will be played this week by someone we can afford." When he was hired to play Wheat, Earl Holliman had great fun doing the two ninety-minute *Alias Smith and Jones* movies, but, at that time in his career, he didn't want to do a series in which he wasn't the lead and he declined to appear in smaller roles.[4] Dennis Fimple was Kyle, one of the dimmer members of the Devil's Hole

Dennis Fimple as Kyle Murtry.

Gang. Like most good outlaws, Kyle frequently had a chaw of tobacco stuck in his cheek and, as he and Lobo watch the ranchers enter the hotel for the game, this episode was no exception. In order to replicate the appearance of tobacco, an actor was frequently given licorice as a substitute. For an appearance in the 1993 series *Harts of the West*, Fimple also played a grubby, chewin' character, with one scene where he was supposed to spit a good stream. There were a lot of takes. Fimple had a sweet tooth, so instead of using the waste bucket to spit it out, he just swallowed and took a fresh wad of licorice for each take. The poor man did not realize until later that, taken in large quantities, licorice serves as a laxative.[5]

WHICH WAY TO THE OK CORRAL?

"Five years from now you won't find two people in the whole country who even remember the Marshal of Tombstone. What kind of name is that anyway – Earp?"
– Hannibal Heyes

STORY:	JOHN THOMAS JAMES
TELEPLAY:	GLEN A. LARSON
DIRECTOR:	JACK ARNOLD
SHOOTING DATES:	JANUARY 18, 19, 20, 21, 24, 25, 1972
ORIGINAL US AIR DATE:	FEBRUARY 10, 1972
ORIGINAL UK AIR DATE:	DECEMBER 17, 1973

The original title was "Whatever Happened to Clementine?" This was meant to be a reference to Clem's seeming to be out of her mind as she makes ever more improbable accusations against the deputy. The title was briefly changed to "Whatever Happened to George?" but George was a new character and the focus on her mental state was softened, leading to a new title.

Heyes is surprised to find Doc Holliday an adequate, but not talented, poker player. Apparently Heyes is unaware that Doc's reputation as a gambler was based on his skill at faro, not poker.

A shot kills Alberto Diego, Señor Armendariz's foreman, as he rides through the gate at Big Mac McCreedy's ranch. The shot awakens Sam Bacon, a scruffy man snoozing nearby. He sees a rider gallop off, then spies McCreedy approaching from the opposite direction. Mac examines the wounded man, then hurries off to get a doctor. Sam makes his way to Diego and helps himself to his wallet and his beautifully decorated rifle.

Hannibal Heyes and Kid Curry search for Sam Bacon on Big Mac's behalf. Questioning the stage dispatcher they learn he's calling himself Morton and he bought a ticket to Tombstone, a destination that causes their hearts to sink. Marshal Wyatt Earp is a man they'd prefer to avoid. Despite their reluctance, they board the stagecoach.

Inside, a woman is asleep, her face hidden by her hat. The stage starts with a jerk, throwing her to the boys' feet and revealing their old friend Georgette Sinclair. George is on her way to Tombstone to be a chanteuse in the Birdcage Saloon, while the boys need to find Sam Bacon in order to prove Big Mac didn't kill Diego. They entreat George not to help them and, offended, George assures them that for the length of their stay in Tombstone, they don't know each other.

In town, George presents herself to Harvey Clifford, owner of the Birdcage Saloon, for her audition.

Heyes and Curry spend the next two days unsuccessfully looking for Sam. Discouraged, they nevertheless congratulate themselves on avoiding Earp, but their luck doesn't hold. "Afternoon, gents," Earp greets them.

In their hotel room, Curry is all for giving up and leaving town. Heyes tries to dissuade him, but Curry worries about what the marshal's greeting meant. There's a knock on the door. Heyes opens it and George bursts in, flinging herself into his arms. A deputy marshal told her to get out of Tombstone or she'd be killed. Heyes urges her to march over to the marshal's office and report it. George agrees that's what they should do and the boys protest her assumption they'll accompany her. "There are Wanted posters on his wall – ours!"

Grumbling about blackmail and extortion, Heyes and Curry follow George to Earp's office where she reports that one of his deputies threatened her. Earp is skeptical, but sends Joe, the deputy on duty, to round up the others. George explains that the deputy, a man she'd never seen before, told her for no reason to leave town on the three o'clock stage. When deputies Harold and Jake make an appearance, George clears them. Earp is losing patience when deputy Bart Russel enters and she says he's the one. Bart denies ever having seen her before and points out that there isn't a three o'clock stage, a fact Earp acknowledges. George is outraged, but Earp turns his attention to Heyes and Curry, wanting to know if they heard the threats. Heyes admits they didn't, but Curry vouches for George's word despite their earlier claim that they just met her on the stagecoach. The marshal demands to know what they're doing in Tombstone. Heyes presents the subpoena for Sam Bacon, which Earp points out is invalid in Arizona. He warns them not to kidnap local visitors or try to get publicity for their lady friend. The boys quickly hustle George out.

George is furious, as are the boys, albeit for different reasons. Curry suggests the safest course would be for her to leave town, but George refuses. After all, she has Hannibal Heyes and Kid Curry to protect her.

In the saloon Heyes plays poker and pumps the other players for information about Bacon. One man recalls him and another suggests that Doc might know more. Doc? The gentleman next to Heyes speaks up. "Holliday is the name. You can call me Doc." Heyes is taken aback.

The game continues. Curry pushes through the crowd of spectators and watches Heyes win. When Doc calls for a break, Curry reminds his partner they promised to be at George's debut, but Heyes, delighted to find that Doc Holliday's reputation as a poker player is overrated, figures he could win another thousand dollars if he stayed in the game. At the mention of money, Curry's attitude changes. "Heyes, you stay right here. I'll take care of George and Sam Bacon."

At the Birdcage, Clifford introduces George to an enthusiastic audience. Curry smiles as he watches her, but his smile fades as he catches sight of his quarry. When George takes her bow, Sam notices Curry's interest in him. He flees with Curry right behind him.

Curry kicks Sam's hotel door in and searches for the fancy rifle that can clear Big Mac. Sam, hands raised, denies having a rifle, but that doesn't stop Curry from serving him with the subpoena, which Sam ignores.

The poker game is still going on. Marshal Earp observes for a while, unhappy that Heyes has bankrupted Doc Holliday.

In their hotel room, the boys compare notes. They're interrupted by a knock on the door. Heyes opens it and George once again flings herself into his arms.

The trio pays another visit to the marshal and this time George reports that she's been robbed – her entire wardrobe is gone. Still suspicious of her story, Earp nevertheless sets out to investigate the crime.

George throws open the armoire doors to show its emptiness. But it's not empty. All her clothes are hanging neatly in their place. Earp is more convinced than ever that her claims are nothing more than an attempt to garner publicity. He promises to throw all of them in jail the next time she pulls such a stunt.

The next morning Curry stops Deputy Bart Russel in the street. He goes for his gun, but Curry outdraws him. Bart insists that George is a liar just out for publicity, like the marshal said. Curry defends George, saying he's known her for a long time. The deputy jumps on his mistake, wondering why he lied to the marshal about meeting her on the stagecoach.

George prepares for her next performance, leery about going along with Heyes and Curry's latest plan to get Sam Bacon to Texas. Curry insists that if she wants them to help her, she has to help them in return.

George begins to sing, then moves off the stage and into the audience. She drifts around until she comes to Sam, then sings only to him. Sam is astonished, but he likes it.

After the show, he accompanies George to her room, where she confesses that she's fallen for him, but sadly nothing can come of it because she'll be leaving Tombstone soon. Sam wonders which way she'll be heading when she leaves. North to Denver, George says. Sam bids her goodnight in the hallway.

As George lights the lamp in her room, she comes face to face with Bart Russel who demands that this time she take him seriously.

In their own room, Heyes and Curry celebrate Heyes's success at poker. With $15,000 they can live high and lay low for a long time. There's a knock on the door. Heyes opens it and for the third time George throws herself into his arms. George announces this time she really believes Bart will kill her and she's leaving town. The boys urge her to stay until they can get Sam on the stage with her, but George is adamant.

Curry follows Bart to Will and Emma McIntyre's ranch. When Bart returned, he deposited $1,000 in the bank. It seems significant, but George has never heard of the McIntyres.

George and the boys call on the couple. Will denies having any dealings with the deputy in response to Heyes's accusation, but as George steps up, she recognizes them as Mr. and Mrs. Cummings, allegedly taken hostage and killed when the express company they worked for was robbed.

That night, Sam comes by George's room. She's leaving in the morning and she'll miss him very much. Sam is torn. He asks if the stage goes through Texas and is pleased to learn it doesn't. "Georgette, I'm going to go with you!"

George reports her success to the boys. A knock on the door surprises them. It can't be George, because she's already with them. This time the visitors are deputies who invite the boys to the marshal's office.

Earp thanks them for their role in arresting three criminals. Then he explains that Doc Holliday is dying and Earp wants to make his remaining days as pleasant as possible. Doc enjoyed a reputation as the best poker player in the territory, but Smith has made him look like an amateur. And Jones outdrew his deputy. That combination should mean something to him, he tells them, pointedly gazing at their Wanted posters. Earp orders Smith to play one more poker game with Doc where he *will* lose the whole $20,000 he won from him, right where everyone can see, after which they will leave town. "And you'll still be able to say, with some satisfaction, that Hannibal Heyes and Kid Curry came up against Marshal Earp and somehow managed to come out ahead."

A hushed crowd watches the poker game. Heyes, mindful of the marshal's ultimatum, bets the full $20,000. Doc reveals an ace-high diamond flush. Heyes gazes sorrowfully at his hand – a full house – before throwing it face down on the table, letting Doc win.

George and Sam ride the stage northward. It stops in the middle of nowhere and a sheriff serves Sam with another subpoena. This one is good because they are, for the moment, in the northwest corner of Texas. The stage dispatcher identifies Sam as the man who had the fancy rifle and the sheriff escorts him back to Red Rock. Heyes and Curry join George in the stage and go to Denver.

GUEST CAST

NEVILLE BRAND	SAM BACON
JOHN RUSSELL	BART RUSSEL
CAMERON MITCHELL	WYATT EARP
BURL IVES	PATRICK J. "BIG MAC" MCCREEDY
MICHELE LEE	GEORGETTE SINCLAIR
WILLIAM MIMS	WILL MCINTYRE
JACKIE COOGAN	HARVEY CLIFFORD
BILL FLETCHER	DOC HOLLIDAY
VIRGINIA GREGG	EMMA MCINTYRE
BILL QUINN	DISPATCHER (JAKE HAWKINS)

Walt Davis	Deputy Jake
Tom Waters	Sheriff
Robert Knox	Deputy
Red Currie	Deputy Joe
Maurice Hill	Cherokee
Bill Bakewell	Baker
Gary Puckett	Saloon Cowboy
Jim Drum	Poker Player #1
Mike Mahoney	Poker Player #2
John Leuger	Poker Player #3
Jimmie Booth	2nd Stage Driver
John Rivera	Alberto Diego

This episode was originally conceived as the second story to feature Heyes and Curry's old friend Clementine Hale. Both Roy Huggins and Jo Swerling preferred to maintain consistency with recurring characters, making every effort to cast the same actor whenever the character appeared. If the actor wasn't available, Huggins would change the character. Thus Clementine Hale became Georgette Sinclair, following in the tradition of Soapy Saunders and his alter ego Silky O'Sullivan. An exception to this policy was Sheriff Lom Trevors who, because of his special relationship with Heyes and Curry, could not be changed into someone else and was ultimately played by three different actors over the course of the series.[6] The dedication they showed to this policy is demonstrated by the brief appearance of Burl Ives, an actor of enough stature to refuse a walk-on part if he wished, reprising his role as Big Mac McCreedy in the opening scene.

Because Sally Field was not available to reprise the role of Clem, the character in the story was changed into Georgette Sinclair. Little was changed besides the name, so George, like Clem, hails from Denver and has a father with a shady past. In early drafts of the script, Clem uses her photo of Heyes and Curry to encourage them to visit the marshal with her. It wouldn't work for George to be in possession of a similar photograph, so the scene was changed so that George threatened to reveal their true identities if they didn't accompany her. Unfortunately this threat was cut from the final shooting script, leaving the audience to wonder just what the boys are referring to when they accuse George of blackmail and extortion.

Huggins felt that a really interesting woman was a good addition to a series and he had several stories planned for Clementine, although they eventually became stories for George. The change from Clem to George was literally accomplished by crossing off CLEM and substituting GEORGE in the dialogue cues in the script. That George seems to be a considerably different character from Clem is strictly the result of differences of interpretation by Michele Lee and Sally Field. Huggins had learned from *Maverick* that using different actors was enough to create a unique character for the audience when, to his amusement, magazine articles appeared praising the conscientious way in which the writers differentiated the characters of Bret and Bart Maverick. "The scripts never used Bret or Bart. The scripts just said Maverick. They were absolutely the same and it was a flip of the coin whether it was played by Jim [Garner] or Jack [Kelly]."[7] That this technique still works is proved by the audience reaction to George. Viewers who are put off by Clem, mostly because of her blackmailing of Heyes and Curry in "Dreadful Sorry, Clementine," have no such reservations about George. As the two characters are absolutely the same, their dislike for Clem and their fondness for George shows they do perceive them to be two different people.

While Heyes and Curry feared Wyatt Earp, portrayed here as the marshal of Tombstone, in reality it was Virgil Earp who was the law in that town. Wyatt Earp had made a name for himself in law enforcement in Wichita and Dodge City, Kansas, but he arrived in Tombstone in 1879 with the intention of starting up a stage line with his brothers. Discovering Tombstone already had two stage lines, Wyatt took a job as a shotgun guard for Wells Fargo. In addition, his interest in gambling led him to partner in the gambling concession at the Oriental Saloon. In 1880 he was appointed deputy sheriff of neighboring Pima County, but still had no official authority in Tombstone. The infamous Gunfight at the OK Corral took place on October 26, 1881, just days after Virgil deputized him in anticipation of trouble with the Clantons and McLaurys. That legendary gunfight and the notoriety Wyatt Earp gained from it ultimately destroyed his political and business opportunities in Tombstone, and within a year Wyatt and his family moved on.[8]

Doc Holliday was a dentist who preferred gambling for a living. He met Wyatt Earp while traveling on the gambling circuit between Texas and South Dakota and the two became loyal friends. Holliday was a violent man, not hesitating to use the guns and knife he carried, but the number of gunfights he actually engaged in was most likely exaggerated. Doc joined the Earps in Tombstone because of the money he could make at the card table. He was completely uninterested in the power plays made by the various factions in the town, yet when the Clantons and McLaurys announced their intention to kill the Earps, Doc's loyalty to Wyatt led him to join in the famous gun battle. He also left Tombstone soon afterwards.[9]

Doc Holliday and Wyatt Earp are probably the most well known historical figures that Huggins used in *Alias Smith and Jones,* although they are by no means the only real people to show up over the course of the series. When asked if using such characters was an attempt to add realism to the show, with a twinkle in his eye, Huggins confessed, "Yeah. I found all those characters very interesting." Huggins always felt the amnesty deal was a bit unrealistic, but he had to work with the premise Glen Larson had established. A touch of history in the form of real life characters from the Old West gave an added dimension to the show as well as providing numerous story ideas.

DON'T GET MAD, GET EVEN

"You are broke? The man who can't lose at poker is broke? The man who quits when other players know what they're doing is broke?"
– Kid Curry

STORY:	JOHN THOMAS JAMES
TELEPLAY:	JOHN THOMAS JAMES
DIRECTOR:	BRUCE BILSON
SHOOTING DATES:	JANUARY 26, 27, 28, 31, FEBRUARY 1, 2, 1972
ORIGINAL US AIR DATE:	FEBRUARY 17, 1972
ORIGINAL UK AIR DATE:	NOVEMBER 5, 1973

The story, originally named "Crack of Noon," was based on a *Maverick* episode titled "Game of Chance." In it, Roy Huggins used a scam taken directly from genuine conman Yellow Kid Weil's autobiography. In Weil's swindle, however, the costly object was a ring valued at $5,000. Marks were happy to "loan" $500 with it as collateral.

According to the Syracuse, New York, *Herald Journal*, the string of pearls was the genuine article and guards were on hand during the shooting to make sure it wasn't stolen.

Hannibal Heyes and Kid Curry, scruffy and bearded, ride into town leading two pack mules. Just back from the mines, they hope their sacks of gold are worth at least $15,000. Unfortunately, their scale was off by half. To make their plan to go to Bolivia work, they have to double the money.

While washing off months of accumulated filth at a public bathhouse, Heyes comes up with an idea. Men play terrible poker at Wheelwright's Palace in Centralia and there's only a $1,000 buy-in. He is so good he can spot any cheating and take advantage of it. Curry agrees it sounds good; he'll stay behind and sell their horses, burros, saddles and equipment.

At Verle Wheelwright's saloon, after long hours of play, Heyes is dealt four kings. He opens with $100. Wheelwright, who also has a good hand, raises to $1,000. The other players pass and the action is between Heyes and Wheelwright. The pot grows. When Heyes finally shows his four kings, the casino owner tops them with four aces.

Heyes stands to leave, angry that Wheelwright passed the opening bid even though he had a pair of aces for starters. Wheelwright, raking in the pot, hopes he's not going away angry. Heyes quotes his grandfather's maxim "Don't get mad, get even" as Wheelwright laughs uproariously.

Heyes finds Curry stretched out on his bed in the hotel room. At Curry's query as to how he's doing, Heyes admits he's broke. Curry is aghast; he thought Heyes knew what he was doing. Heyes says he was ahead $4,000, then Wheelwright brought in a mechanic who must have "palmed the entire deck after the cut and dealt from the one he'd stashed." They set Heyes up for just the one hand. Curry falls back onto the bed and quotes their Grandpa Curry, "You show me a poor man and I'll show you a man who ain't got any money."

Heyes promises to get their whole $12,000 back and thinks of a plan. Curry needs to go to Denver and bring back Georgette, while he heads to San Francisco to see Silky.

A few days later, Curry signs himself and Georgette into the hotel as Chauncey Gaylord Brandon and his sister Charlotte, upper–class folks from Atlanta who may be moving permanently to Centralia.

As Georgette unpacks, there's a banging on her door. Unshaven and dirty from sleeping in the livery, Heyes strides in, upset they are two days late. A kiss from her improves his mood.

From one pocket, Heyes whips out a pearl necklace. From his other pocket, he proffers an identical, but fake, necklace. She demands to know what she has to do to earn her $3,000. Surprised by news of this added expense, Heyes says they now have to take Wheelwright for $15,000. Patiently he explains the plan . . .

At dinner, Wheelwright approaches the Brandons' table and joins them for a drink. Chauncey tells him their father left them money to invest. The area seemed like a good place to do that. Tugging at her necklace as she laughs at a comment by Wheelwright, Charlotte breaks it and the pearls scatter. Because she was laughing at his joke, Wheelwright offers to have them re-strung.

The jeweler estimates the necklace to be worth $50,000.

Curry and George kill time playing cards in her hotel room. At a knock, Curry leaves through an adjoining door. When Wheelwright enters with her necklace, Georgette acts tearful. Since she's packing to leave, she puts the pearls into her suitcase and explains that she and her brother have to return to Atlanta because a Yankee nephew of her father is challenging the estate. Having switched the real and fake necklaces, Georgette, as if inspired, asks Wheelwright to take her necklace as collateral on a loan of $15,000 to fight the nephew.

Wheelwright agrees and they draw up the papers immediately. He'll hold her necklace in a safe behind the bar. The casino never closes, so it's never been robbed. Since they are now business partners, Verle Wheelwright asks Miss Brandon if he may call her by her first name. As he escorts them to the stagecoach, Wheelwright asks if he may also call Mr. Brandon by his first name. Curry acquiesces and introduces himself as Chauncey Beauregard Brandon. In the stage, they realize that he signed the hotel register as Chauncey Gaylord Brandon. Hopefully no one, especially Wheelwright, will notice.

Heyes greets their coach in Westfield. They'll wire the $15,000 to San Francisco and Curry will guard the real necklace with his life until they get it back to Silky.

Meanwhile, Wheelwright drapes the pearls on a lady friend and takes her to dinner. The jeweler, who is dining nearby, notices and comes to their table. Something is wrong. He examines the necklace and proclaims it to be a worthless paste duplicate!

On the stagecoach to San Francisco, Curry and Georgette play blackjack. The coach slows and stops at the cries of four men. It's a hold-up. Heyes hastily wraps the necklace in the coach's window shade. One robber frisks the passengers while another locates the hidden necklace.

Continuing on, the depressed Heyes and Curry figure "Wheel-wrong" must have discovered the necklace that George gave him was fake. When they reach Silky's mansion in San Francisco, he is killing angry that his pearls are gone. Heyes promises to get them back, but first they need to borrow $15,000.

Back in Centralia, Charlotte admits to Wheelwright that she tried to swindle him, but her evil brother Chauncey forced her into it. To undo what she did, she offers Wheelwright $15,000. Wheelwright laughs in her face and refuses, but he will return the *fake* necklace that she gave him. Charlotte pretends to cry as Wheelwright laughs again and walks away.

At the hotel, Heyes figures it's time for Plan B, a frontal assault. George wants to be counted out; she couldn't stand to hear Wheelwright laugh again.

The casino owner is surprised to see Mr. Smith and Chauncey Brandon, realizing he should have put them together before this. Curry informs Wheelwright that he can't sell the necklace, it's too well-known and he'll be in trouble for not taking the money back from the lady and returning her pearls. Heyes repeats Charlotte's offer to buy the real necklace for $15,000. Wheelwright again refuses and calls over his hired guns to throw the boys out. Heyes and Curry won't be thrown out and Curry draws on the men. Wheelwright orders his gunmen to back off, but the answer is still no.

They put Plan C into effect. Charlotte approaches Wheelwright, this time offering $30,000. With that amount, he is interested. A short time later, Heyes, Curry, and George meet him at his table. Heyes hands over the $30,000 in an envelope and Wheelwright proceeds to count it. He's satisfied that it's all there and licks the flap to seal it.

Charlotte would like to see her necklace and when she does, protests that it's the fake one. Wheelwright stands and pulls the fake pearls from his other pocket and hands them over. While he's distracted, Heyes switches envelopes. Mollified, Charlotte apologizes, she's learned that you can't cheat an honest man. The trio turns to leave as Wheelwright throws Heyes's words back at him – "Don't get mad, get even."

Wheelwright is about to put the money into his safe when he reconsiders and opens the envelope. He finds it full of pieces of cut newspaper!

Heyes, Curry and George ride furiously out of town. Hot on their heels come an angry Wheelwright and his men. At a railroad water tower, he discovers their horses and a note. "Dear Verle, I didn't want to go away mad. J. Smith."

Sprawled in a boxcar on the way to Silky's with the money and the pearls, Curry wonders how Heyes knew Wheelwright was going to seal the envelope when he switched them. Heyes reveals that he increased their chances by having along an unsealed envelope of cut paper. Delighted with their triumph, Curry tosses the paper into the air like confetti.

The script originally called for a reunion of characters met in previous episodes. Clementine, not Georgette, was to help the boys out, Diamond Jim Guffy, not Silky O'Sullivan, was to supply the money and necklace. In addition, Curry and Clem were to reprise their aliases of "Rhett" and Charlotte Brandon from "Dreadful Sorry, Clementine." Heyes and Curry, who previously had considered going to South America to sit out their amnesty year, planned on going to Australia instead.[10] Things had drastically changed by the final script revision.

Huggins's script became a vehicle for him to not only experiment with the personality of his characters, but to play with names as well. Role reversal is one of the first things noticeable in this episode. Their friend Silky O'Sullivan, the wealthy, retired con man, still has a few tricks up his sleeve. Heyes knows how to get and use them. Previously quite pleasant, Silky turns menacing when the boys return without his jewels. He even goes so far as to threaten murder if his pearls are not returned, a side of the kindly old gentleman the audience hasn't seen before. As for Heyes, his silver tongue fails to convince Wheelwright to return the pearls throughout Plans A, B, and C. It is Curry who forcefully, though unsuccessfully, reminds Wheelwright of the near impossibility of trying to sell the pearls. Somewhere Curry learned that the pearls, if sold separately, would bring in less than if they remain in the matched, albeit recognizable, string. Wheelwright is the one character who remains consistently obnoxious from the get-go. Huggins wanted him to be "a really interesting heavy, a man like Sidney Greenstreet. He has size and a cool menace – a worthy adversary."[11] Heyes learns right off how devious he can be and he, Curry and Georgette regard him not as Wheel-right, but as Wheel-wrong. Finally, for Otto, the jeweler, Huggins wanted him to have a European accent to give him authority.[12] John Banner, familiar to television audiences as Sgt. Schultz from *Hogan's Heroes,* was hired.

Though not named in the aired episode, according to the script, the four men who stop the stagecoach purposefully looking for the pearls are named Art, Bart, Fargo and "the Leader."[13] The hired gunmen who arrive at Wheelwright's table to throw out Heyes and Curry are Ferman, Herman and Vermin.[14] When Wheelwright checks the envelope and discovers the cut newspaper, in the January 24 revision of the script, he "screams" for "Jo, Steve, Art!" to ride with him in pursuit. The three are no doubt Huggins's idea of a joke on Jo Swerling (Associate Executive Producer), Steve Heilpern (Associate Producer), and Art McLaird (Assistant to the Producer).

Besides his using off-the-wall names, Huggins managed to bring in references to real people as well. Wheelwright tells Chauncey that his sister cries better than Sarah Bernhardt. The French actress had begun to travel with her own company by 1879, appearing regularly in London and New York City and touring North America in 1886-87 and 1888-89, famous for her beauty and bell-like voice. Heyes compares the talents of the card sharp with Paganini, a famous Italian composer and violin virtuoso who died in 1840. His playing astonished the listeners of his day, as he performed complex works using only one of four violin strings.[15] It's no wonder Heyes missed the card switch if the sharp were twice as talented! Finally, Wheelwright tells the Brandons over dinner that he met Mark Twain when he was a struggling young reporter. This would have been around 1862 when Twain reported for the *Territorial Enterprise* in Virginia City, Nevada.

Three times within the first eleven minutes, Huggins reiterates for viewers that Curry and Heyes share a common Irish grandfather. Though he had presented them as cousins early in the series and had already changed the introduction from "latter-day Robin Hoods" to "Kansas cousins," Huggins seems to have played it up more after Roger came on board. It couldn't hurt, he thought, to explain away the similar coloring of Roger and Ben by re-enforcing their characters' blood relation.

WHAT'S IN IT FOR MIA?

"When you took The Clarion from me, Miss Bronson, you presented me
with a monstrously simple choice – sin or starve.
I chose sin because it presented the greater challenge."
– George Austin

STORY:	JOHN THOMAS JAMES
TELEPLAY:	WILLIAM D. GORDON AND JOHN THOMAS JAMES
DIRECTOR:	JOHN DUMAS
SHOOTING DATES:	JANUARY 10, 11, 12, 13, 14, 17, 1972
ORIGINAL US AIR DATE:	FEBRUARY 24, 1972
ORIGINAL UK AIR DATE:	DECEMBER 10, 1973

The King City barber shop has a three hour wait, so Hannibal Heyes and Kid Curry while away the time playing poker at the Diamond Horseshoe Casino. They lose every hand. Heyes notices a well-dressed woman, Mia Bronson, coming out of the office and asks the other players if she's the proprietor. Learning she is, he scoops up the cards over the protest of the dealer and he and Curry make their way over to her.

This story was originally titled "How to Change A $10 Bill." At that time, the proprietor of the casino was Fred Bronson.

Mia leads them into her office for privacy, but has two of her men, Max and Cliff, join them, not trusting the unkempt cowboys. Heyes offers to sell her the deck of cards for $250. Mia isn't interested; she buys cards for twenty-five cents a pack. Not like these, Heyes assures her. "These are different. Unique. Marked." Mia challenges him to show her the marks. Heyes can't, but he knows they're marked because seconds were being dealt. If she returns their $250, they'll be on their way; otherwise, they'll let everyone in town know she cheats. Mia's two bodyguards start to draw, but Curry beats them to it. Unfortunately, the crooked dealer has entered the room and gotten the drop on the boys. Mia orders her men to take the two tramps out of town and dump them, making sure they know better than to ever return to King City. She watches in satisfaction as the beating begins.

Max and Cliff dump the unconscious Heyes and Curry in a ditch outside of town.

Later, having been found and brought home by George Austin and his daughter Charlotte, Heyes and Curry moan restlessly as she keeps vigil over them. Charlotte returns to the bedroom after a short break to find Heyes awake and confused. She soothes him as her father, drawn by the voices, enters the room. He introduces himself and explains how the boys came to be there, then urges Heyes to go back to sleep. Heyes takes his advice.

In the morning Curry peers out the window, wondering where they are. He wakes Heyes and learns about the Austins, but are they back in King City? Maybe they'd better find out.

The boys *are* in King City. The Austins aren't surprised to learn that Mia Bronson is responsible for their injuries. She ran George Austin out of business and stole a fortune from them. Austin assures them that, as he's no longer a threat to Mia, it's safe for them to stay.

That night, Heyes talks to Austin while Curry helps Charlotte in the kitchen. She explains that Mia drove away the advertisers, forcing her father to sell his newspaper. He had invested $30,000 in it and sold it for only $10,000. Charlotte is attracted to Curry. They share a leisurely kiss.

Austin tells Heyes it was his printed criticism of Mia Bronson that caused her vendetta against him. After selling the newspaper, Austin discovered the buyer worked for Mia. The advertisers have returned and the paper is once again making money.

Charlotte and Curry join them at the table. As Curry passes the sideboard, he notices a piece of paper on which is printed, in reverse image, a $10 bill. He shows it to Heyes who remarks that, if Austin is a counterfeiter, he sure is a good one. With a smile Austin invites the boys into his workshop.

Austin has never seen a printing press that wasn't cumbersome. He'd always wanted to come up with something better and once he lost the newspaper, started pursuing his dream. He's made great progress on developing a chemical printing process. He demonstrates it for the boys, printing another fake $10 bill, explaining that the high quality of the ink in money makes it ideal for his tests. However, he couldn't use it for counterfeiting even if he wanted to, because of the reversed image and the pulpy paper he must use.

Heyes grows quiet, prompting Charlotte to worry that he's bored. Heyes assures her he's always quiet when he's coming up with something brilliant. Heyes asks Austin how he'd like to get even with Mia Bronson and go back east with a pocketful of money. The idea appeals to him, although he hopes Joshua hasn't got anything violent or illegal in mind. When Austin points out that Mia doesn't just have people beaten, sometimes she has them killed, Heyes admits his plan is dangerous. Austin wants to hear it anyway.

Clean-shaven and dressed in their city clothes, Heyes and Curry are unrecognizable as the troublesome tramps Mia dealt with earlier. They buy into the poker game with stacks of crisp new $10 bills. It's not long before Cliff informs them Miss Bronson wants to see them in her office.

The money they bought into the game with has a peculiar odor that has piqued Mia's curiosity. Although the money looks real, she's noticed two of the bills have the same serial number. Jones berates Smith for not waiting another day for the bills to air out, but Smith wants to know what that has to do with serial numbers. "You can't smell serial numbers!" Jones retorts. Mia is interested and, with gun in hand, demands to know more. They earnestly plead to buy back the counterfeit bill. Their admission that the money is counterfeit reverses her attitude. She invites them to share her Napoleon brandy.

In Austin's workshop, Mia avidly watches as Austin mixes his chemicals. She offers him a brand-new bill to use, which he quickly switches when Curry diverts her attention by paying her for it. Mia is delighted to find that the sanctimonious journalist has become a counterfeiter. Austin completes the printing and shows her the result. It's backwards, she protests. "Negatives always are," Austin answers. Curry explains that the whole process is complicated, taking up to sixteen hours to complete. Immediately, Mia becomes suspicious, accusing them of trying to pull a switch on her. Curry reminds her she invited herself in on this deal and urges her to invite herself out. Heyes steps in as peacemaker. He has Mia note the serial number of the bill, then convinces her to stay while Austin mixes up the chemicals for the final step. She dutifully recites the number and watches as Austin puts the bill in the press and adds a piece of litmus paper. If she wants to see the final result, she can drop by the next day.

As soon as Mia leaves, everyone hurries back into the workshop. Heyes takes one of their own bills and begins altering it. When he's finished, he gives it to Charlotte to compare with the bill that was in the press. She can't tell the difference. They both have the same serial number, but she can't tell which one he changed.

Austin exchanges the litmus paper for a piece of red paper to make it appear that the litmus paper changed color.

The next day, Mia comes to see the counterfeit money. She compares the two bills and announces that they have made a believer out of her. She can't tell which is real and which is fake. Smith offers to let Mia in on their plan to market the counterfeit money in neighboring towns at the rate of $1,000 per week. They'll cut her in for twenty percent. Mia refuses. That's small time. She wants them to print her $20,000 and then she'll leave them alone.

When Mia has gone, Austin and Heyes decide to split the $20,000 fifty-fifty while Curry and Charlotte make plans for their getaway. They'll take the train to Denver, then buy tickets for another destination. They'll be long gone before Mia realizes she's been swindled. Curry has one more plan in mind, if Austin will show him how to use his old printing press.

Mia arrives the next day with twenty new $1,000 bills for them to copy. They form an assembly line and soon have the printing press loaded with money and paper. The process is automatic from this point, although they do check on it from time to time. Mia is satisfied. She puts a carpetbag on the table and places the press inside. She'll keep it in her room at the casino and bring it back when the litmus paper turns red. Austin and the boys are taken aback and scramble to find excuses to keep her from taking the press. None of them work and they watch in dismay as she leaves with the money.

Afterwards, they lament the plan's failure. Charlotte has everything ready to go, so they might as well catch the train. But Heyes comes up with another plan, a dangerous plan that might not work at all. He'll accuse Mia of opening the machine, thereby ruining the process. "If you claim that she opened that press and she didn't, you're never going to get out of that saloon alive," Curry warns him. Heyes is willing to take that chance.

Early the next morning, Smith and Jones visit Mia to check on the press. Smith examines the machine and declares it's been tampered with. Mia indignantly denies opening it, then, at Smith's skepticism, reluctantly admits she did open it to check just the top bill. Smith explains the transfer process stopped when she released the pressure and let in air. Luckily, the ink is still good on the $1,000 bills. Jones tells her to let them dry and bring them back later.

That night the men set up the press again, but this time they're ready for her. When Mia turns to get her carpetbag, they switch presses and send her off with an admonishment to keep her hands off until the litmus paper turns red.

Charlotte, her father and the boys board the train to Denver with $20,000 between them. Heyes and Curry are playing poker in the parlor car when Charlotte asks to talk to them in private. She's glad to hear they're winning at poker, because she wants them to give her father their half of the money, which by rights should be his. Heyes can see her point, but they can't afford to be that generous. She was hoping they'd give up the money as a noble gesture, but if they don't, she can get the money another way. When they were delirious they were talking to each other, using their real names. She was curious and discovered they are worth $10,000 a piece. Curry tries to charm her, reminding her of the kisses they shared. It was exciting kissing Kid Curry, she admits, but she knew all along the relationship couldn't go anywhere. Charlotte is adamant; there's a US Marshal on board the train and she'll turn them in if she has to. Heyes and Curry make the noble gesture.

Meanwhile, back in King City, Mia is faced with thousands of flyers offering a $1,000 prize to the first man who figures out how she marks the cards in her casino. "Apply for prize money to Mr. Joshua Smith and Mr. Thaddeus Jones, 1600 Pennsylvania Avenue, Washington, D.C." With a cry, she rushes to the press and frantically opens it, finding only blank paper.

GUEST CAST

IDA LUPINO	MIA BRONSON
BUDDY EBSEN	GEORGE AUSTIN
SALLIE SHOCKLEY	CHARLOTTE AUSTIN
GEORGE ROBOTHAM	MAX
ALLEN PINSON	KARL
BUD WALLS	CLIFF
JOHN KELLOGG	DEALER

Although this was the fourth episode with Roger Davis to be aired, it was shot just after "The Biggest Game in the West," and thus was the first one in which he was free to give his own interpretation to the character of Hannibal Heyes instead of having to mimic Peter Duel's characterization. Left to his own creative instincts, Roger played Heyes much differently than Peter had, so much so that many viewers feel that the character was thereafter written differently to accommodate him. When asked if that was the case, Huggins immediately denied it. "I would have a professional rejection of the idea that when you get a new actor you have to change the character."[16] The outlines, story notes and rewrite notes for the post-Duel episodes bear this out. The character did not change, only the actor's take on it.

"The Biggest Game in the West" and "What's in It for Mia?" share a common ancestry – an episode of *Maverick* called "Rage for Vengeance." That story features a woman who uses counterfeit money placed in a bank for safekeeping (but not deposited) to open a newspaper and expose the corruption of a local cattleman.

The genesis of this story goes back to 1957 when Howard Browne had an idea for an episode of *Maverick* in which Bret would play poker for counterfeit money. Browne tried various tacks but ultimately couldn't make the story work. He turned the idea over to Roy Huggins, who also played around with it and came up with the story told in "Rage for Vengeance," which had counterfeit money and lots of action, but no poker game.[17] After almost fifteen years, Huggins found a way to make the original idea work and the poker game was finally incorporated into a story about counterfeit money in "The Biggest Game in the West." Never one to let a good story go by, Huggins then took the portion of the story regarding the newspaper owner battling corruption, gave it a twist and fashioned it into this episode. It's quite fitting, given this history, that Mia Bronson gets her comeuppance through counterfeit money.

Though this script went through five drafts, there weren't many changes made to the basic story. Instead, Huggins guided writer Bill Gordon towards simplification, urging him to eliminate subtle details in the opening sequence that would "take too much coverage and are time-consuming to shoot" and suggesting less complicated ways of conveying information to avoid what he called "too much connective tissue."[18] Huggins was also concerned that Gordon hadn't been clear that Austin's process was not a successful method of counterfeiting. Besides Austin being a law-abiding citizen, Huggins wanted to make sure the plan belonged to Heyes, saying, "If we get the impression that Austin is already close to counterfeiting, what Heyes does doesn't become very interesting. . . .Austin should state the difficulties very clearly. . . .But Heyes is still thinking. Thus we can hook the interest of our audience: what could he possibly be thinking?"[19]

The most significant change made during the final rewrites was to switch the crooked casino owner from a man named Fred to a woman named Mia. By doing this, a serviceable and somewhat predictable character became much more intriguing. The dialogue originally written for Fred was retained, a decision which added depth to the boys' now-female adversary. The "man who owns the town" is a standard character in westerns. He's expected to be violent and powerful. To see these same traits in a woman goes against the tradition of the genre, where woman are most often the civilizing influence on the men around them, and the audience will sit up and take notice when the cliché is broken. Rather than the predictable bad guy, Heyes and Curry face the more unusual Mia Bronson, making the story more interesting and the ultimate defeat of Mia more satisfying.

BAD NIGHT IN BIG BUTTE

"A stolen diamond does not belong to the heirs of the thief that stole it!"
– Kid Curry

STORY:	JOHN THOMAS JAMES
TELEPLAY:	GLEN A. LARSON
DIRECTED:	RICHARD L. BARE
SHOOTING DATES:	FEBRUARY 3, 4, 7, 8, 9, 10, 1972
ORIGINAL US AIR DATE:	MARCH 2, 1972
ORIGINAL UK AIR DATE:	JANUARY 14, 1974

Hannibal Heyes and Kid Curry mosey into town worried that they're being followed by one Boot Coby. When Coby veers off, the boys are relieved and

Heyes's Great African Diamond Hunter. He invented the name *Africanus Phodopus*. The true scientific name of a hamster is *Cricetinae Phodopus*.

Heyes wants to leave while the going's good. But Curry reminds him they've spent the last month looking for Georgette and they can't give up her trail now.

Coby asks the sheriff about a man named Skeet Jenkins and learns he has been dead for two days. His daughter has come to town for the funeral.

Heyes and Curry query the hotel desk clerk and learn that no Georgette Sinclair checked in, but a Georgette Jenkins did. They find the lady at the cemetery and debate whether it's "their" Georgette or not. When she raises the black veil that hides her mournful face, they recognize her, then watch as she persuades the undertaker to open the coffin and search through the dead man's pockets for a letter. Unobserved, Boot Coby watches, too.

The boys approach as she heads for her carriage, letter in hand. Offering their sympathies, they wonder who Skeet Jenkins is.

Skeet was her father's best friend from his more crooked days, she tells them. As she trails off sadly, the boys change the subject and say they've looked her up to borrow $3,000 for a poker stake. She refuses; poker is not her idea of a sound investment. As they help her aboard the stagecoach for Big Butte, Heyes and Curry spot Boot Coby still watching. George, also seeing Coby, suddenly changes her mind. The way Heyes plays poker is more like investing in an accounting firm than gambling. She has only one condition – that they help her out for one night in Big Butte. She won't say whether it has anything to do with the envelope she retrieved from Jenkins's pocket.

In Big Butte, George hopes to get the hotel's front corner room on the top floor but it's already been rented to Mr. Smith and Mr. Jones. The boys specifically asked for it because of its view of the sheriff's office and the main street. George hastens in, laments how small it is, and offers to trade. She peeks through the curtain and spies Coby riding into town.

It's the Fourth of July and Big Butte celebrates in a big way. After dark, the town hurrahs the holiday with fireworks, firecrackers and noisy gunplay.

Heyes and Curry head out of their room for dinner with George, unaware that she's watching them from around the corner. As soon as they've headed downstairs, she picks the lock on their door and enters. Pacing off the room, she locates a spot and begins to hack at the ceiling above it with an axe. After chopping a good-sized hole, she stands on the bed and reaches up into it but can't locate what she's after.

Meanwhile the boys wait for her in the hotel dining room, worried that Boot Coby is after them. If so, why hasn't he nabbed them? They conclude that maybe he's not after them and they'd better find out what George is up to.

When she finally joins them, Coby takes a seat at a nearby table. They tell her that his business is turning people like them in and recovering stolen property. She nervously denies that she's into anything in which money is involved. At this

obvious lie, the boys stand to leave
and she admits there may be *some*
money involved. They want fifty
percent of whatever they're talking
about. She counters with a flat
thirty percent.

Back in their hotel room, Heyes
and Curry stare at the damage in
the ceiling. Coby comes by and
orders them to the sheriff's office.
There, Coby, the sheriff and the
deputy go through Heyes's and
Curry's clothes as the boys stand in
a jail cell wrapped in blankets.
When they ask what the men are
looking for, Coby scoffs at their
ignorance. They just happened

Georgette Sinclair, played by Michelle Lee.

into town on the night the statute of limitations runs out on a famous robbery,
stay in the hotel where the robber was captured, and tear up the room? Curry
admits it sounds too coincidental, but that's what it is. Disgusted, Coby asks if
they never heard of the $200,000 Thurston diamond.

Not finding anything, the sheriff unlocks the cell. The boys plan to leave
town, however, the sheriff orders them to stay until somebody pays for the
damage to the hotel room.

Coby is angry the sheriff released them but he has no reason to hold them
since they don't have the diamond. The room that was torn up was not even
there seven years ago when the robbery took place. The third floor was only
added a year ago. The sheriff suspects that Coby, on the trail of the diamond,
would not turn it over to the state if he locates it nor would he settle for the
ten percent finder's fee. For his part, Coby accuses the sheriff of wanting him
out of town so he can collect the fee. The lawman argues that, as a public
official, he will only get thanks from the governor if he turns in the gem. Coby
doesn't believe him.

While the sheriff is searching Heyes and Curry, a frustrated George paces off
the steps in their room, checking the placement of the ceiling hole. They return
to the hotel and badger the desk clerk for a new un-damaged room. When he
refuses, they threaten to sue because the damage looks like an inside job.
Acquiescing, he offers them the room directly under their old room.

Just missing them, George descends the stairs to the lobby. Feigning fascination
with desperadoes, she queries the desk clerk who explains about robber Skeet Jenkins.
The sheriff fell off the roof chasing Jenkins and ended up with a wooden leg.

"The sheriff fell off a three-story building and only lost a leg?" George
wonders. The clerk clarifies that it was only a two-story building then. She grins

as realization dawns. "That would mean seven years ago the second floor was the top floor!"

Curry undresses for bed arguing that they should leave because, in the past seven years, someone was sure to have found the diamond. Maybe not, Heyes says. It may be only as big as a .45 caliber slug and easy to hide.

The noise of exploding firecrackers covers the creaks as George pries up floorboards. Soon she's got a sizable hole directly under the one she chopped in the ceiling.

As Heyes begins to undress for bed, Coby knocks on their door. Because Curry is already asleep, Heyes steps into the hall to talk with him. Coby thinks that they or their lady friend know where the diamond is and says they'll have to go through him to get it out of town.

While they're talking, George's crowbar slips and dislodges the diamond. It falls smack into the sleeping Curry's navel. Heyes spots it as soon as he reenters their room. Peeking through the hole in their ceiling, her floor, George claims it. She reasons that it's hers because it was willed to her by the man who stole it. Seven years ago, Wilton R. Thurston made some bad investments and all he had left was the diamond. He hired Skeet Jenkins to steal it so he could collect the insurance. Skeet died on his way to retrieve it, so it belongs to George. Curry points out that a stolen diamond does not belong to the heirs of the thief that stole it; it belongs to the heirs of the victim. There were no heirs but Heyes argues that it still doesn't belong to her. "All right," she says, "maybe it just belongs to whoever finds it. And that's me!"

She plans to sneak out of town with it. When they shimmy down a knotted sheet thrown out the hotel window, the sheriff and two deputies greet them, armed with rifles.

George, Heyes and Curry are once again stripped and locked in jail cells while their clothes are searched to no avail. George says they didn't find the diamond but were sneaking out of town to avoid this sort of humiliation. The sheriff isn't buying it. Heyes deals for their release. But the only deal the sheriff will make is the keys to the cell in exchange for the diamond.

At that, Coby calls for a conference with the sheriff. Coby sees through him; the sheriff wants the diamond, not because he will get a letter from the governor, but because he lost a leg. If the sheriff cuts Coby out, he threatens to track the lawman down. If they work together, half of $200,000 is better than nothing.

The sheriff offers his prisoners a new deal. Since the diamond rightfully belongs to the state, and he's a duly authorized representative, he'll give them $1,000 reward each. Curry and George scoff at the ridiculous offer, but Heyes says he'll take it. They don't have the diamond, but to get it, they'll have to let him out of jail. The sheriff reluctantly acquiesces but will hold Curry and George.

Heyes boards the train as Curry and George kill time playing cards through the bars of their adjoining cells.

Three days later, Heyes returns from the Denver zoo with a cage. In it is an

Africanus Phodopus, a great African diamond hunter. Coby and the sheriff don't believe it, but pretend to go along.

As soon as it's dark, since that is when rodents do their best work, Heyes heads for the hotel, cage in hand. He enters the room alone and covers the keyhole with tape. He lights a lamp and unscrews the doorknob to the adjoining room's door. The diamond falls into his hand.

Coby and the sheriff, frustrated at their inability to peek through the keyhole, enter the room with guns drawn to find Heyes gazing dejectedly at the phodopus, who didn't find the diamond.

Once more, Heyes, Curry and George are searched, while Coby turns the room inside out. Once more, the search is futile. With no choice, the sheriff turns them loose. Ready to leave, Heyes can't understand why the phodopus failed. "He must not be a purebred."

Safely out of town, the trio buggy to an abandoned out-building where Heyes retrieves a homing pigeon. Attached to its leg is the Thurston diamond.

Sometime later they take the jewel to Soapy Saunders for evaluation. "Well, well, well," he says, examining it through an eyepiece.

"Well?" asks Heyes.

"Well?" asks Curry.

"Well?" asks George.

"Well," says Soapy, it's quartz and worth only $50!

Georgette is dismayed and walks out but the boys remind her of the poker stake money. They still expect her to fund the game. What has she got herself involved with, she asks the audience, a bunch of crooks?

GUEST CAST

JACK ELAM	BOOT COBY
MICHELE LEE	GEORGETTE SINCLAIR
ARTHUR O'CONNELL	SHERIFF, BIG BUTTE
PAT BUTTRAM	SHERIFF
SAM JAFFE	SOAPY SAUNDERS
MILLS WATSON	DEPUTY SHERIFF SAM PERKINS
DAVE WILLOCK	CLERK, BIG BUTTE
ROBERT NICHOLS	DOC
PAUL SCHOTT	HOTEL CLERK
FRANK FERGUSON	BILLINGS
LAURA ROSE	MOXIE
DONNY SANDS	DRIVER
AMANDA REISS	MARIA
WALT DAVIS	MINISTER

Mark Twain opens Chapter 17 of *Pudd'nhead Wilson* with a quote about July 4th. "Statistics show that we lose more fools on this day than in all the other days of the year put together. This proves, by the number left in stock, that one Fourth of July per year is now inadequate, the country has grown so."[20] It is appropriate that this episode is set on the Fourth of July because it is filled with foolishness.

In his as-yet-unpublished autobiography, Roy Huggins wrote that the kind of humor he liked "is the kind that comes out of character and is funny only if the actor understands how that character would read the line and why."[21] Knowing his actors, in his rewrite notes for Glen Larson, Huggins consistently challenged Larson to come up with funny lines for them and the humor in the episode is the result of Larson's trying really hard. So, the attempts at humor in the dreadful exaggerated facial expressions and breaking of the "fourth wall" between actors and audience in this episode cannot be blamed on the writer but must be laid at the feet of the director. When Heyes and Curry ask Georgette just who the dead Skeet Jenkins was, she looks into the camera and the audience hears a BOING going off in her head. (A similar note was sounded in "Don't Get Mad, Get Even" when the jeweler examines the necklace hung on Wheelwright's woman. His eyepiece falls with a BOING as he realizes it's fake.) In the final scene, Georgette wonders what she's got herself into and, with eyes wide facing the camera, appears to ask the audience. The two directors responsible for these juvenile attempts at humor were not involved in any other *Alias Smith and Jones* episodes.

Other nonsensical particulars should have been worked out before final shooting. When the sheriff and Coby are searching their clothes, Heyes and Curry are wrapped in full-length blankets. Georgette, presumably a proper lady of the 1880s, was given a short blanket that leaves her shoulders and legs exposed. Gentlemen that they are, or perhaps single-minded in their hunt for the diamond, neither Coby nor the lawman leers suggestively at her. The phodopus, a typical rodent active at night, is supposed to work best in the dark. Heyes tapes the keyhole shut so Coby and the sheriff cannot peek in to see him light a lamp. Don't they see the light stream out under the door? How did Heyes carry the homing pigeon in the same cage as a hamster without a lot of fluttering and screeching from the two animals? Since when does a zoo lend out its animals? How did Heyes train a homing pigeon in the three days he was gone to Denver? Huggins might shrug, assuming these conjectures to be "overthink." But it can be argued that they are instead examples of the writer's and director's "non-think."

The story line went through drastic changes throughout numerous revisions. Initially, the title was "The Girl with the Empty Box," in which a woman named Justine Plunkett coerces the boys into accompanying her to the town of Providence. When she chops a hole in her hotel room floor looking for hidden money, dollar bills float down, forming a "hundred thousand dollar patch quilt of greenbacks" on the sleeping Curry.[22] By Huggins's rewrite notes of January 13, 1972, Clementine Hale had become the female lead and the boys are tracking her down to retrieve the photograph of the three of them. When Sally Field did not reprise her role for this episode, the female lead was given to Michele Lee as Georgette Sinclair. The boys are looking for Georgette to borrow money for a poker game, an unlikely but still plausible theory. Don Ameche was not available either and, instead of Diamond Jim Guffy as originally planned, the trio takes the diamond for evaluation to old friend Soapy Saunders. Jim Guffy, Soapy Saunders and Silky O'Sullivan are rich gentlemen to whom Heyes and Curry can turn to get money, advice or scam props. They appear to work interchangeably in the scripts depending on which actor was available. Huggins used the same tack in *Maverick,* creating the character of Gentleman Jack Darby when Efrem Zimbalist, Jr. was unavailable to reprise his role of Dandy Jim Buckley.

From the beginning, Roy Huggins worried about the logic of the diamond belonging to whoever possesses it after midnight on July 4. He insisted it must be clear that it belongs to the state before that. "This is a fairy tale that we must hope the audience will believe. They will — because it takes a lawyer to answer that question."[23]

Thirty years after the episode aired, Jack Elam had no recollection of his role of Boot Coby. "I can only say that in any show that long ago — I was mean! Bad and mean!"[24]

CHAPTER 8

It Was a Good Life, but Times Were Changing

By some miracle, Peter Duel's suicide had not destroyed *Alias Smith and Jones* and the network ordered a third season. Universal decided to make the new season something special and do what they had never done before – send the production out on location. While the show did spend some time off the studio backlot during its first two seasons, the locations had always been local, no more than an hour or so from Universal. This time the cast and crew would trek to the wilds of Utah.

Jo Swerling remembers that after Peter's death, "we wanted to come on very strong with our new cast . . . we wanted to give the shows, those first shows, a kind of a John Ford western movie look because it's very spectacular." John Ford had created a signature style by shooting on location in Monument Valley, Utah, in which the grand rock formations became as important to his films as the actors and the script. But the *Alias Smith and Jones* team decided Monument Valley was too limited for their purposes and instead chose to take their production to Moab. "Moab had a lot of those same kinds of rock formations and mesas . . . but it also had mountains with snow and things like that so we felt that if we headquartered ourselves there, we'd get a wider variety of looks," Swerling explains. Besides a wider variety of scenery, Moab was also logistically a better choice than Monument Valley, with the town reasonably close to the chosen locations and with easy transportation in and out of the area. The time spent in Utah eventually stretched to three weeks, longer than originally planned. "I got yelled at on that one," Swerling remembers with a grin.[1]

With the crew scheduled to begin third season production with the Utah shoot, Roy Huggins needed to get the season's scripts ready earlier than usual. The time in Utah would be limited, but with advance planning, footage could be shot for all the episodes. ABC's third season renewal had been a short order – twelve episodes – with the possibility of an order for the "back nine" later on. Huggins wanted all twelve episodes already committed to to have the advantage of Moab footage to maintain the high production values and special wide-open-spaces look. During the last two weeks of April 1972, Huggins concentrated on stories, holding two or three story conferences a day. The pace slowed down after that first flurry, but by the time production began, all twelve scripts were in some stage of development. "The Long Chase" would open the season, followed by "High Lonesome Country." These two episodes were mostly outdoor stories and would be shot entirely in Moab. New opening title sequences and portions of all episodes except "The Strange Fate of Conrad Meyer Zulick," "The Day The Amnesty Came Through" and "McGuffin" would be shot on location with the interiors done in the studio soundstages later. Generic footage of Heyes and Curry riding through the area became the basis of the tags for each episode, the particular dialogue for each being looped in later. In this manner, even those scripts which weren't a

Ben Murphy as Kid Curry in Moab.

part of the location shooting schedule would still have a share of Utah's majestic vistas. Besides splendor, this footage added a sense of space to Heyes and Curry's wanderings and enhanced their characterization with the audience becoming privy to the boys' life on the trail as they argued and teased their way from town to town. This tag format, not incidentally, also accommodated the new policy of "dispensable" tags that the network affiliates demanded. In some markets, the affiliates wanted to carve out additional commercial time to enhance their revenue and the easiest way to gain an extra minute and a half was to lop off the tag at the end of the show. During the first and second seasons, the tag was often the final story element and eliminating it left the episode incomplete. In the third season, the tags became lagniappe, adding punch but no longer essential to the story.

On June 30, 1972, Jo Swerling took charge of a cast and crew eighty-five persons strong as they settled into their quarters in the little town of Moab. Not many problems arose which required Swerling's intervention, but "somebody had to be there to make sure we didn't go too far over schedule or budget," Swerling explains. "And keep pointing at the sun that's setting . . . ." Most of the locations where they would be working were within the boundaries of the Manti-LaSal National Forest and Swerling was the point man, working as a liaison between the production and the park rangers, who were happy to see the company, but concerned about possible damage to the land. Adding to the complications of shooting on location were the constraints of respecting the protected environment. Swerling elaborates, "[We] had to be careful we didn't disrupt anything, knock any rocks over, that sort of thing. There were a lot of rangers around, kind of keeping an eye on us."[2]

Alex Singer was the director chosen to lead the Moab production team. He recalls the experience fondly. "It was a magical place. Moab must be one of the most beautiful places in the world. I felt very pleased." But while the scenery around Moab was beguiling, the environment was brutal. It was early July – the temperature climbed to over 120 degrees Fahrenheit and stayed that way. Yet, as Singer points out, "it was the driest heat I've ever known, which meant that once you sort of got used to it, it was very tolerable." Getting used to it required drinking lots of water. Singer made sure that every member of the cast and crew drank at least a gallon a day.

While keeping hydrated was essential, Singer felt that actually going to fetch water, or having someone bring it to him, was a waste of time. He solved the problem by carrying a canteen. And as he was constantly referring to his scripts, he decided it would be nice to carry them with him at all times, too. He had a pouch made to hold the scripts and found that it was also a good way to carry his wallet, his glasses, Kleenex, chewing gum and any other essential he might need. "I was completely independent as I moved through time and space," Singer recalls. "I looked like I was going to war."

And move through time and space he did. It was against his principles to ever have the crew see him sit down on the theory that if the boss didn't sit down, the crew wouldn't either. But film production is an arduous task, especially when coupled with the heat and dust of a desert summer. "People are tired, they're physically tired," Singer explains. "It's very easy for the set to kind of decline into paralysis unless there's something going on. So, I felt I was duty-bound to be the *tummler*. It's a Yiddish word and it means the guy who makes the noise." Singer's efforts to "make the noise" and keep things lively endeared him to the crew and they started to play games with him.

They started in a simple and subtle way. Because of the heat, Singer had developed the habit of wearing a sweatband under his wristwatch to keep it from sliding around. One day the crew imitated him, each person wearing a sweatband under *their* watch, then using exaggerated gestures as they worked to draw his attention to their wrists. On another day, Singer wore pants that were a little too long. Afraid he would trip over them as he rushed around the set, Singer rolled up his cuffs a couple of inches and was able to move about unhampered. The next day the entire crew rolled up their cuffs, creating a new fashion trend on the set. "They made me laugh," Singer remembers. "And they made themselves laugh a lot."

Pleased with the success of their teasing, the crew planned a bigger joke, involving not only the crew, but also Singer's wife Judy and the staff of a local

Chinese restaurant. Singer ordered a complicated entree, so when his dinner came a bit later than everyone else's he didn't think too much about it. At last the waiter brought his meal, placing it in front of him with an elaborate flourish and a straight face. The dish looked beautiful, garnished with parsley and other greens. "It was an interesting arrangement of things," Singer muses. "Chinese food is a little bit exotic in some of the ways in which it is prepared, so I allowed for that and kind of examined it." The entire room was dead silent as everyone watched the director closely. "I tried to get a hold on something that looked like I should hold it," he continues with a laugh. "And there was nothing but chicken bones artfully put together." The crew roared with laughter at his confusion. It took great daring for a crew to play such a trick on their director, but it was great fun and a total success. "They were very proud of themselves," Judy Singer adds. The director was also proud of them. Singer approaches directing as performance art, communicating a certain euphoria to the crew that creates excitement and a sense of fun. "It was a way for me to be able to push them without being aggressive and without being personal," Singer explains. "I got a marvelous reaction from this crew."[3]

The time in Utah wasn't all fun and games, though. In fact, at times it was downright dangerous. After a long, tiring day of shooting, cast and crew would return to town for dinner and a bit of relaxation. Having a film company in town was a boon for local business owners, but for the local cowboys, these Hollywood interlopers soon wore out their welcome. The cowboys watched in frustration as their starry-eyed girlfriends gravitated toward the visitors, flirting and fraternizing with the glamorous film crew. The situation became so tense, Jo Swerling took to traveling in the company of the unit's stuntmen, Jimmy Nickerson and Sonny Shields, for protection. It was a wise decision. One night while walking from the hotel to a nearby restaurant, two cowboys in a pickup truck stopped at the intersection where the three men were waiting to cross the street. The driver rolled down his window and greeted them with a sneer. "Hollywood faggots!" Shields sauntered over to the truck and challenged him. "You got something to say to me?" The driver replied with another choice epithet. "Step out of the car," Shields demanded. The cowboy opened the door, put one foot on the ground and folded up in a heap. Shields's left hook had been so fast, neither Swerling nor Nickerson had seen it. Ignoring the man at his feet, Shields addressed the passenger. "Have *you* got anything to say?" The cowboy shook his head, slid behind the wheel and took off, leaving his buddy in the street.

Ben Murphy may have played the "fastest gun in the West," but he had no desire to become a target for irate cowboys, or even cowgirls, in Moab. "I just knew instinctively – don't go out in public. I knew people'd come gunning for me and I'm no fighter," Ben admits. One night he did leave his hotel room, going to a local bar where Monty Laird was to perform his gun-twirling routine. The phalanx of crew members surrounding the actor didn't deter a hostile woman from approaching him. "Oh, you're Ben Murphy! Ya wanna fight?" Ben realized

Monty Laird.

the woman was just drunk and being ornery; he diffused the situation by being polite. Laird wasn't so lucky.

Laird's gun-twirling routine didn't endear him to the local cowboys. After the show, as he was leaving the bar, three cowboys jumped him and started to beat the tar out of him. But Laird, though rather slight of stature, was wiry and tough. He was also a fighter and never went about unarmed, as the cowboys learned to their shock. Laird managed to reach his boot, pull out his knife and sink it into one of his attackers. He made his escape and the cowboys disappeared with their buddy, the knife still sticking in him, much to Laird's disgust. "I lost my best knife that night," he regretted. The next morning he related the incident to Swerling, who wondered how soon it would be before the police came calling. No one knew how badly injured the cowboy was, but Swerling eventually decided it must have been minor and the cowboy so humiliated that he didn't talk about it. "There was never a peep out of anybody. He didn't die or anything," Swerling explains. "I think there would have been major consequences if that had happened."[4]

Being in Utah, far away from the watchful eyes of the Black Tower and the limitations of the Universal backlot, was invigorating. Singer and cinematographer Gene Polito no longer had to frame their shots in such a way as to avoid showing nearby power lines or the castle battlements on the back side of the western sets. While Singer always enjoyed the challenge of filming the great outdoors within the backlot boundaries, he was excited to be shooting a Western the way it ought to be shot – in rocky canyons and remote hillsides, where every turn offered a new and unexpected surprise. "The locations were really exotic, really remote. . . . They had exactly that quality that you want from a western where you don't know what's around the other side of the rock over there and the rocks are so beautiful that it almost doesn't matter what's around the other side," Singer rhapsodizes. He took full advantage of the countryside, giving the show a sense of reality lacking in its first two seasons. He was excited by the beauty of the surroundings as well as the challenge of shooting half a dozen episodes at once, each of them essentially an action film. "The physical freedom just gave the

(Courtesy of Ben Murphy)

Relaxing between scenes.

whole show, the shows, a lift in spirit that was very special," Singer recalls.

Singer had been the director who shepherded Roger Davis through his first days in the role of Hannibal Heyes. Now he was the director breathing new life into the series. Having also directed several episodes with Peter Duel in the role, he was in the perfect position to judge the performance of both actors. He had been impressed by Peter's talent, his ability to read the lines with real understanding. "That makes doing a kind of an out-of-the-side-of-the-mouth comedy, which is what this was, a pleasure because you have somebody who really touches the right notes and [gets] it straight," Singer says. Roger Davis gave a different interpretation. Singer recalls Roger had a sweet nature that was very different from Peter's take on the character. "It was a kind of openness and accessibility that I think worked very well for the character."

Pleased as he was, he was somewhat dismayed by a quirk of Roger's. "He managed to get himself injured in ways that simply astonished everybody," Singer explains. "He could fall in places where you'd say 'There's nothing to fall from.' He could trip over things where there's nothing to trip over . . . [The crew was] always on the edge of their seats every time he did something." Luckily the injuries, though frequent, were minor and none of them show on film. "Once or twice they were a little scary," Singer recalls. "The crew tried so hard to avoid any difficulty. The guys doing the special effects and the stuntmen would do anything to keep him from getting hurt. He got hurt anyway, but I don't think he was ever out of action completely."

Monty Laird remembered one such scary incident. The scene called for Roger and Ben to gallop down a hill full out. At the bottom they were to make a quick left and go through a wide gate. Laird checked Ben's horse and tightened his saddle, knowing the competitive spirit between Ben and Roger would turn the scene into a race no matter what the director had in mind. Always protective of Ben, Laird advised, "Okay, now when you get down to the bottom of that hill and you get ready to make that left to go through that gate, lean to the left and bring your horse around into it." Ben listened to the advice, as he always did. Laird then went over to Roger and asked if he could check his saddle. "No! I checked it," Roger retorted, reluctant to take advice from anyone other than the director. The two actors mounted their horses and took off "like two race jockeys coming out of the chute." Ben followed the advice and made the turn. "Roger made that turn sitting straight in the saddle, went over to the left, the saddle twisted on the horse, he got hung up in the stirrup and it drug him, oh God, thirty or forty feet," Laird recalled. Roger finally broke loose of the stirrup as members of the crew ran through the clouds of dust to rescue him and capture the horse. The fall was spectacular, but fortunately Roger suffered only bruises.[5]

Roger Davis and Ben Murphy.

Ben and Roger were getting used to working together. They didn't have the natural chemistry that had existed between Ben and Peter and the circumstances of their pairing didn't help the situation. "I liked Roger. He was a personable fellow," Monty Laird mused. "But him and Ben just didn't click." Part of the reason they didn't click was that neither one of them understood how the other one worked and neither one of them took the time to find out. It was a new season, but Roger still felt insecure in his position as the replacement for the well-liked Peter Duel. *Alias Smith and Jones* was, as everyone who worked on it agrees, a fun show. But not for Roger. "The problem with *Smith and Jones* was that, for me, for the most part it was hard and I wasn't having a good time," Roger remembers. "And there was an element of Ben's enjoying that I wasn't having a good time . . . at least from my paranoid perspective."[6]

(Courtesy of Ben Murphy)

Roger performed best when reacting to another actor. He looked to Ben to give him that support and was constantly frustrated when it wasn't forthcoming, leading him to feel Ben was deliberately making things hard for him. Ben also had his moments of frustration with his co-star, but his lack of response to Roger was not caused by a conscious desire to irritate him. It happened because, most of the time, Ben couldn't see him well enough to be able to play off the nuances of his performance. While Roger knew Ben was nearsighted, he had no concept of just how poor his eyesight was. Normally Ben wore contact lenses, but that quickly became impractical in Moab. "You don't want to wear lenses in all that dust," he explains. "It was just one pain in the ass after another out there."

Without his contacts, Ben could have been giving his own performance to a wall. "I don't care who's feeding me lines. I don't see them anyway." But it was driving Roger crazy. "I would think that Ben was enjoying it," Roger expounds. " . . . and I would come over to him and I'd say, 'Jesus, you're just standing there!' And he would go, 'I don't even see you. I've had my glasses off.'"[7]

Ben admits that, although he realized how difficult it was for Roger to replace Peter, he didn't do much to ease the tension between them. And, in truth, he did find an element of enjoyment in Roger's daily mishaps. He shrugs, "Roger's one of those guys who just kind of got in his own way a little bit sometimes, but once you didn't let it bother you, it was hysterical to watch."

Neither Ben nor Roger were expert horsemen, but at the studio that wasn't important. The horses were well trained and experienced in film work and the actors could perform without having to expend a lot of effort controlling their animals. In Utah, that changed. The studio did not send their stable of trained animals with the production team, but instead hired horses from local owners. Naturally these horses were not camera-savvy, as Roger and Ben learned one day.

The scene called for Roger to ride up to Ben, stop, deliver his lines, then turn and gallop off. Ben and Roger were in place on one ridge, while the camera was set up some distance away on another ridge. The actors wore microphones and also had walkie-talkies to communicate with the crew. The first take began. Roger rode up, stopped, delivered his lines, then galloped off. But there was a technical glitch and they had to do it again. Once more Roger rode up, said his lines and rode off. Again something went wrong and the scene had to be re-shot. Ben grins as he remembers what happened next. "By the time you do something with a horse two, three, four times, the horse has got it down." The horse had learned the drill and had no patience with the tedious repetitiveness of filmmaking. On the next take, Roger rode up, got out half the dialogue and suddenly the horse turned and took off. Through the walkie-talkies the actors could hear the crew burst out laughing. They tried it again, but the horse wasn't interested. Over and over they tried to get the scene done and, despite Roger's best efforts to control him, over and over again the horse hurried them along. It was getting late, they weren't getting the shot and Roger was growing more and more embarrassed as the crew laughed ever harder. Ben continues the story, " I remember he's riding up again, he stops the horse, he starts to say his lines and the horse then does the usual – starts to turn and take off again – and I remember seeing Roger's eyes just roll up to the back of his head. Only I saw this, the camera couldn't see it, but you could just see this man and all of a sudden it was like, 'Oh fuck.'" That was the last straw. Ben, who had maintained his composure though take after take, gave up the struggle. He laughed so hard he fell off his horse. Finally giving in to the stubborn animal, the director called it a day. The dialogue was looped in later.[8]

Thirty years and seven hundred fifty miles from Moab, Ben and Roger now laugh at the memories. On a pleasant Saturday afternoon in Malibu, Roger jokingly accuses Ben of having wanted the show to become *Alias Jones*. "I'm sure that that was completely true, but I couldn't laugh about it at the time," Roger admits. Ben promptly denies the charge. He never likes to be the sole lead in a show, a position he declares the "loneliest experience in the world." Ben prefers to be part of an ensemble cast as he was in *The Chisholms,* a situation where he felt secure. "I was never at home [starring] alone, even though I may have been competitive and wanted to be better than all [of them]." That competitive spirit was something that had bothered Peter, who once told Roger the only thing he disliked about working with Ben was that sense of competition. Peter was always ready to help his fellow actors and he was bewildered by Ben's attitude. He didn't understand where it was coming from and, being Peter, assumed he had done something to cause it. But the real source of the rivalry was Ben's insecurity. He said of Peter, "I thought he was so much better than me and it was a jealousy that I had, of not being up to his level." As a result, Ben constantly pushed himself to outdo his co-star and never realized Peter was aware of what he was doing. "[Peter] never saw that," Roger explains, "because he didn't like himself very much and he didn't think he was very good." Ben ponders that for a moment. "Ah, but *I* knew he was."[9]

The location shooting in Moab added a sense of realism to the third season episodes. The blue sky and red earth, stunning rock formations, forests and canyons gave a true feeling of the Old West to Heyes and Curry's adventures. Ben and Roger were beginning to develop their own chemistry and, while different from that between Ben and Peter, it worked. The magic of the Utah landscape and the combination of the people, the time, and the show itself, all added up to a special feeling that was communicated in the texture of the third season episodes.

CHAPTER 9

THE GOVERNOR MIGHT SEE FIT TO WIPE THEIR SLATE CLEAN
THE THIRD SEASON

SEPTEMBER 16, 1972 – JANUARY 13, 1973
Third Season Credits (1972-73)

DIRECTOR:	ALEXANDER SINGER, JACK ARNOLD, EDWARD M. ABROMS, JEFF COREY, RICHARD BENNETT, JEFFREY HAYDEN
CASTING:	JOE REICH, MILT HAMERMAN
UNIT MANAGER:	CARL BERINGER
ASSISTANT DIRECTOR:	JOHN GAUDIOSO, ALAN CROSLAND, DICK BENNETT
2ND ASSISTANT DIRECTOR:	CHARLES DISMUKES, WIN PHELPS (TRAINEE), DICK BENNETT, HERB DUFINE
ART DIRECTOR:	PHIL BENNETT
ASSISTANT ART DIRECTOR:	IRA DIAMOND
SET DECORATOR:	BERT ALLEN
PROPS:	JACK HAMILTON, BILL SMALLBACK, VIC PETROTTA, JR.
SCRIPT SUPERVISOR:	DELL ROSS
CAMERA:	GENE POLITO
SOUND:	ROBERT BERTRAND
WARDROBE – MEN:	HARRY PASEN, JACK TAKEUCHI
WARDROBE – WOMEN:	GENEVA RAMES, GRETCHEN FUSILIER, LEAH RHODES, LOUISE CLARK
PUBLICITY:	BOB PALMER
COORDINATOR:	CHARLES JOHNSON
EDITORIAL SUPERVISION:	RICHARD BELDING
EDITOR:	GLORYETTE CLARK, JOHN DUMAS, ALBERT ZUNIGA, TOM McMULLEN, CHARLES McCLELLAND, BOB SHUGRUE
ASSISTANT EDITOR:	WALT SEGALO, GENE CRAIG

MOAB CREW (JULY 1972)

DIRECTOR:	ALEXANDER SINGER
UNIT MANAGER:	CARL BERINGER
1ST ASSISTANT DIRECTOR:	JOHN GAUDIOSO
2ND ASSISTANT DIRECTOR:	CHARLES DISMUKES
ASSISTANT DIRECTOR TRAINEE:	WIN PHELPS
SCRIPT SUPERVISOR:	HOPE MCLAUGHLIN
EDITOR:	JOHN DUMAS
ASSISTANT EDITOR:	JERRY LUDWIG
DIALOGUE COACH:	STEVE GRAVERS
CAMERAMAN:	GENE POLITO
CAMERA OPERATORS:	SERGE HAIGNERE, TOM CROSS
FIRST CAMERA ASSISTANTS:	JOHN THOENY, CHARLES MILLS
SECOND CAMERA ASSISTANT:	GENE LUCE
CAMERA MECHANIC:	JOHN WALKER
GAFFER:	RON MCLEISH
BEST BOY:	JOHN TODD
LAMP OPERATORS:	BEN GRAHAM, CHARLES RAFFINGTON
GENERATOR OPERATOR:	HARRY JUKES
KEY GRIP:	KENNY SMITH
SECOND GRIP:	JERRY KING
DOLLY GRIP:	JOHN BLACK
GRIP:	GARY PARKER
MIXER:	BOB BERTRAND
BOOM OPERATOR:	MERT STRONG
RECORDER:	BILL GRIFFITH
PROPERTY MASTER:	JACK HAMILTON
ASSISTANT PROP MAN:	STAN BENBROOKS
ART DIRECTOR:	PHIL BENNETT
ASSISTANT ART DIRECTOR:	IRA DIAMOND
SET DRESSER:	BERT ALLEN
LEADMAN:	JOHN LOWERY
SPECIAL EFFECTS:	DON COURTNEY
CRAFT SERVICEMAN:	LOU PERNA
GREENSMAN:	JOHN HUDSON
MAKEUP:	MIKE WESTMORE, WERNER KEEPLER
HAIRDRESSER:	CAROLYN ELIAS
MEN'S WARDROBE:	JACK TAKEUCHI
WOMEN'S WARDROBE:	NEVA RAMES
STUDIO WRANGLER BOSS:	RUSTY MCDONALD
KEY WRANGLER:	ROY WILLIAMS
WRANGLER:	HUTCH HUTCHINSON
UNIT PUBLICIST:	BOB PALMER

CASTING DIRECTOR:	JOE REICH
SECRETARY:	KAREN REITZ
TRANSPORTATION CAPTAIN:	MEL BINGHAM
DRIVER HORSE TRUCK:	DANNY ANGLIN
DRIVER WATER WAGON:	JIM BURRIS
DRIVER #498:	BILL ESSEN PRIES
DRIVER #618:	CECIL MOON
HONEYWAGON DRIVER:	BOB MUNSON
FIRST AID:	JIM RAWLINS
AUDITOR:	PAUL RIGGS
TIMEKEEPER:	DAN YOUNG
STAND IN (MURPHY):	MONTY LAIRD
STAND IN (DAVIS):	CECIL COMBS
STUNTMAN (MURPHY):	JIMMY NICKERSON
STUNTMAN (DAVIS):	SONNY SHIELDS
COURT FOREMAN:	JIM WOOD
CARPENTER:	JIM WALKER
A.H.A. REPRESENTATIVE:	CHICK HANNON

THE LONG CHASE

"Can you imagine that? Harry Briscoe incompetent?"
– Harry Briscoe

STORY:	JOHN THOMAS JAMES
TELEPLAY:	JOHN THOMAS JAMES
DIRECTOR:	ALEXANDER SINGER
SHOOTING DATES:	UTAH – JULY 12, 13, 14, 15, 17, 18, 19, 20, 21, 1972; STUDIO – JULY 24, 25, 26, 1972
ORIGINAL US AIR DATE:	SEPTEMBER 16, 1972
ORIGINAL UK AIR DATE:	OCTOBER 29, 1973

Two bandits, Mugs McGeehu and Hank Silvers, dash out of the Bank of Cottonwood. Townspeople scatter as the men leap on their horses and ride off.

Hannibal Heyes and Kid Curry ride through the desert. They are recognized by Moroni Stebbins who works at untangling his horses' reins at the side of the road. Stebbins jumps in his wagon and races towards town. The boys race off in the opposite direction.

Soon a posse is on their trail.

The boys reach the town of Sagers. Bursting into the livery stable, they claim to be deputies on the trail of three outlaws and exchange their exhausted mounts for two fresh horses. As they switch their saddles to the new animals, Curry asks the proprietor if he rents horses. The idea is preposterous but, when pressed, the

Frank Sinatra, Jr. guest stars as Deputy Wermser in "The Long Chase."

proprietor suggests fifty cents an hour as a fair price. The boys drive the remaining horses out of the stable, handing the proprietor enough money to cover their "rental" before riding out.

The posse, led by Deputy Wermser, arrives seeking fresh horses and is dismayed to find the stable empty.

Heyes and Curry watch and wait as a train takes on water. As it begins to move, they run and jump into a boxcar. Inside they find their old friend Harry Briscoe, rumpled and miserable.

The posse reaches the railroad tracks and begins following the train.

Harry tells the boys he's been fired from the Bannerman Detective Agency for incompetence. Heyes observes they've met a lot of Bannerman detectives and Harry is no more incompetent than they are. Harry smiles, his spirits lifted. Hearing horses, the three men slide open the boxcar door and take a look. Mystified, the boys watch as a member of the posse climbs a telegraph pole. Harry explains that with the proper equipment the man can send a message from there.

Heyes and Curry discuss their options – jump off the train in the middle of the desert or stay on board until the train reaches the town the posse has just telegraphed. Neither is acceptable. But Heyes has an idea that will work if Harry still has his Bannerman credentials. He does.

Heyes and Curry spruce Harry up, brushing the dust off his clothes and giving him a shave. Soon he looks respectable again.

> This story was originally called "The Big Chase."
>
> *Alias Smith and Jones's* new timeslot put them opposite CBS's powerhouse *All in the Family*, a show which gave the conservative CBS censor fits. That censor's name was William Tankersley, a grave Texan more commonly known as Mr. Prohibition. Given Roy Huggins's dislike for most network executives, it is probably not a coincidence that he named his grave, humorless sheriff "Tankersley."

The train pulls into Little Grande. Sheriff Tankersley and his men are inspecting the cars when the boxcar door opens. Hands raised, Heyes and Curry jump out, followed by Harry, gun in hand. Tankersley inspects Harry's credentials, then reluctantly accepts that Heyes and Curry are in his custody.

While the sheriff sends a telegram, the trio waits outside, worried that he is checking up on Harry. Tankersley joins them and announces that Deputy Wermser will accompany them to Cheyenne.

As the stagecoach heads north, Wermser details the social events he'll be missing and Curry threatens to live up to his reputation unless the deputy quits complaining. Wermser explains that he wouldn't be on this trip if the sheriff had gotten an answer to his telegram about Harry. Harry and the boys exchange anxious looks.

The answer finally came and it wasn't good. Sheriff Tankersley and his men follow the stagecoach with grim determination.

Heyes and Curry silently beseech Harry to come up with a plan. Harry thinks hard. Leaning out the window, he urges the driver to speed up because dust behind them is most likely the Devil's Hole Gang. Wermser looks, but doesn't see anything. Harry explains that superior vision is a special qualification necessary for BDI men. Wermser takes another look. "By golly, there is something out there." Harry, trying hard not to show his surprise, leans out for another look. In the distance there really is a cloud of dust.

Heyes and Curry play it up, insisting it's their gang following them, all the while hoping Harry can come up with a plan. Harry struggles to think of something. In desperation, he asks Wermser if there's a ranch nearby.

Sheriff Tankersley and company continue to follow the stagecoach.

At the road to the Circle Y Ranch, Harry and the boys get out. Over Wermser's protests, Harry convinces him to stay aboard to act as a decoy. The stage takes off and the trio heads for the ranch where Harry asks for horses and gear, promising reimbursement from the BDI. Learning the prisoners are the notorious Heyes and Curry, the rancher obliges.

Tankersley catches up to the stagecoach, angry to find Wermser alone. The deputy's feeble explanation does not appease him. "Stay with the stage, Wermser," Tankersley orders coldly. "Go to Cheyenne. Don't ever come back."

Heyes, Curry and Harry, having headed north from the Circle Y for the sake of appearances, now turn south to head for the railroad.

The posse stops at the Circle Y where the rancher informs Tankersley that the outlaws were handcuffed and Briscoe had them covered. They headed north, he tells the sheriff, toward Cheyenne.

The posse continues the chase, finding the point where their quarry turned south.

Curry's horse comes up lame, forcing him and Heyes to ride double, slowing them down. All the while Harry complains about being on the run, certain to be caught and sent to jail. They reach the railroad tracks in time to catch a passing train, hopping aboard even though it's heading back to Little Grande.

Inside the boxcar they find two scruffy men already in residence. After wary introductions, Harry sits down near Heyes and begins to poke his thumb into Heyes's back while commenting to the men that his friends are going to have to jump off the train before it reaches Little Grande. Curry is certain Harry has lost his mind and isn't reassured when Harry next announces that they like him in Little Grande, so it's safe for him to stay on the train. Curry is even more confused when Heyes agrees with Harry. The shorter man asks why they aren't welcome in Little Grande. Disturbing the peace, Heyes offers. His friend has a drinking problem. "When he drinks he thinks he's Kid Curry." The two burst out laughing as Curry scowls.

Heyes and Curry jump off the train ten miles outside of Little Grande. They find some shade and settle down to wait for Harry to return with food, water and horses. Curry wants to know what they're doing. Heyes admits he's not sure himself, but Harry had something in mind. Curry is appalled. "Harry had something in mind? Is that what I heard you say?" Sheepishly Heyes admits he lost his head, but with Harry continuously poking him in the back, he got the impression that Harry had a plan.

They debate the merits of attempting to jump on a train moving at full speed, risking having their arms ripped off, versus walking ten miles to town under cover of darkness. "I think I'd rather get my arm ripped off," Curry decides. They hear horses approaching and duck down just as the posse passes by.

In the boxcar, Harry pulls out his gun and gets the drop on the two men – Mugs McGeehu and Hank Silvers – whom he has recognized. They're under arrest.

When the train pulls into Little Grande, once again the sheriff is startled at the boxcar door opening during his inspection. Hands up, out jump McGeehu and Silvers, followed by Harry, gun at the ready. He introduces his two new prisoners to the sheriff, stating that they're wanted for grand theft in Colorado. Tankersley counters with the information that they're wanted for murder here in Utah. The deputies escort the outlaws to jail while the sheriff pulls Harry aside. What happened to Curry and Heyes? Harry feigns surprise at learning it was the sheriff who was following the stage, then explains that Curry and Heyes jumped him and escaped. Tankersley is skeptical, wondering why they left him his gun. "Because they took the bullets out first, Sheriff." Harry offers his empty gun as proof. The sheriff is almost convinced, but when the BDI finally answered his telegram, they denied Harry worked for them. Harry forces a laugh. That's standard procedure, designed to protect their agents, he bluffs. If Harry sent a telegram and used the right code word, their answer would be different. The sheriff hauls Harry to the telegraph office.

Meanwhile, Heyes and Curry wait miserably under a tree. They'll catch the train east if they don't starve to death before it comes by.

At the telegraph office, the sheriff reads the response from the BDI congratulating Harry on the capture of McGeehu and Silvers and claiming the reward for the company. Sheriff Tankersley now understands what Harry meant

Harry Briscoe, a Bannerman Detective, portrayed by J.D. Cannon.

by the right code word. Harry lost him the popular Heyes and Curry, but delivered the despised McGeehu and Silvers. The sheriff is ahead on the deal, so he's going to let Harry go.

Heyes and Curry dash for the eastbound train, noting with annoyance Harry waving at them from the comfort of the passenger coach. The train is moving at full speed as they struggle to grab hold of the passing boxcar rail. Heyes makes it but Curry loses his grip and falls. When he doesn't get up, Heyes jumps off the train and races to his side. He leans over his unconscious friend, worried and scared. It looks bad. After a time, Curry stirs and opens his eyes. With a relieved smile, Heyes helps Curry to his feet and they retreat to their "office" to make new plans, first of which will be to torture and kill Harry Briscoe.

That night Heyes and Curry begin the long walk to town. They meet a boy leading two horses. He's taking them to some very important people, he says, and he promised the man who's paying him that he wouldn't let anything go wrong. "That man wouldn't happen to be Detective Harry Briscoe of the BDI, would it?" Curry asks. It would. The boy hands over the horses, along with canteens and saddlebags full of food. Heyes and Curry wonder how Harry was getting along with the sheriff. Real good, the boy tells them, since he brought in those two killers. Heyes and Curry exchange astonished looks.

The next day Heyes and Curry ride through the desert. The countryside is too beautiful to keep riding through in such a hurry, they decide, and slow their horses to a walk, the better to look and appreciate. They offer a friendly greeting to a man passing by. It's Moroni Stebbins again. Alarmed, he whips his horse and hurries towards town. Heyes and Curry spur their horses in the opposite direction.

GUEST CAST

JAMES DRURY	SHERIFF TANKERSLEY
J.D. CANNON	HARRY BRISCOE
LARRY STORCH	MUGS MCGEEHU
FRANK SINATRA, JR	DEPUTY WERMSER
GEORGE KEYMAS	HANK SILVERS
DAVE GARROWAY	MORONI STEBBINS
STEPHEN HUDIS	BOY
JON LORMER	PROPRIETOR
TOM WATERS	RANCH OWNER
LAURIE FERRONE	FIRST GIRL
RENEE TETRO	SECOND GIRL

While Roy Huggins provided the stories for almost every episode of the series, there are very few which he did not hand over to another writer to turn into a teleplay. Even on those episodes where John Thomas James receives a full "written by" credit, drafts written by others were often part of the development process. "The Long Chase" is one of only three that Huggins wrote completely by himself, never even telling the story to another writer.[1] As the executive producer, Huggins had no one to answer to but himself when it came to the script and, because of this, he was free to indulge his sense of humor. The teleplay for this episode is full of wry comments and extraneous information that goes against a basic precept of screenwriting, which is that if it's not shown on the screen, it's not written on the page.

This episode was the third season premiere and the audience would, for the first time, enjoy the results of the location shooting in Moab. It would also mark the shift in timeslots from Thursday night at 8:00 p.m. to Saturday night at 8:00 p.m. Huggins acknowledged this in his scene description setting up the Utah countryside that would play such a big part in this story. "If you are seeing all this in living color in an air-conditioned twentieth century home on a quiet Saturday evening, it probably looks monumentally beautiful . . ."[2] While in most cases, the town of Little Grande would be described in prosaic terms that allow the set designers and sign painters to do their job, Huggins elaborated. "Little Grande is a hot and miserable community of several hundred souls who will become known to history as hardy pioneers, too late to give them any satisfaction, but in plenty of time to make their grandchildren feel an uneasy, enduring sense of inadequacy and guilt."[3] Huggins later describes Curry jumping out of the train outside of Little Grande with a nod to the realities of filmmaking. "A truly spectacular and bone-rattling jump is made at no risk to our star."[4]

Huggins always liked stories that were about nothing. This sounds strange coming from a master storyteller, but the stories "about nothing" are really those that concentrate on the characters of Heyes and Curry rather than the mechanics of an intricate plot. It doesn't matter what they're doing; we're interested because we like them. So in this story "about nothing," Huggins focuses on one of the problems the boys often face, being chased by a posse, and treats the audience to one long chase through the hot, dusty desert, throwing Heyes and Curry up against a tough sheriff, a hapless deputy, a pair of scruffy outlaws and the always bumbling Harry Briscoe.

Huggins loved the character of Harry Briscoe. "I . . . saw what his potential was and brought him back to exploit that potential," he recalled. Harry is once again down and out, a man who seemingly can do nothing right, yet who nevertheless always lands on his feet with a little help from his friends, Heyes and Curry. In this story, though, it's Harry's turn to save the day. Knowing the boys are depending on him to keep them out of the clutches of Sheriff Tankersley, Harry manages to come up with a plan and bring it to fruition. Along the way, Huggins gave him a lot of funny moments: his attempt to whisper into the sheriff's ear when asked if he knows who his prisoners are, his surprise when his imaginary dust becomes the real posse, his arrival in Little Grande with two new prisoners. Huggins explained, "It was dangerous because he was right on the verge of being farce and you have to be very careful to avoid that."[5] J.D. Cannon played the role with relish, but not over the top, also recognizing the need to avoid farce but still have fun.

During the chase, we see Heyes and Curry perform effortlessly as a team. There is no time wasted when they "rent" all the horses in the livery stable or when Heyes lends a hand to help Curry mount his horse when Curry's comes up lame. Their long partnership allows them to function as one. With the situation looking bleak, they resort to bickering while waiting for Harry, but when Heyes suggests splitting up, Curry immediately vetoes the idea, ostensibly because it's impractical at that moment, but in truth because it's unthinkable. When Curry falls from the train, Heyes races to his side, tears in his eyes, all bickering forgotten. Reunited once again in their ambition to get even with Harry for what they interpret as his betrayal, they enjoy trading ideas for his demise, and then are pleasantly surprised when Harry comes through with horses, food and water. The chase has indeed been long, but no matter what the difficulties, it's obvious that nothing will split this pair up.

HIGH LONESOME COUNTRY

"Wouldn't it be more of a partner thing to do if we flipped a coin?"
– Kid Curry

STORY: JOHN THOMAS JAMES

TELEPLAY:	DICK NELSON
DIRECTOR:	ALEXANDER SINGER
SHOOTING DATES:	STUDIO – JUNE 28, 29, 1972; UTAH – JUNE 30, JULY 1, 3, 5, 1972
ORIGINAL US AIR DATE:	SEPTEMBER 23, 1972
ORIGINAL UK AIR DATE:	OCTOBER 23, 1973

Hannibal Heyes and Kid Curry ride into town and are soon engrossed in a poker game. After some time the other players leave for their ranch and the game dissolves. Phil Archer remains behind and wonders what the boys do for a living. Curry suggests they might be unemployed trappers. To their dismay, Archer came into town specifically looking for trappers. He's overjoyed. Heyes and Curry eye each other wondering what they've just gotten themselves into.

> Roy Huggins first suggested the title be "The Big Trap: A Game of Silent Waiting" or "The Waiting Game."
>
> Rod Cameron was not well during filming and used a breathing apparatus when he was off-camera.
>
> When Billings tracks Heyes and Curry, stock shots of rabbits, squirrels and deer running away symbolize just how dangerous a man he is.

As they follow Archer to his ranch, the boys argue about the situation, Heyes reminding Curry that "unless the conversation is about guns or something very simple and unimportant," he should let Heyes do the talking, not that Heyes talked them out of this. There's a depression on, though, and their wages will cover the cost of equipment with a little extra when they sell the traps back.

Helen Archer greets her husband with a smile until she sees who he's brought home. She recognizes Kid Curry from the Buckton courtroom. Her husband rightly assumes the other man must then be Hannibal Heyes. What should they do? Outlaws like Heyes and Curry won't be taken easily, but Archer is already thinking about the $20,000 reward on their heads. For now, though, he'll just let them start trapping.

As Heyes and Curry set traps out, they worry about running into the smart old cat that Archer will pay a $50 bonus for. Curry wonders at the strange way Mrs. Archer was looking at him, like she was scared.

Meanwhile, back at the ranch house, Luke Billings comes by. He heard Archer was looking for a trapper. Archer tells him he's already hired two men but he knows Billings's reputation as a hunter and wonders if he'd like a job that would pay $10,000. For that price, it would be men Billings would be hunting and he doesn't hire out to kill men, he says. But when he leaves, Billings heads for the foothills where Archer told him Heyes and Curry are trapping. Archer suspects he may have just been double-crossed.

At their campfire, Heyes and Curry hear unsettling noises in the dark. At the increased skittering of the horses, they grab rifles and, after a short pursuit, Curry fires at a cougar, wounding it. It's grown too dark to follow the cat, but the next day, they follow its bloody tracks as Billings, who has arrived in the area, changes his riding boots for moccasins.

Heyes and Curry track the cougar but it has them in its sights as well. Suddenly the cat springs from a large boulder onto Curry's back. Man and animal wrestle for superiority. Heyes takes careful aim so as to miss Curry and kill the cougar. His shot alerts Billings to their whereabouts. Ready to quit trapping

after the scare, the boys slide down a slope and a bullet blows Curry's hat off. Billings missed killing him only because Curry slipped when he fired. Now they know why Mrs. Archer was looking at them funny. Somehow Archer has figured out who they are and hired someone to kill them.

Since there was only one shot, they figure there's only one man, so they separate, planning to work their way back to the wagon. Shots ring out occasionally as Billings spots one or the other. As he nears the wagon, Curry hears another shot and Heyes moans as he falls. An angry, determined look crosses Curry's face as he strips off his jacket and readies his pistol.

Quietly tracking the sniper, Curry comes up behind Billings and orders him to drop his weapons and run to see how badly his partner is hurt. They find Heyes with a shoulder wound. While Curry holds a gun on him, promising to bury him next to his partner if Heyes dies, Billings uses his knife to dig out the bullet.

After the surgery, Curry ties Billings up and questions who he is and why he came after them. Billings will talk only if they tell *Mrs.* Archer where he is. He figures Mr. Archer won't be happy he's been double-crossed.

That evening, Heyes and Curry surprise the Archers and inform them about Billings. All four of them will stay together for the night; in the morning they'll head for the nearest railroad. Only then will they separate.

They ride out in single file. Curry, bringing up the rear, raises his hands to fend off a buzzing insect just as a bullet blows off his saddle horn. At the shot, all four scurry for cover in a gully. Billings must have gotten loose. He's got a Sharps buffalo rifle, accurate up to a thousand yards. Because it takes an expert five seconds to reload the single-shot rifle, Curry has time to stand up and look for where Billings may be. He ducks down in time to avoid being shot.

With ten hours of daylight, Billings could move and get a clear shot at them from another angle. Archer is not willing to wait and is going for help. They decide Curry will shoot his hat off to make Billings think he's trying to escape from the outlaws. Archer reaches his horse but a bullet from Billings's rifle causes the horse to rear, throwing Archer off and breaking his leg. Helen Archer runs to her husband, checks on him, then mounts the horse and rides away. Billings is so surprised, by the time he reacts, she's out of range.

Archer must be okay so Heyes and Curry agree they must give Billings twenty minutes to move, then one of them will have to play decoy. They argue over who it will be. Curry can run faster than Heyes, but not when they're scared. Heyes complains about his wounded shoulder. At the end of the first twenty minutes, Heyes contends that Curry should run because he's younger. Being only a couple years younger is no difference, Curry counters. Heyes suggests alphabetical order but Curry will agree only if they're talking about Joshua and Thaddeus. They decide it would be fair to flip a coin. When Curry loses the toss, he pulls off his boots. Puzzled, Heyes reminds him he always wanted to die with his boots on.

Curry runs and, at Billings's missed shot, turns around and races back to the gully. Billings hasn't moved.

Who runs next? It seems fair to flip a coin, Heyes answers, a precedent has been set. Curry will have none of that. He insists that Heyes will run next.

Heyes gets ready to run, removing his vest, gloves and boots. His mad scramble out and back proves Billings remained in the same place.

Twenty hot, dusty minutes later, Heyes announces it's Curry's turn to run. Oh no, says Curry, they flipped and he lost, so he ran, then Heyes ran. Now they flip again.

No, argues Heyes, the principle is that they take turns. Heyes refuses to run; he's weak from loss of blood. Curry thinks for a moment then suggests they flip to decide if they should flip again. Heyes stands firm and Curry concludes, with no help coming for a long time, they'll have to just keep doing this, so he takes his turn and runs.

As Curry slides back down into the gully exhausted, Heyes figures they only have to do it one more time. It'll be his turn, all nice and even. By then Mrs. Archer should be back with help.

"Look, Kid," Heyes says, "if Billings get me, I want you to turn in my body for the reward. I don't want him to get it." "*What?!* How can I do that, Heyes? Who gets the reward on me when I'm gettin' the reward on you?" In the middle of the new argument, they hear two pistol shots. Mrs. Archer, instead of going for help, circled around behind Billings and shot him.

After checking on Archer, Heyes and Curry ride toward town. Curry anticipates selling the traps back and recouping their money. Heyes takes a dim view of this prospect and leans on a hardware store post watching Curry wheel and deal. The merchant insists that once the traps leave the premises, they are used but reluctantly offers a twenty-five percent return. Outraged, Curry demands seventy-five percent because the traps were new only six days ago and some were hardly used at all! No deal, says the store owner, once they leave the premises, they are *used*. Curry counters, how about fifty percent of their money back if they throw in a dead cougar?

Guest Cast

Buddy Ebsen	Phil Archer
Rod Cameron	Luke Billings
Marie Windsor	Helen Archer
Walt Davis	Clyde
Monty Laird	Bill
Clarke Gordon	Storekeeper

The episode was born in April 1972 when Roy Huggins told the story to Tony Barr, a programming executive at ABC who had the contractual right to approve stories. In Huggins's case, it was "pretty much of a rubber stamp. . . .They'd had a long-standing relationship with Roy on the show . . . and they knew that he worked out these stories in great detail."[6] Director Alex Singer knew a good writer like Huggins set something up for the audience to anticipate. Viewers will "sit still for the relatively quiet stuff because they know that there are two payoffs here that they've already installed. One is that these guys are really in danger of being captured by a very shrewd man who isn't at all the kind of easy-going, farmer-type he pretended to be, and secondly, there's a cat that's a bit of a question mark. . . ." Tension builds not only for Heyes and Curry, but for Archer who has to contend first with the outlaws, then with Billings who ratchets up the anxiety. When Mrs. Archer argues with her husband over killing Heyes and Curry, she also becomes a component Archer must deal with.

When Huggins re-told the story for writer Dick Nelson, he added that the boys were being hired to trap a cougar. Huggins knew cougars are called painters in Montana, and the boys could be hired to trap a painter. This was dropped as no one outside of Montana would know the term. Reminding the writer that stock footage of a cougar existed from "The 5th Victim," he also insisted no souvenirs be taken of the dead cat. "We don't want to see our boys cutting off an ear or anything like that."[7] The cinematographer shot Ben Murphy's wrestling with the dummy cougar from a discernible distance. However, some of the intercut shots are of a trainer working with a real cat whose jaws had been tied to keep it from biting. The filming came out well, and Singer recalled, "I know that they all enjoyed it. It's a naked piece of action and they could look like heroes."[8]

Villainy in the episode is assigned to Billings, a huge man in animal furs. At no point did Billings announce he was a tough guy; he said very little, but his presence was powerful. Huggins wanted to hire "the biggest actor we can find and the scrawniest-looking horse we can find." Singer exaggerated Billings's threat by shooting from a low camera angle, making him appear even larger and meaner. "You create the entity by the kind of shot that you do, by the actor's presence in the makeup and so on."[9]

Billings's Sharps rifle was favored by buffalo hunters for its heavy bullets and long range, about three times that of a regular rifle. Invented in 1848 by Christian Sharps, it was a breech-loading firearm manufactured in great numbers for Civil War use. The single shot weapon had to be loaded by pulling down the trigger guard, releasing the breechblock. When the chamber was laid open, the cartridge was inserted. The breechblock was then closed cutting off the end of the cartridge exposing the powder. The trigger was pulled, the powder ignited and the gun fired.[10] All of this took time in the hands of even an expert shooter.

To test Billings's position, Curry wouldn't have wanted to run in his boots, particularly if they had any heel height. The high narrow heels on boots prevented the foot from slipping through the stirrup, especially on fast turns and stops. Riding was less tiring when the weight fell on the balls of the feet or the toes. The pointed toes of cowboys' boots made them easy to insert into the stirrups and the stitching kept the boot together when the leather wore thin. Thus, while very practical in the saddle, boots were often uncomfortable for walking or running. However, when the scene called for them to run bootless, protective gear was put into the actors' socks because no actor could perform well while running over rocks.

When Heyes reminds Curry he wanted to die with his boots on, a nice throwback to the old western cliché, Curry's scripted reply was "Heyes, sometimes I wonder why I like you. And the times I wonder, I *don't* like you."[11] The line was deliberately cut during editing. Singer believes the producers "didn't want to muddy the waters, that 'I like you' was enough of a sour joke at this particular time." The argument over who would play decoy appears to reflect the tension between the two actors, but Singer didn't see it that way. "If somebody showed me this show and I'd never seen it before, I would assume that they were good friends who had a kind of running argument about who takes the chances and who cons the other out of whatever. But I would not assume that there was any real unhappiness between them as people." To add to the conflict, Ben, Roger and Singer all vividly remember how hot it was during that scene – about 120 degrees. Because it was actually dark in the gully, the crew used huge lights, raising the temperature even more – enough to make anyone testy with those nearby.

In *The Young Country,* Roger Davis played an innocent guy who was kind of shy. "*Smith and Jones* was not that at all. But," he believed, "if I'd brought that [shyness] to the role it would have been interesting and more in contrast to [Ben]." Rather than both of them trying to one-up the other, "it would have been better if I'd stayed with that character." All actors eventually learn the effort to outdo another actor is self-defeating. "What we were doing in *Smith and Jones* could have, in a way, kept us from really being great. . . .I think that Ben and I had some really wonderful moments in *Smith and Jones*; nobody ever talks about them much, but in that ditch was one of them. I *know* it. And there were others."[12]

THE McCREEDY FEUD

"Sometimes I get the feeling Big Mac's not too well liked."
"Sometimes I get the same feeling about us."
– Hannibal Heyes, Kid Curry

STORY:	JOHN THOMAS JAMES
TELEPLAY:	JUANITA BARTLETT
DIRECTOR:	ALEXANDER SINGER
SHOOTING DATES:	UTAH – JULY 14, 1972; STUDIO – AUGUST 7, 8, 9, 10, 11, 14, 1972
ORIGINAL US AIR DATE:	SEPTEMBER 30, 1972
ORIGINAL UK AIR DATE:	DECEMBER 3, 1973

This was Juanita Bartlett's first writing credit. She went on to a successful career as a writer-producer on such shows as *The Rockford Files, Scarecrow and Mrs. King,* and *In the Heat of the Night.*

Katy Jurado is the only Mexican actress ever to be nominated for an Academy Award.

Hannibal Heyes and Kid Curry travel through the Mexican desert on their way to Señor Armendariz's ranch, Curry complaining bitterly all the way. Heyes tries to soothe him by pointing out how cordial Armendariz was the last time they were there, but Curry doesn't consider being bound, gagged, threatened and darn near killed a friendly welcome. They're met on the trail by Armendariz's men who hail them with a cordial "Manos arriba!" ("Hands up!")

At the hacienda, Heyes and Curry ask for Señor Armendariz, but are informed by his sister Carlotta that he's out. She apologizes for the unconventional way they were brought to the house, but wonders why they ignored the "No Trespassing" signs. They've come on legitimate business, Heyes explains. Can they wait for her brother? She

((Sagala collection))

Roger Davis, Burl Ives, Ben Murphy in "The McCreedy Feud."

insists they do. Heyes makes the mistake of mentioning Mr. McCreedy and her cordial, though cautious, welcome turns distinctly cold. The boys are locked in a room with guards posted outside.

Many hours later the boys are released. Señor Armendariz refuses to talk to them, uninterested in anything McCreedy has in mind.

Back in Red Rock, McCreedy is unhappy that Heyes and Curry have failed to set up a meeting with Armendariz. Fighting him over the ever-shifting boundary between their ranches is costing too much money, too much time, his good disposition and his stomach, McCreedy grumbles, punctuating his words with a belch. Mac thanks the boys for trying, but doesn't pay them the $500 he promised. Curry starts to protest, but Heyes cuts him off. Mac immediately wants to know what Heyes won't let Curry say. Heyes says they've figured out how to solve Mac's whole problem, but it will cost him $5,000. Mac agrees. Heyes explains that Armendariz has a sister, but Mac is already aware of that dried-up, ugly old maid. "Ugly? Obviously you've never seen the woman," Heyes exclaims. The boys talk up Carlotta's beauty, strength and pride, adding that she has taken an interest in Mac and once they meet will surely speak to her brother on his behalf.

Heyes and Curry return to the Armendariz hacienda where Carlotta greets them once again. Heyes relays Mac's regards, prompting her to ask why they keep speaking to her of a man for whom she has nothing but distaste. "Fat, cowardly . . ." Carlotta scoffs. Heyes acknowledges that Mac is carrying a few pounds more than he should, but that's because he's a wealthy man who enjoys fine living. Far from being cowardly, Big Mac has tamed dangerous men with nothing more than a look. Heyes piles it on, claiming Big Mac is charming and witty and that he greatly admires Carlotta. She is skeptical. "Does he honestly believe I can be flattered into influencing my brother on his behalf?" Carlotta leaves them. Since Big Mac is not charming or witty, Curry is surprised Carlotta didn't laugh in their faces. But Heyes is pleased to notice she didn't laugh, she listened.

Señor Armendariz allows the boys to deliver Big Mac's message. McCreedy will sell the disputed land, currently on his side of the river, to Armendariz. Then when the river changes course, it will continue to be Armendariz's. His answer is no. He invites the boys to leave.

Heyes and Curry leave, but circle back and return to the hacienda at night. Heyes picks out the window he believes is Carlotta's and taps on it. It's opened by a man wielding a shotgun, demanding they raise their hands as he calls for the guards.

Señor Armendariz is angry they've returned and is unconvinced by their explanation that they got turned around in the darkness. He will have his men escort them to the border in the morning. As Armendariz and his sister turn to leave, Heyes speaks up. Could they have something to eat?

Curry can't believe Heyes had the nerve to ask for food, but Heyes is sure that Carlotta will bring it, giving them a chance to talk with her alone. Besides, he's hungry.

When Carlotta returns, Heyes works on her feelings, telling her Mac is even more impressed with her now that they've filled in the details on what kind of a woman she is – strong, proud and dignified. Carlotta is amazed they would assume she has any interest in meeting the man, much less marrying a Yankee Protestant. McCreedy is Catholic, Heyes assures her. Carlotta shakes her head in disbelief as she leaves. The boys are discouraged.

The next morning Carlotta hails them in the courtyard. There's no Catholic church in Red Rock, so she invites McCreedy to attend the church in Mataska. She's not interested in McCreedy as a man, but as a Christian she has concern for his soul. She'll be at the church on Friday, her saint's day. As the boys ride out, Heyes smiles with satisfaction.

Heyes and Curry return to Big Mac with news of their progress. They also admit they told Carlotta that Mac is Catholic. "How'd you boys know that?" Mac whispers in shock. Taken aback, Heyes covers his surprise by claiming they have their way of finding things out, but his secret is safe. After all, he knows some-thing even worse about them.

On Friday, Carlotta, along with several companions, heads to Mataska. Before they arrive, the carriage is overtaken by armed bandits.

Mac goes to the church in Mataska to meet Carlotta. Heyes and Curry come with the news that she has been kidnapped. Mac's first thought is that Armendariz will kill him on the assumption he was responsible. He wants to head back to Red Rock immediately, but the boys convince him it would be better to help find her. With Mac's money, they should be able to buy information leading to the kidnappers.

Carlotta and her companions are being held in an old adobe shack, where she paces and rants. The sound of gunshots brings her to a halt. She knew her brother would rescue them!

The door opens and Big Mac enters. He introduces himself to Carlotta and assures her she's safe. Carlotta is suspicious. "How did you find me?" Mac explains that Mataska is talking of nothing else. He was in church when he heard the news and he immediately took steps to rescue her. Heyes and Curry enter and report that the bodies of the kidnappers have been removed and the team hitched to the carriage.

Mac would like to see Carlotta home, but fears her brother would object.

Burl Ives starred as Big Mac McCreedy in three episodes.

Carlotta is sure her brother will want to thank Mac personally for saving her life, but he feels that she should break the news to him slowly. Mac is truly smitten with Carlotta and he tells her his friends didn't come close to doing her justice when they told him about her. Carlotta is also impressed with Mac. While the boys spoke of his courage, they neglected to mention his gallantry.

As Mac escorts Carlotta home, the boys stay behind to make certain everything is wrapped up. They inform the "kidnappers" the coast is clear. Rising from their hiding place, the Devil's Hole Gang hurries to their horses.

The next morning Heyes, Curry and Mac ride back toward Red Rock. At the sound of shots, they realize Armendariz's men are pursuing them. When Heyes's horse goes down, Curry stops to help him while Big Mac disappears in a cloud of dust. Surrounded by vaqueros, Curry helps Heyes to his feet and they wearily raise their hands.

An enraged Armendariz demands the truth from the boys. He doesn't believe the story about Mac's heroic rescue of his sister. Obviously, McCreedy was behind the kidnapping. Ordering the vaqueros to aim their weapons at the boys' heads, Armendariz demands the truth. Heyes and Curry would love to tell him that McCreedy was behind it, but they can't because he wasn't. The standoff is interrupted by a man with news that Carlotta has disappeared. Heyes and Curry are locked in the little room while Armendariz investigates.

Armendariz returns and outlines his plan. One of them will go get McCreedy. The other will stay as a hostage. If McCreedy does not come, Armendariz will shoot the hostage. He gives them five minutes to decide who will go. Because he blames Heyes for the mess they're in, Curry will go.

He rides like hell to Red Rock, and rushes in the ranch house without knocking. To his surprise, he finds a wedding ceremony in progress. Mac and Carlotta, in the presence of a handful of friends, have just become husband and wife.

Later, Mac counts out $500 for the boys as he explains how the boundary dispute has been settled. Armendariz doesn't own that land any more, but neither does Mac. It now belongs to Carlotta. Curry protests that Mac is short in his payment; the deal was for $5,000. Mac's not going to pay for something the boys had nothing to do with. They set up a meeting in Mataska, but Carlotta didn't make it. It was Fate that led to the happy ending. Heyes contradicts him. They set the whole thing up and if Mac will just step outside, he'll prove it.

Outside, Heyes and Curry introduce Mac to the Devil's Hole Gang. They were the kidnappers that Heyes and Curry "killed" during the rescue of Carlotta and Mac owes them $100 each. Mac pays, hoping his wife never finds out. Carlotta will never find out, Curry promises, because they wouldn't tell for love or money. "Well, maybe for money," Heyes muses. Mac slowly pulls his wallet out and counts out $5,000.

Heyes and Curry, flush with cash, head for Santa Marta. There they'll settle down and wait for their amnesty. Something's missing, though. "Our gal, Clementine," Heyes announces. The boys change direction and ride off toward Denver.

GUEST CAST

BURL IVES	PATRICK J. "BIG MAC" MCCREEDY
CESAR ROMERO	SEÑOR ERNESTO ARMENDARIZ
KATY JURADO	CARLOTTA ARMENDARIZ
RUDY DIAZ	MAN
LOU PERALTA	GUARD
DENNIS FIMPLE	KYLE MURTRY
CLAUDIO MIRANDA	PRIEST

Roy Huggins's influence on television was profound, not only because of the numerous shows he created, but also because of his method of storytelling. "Huggins . . . introduced a plot device that has since become a Hollywood obsession: the backstory. . . .Huggins realized early that you can blend one important story with a second, usually character-based, story, weave them together carefully and give the audience the subliminal feeling they've gotten two shows for the price of one."[13] In this case, Huggins wove together three separate adventures for Heyes and Curry involving McCreedy and Armendariz to create a story arc that crossed through three seasons. This episode is the culmination of the story that began with "The McCreedy Bust" and continued with "The McCreedy Bust: Going, Going, Gone." Although many recurring characters pop up to take part in the boys' adventures, only Big Mac McCreedy and Señor Armendariz have a continuing storyline of their own.

Backstory is a concept writers use to give their stories and characters a sense of realism. While the story itself is concerned only with the events currently taking place, the backstory provides the history of all that has come before and brought the characters to where they are now. Often the backstory is known only to the writer, used for character development but not explicitly shared with the audience. In this episode, Heyes's plan depends on Carlotta Armendariz wanting a husband. This is a reasonable assumption for a nineteenth century single woman, but in the backstory Huggins provides a more detailed explanation of Carlotta's past and present desires. "Note: it turns out they have learned something offscene – Carlotta has been living in Mexico City and she's come to live with her brother now. She had gone to Mexico City on the theory that if she went there she might find a husband, but she didn't find one."[14] Carlotta's life in Mexico City is never mentioned in the episode, but it influences her reaction to Heyes and Curry's matchmaking.

The feud between McCreedy and Armendariz began long ago and revolves around the fact that the boundary between their ranches is the Rio Grande, a bit of backstory shared with the audience in "The McCreedy Bust." In a departure from the traditional American ethnocentrism found in most westerns, Huggins made the Mexican rancher, rather than the Texan, the more admirable character, imbuing Armendariz with class and style as well as strength. For this episode, he stressed the need to avoid ethnic stereotypes in the outline given to writer Juanita Bartlett. "The Mexicans are not ragged, not unshaven, and not dirty. Armendariz has great class – and these are his top men."[15]

In contrast to the honorable and gracious Armendariz, McCreedy is a brash and devious man. He has no sense of honor as evidenced by his actions throughout the story arc – selling the disputed land when it was on his side of the border, hiring Heyes and Curry to steal the bust from Armendariz, using an obscure rule in Hoyle to cheat the boys out of the money he paid them and using his knowledge of their true identities to coerce them into helping him whenever he needs them. Here he uses the boys as go-betweens to set up a meeting "because Big Mac thinks Armendariz kind of likes them,"[16] then refuses to pay them because they were unsuccessful. In the first draft script, Curry, concerned they'll be fatally unwelcome at the Armendariz hacienda, wonders why they're doing such a big favor for Mac. Heyes responds, "If we said 'no', Big Mac knows who we are . . ."[17] and it's clear they believe Mac would turn them in if it suited him.

In this final chapter, McCreedy is redeemed by his response to the match-making plan. While it seems at first that Mac is going along just to win this latest battle, when he meets Carlotta he truly falls for her. In the backstory, Mac has never married because he's never met a woman with strength to match his own. Now he has and he's enchanted. Huggins insisted that Mac be sincere in his admiration of Carlotta, noting that the scene in which he tells Carlotta he'd like to ask her brother for permission to call on her "should be played terribly straight. At this point I want the audience to believe that McCreedy means what he is saying."[18] Carlotta believes him, too, and decides that she has finally met the man she's been waiting for. With the marriage of Mac and Carlotta, the threads of both story and backstory are woven together into their final pattern. A story three seasons in the telling comes to a close. The feud has ended.

The Clementine Ingredient

"Somehow it's always easier to talk brave than to be brave."
– Hannibal Heyes

STORY:	JOHN THOMAS JAMES
TELEPLAY:	GLORYETTE CLARK
DIRECTOR:	JACK ARNOLD
SHOOTING DATES:	UTAH – JULY 14, 1972; STUDIO – AUGUST 16, 17, 18, 21, 22, 23, 1972
ORIGINAL US AIR DATE:	OCTOBER 7, 1972
ORIGINAL UK AIR DATE:	NOVEMBER 12, 1973

The original title was "The Day They Married Clementine."

It is ironic that Clementine tells the Alcalde, "I've never met anyone like you before." In fact, Sally Field and Alejandro Rey worked together in her series *The Flying Nun*.

Hannibal Heyes and Kid Curry canter through the arid landscape halfway to Mexico when Heyes pulls up short. He's decided the two of them would look suspicious settling down in Santa Marta. They're missing a vital ingredient – Clementine. Curry thinks Heyes's missing ingredient is brains.

After miles of travel, they arrive at Clementine's house. Welcoming them with smiles and kisses, she says it's good they didn't come around a month ago because men were watching her house. As she rustles up some food, they tell her they're headed to Mexico with money from a job they did for Big Mac McCreedy. They've stopped to invite her to go along but she has to pretend to be married to one of them. They'll stay in cool, green Santa Marta in a villa they can rent for $50-60 a month and may be there awhile because the situation isn't good for Governor Warren to grant them amnesty just now.

It sounds wonderful to Clem but she suspects they're still after the photograph she has of the three of them. Curry agrees that's important, but they wouldn't *marry* her to get it.

The next morning, they play a hand of showdown to decide who pretends to be married to Clem. Heyes turns up a pair of tens to Curry's pair of fours. "Mrs. Joshua Smith sounds nice," Clem purrs. "I won, you're Mrs. Thaddeus Jones," Heyes points out. Clem is outraged that the loser gets her.

She begins to argue when a shot fired from outside shatters the lamp on the table. The men who had been watching her house have returned and they know Heyes and Curry are inside. Calling out to the leader, the boys suggest making a deal. They'll send Clementine out if the leader comes in to talk.

Before Clem goes out, Heyes asks for pencil and paper. She walks out the door and is met by the man in charge. As long as his men have Clem, Curry promises, it'll be safe for him to come inside.

The leader, Ted Thompson, tells Heyes and Curry that twenty men formed a club to watch Miss Hale's house. They plan on splitting the $20,000 reward. Heyes has a bigger deal for him, reminding Ted that the Red Gap bank was robbed and they got away with a half million dollars. They're going to give it to Ted as a bribe to get out of their predicament. Heyes produces his half of the freshly-drawn map showing where the money is buried. Curry withholds his half until Ted agrees to go along. The prospect of the loot convinces Ted to shut out the rest of the club, which in actuality numbers only six.

Ted calls to two of his men, inviting them into the house to help him decide what to do about Heyes and Curry's deal. Once inside, the boys get the drop on them. His partners threaten Ted with death as he ties them up, but he convinces them he was under the guns of the outlaws and had to do what they said.

For show, Curry threatens Ted before he sends him out the door again with a whiskey bottle to invite the rest of the club in. The ruse works and, as the four men step onto the porch, Curry and Heyes corner them with guns drawn.

After a long journey, Heyes, Curry and Clementine arrive in Santa Marta. The alcalde greets them and apologizes for the way they were treated the last time they were in his town. He even offers to drive them to the villa in his own coach. Clementine is immediately taken with his charm and good looks and openly flirts with him.

At the villa, Curry already acts the part of a newlywed husband, berating his "bride" for the way she acted around the alcalde. She *must* pretend to be a married woman or they can't hide out there.

That evening at dinner, the alcalde wonders that Mr. Smith is so young to be retired from banking and railroads. Smith explains they're really speculators who are taking a year off. Curry chimes in with how much they love the town and Clem, watching the alcalde, agrees that the town is so handsome, er, beautiful.

Back at the villa, Curry once again scolds Clem for her behavior toward the alcalde. He doesn't like the way it makes him feel, like a . . . lost for words, he looks to Heyes. "Husband," Heyes supplies. Clem apologizes again; she can't help herself. The alcalde is just so charming.

One day while Clementine is on her way to town in a buggy, a sudden gust of wind spooks her horse. She is unable to control him as he bolts. The alcalde, on the way out to the villa, spots the runaway and manages to stop the horse. Grateful, she allows him to drive her back home.

While Clem is gone, Heyes and Curry search her room for the photograph of them. She returns to find them hard at it. They emphasize how important it is that the photo not get into the hands of a lawman, but seeing her disappointment in them, Heyes promises they won't ever think of it again. Clem fibs, it's where it belongs, in her safe deposit box in Denver.

A little later, she seals the photograph in an envelope and heads back to town. At the alcalde's office, she asks him to put the envelope in his safe. Before she leaves, Clem admits she's never met anyone like him before. He echoes her feelings and they kiss. Breaking away from her, the alcalde is remorseful but Clem insists it's her fault for acting "unwifely." When he calls her warm and womanly and honest, Clem refutes that she's honest and leaves, teary-eyed. She returns to the villa and admits to Heyes and Curry what she's done. The alcalde kissed her and she kissed him back. Curry is flummoxed. What does he do now – challenge him to a duel? Clementine insists they have to leave Santa Marta; she can't stay there feeling as she does about Ramon, the alcalde.

Meanwhile, Ted Thompson has been on their trail and finally arrives in Santa Marta. A friendly Mexican points him in the direction of the Carruthers's hacienda where the gringos are staying. He arrives in the middle of the argument and catches the boys without their guns handy, then takes the three of them to jail. When the alcalde arrives, Ted shows him arrest warrants on Hannibal Heyes and Kid Curry for bank and train robbery. Clementine Hale is wanted for aiding and abetting. Clem admits to Ted's claim that she's not married but agreed to pose as Mrs. Jones in public. Despite Ted's protests the alcalde orders her released.

Over dinner, the alcalde admits his confusion. Clementine didn't act like a wife, though she clearly liked Mr. Jones. She loves both of them, she says, they are like family. Clem argues for their release. Prisons are supposed to reform people but Heyes and Curry have already reformed. Governor Warren even promised them an amnesty.

The alcalde is torn. He cannot let them go and break his solemn vow to uphold the laws of Santa Marta.

Early the next morning, Ted Thompson demands to see his prisoners. When he's let into the jail, he discovers an empty cell and accuses the acalde of letting them escape.

Outside of Santa Marta, Heyes and Curry hail a passing stagecoach whose lone passenger is Clementine. She tells them the alcalde showed up at the villa and told her he had to pay a penance. Though he didn't say it in so many words, it was that he had to give her up. Heyes and Curry exchange glances, then divulged that the alcalde made each of them contribute $2,000 for a new school before he let them go.

About the photograph they promised not to bring up . . . As they board the train with Clementine, they vow to forget about it for good, but Curry entreats Clem not to lose it.

Clem has gone back to Denver and the boys are finally alone again. Heyes suggests he and Curry pull one more robbery – stealing the photo from Clem's safe deposit box. Curry wants no part of it, saying he'll be in Moose Jaw, Saskatchewan. Besides, he still thinks the missing ingredient is Heyes's brains.

GUEST CAST

SALLY FIELD	CLEMENTINE HALE
ALEJANDRO REY	ALCALDE RAMON CORDOBA
RAMON BIERI	TED THOMPSON
MILLS WATSON	CHESTER
JOE HAWORTH	TAD
CODY BEAR PAW	INDIAN
WALT DAVIS	CLERK
DAVE MORICK	CLERK
JESS FRANCO	GUARD
REF SANCHEZ	STABLE KEEPER
JERRY BROWN	STAGECOACH DRIVER

If Hannibal Heyes and Kid Curry are loosely based on Butch Cassidy and the Sundance Kid, then Clementine Hale can claim Etta Place as her fore-mother. Even more directly, "Clementine Hale" was originally a character in Huggins's *The Young Country.* As Huggins admitted, "I was stealing from myself."[19] Both women are single and live alone. Butch and Sundance come by to invite Etta along to Bolivia; Heyes and Curry hope Clem will accompany them to Mexico. Clem does not have the discouraging "bottom of the pit" outlook of being twenty-six, single, and a schoolteacher as Etta; she seems perfectly happy in her chosen life. However, both women jump at the chance for a new adventure and agree to accompany their two handsome companions. In the end, both women go off leaving their menfolk to carry on and have continuing adventures. In 1959 novelist Frederick Woods observed that in westerns "Time after time, one can detach the females without endangering the structure of the main plot,"[20] an unfortunate truism.

Even William Goldman, who gave Etta Place life in *Butch Cassidy and the Sundance Kid,* observed that "Girls are a drag in Westerns." Seeing as how Etta was a necessary part of the story, though, he solved the dilemma of how to deal with her by making her a surprising character.[21] Huggins did the same for

Clementine. She never shows up unless she has a scheme in which to embroil Heyes and Curry and Huggins felt that Sally Field "was so good that you knew here was a real star. She had whatever it is that makes a star – which is something indefinable. It's just there. . . [I] realized how good she was, so then I brought her back."[22]

Both Etta and Clementine represent a new breed of western women. On their own in the West, they are neither prostitutes nor dance hall girls, nor prim married ladies. If the men's attraction to them is self-serving, perhaps turn-about is fair play.

Gloryette Clark, the teleplay writer, managed to mix and match that connection to real history with references to *Alias Smith and Jones's* history. Since all turned out well in "Miracle at Santa Marta" when Curry was accused of murdering Mr. Hanley, the race horse owner, they have no qualms about returning. They have the money to take a year off in the beautiful Mexican town because they've been paid by Big Mac McCreedy for resolving his and Armendariz's land dispute. Clementine suspects the boys have only come to retrieve the photograph of the three of them. They learned that she has it in "Dreadful Sorry, Clementine," when she used it to blackmail them into helping her scam Winford Fletcher. When Ted Thompson and his club turn up at Clem's, Heyes reminds him that, according to the newspapers, in Red Gap they got away with the biggest robbery west of the Mississippi.

The only confusing continuity point is the new actor playing the alcalde. Jo Swerling remembers that they first cast Nico Mindardos as the Mexican mayor in "Miracle at Santa Marta." Because they felt the episode was "one of the best last season," they devised a sequel.[23] The script for "The Clementine Ingredient" sent the boys back to the Mexican town, and Swerling and Huggins cast Minardos again. But in the intervening year, two organizations had been formed as a sort of watchdog for Latino actors – *Nosotros* and *Justicia O Muerte*. When the head of *Justicia* learned that Minardos would reprise the role, he protested a Greek actor playing a Mexican mayor. He thought Universal was disrespecting the Latino community and promised that, if the part were not recast, he would lead a demonstration to disrupt the Universal Studios tour center. Roy Huggins took offense and phoned the man to refute his charges. Huggins clarified that he wanted to be conscientious about the Latino community because his wife was Latina and mentioned a dozen other Latinos he had hired. The director of *Justicia* would not be pacified, discarding each name for trivial reasons – "She's a lousy actress," "We don't like him anymore," "She's a Jew."

ABC's hiring practices were also criticized by the Screen Actors Guild as "reverse discrimination." SAG, holding that the Minardos affair "is part of a sensitive, overall picture," demanded the network "clarify its policy and comply with genuine 'fair employment.'" The bottom line of the whole harangue was that Universal caved in to political pressure, paid Minardos off and hired Alejandro Rey to play the part.[24]

BUSHWHACK!

"The day I can't outshoot anyone and everybody on that list,
especially Hannibal Heyes, I'll go east and become a preacher."
– Kid Curry

STORY: JOHN THOMAS JAMES
TELEPLAY: JOHN THOMAS JAMES AND DAVID MOESSINGER
DIRECTOR: JACK ARNOLD
SHOOTING DATES: AUGUST 24, 25, 28, 29, 30, 31, 1972
ORIGINAL US AIR DATE: OCTOBER 21, 1972
ORIGINAL UK AIR DATE: NOVEMBER 19, 1973

Hannibal Heyes and Kid Curry have been in Rock Springs too long. As Heyes packs their gear, Curry complains. It's a quiet town, the sheriff doesn't know them, no one has been unfriendly. Why leave? Heyes, long-suffering, lets him grumble until he runs out of steam, then calmly asks, "You ready, Kid?"

After disappointing the hotel desk clerk by refusing to stay longer, Heyes and Curry ready their horses. Across the street Jake Horn hangs out, rolling a cigarette and watching the street traffic. The boys wonder if he's watching them in particular. As they head out of town, Jake hurries over to where his partner Phil Westerly is waiting with their horses. They follow the boys.

As Heyes and Curry meander toward Sweetwater, Jake and Phil gallop madly across country, eager to get ahead of them.

From the other direction, Marty Alcott rides along. Seeing two horses tied up by the side of the road, he stops to investigate.

> Early titles for this episode are "The Bushwhackers" and "Sweetwater Drygulch."
>
> Contrary to Curry's observation, Rock Springs, Wyoming, was not always a quiet town. On September 2, 1885, a mob of white coal miners attacked their Chinese co-workers after they refused to participate in a strike for higher wages. Twenty-eight Chinese were killed, fifteen wounded, seventy-nine homes set on fire and hundreds of Chinese workers fled. Federal troops were called in to restore order. The event became known as the Rock Springs Massacre.

From their hiding place among the rocks, Jake and Phil watch Heyes and Curry approach. They're nervous but ready to bushwhack the boys, planning to shoot them in the back to avoid any chance of them returning fire.

Marty steps up behind them. "Hey, Phil, Jake . . ." he says and shoots them both when they turn in surprise. He then hurriedly fires each of their guns into the air.

Heyes and Curry draw their guns, trying to see where the attack is coming from and take cover. Marty hails them from atop the rocks, assuring them it's safe. He's taken care of the bushwhackers. Cautiously the boys join him.

They gaze at the bodies as Marty explains they were Stockgrowers Association detectives who had recently been fired. Marty saw them about to bushwhack the boys and when he told them to freeze, they started shooting. He had to kill them.

Curry looks skeptical, but doesn't argue.

Heyes and Curry thank Marty, who offers to let them buy him a drink in Rock Springs after they report this incident to the sheriff. The boys exchange dismayed glances, then regretfully refuse to return to town. The sheriff will want to know why Jake and Phil were trying to bushwhack them and they don't have a good answer. Shrugging, Marty accepts their decision and invites them to his ranch for supper.

Marty's wife Ellie is on the porch to greet them. As they enter the house, Marty pulls his gun and orders her to disarm their guests. Surprised, Ellie complies as Curry asks, "You do this for all your supper guests?" He needs the boys to back up his story because it's too well-known that he hated Jake Horn and Phil Westerly. The sheriff might not believe him without witnesses. He saved their skins, now they've got to save his.

Heyes and Curry retreat to the bedroom to talk it over. Only one of them will need to go back to town, so they flip a coin. For once, Curry wins. Heyes will go to the sheriff with Marty.

Marty's partner, Cress Truett, bursts into the house and shoves a newspaper at him. The Livestock Commission has empowered inspectors to seize all cattle shipped by men known to be rustlers and impound the money from the sale of the cattle until the shipper can prove ownership. Ellie is indignant, but surely that law doesn't apply to them, as Marty and Cress aren't rustlers. Marty points out that to the Wyoming Stockgrowers Association anyone with less than three hundred head of cattle is a rustler. By the time some court decides the Commission's actions are illegal, Marty and Cress will be ruined. As the ranchers sink into an angry, despairing silence, Heyes speaks up. "If it will make you feel any better, I'm going back into Rock Springs with you." But Marty has a new plan. If they'll help him cut his cattle out of the upcoming roundup and drive them to Montana, he'll let them off the hook and pay them $200 each. The boys agree.

The roundup begins. After the animals have been herded together, Marty announces to foreman Mike McCloskey that he'll be cutting his cattle out. McCloskey objects. It's against the Association's rules. Marty angrily insists they're his cattle and no one can force him to sell them this year. McCloskey sizes up Heyes and Curry, deciding they're hired guns. Again he cites the rules, adding that his men will back him up. The two stock inspectors are ready to follow his orders, but the rest of the cowboys are not so eager. Marty challenges the foreman to settle things with guns right now or else leave them alone. McCloskey orders the stock inspectors to arrest them and they reach for their guns, but Curry's fast draw stops them. Marty, Cress and the boys ride off. McCloskey sends Pete, one of the inspectors, to inform Teshmacher, a WSGA cattleman.

Heyes, Curry, Marty and Cress watch Pete gallop away, wondering if they'll be able to cut all of Marty's cattle out of the herd before he gets back.

They round up the cattle and start moving them north. Ellie joins them on the trail, bringing provisions. Cress is upset that Marty has allowed her to come, feeling she'd be safer at home, but Marty declares it's a family decision. Heyes and Curry worry about how long it will be until the Association sends more inspectors after them.

Pete arrives in Rock Springs, relaying the news of Marty's actions to Sheriff Wiggins and Teshmacher, who is astonished that four men were able to take over the roundup. He's determined they won't make it to Montana. Sheriff Wiggins is eager to speak to Marty as well. He's found the bodies of Horn and Westerly.

The next day Ellie tries to smooth things over with Cress while Marty tries to get Smith and Jones to reveal their real names. He figures they must be outlaws since they didn't want to talk to the sheriff.

In Rock Springs, five stock detectives get their orders from Teshmacher. They hook up with McCloskey, who's disgusted there are so few of them.

Young Alonzo, Marty's neighbor, rides up to warn him he's in big trouble and the sheriff is looking for him. Cress urges the boy to hurry home before all hell breaks loose.

The drive continues. That night when Marty wakes Heyes and Curry to take their turn on watch, he insists he has to change the deal. One of them will have to go to the sheriff with him after all. He confides that Ellie is pregnant, so he can't run or risk being hanged. They've got to clear him.

Heyes and Curry discuss it privately. They had already decided by the legal flip of a coin that Heyes would accompany Marty, but now Heyes wants to flip again. He loses and once again he will be the one visiting the sheriff.

In the morning Marty announces that if they push the cattle they'll reach Montana that day. A sudden shot rings out and he pitches out of his saddle. The stock detectives have caught up with them. Cress, Heyes and Curry return fire as Ellie tends to Marty. The battle is fierce.

Heyes is hit in the temple and he falls to the ground, blood flowing down his face. Fearing his friend is dead, Curry is overcome with cold anger. He grabs Heyes's gun, then Marty's. Ordering Cress to keep him covered, Curry races off in a suicidal assault on their attackers. He fires each of the three guns he carries until they're empty, wounding two of McCloskey's men. He dives behind a rock to reload, then continues his barrage until McCloskey's men retreat. Curry watches them go, firing into the air to hurry them along.

Heyes pulls himself up, joining Cress in watching Curry. Cress is awed by the sight. "You should see him when he really gets mad," offers Heyes.

Curry returns, emotionally drained. He wipes the blood off Heyes's forehead, noting that the wound is little more than a scratch. Still, Heyes should be more careful, he suggests. A half-inch to the right and the bullet would have gone through his head. Heyes prefers to look on the bright side – a half-inch to the left and it would have missed him completely.

Ellie cries out for help. Marty has taken a turn for the worse. Cress prepares to dig for the bullet in his friend's chest, but it's too late. Marty dies.

They bury him on the trail and continue the drive to Montana. Cress sells the cattle, then pays the boys. If they are ever in Wyoming again, they promise to look Ellie up, but she demands they return to Wyoming now. Her baby will be raised there and she won't have folks claiming her child's father murdered two men in cold blood. Heyes explains he was willing to risk a twenty-year prison sentence when Marty was alive because he owed him, but not anymore. Ellie insists he pay the debt.

Curry draws Cress and Heyes aside for a private talk. When Curry fired Marty's gun, he finally figured out what had been bothering him about Marty's story. On the day of the attempted bushwhack, the boys heard two shots close together, then there was a pause followed by two more shots. The bushwhackers' guns were Colt .45s, but the first two shots came from a .38, Marty's gun. Marty didn't kill Horn and Westerly to save Heyes and Curry, he just killed them. Cress absorbs this news. He'll talk to Ellie and assures them they won't have to return to Wyoming.

Before leaving town the boys talk to Cress again. How did he fix things with Ellie? First, Cress convinced her the two of them could tell Marty's story to the sheriff themselves. Enough people saw Marty with the boys to make the sheriff believe them. Second, there won't be any trouble with the baby's name because it isn't going to be Alcott, it's going to be Truett. The boys wish him luck.

Heyes and Curry ride through the desert. Curry is worried because he doesn't feel like they're being watched. Now Heyes is worried because Curry's being worried that there's nothing to be worried about worries him. What Heyes said doesn't make sense to Curry. He tells his friend, "You know, you're really beginning to worry me."

GUEST CAST

GLENN CORBETT	MARTY ALCOTT
CHRISTINE BELFORD	ELLIE ALCOTT
FRANK CONVERSE	CRESS TRUETT
MARK HOLLY	JAKE HORN
EUGENE "SONNY" SHIELDS	PHIL WESTERLY
MICHAEL CONRAD	MIKE McCLOSKEY
TODD MARTIN	PETE
BUDDY FOSTER	ALONZO TAYLOR
CHARLES H. GRAY	SHERIFF WIGGINS
FORD RAINEY	TESHMACHER

"The history of the Wyoming Stockgrowers Association is a vile history, and we can say so,"[25] Roy Huggins told writer David Moessinger. The plot of this episode revolves around the battle between the small ranchers and the cattle barons that was a part of life in Wyoming throughout the 1880s and eventually led to the infamous Johnson County War in 1892.

In the 1880s, the cattle industry was booming and fortunes could be made. This proved attractive to investors and between 1880 and 1884, a stream of cattle corporations, many of them foreign-owned, set up shop in Wyoming. To protect their interests, these cattle barons formed the Wyoming Stockgrowers Association, a powerful group that soon controlled not only the cattle industry, but also politicians, newspapers and courts. They instituted rules governing every facet of the cattle business, rules designed to drive out homesteaders with small herds.

The Association's desire to get rid of the small ranchers derived from their own greed and shortsightedness. To increase their profits, they increased the size of their herds, giving no thought to what the land could support. By 1885 the range was severely overstocked, driving down prices and contributing to a depression. The ranchers were faced with more problems in 1886, when a summer drought, which weakened the cattle, was followed by an exceptionally harsh winter. Sixty percent of the herds perished. To save money, the cattle barons cut wages, began laying off cowboys during the winter and refused to honor the institution of grub line riding (providing food for hungry, out-of-work cowboys) unless a cowboy paid fifty cents for the meal. Cowboys who had the temerity to start their own homesteads and herds were declared rustlers because they often started those herds by rounding up stray cattle, especially calves, and branding them, thereby declaring ownership. This infuriated the Association and the Wyoming legislature obligingly passed a "maverick law" making this practice illegal.[26]

With this history as a basis, Huggins developed the story of Marty and Cress, two homesteaders partnering to make a living as independent ranchers. While the story is a straightforward tale, understanding Marty's motivation is dependent on understanding the corrupt practices of the Wyoming Stockgrowers Association. Moessinger was not successful in relating this history to the audience in his first draft script, being somewhat confused about it himself, and the second story conference turned into a history lesson, with Huggins explaining in great detail the difference between the Wyoming Stockgrowers Association and the Livestock Commission, making sure his writer learned that "the Commission was three men in the legislature – all members of the Wyoming Stockgrowers Association, and puppets of that Association who passed rules and issued orders under the instructions of the Wyoming Stockgrowers Association."[27]

Huggins had other quarrels with the first draft, noting that the attitudes of the characters are very important. The story wouldn't work if the audience didn't like them. "In the present draft we don't like Marty very much because of his cocky attitude. We also don't like the boys very well because they say, 'Well, gee, we've got problems of our own –' and they're saying this to a man who saved their lives."[28] In the scene where Marty tells the roundup foreman he's removing his cattle, the foreman draws on them, showing his disdain of Marty's "hired guns." Curry responds with a threat. "Do that again. . . I'll cut you in half before you can even thumb back your hammer."[29] The foreman found the threat convincing, but Huggins didn't, complaining "it makes Curry look like a troublemaking crumb."[30] The second draft of the script still didn't satisfy him and after covering almost every page with scribbled rewrites, Huggins gave it to his secretary with the note, "Do a complete re-type on this so I can re-write it *again!*" It took two more drafts to get the script where Huggins wanted it to be – a careful balance of story, characters and history.

WHAT HAPPENED AT THE XST?

"What could go wrong?"
– Kid Curry

STORY:	JOHN THOMAS JAMES
TELEPLAY:	JOHN THOMAS JAMES
DIRECTOR:	JACK ARNOLD
SHOOTING DATES:	UTAH – JULY 20, 21, 1972; STUDIO – SEPTEMBER 11, 12, 13, 14, 15, 18, 1972
ORIGINAL US AIR DATE:	OCTOBER 28, 1972
ORIGINAL UK AIR DATE:	DECEMBER 26, 1973

Roy Huggins liked the name Gorman. He used it as a character's name in this episode as well as in "Shootout at Diablo Station" and "Exit from Wickenburg."

The real Frank Canton a.k.a Joe Horner.

"Frank Canton was Sheriff of Johnson County, Wyoming from 1883-1887. When he died in 1932, full of honors, he was Adjutant General of the State of Oklahoma, and still calling himself Frank Canton – which was not his real name."

Those words scroll on the screen as Hannibal Heyes and Kid Curry make their way to Buffalo, Wyoming. Passing a woman driving a buggy, they're glad to learn from her that Frank Canton is the sheriff there and even happier to realize they don't know him.

Deputies Burk Stover and Orville Larkin take special note of Heyes and Curry as the boys play poker in a Buffalo saloon.

Back at their hotel, Heyes and Curry inquire of the desk clerk if a man named Gorman checked in yet. He hasn't.

When Heyes and Curry enter their hotel room, the same two deputies are waiting for them, wondering what they're doing in Buffalo. Just passing through, they say, their friend Gorman may be meeting them here. The deputies aren't interested in Gorman, but they strongly urge the boys to leave town. If they don't, the deputies will selectively enforce the law prohibiting firearms to be carried and will throw them in jail.

Heyes laughs after the deputies leave. If they knew who they really were, they wouldn't be inviting them to move on. Heyes isn't even curious about why they're not wanted in town. "Curiosity's a vice, one of the few I don't have," he confesses much to Curry's consternation. However, it's April 9 and Gorman isn't supposed to arrive in Buffalo until the twelfth. They'll leave town, then sneak back in in three days.

Curry doubts the wisdom of meeting up with Artie Gorman. He probably has a scheme that's illegal and stupid. But Heyes reminds him they owe Artie a large favor.

Next day as they meander on horseback through the dry landscape, Curry sings all the verses to "I'm a Poor Lonesome Cowboy." Listening patiently, Heyes knows for sure why the reward on Curry is for "dead or alive." If he sings one more chorus, though, Heyes promises to turn him in himself. Disregarding his partner's lack of musical appreciation, Curry sings on.

Three days later, Heyes and Curry pay a boy fifty cents to ask the hotel desk clerk if Artie Gorman has checked in. No one fitting the description has come to the hotel desk. Curry is hungry, tired, and needs a bath so he plans on getting a room in spite of the possible danger. A little later, from around a corner, Deputies Burk and Orville watch them exit the hotel. As Heyes and Curry walk down the sidewalk, Orville calls to them and puts them under arrest. Heyes explains they only returned to see if their friend Artie showed up. They'll leave in the morning.

Orville points the way to the jail. As they pass an alley, he shoves them into it and a fight ensues between Heyes, Curry, and the deputies.

The boys lose the fight, are knocked unconscious and come to to find themselves dumped out of town. A note pinned to Heyes's vest advises them to head to Sheridan or Gillette, just not back to Buffalo. The first thing Curry plans on doing is returning to bruise the deputy like he got bruised and to find out why they're not wanted in town.

They get Deputy Burk alone and beat on him until he reveals what Buffalo's got against them. Burk says Sheriff Frank Canton ordered them to encourage the boys to leave town. Orville appears and gets the drop on them. Taking their gunbelts, the deputies lead the boys to jail. When the lawmen leave, Heyes begins to work on the cell lock with a pick he had hidden in his boot.

He stops as the door to the jail opens and a man enters whom Heyes and Curry know as Joe Horner. Horner opens the cell door. Heyes and Curry are eager to leave because Frank Canton will be coming soon. "You're looking at him," Horner says. Horner is sheriff of Johnson County and is very popular. The Stockgrowers even want to make him chief of detectives, but everyone knows him as Frank Canton. He asked his deputies to get Heyes and Curry out of town because he can't have them calling him "Joe Horner" when they see him on the street.

Canton wonders who Artie Gorman is. They say he's an old friend who was in prison in Utah but they don't know exactly why Artie wants to see them. After promising Canton not to get into trouble in his town, they head to the hotel where Gorman has finally arrived.

The hotel clerk has put him in the boys' room and when they enter, they hardly recognize the sleeping man. Years in prison have changed Artie. After Heyes fetches a bottle of whiskey, Artie begins his story. He and Old Jack Cheseboro had stolen $80,000 from a North Platte bank and buried it thirteen miles from Buffalo. They got caught pulling another job and went to jail. Jack was on his way to dig up the money after he got out of prison but died before he could get to it. In the meantime, a rancher had built an icehouse right on the spot. It's not dangerous or illegal to dig up the money because the statute of limitations has run out on the crime.

The boys are reluctant to help retrieve the money because it wouldn't be honest. Artie can't believe his ears. He acknowledges that they're trying to go straight but says they owe him. If he hadn't taken them in when they were sixteen, they wouldn't have made it to seventeen.

Heyes sends Artie out to get his own room while they discuss his proposition. They realize they do owe him a lot and finally agree to help dig up the loot.

The next afternoon, Artie rides up to the ranch to sound an alarm. He announces that the sheriff has Hannibal Heyes and Kid Curry holed up at the KC and will split the reward with everyone who shows up to help. The ranch hands scurry for their horses and ride off as Heyes and Curry watch from atop a ridge.

At the icehouse, the three men gather with picks and shovels. Heyes says he worked the line crew out of Denver once and learned the secret to a job like this. "Just keep digging." The boys take turns while Artie supervises. After a long, hot, exhausting time, Curry's shovel snags the prize. He pulls out a satchel.

Artie gleefully hollers, "That's my money." A voice behind him disagrees. They look up to see the Buffalo deputies, guns drawn. The lawmen order them to toss away their guns and head for the barn. Orville commands Artie to tie up Smith and Jones while Burk checks the satchel and counts the money. Then Orville ties up Artie.

Before they leave with the $80,000, Burk wants to kill the three men because they're witnesses, but Orville knows they are no threat. They can't accuse the deputies of taking the money without admitting they stole it themselves. He pushes Burk out the door.

The boys immediately begin to fight their bindings; the crowd of cowboys will be on its way back, "saddle sore and slayin' mad" at the false alarm.

Artie works his way loose and unties his partners. They're soon on the deputies' trail and after awhile, they come upon Orville's corpse and bloody tracks leading off in another direction. Curry can tell by the blood drop spacing that a horse got hit.

Further along, they find Burk's dead horse. After another short ride, Burk ambushes them. They run for cover. Ordering his friends to stay put, Artie heads up the hill after the deputy. Two ominous shots later, Heyes and Curry run after him. They find Burk dead and Artie wounded. Heyes starts to go after a doctor but Artie dies in Curry's arms.

Around their campfire that night, Heyes and Curry admit they know what they have to do – take the bodies and the money back to Frank Canton.

Sheriff Canton listens to their story but is not sure they're really trying to go straight. He realizes they're feeling pretty stupid about the whole thing but he's going to let them go mainly because they keep calling him "Joe." They can take the money too because it's worthless. The bank that issued it went bankrupt. The boys decline.

At Artie's funeral, the minister asks what was in the canvas bag buried with the deceased. Heyes doesn't answer directly except to quote Job 1:21 – "We brought nothing into this world and we carry nothing out." Frank Canton also attends the funeral lest Artie be buried with no one to mourn him. They thank him for letting Artie take the money with him. As they get ready to leave, Canton wonders if it would do any good for him to mention to Governor Warren that two good, honest men, Thaddeus Jones and Joshua Smith, came passing by Buffalo. It might help, they say, though they can't tell him how or why.

Riding along, Curry poses a hypothetical question to Heyes, "If no one had got killed, would we have turned the money in?" Heyes's hypothetical answer is to ask if they would have kept it.

GUEST CAST

KEENAN WYNN	ARTIE GORMAN
ED NELSON	FRANK CANTON
WILLIAM SMITH	DEPUTY ORVILLE LARKIN
GEOFFREY LEWIS	DEPUTY BURK STOVER
EVE McVEAGH	WOMAN
DAVID GRUNER	BOY
WILLIAM D. GORDON	REVEREND SIEVER
DAVE MORICK	HOTEL CLERK

Any one episode of *Alias Smith and Jones* could inspire viewers to inquire more deeply into some historical facet of it. In the teleplay for "What Happened at the XST?" Huggins provided historical background for the actors and director. In scene four, before we see Heyes and Curry, Huggins described Buffalo as having evolved as a result of the building of Fort McKinney, headquarters of the 6th Cavalry. He put soldiers walking around the streets because the fort was only five miles west of town. The only other reason Buffalo existed was to "serve the cattlemen of Johnson County, large and small, and their cowhands. It was a town of just over 1000 in 1885."[31]

Canton, he wrote, has "a moustache which turns down in a curl at each end. He has light blue eyes, light brown hair and a slender, strong-jawed face. He is lean and well over six feet in height. Canton was thirty-six at this time . . . he liked to smoke a pipe and had one in his hand or mouth about twelve hours a day."[32] No physical descriptions exist for the deputies, but Huggins wanted Burk, in particular, to come off as "a mean sonofabitch. He does not make a good first impression."[33]

The real Joe Horner was under indictment for cattle rustling in October 1874. He had also robbed a bank in Comanche, Texas, for which he received a ten-year sentence, but he broke out of prison and held up a stagecoach. This time he was sent to Huntsville Prison with another ten years tacked onto his sentence. Two years later, Horner escaped while working on a chain gang. He disappeared and changed his name to Frank Canton.

Meanwhile in Johnson County, Wyoming, cattle barons aimed to stop small ranchers from doing business. They imported Texas gunfighters and deployed them against local ranchers and homesteaders they accused of being cattle thieves. They also recruited some local talent including Frank Canton who'd recently served two terms as sheriff of Johnson County. Even with the legendary lawman on their side, the cattle barons lost the war. A stand of two hundred local settlers massed against the gunfighter army and restored legitimate law and order to the county. Canton was prosecuted on two separate murder indictments for shooting Nate Champion and Nick Ray, but after a year of legal maneuvering, the charges were dropped. Canton left Wyoming.

In 1894, he sought an audience with Texas governor James Hogg. In a startling confession, Canton revealed that he and Joe Horner, who had terrorized Texas in the 1870s, were one and the same. Governor Hogg granted him a full pardon. Although he had made peace with his past, Frank Canton would remain a shadowy figure in the history of frontier justice. Huggins was aware that Canton had been a cold-blooded killer but that "does not have to be brought out in our story."[34]

For many viewers, the title is confusing. Some fans, though, may have reasoned out that XST could stand for est, Erhard Seminar Training, an awareness program first taught by Scientologist Werner Erhard in 1971 that offered attendees a new life after a marathon $250 seminar. According to Erhard, the program would force you to "throw away your belief system, tear yourself down, and put yourself back together again." A person trained in est comes to view the entirety of his life as superfluous to who he really is and glorifies the self at the expense of all social connections. est teaches how to ignore a problem in such a way as to deny that something is being ignored.[35]

Artie Gorman was happy to ignore the problems that went along with retrieving the stolen money, leaving those details to Heyes and Curry. What happened at the XST is that three men died because of Artie's and the deputies' greed. Heyes and Curry were "saved" because they did not throw away their belief system. Instead, they kept on the track that they had set for themselves of becoming honest citizens.

Roy Huggins explained his title like this: "[XST] is an existentialist story. Everything is meaningless. . . . The ultimate meaninglessness is that even the money isn't worth anything. People have died, and everything else has happened. . . . It's a meaningless title. At the end, our audience might be wondering what the XST was – and a few people in our audience might guess."[36]

Keenan Wynn plays a greedy man in each of the three *Alias Smith and Jones* episodes he guest starred in. In "Dreadful Sorry, Clementine," as Horace Wingate, he owns Golden Meadows land and gets fleeced by Clem. In "Stagecoach Seven," he's not willing to split the reward money on our boys with the Weaver gang. It appears that some of Wynn's remarks in this episode, e.g. when they're in the barn tied up and he complains that his back is bad and his knees aren't too good either or his "Shut up" to Curry's protest about his tying the knots good, are really adlibbed remarks to Ben Murphy and to William Smith; they are not in the script. When the boys are digging under the icehouse, dialogue is missing from the script. The lines are rare instances of adlibbed dialogue which Huggins allowed because they don't alter the story in any way, but are merely Wynn's comments while watching Ben and Roger dig.

THE TEN DAYS THAT SHOOK KID CURRY

"I knew [Mr. Jones] didn't have enough brains or imagination to kidnap someone and rob a bank, so I figured it had to be the other way around."
– Hannibal Heyes

STORY:	JOHN THOMAS JAMES
TELEPLAY:	GLORYETTE CLARK
DIRECTOR:	EDWARD M. ABROMS
SHOOTING DATES:	SEPTEMBER 20, 21, 22, 25, 26, 27, 1972
ORIGINAL US AIR DATE:	NOVEMBER 4, 1972
ORIGINAL UK AIR DATE:	JANUARY 21, 1974

A posse chases Hannibal Heyes and Kid Curry. Pausing to consider their desperate situation, Heyes decides splitting up is their only chance to escape. Curry feels this is one of Heyes's flabbier ideas, but agrees to meet in Ashford.

Curry arrives first – dirty, hungry and nearly broke. The distrustful hotel clerk makes him pay in advance before handing him the key.

After cleaning up, he heads for the saloon and spends his last nickel on a beer. He notices Doc Holliday at a nearby table playing solitaire and joins him, introducing himself as a friend of Joshua Smith, the man who lost $20,000 in that Tombstone poker game. Doc's curt attitude mellows as he recalls his biggest win. Curry suggests a game and wonders aloud what the odds are that he can make five pat hands out of twenty-five cards. Doc is angry at being thought a sucker, especially since he invented that trick. Curry apologizes and Doc suggests trying it on Jorgenson, a stupid man who doesn't know he's stupid.

The schoolteacher and the bank teller went through several name changes: From Ellen to Phoebe to Amy Martin and from Joe to Elmer to Willard Riley.

"We will have an exciting, action-filled (but not violent) climax in which Heyes gets Curry out of this spot and in which, in fact, Curry helps himself out of it – once given the edge that Heyes gives him. We don't want Curry to be too passive in this show." – Story notes, Jun 1, 1972.

Jorgenson is interested in the bet. He's eager to up the stakes to $100, but Curry refuses. Ten dollars is all he's willing to risk. After Jorgenson deals the cards, Curry begins to arrange them. An hour later, Jorgenson complains about how long it's taking. Doc points out to Curry, sadly, this is the one time in ten it can't be done.

Judge Morrison fines Curry $10 for trying to pull a con game, but since he doesn't have any money, sentences him to five days in jail.

The judge calls the next case, a man accused of being drunk and disorderly. Amy Martin, the local schoolteacher, speaks on his behalf and the judge agrees to send the man home to his wife rather than throw him in jail. Amy then offers to pay Curry's fine, arguing that his only crime was being hungry and broke. "My, my, the milk of human kindness is getting awfully deep in here," the judge remarks, but he allows her to pay the fine.

Amy hurries to the bank to withdraw ten dollars. She informs the teller, Willard Riley, that she's found someone. Can it be done tonight? Riley agrees.

Curry is returned to the courtroom and informed of his good fortune.

Outside, he thanks Amy. She explains that she felt sorry for him and invites him to come to the schoolhouse that night. She might be able to help him again.

Later, when Curry knocks at the schoolhouse door, Amy ushers him into her private quarters, taking his hat and suggesting he'd be more comfortable if he removed his gunbelt. Not sure where this is heading, Curry obligingly removes his gun and sets it on a nearby table while Amy carries his hat into the bedroom and places it on the bed.

Riley emerges from the shadows and scoops up the hat. Then, as Curry and

Amy chat, Riley bursts into the room, gun aimed at Curry. Riley orders him to turn around, then hits him on the head.

Riley and Amy have outfitted an old mine shaft as a hideout. Curry is tied to a chair. Amy assures him he won't be mistreated in any way during the ten days he'll be held there.

The next day Heyes arrives in Ashford, wondering at the excitement in the street, but intent on getting a drink. In the saloon he learns the bank was robbed the night before. Doc Holliday spots him and calls him over, informing Heyes it was his friend Thaddeus Jones who robbed the bank. Doc explains about the con game gone awry, Jones's arrest and the schoolteacher paying his fine. Then that night, Jones kidnapped the banker's stepson and forced him to empty the safe, netting $70,000. Not satisfied with that, he then left a ransom note demanding $100,000 more. "It wasn't Thaddeus Jones, Doc," Heyes insists. "He hasn't got that much greed or that much imagination." All Doc knows is that Jones is gone and his hat was found in the alley behind the bank. Heyes is worried. He asks Doc not to tell anyone he knows Thaddeus, then wonders if the schoolteacher makes a habit of paying people's fines. No, Doc doesn't think she does.

In the hideout, Riley feeds Curry a sandwich. Curry throws himself, chair and all, at his captor. They crash to the ground, where Curry tries to overpower Riley as best he can, but Riley crawls free and grabs his gun, firing several shots. Riley promises to blow Curry's head off the next time. "You're going to kill me sooner or later anyhow," Curry reasons. "So why not now?" Because Amy only agreed to do this if their victim was released at the end. Curry doesn't believe him. How can they leave him alive to tell what really happened? Riley says Amy feels that Jones is smart enough to disappear when they release him, given the evidence against him. Besides his hat at the crime scene, Riley's bloodstained coat will be found at the river. Curry agrees he won't buck those odds but wonders what they're waiting for. In six days school will be over and Amy's leaving town won't be suspicious. This is unwelcome news for Curry and Riley confirms his fears. "That's right. She won't be here when you and I say our goodbyes."

A man in search of a doctor dashes into the saloon, barreling into Heyes in his haste. Mr. Schwedes is hurt bad, the doctor is needed right away. Heyes asks the bartender if Mr. Schwedes has any children in school and learns he has a son.

Heyes picks the boy up from school and takes him home.

Mrs. Schwedes is grateful to Mr. Smith. Heyes notices her shelves filled with books of poetry which Mrs. Schwedes admits she also writes. Heyes asks if she'll allow him to read some of them.

That night in his hotel room, Heyes studies her poems. He paces the room, reciting them over and over until he has them memorized.

The next day Heyes visits the schoolhouse, reminding Amy that they met when he picked up the Schwedes boy. He asks a favor of her. He writes poetry, Heyes explains, but the poems are all in his head. He never learned to write and is hoping she will write them down for him. When Amy agrees, he recites one of the poems he memorized. Amy sits entranced, swept away by the beauty of the words. She's surprised such an uneducated man has so much sensitivity. She transcribes the poems as he recites them to her. Finally Heyes confesses that he really came to see her. She invites him to return the next evening. As Heyes leaves, a look of shame crosses his face.

Riley calculates the interest he will earn on $70,000, but Curry points out that he hasn't calculated the cost of bad dreams.

Heyes visits Amy again, sharing more poetry. Amy is falling in love with him.

The next morning, when Heyes enters the saloon, Doc wonders what he's been up to that makes him so miserable. Heyes says he is worried about his friend Jones.

That night Heyes once again visits Amy, not for poetry, but for lovemaking.

The next day Heyes asks Doc how much money he could raise. If it's in a good cause, Doc says, he could come up with about $7,000. That's plenty, Heyes assures him. Tonight they'll play poker and Heyes will win the whole amount. After the game, Heyes will return the money privately. Doc doesn't understand, but agrees to the plan.

Curry works to free his hands while Riley explains the plan was his idea, not Amy's. If he wasn't a cynic, Riley muses, he might say he's in love with Amy. Curry reminds Riley that the plan doesn't include killing anyone. "Me, for instance."

After Heyes "wins" the money from Doc, he pounds on the schoolhouse door, sweeping Amy into his arms when she answers. In three days when school ends, they'll leave and go to Santa Marta. Amy is hesitant. "We'll be married, of course," Heyes tells her. At this, Amy hugs him, but she worries that they have no money. Heyes informs her that he just won $7,000 playing poker. Amy kisses him ecstatically, but Heyes seems not to share her joy.

Later, he hides in the bushes outside the schoolhouse. Eventually Amy comes out, gets her horse and rides off.

In the hideout, as Riley sleeps, Curry works harder on his bonds, struggling to free his hands. His efforts cause the chair to scrape across the floor, breaking the silence. Riley wakes, wondering what he heard. You're just having one of those bad dreams I told you about, Curry suggests. Amy's arrival interrupts further conversation.

She tells Riley she's not going through with their plan. Dumbfounded, he demands to know why, as Curry, his hands free at last, leaps for Riley's gun on the table. As the two men fight over it, Amy picks up a crowbar and hits Curry until he's forced to drop it. With an arm around his captor's throat, Curry urges her to leave Riley to him, but she holds the gun unwaveringly, threatening to shoot. Reluctantly, Curry releases his stranglehold. Amy extends the gun to her accomplice, but a voice intrudes. "I sure wouldn't take that gun," Heyes advises Riley, urging Amy to give the gun to him as he moves closer. Curry is delighted to see his partner.

Heyes apologizes to Amy. In case she hasn't figured it out, his ruse was a way to save his friend. Heyes ties up Riley, then outlines his plan. Riley will turn himself in, clearing Mr. Jones but making no mention of Amy's part in the robbery. Riley has no intention of taking all the blame, but Heyes points out that doing it his way will get Riley out of trouble as well.

In the morning Riley and Curry cause quite a stir in Ashford as they ride into town and enter the bank.

Heyes sees Amy off on the stagecoach wondering if she will ever be able to forgive him. She assures him that she can, because he taught her that she is capable of loving someone. She hadn't believed she could fall in love before this. Heyes says goodbye and sadly watches as the stage pulls away.

As they ride out of town Curry notices that Amy got a lot closer to Heyes than he expected. Heyes admits Amy will probably get over him sooner than he'll get over her. Then Curry changes the subject. How did Heyes deduce that the schoolteacher was the answer? You just can't explain genius, Heyes brags. Of course, it helped when the stableman told him Curry rode out toward the school-house the night the bank was robbed. Curry exclaims, "Heyes, you *are* a genius!"

GUEST CAST

SHIRLEY KNIGHT	AMY MARTIN
EDD BYRNES	WILLARD RILEY
BILL FLETCHER	DOC HOLLIDAY
BARBARA BOSSON	MRS. SCHWEDES
RALPH MONTGOMERY	CLERK
FREDERIC DOWNS	JUDGE
TED GEHRING	JORGENSEN
BILL QUINN	HOTEL CLERK
STEVEN GRAVERS	BARTENDER
JOHN MCDONALD	MR. SHAEFFER
RANDALL CARVER	YOUNG MAN
MONTY LAIRD	STUNT DOUBLE – RILEY
JIM NICKERSON	STUNT DOUBLE – CURRY

"There is a theme in this story which is something about love," Roy Huggins noted in his original outline.[37] For a story about bank robbery and kidnapping, this is a startling statement. But, in truth, this story is about love, or more accurately, about what love can drive a person to do. Love drove Riley to rob a bank, Amy to betray her partner and Heyes to prey on a vulnerable woman.

Amy Martin has always thought herself incapable of love. Rather than admitting she has just never found the right man, she assumes her soul is lacking the necessary emotions and settles for a life of well-heeled companionship with Willard Riley. Riley, who has his own issues with love, considers himself incapable of feeling love, and also of being loved.

The kidnapping plot hinges on the fact that Riley knows his stepfather wouldn't pay ten cents for him, let alone the $100,000 ransom. When Curry questions his mother's reaction, Riley is convinced she would make only a token protest by threatening to leave her husband, an event the man would most likely welcome. With his fate a matter of indifference to his family, Riley can stage his own murder and disappear with Amy and the money, secure in the knowledge he will never be sought.

Riley and Amy made their plans carefully, content to wait for a drifter who would fit their purpose. Naturally this drifter must be alone in life, just as they are. Amy mistakes Curry for such a man, not realizing that Curry does have someone who cares for him – Heyes.

Heyes's arrival in Ashford adds a twist to this odd love story. With the school-teacher the only clue in Curry's disappearance, Heyes searches for a way to force her to lead him to his partner. The weapon he chooses is love. Making Amy fall in love with him will lead her to betray Riley, a man who truly loves her despite his cynical claim that their relationship is only a profitable, life-time arrangement.

Heyes's plan, while clever, is less than admirable. Desperate to find Curry, he steals Mrs. Schwedes's poems. Then, reciting the poems with great intensity, Heyes convinces Amy that he's a sensitive and romantic man who loves her. Riley's love for Amy led him to rob his stepfather's bank; Heyes's love for Curry leads him to deliberately play on her emotions. As Huggins explains, "This woman had never been in love in her life. . . .But she falls truly in love for the first time now – and that is the thing that lifts this story, because Heyes is doing something cruel for his friend."[38]

In most love stories the lovers go off to live happily ever after. Not so here. Amy has learned to love and "is a completely different human being."[39] She happily goes off alone to start a new, more promising life. Riley, devastated to learn that Amy never truly loved him, agrees to turn himself in and returns to his loveless existence. Heyes is left suffering from an unintended consequence of his scheme – he "has fallen a little in love with [Amy]. Having gone through all this, he couldn't have gone through it coldbloodedly."[40] The only relationship to remain intact is that between Heyes and Curry. They leave Ashford, inseparable as always.

Gloryette Clark had worked on *Alias Smith and Jones* since the first season, but as a film editor, not a writer. Her first foray into writing had come several years earlier when she pointed out a newspaper article she felt would make a good story for the Lawyers segment of Huggins's show *The Bold Ones*. Huggins insisted she write a treatment and then bought it, giving Clark her first story credit. From then on, if Huggins needed a writer in a hurry, he would often turn to her. Huggins first told the story of "The Ten Days That Shook Kid Curry" to Juanita Bartlett but, as she was still busy with her first script, "The McCreedy Feud," he needed another writer. Since third season shooting had not yet commenced, Huggins turned to his favorite film editor. "He knew that I was there and available, so it was at his behest," Clark recalls of her sudden script assignment. "Naturally, he wanted me where I could be most useful, so it was never when he wanted me in the cutting room."[41]

Both Huggins and Clark loved poetry and continued to share their favorites with each other until Huggins's death. However, the fast pace of television production precluded the writing of original poetry for Heyes to recite. Instead, they turned to nineteenth century poems that are in the public domain, among them "The Dream" by Caroline Norton, granddaughter of Richard Brinsley Sheridan, and "Twenty-fourth Sunday after Trinity" by John Keble.

THE DAY THE AMNESTY CAME THROUGH

"Heyes, I hope you know what we're doin'."
– Kid Curry

STORY:	JOHN THOMAS JAMES
TELEPLAY:	DICK NELSON AND JOHN THOMAS JAMES
DIRECTOR:	JEFF COREY
SHOOTING DATES:	OCTOBER 2, 3, 4, 5, 6, 1972
ORIGINAL US AIR DATE:	NOVEMBER 25, 1972
ORIGINAL UK AIR DATE:	JANUARY 28, 1974

Hannibal Heyes and Kid Curry ride into Fort Morgan, Colorado, and soon are playing poker in the saloon. They consider taking a job cutting two thousand railroad ties for $150, but a reply to their telegram to Lom Trevors changes everything.

"What you have been waiting for so long has finally come through!" it reads. Elated, they ride hard to meet Lom at the Nolan ranch.

Instead of happy congratulations on receiving their amnesty, Lom notifies them that the president removed Governor Francis Warren from office. Over what should

The taciturn Black Henry Smith was played by Sonny Shields, one of the stunt doubles for Ben Murphy and Roger Davis. Monty Laird remembered that Shields used to be a punk fighter.

The story was originally titled "The Day of the Amnesty."

have been drinks of celebratory champagne, Lom tells them about the new governor, George W. Baxter. He promises to get the same amnesty deal for them from him.

At midnight in Cheyenne, Wyoming, dressed in their best suits, Heyes and Curry are hiding in an alley lest they be recognized and tossed in jail. Lom finds them and escorts them into an audience with Governor Baxter, who is surprised to see the two men who don't look at all like his concept of outlaws. He is inclined to go along with Frank Warren's promise to them. The thing is . . .

Baxter has a friend named Eric Anderson whose daughter is missing. Anderson thinks she's been kidnapped, but Baxter has information that she ran off with Ed Starr of the Red Sash Gang. If Heyes and Curry will ride into the

Little Bighorns and check out the situation, Baxter will consider their amnesty and won't make them wait two years. He just wants to know if she's there of her own free will or if she's been kidnapped and he should send the militia in to rescue her. Their knowing Charlie Taylor of the Red Sash Gang will help.

Heyes and Curry leave that night, neglecting to mention to the governor that Charlie Taylor hates Curry. Heyes offers to let his partner ride in first so Heyes's back is exposed. After all, Heyes has no problem being courageous. "True," Curry says, "every time you decide to get courageous, it becomes a problem for me." Another Red Sash member, Black Henry Smith, is the silent type. Heyes admires that, recalling that their granddaddy used to say, "A loud mouth is a sure sign of a small brain." Curry's off-key singing verifies granddaddy's belief.

Arriving in the Little Bighorns, Heyes and Curry announce themselves to gang members stationed as lookouts. Skeptical of the pair really being Heyes and Curry, the men take their weapons and introduce themselves as General Grant and Stanley and Livingstone just back from Africa. Then they lead them through the mountains, across a river and finally into camp where the rest of the gang comes out to greet them. Face to face with Curry, Charlie admits he can't remember why he was mad at him and the boys are welcomed. Their cover story is that things got hot in Carbon County and they're looking for a cooler climate to hang out in.

As the gang enjoys a meal, Ed Starr bursts into the cabin with pretty Ellen Anderson. She heads for her bedroom and slams the door. Charlie explains their spats provide entertainment for the rest of the gang and usually involve her wanting Ed to fetch a preacher to marry them.

That evening, Heyes and Curry discuss the situation. They already found out what Governor Baxter wants to know. However, if they take back the girl instead of just a message about her it may put them in better stead. They can't kidnap her but Curry suggests he turn on his charm and win her away from Ed. Heyes insists that women are *his* strong point and he should win her over. Curry points out that Ed is very good with a gun and is a sore loser. Would Heyes like to take on Ed Starr? Heyes concedes.

While the gang plays poker, Curry steps outside with Ellen and begins his seduction. Ed had promised to ride with her to the top of the next ridge in the moonlight to see the lovely view. Curry offers to accompany her, but she declines knowing Ed wouldn't understand. Ed doesn't realize how lucky he is to have her, Curry says, and repeats his offer to ride with her. This time she accepts.

Instead of admiring the view, Curry admires Ellen. He tells her he knows of her father and believes she's making a mistake with Ed Starr. She deserves better than him. Ellen sees that Curry is coming on to her and wants to head back.

Ed is waiting for them and sends Ellen into the cabin. He cautions Curry to leave her alone.

Next morning, as Ellen hangs laundry, Heyes comes by to say how much Curry likes her. Curry has gone fishing and would have asked her to go along, except for Ed's warning. She decides to go fishing to show that Ed has no hold on her. When Heyes purposely lets it slip to Ed that Ellen has joined the Kid fishing, Ed is furious and tells Heyes to keep the Kid away from her.

After breakfast, Heyes and Curry watch Ed practice his quick draw. Curry realizes Ed may be better than he is. For his part, Heyes is glad Curry talked him out of winning Ellen away from Ed and he wants to head back with only the information about the girl. Curry insists it would be more advantageous to return with Ellen and promises to stay away from her. Heyes should just keep pointing out to Ellen how much the Kid likes her.

The boys are fixing bridles when Ellen appears with her mending. Curry leaves, ignoring her. Heyes mentions to Ellen that they're leaving in the morning. The Kid is wild over her, he tells Ellen, and would like her to go with them but he can't ask her because of Ed. Ellen is confused; she never gave him reason to be crazy about her.

At supper, Curry smiles at Ellen who smiles back. Watching the exchange, Ed bangs on the table in anger. He orders Ellen to her room and warns Curry that he'll kill him if Curry doesn't stay away from her. Curry diffuses the situation with a request that Ed pass the biscuits.

The next morning, when Curry is chopping firewood, Ellen apologizes to him for the night before. Ed sees them talking and challenges Curry to a gunfight. After a few tense moments, Ed draws and fires but Curry is faster and shoots the gun out of Ed's hand. Ed is disgraced.

As the boys saddle up to leave, Ellen apologizes yet again. But Curry tells her the whole story – that they came to take her home. Her father wants her back and the governor would have sent the militia in after her. Having seen Ed at his worst, she agrees to return with them.

The boys telegraph Lom to meet them near Rock Creek. When they arrive, Lom has the same hang-dog expression on his face he had at their last meeting. President Cleveland removed Governor Baxter from office two days previously. Heyes and Curry are disgusted. They refuse to continue on and meet Ellen's father because he's probably been replaced by her uncle. They don't need any more friends like Lom or Baxter because all their friends get removed from office.

Nevertheless, they have second thoughts and later agree to meet Lom at the Nolan ranch. As they chew on a tough sage hen supper, Lom arrives. Guess what happened! Wisconsin replaced Wyoming? Curry wonders. Lom announces that the new governor is Charles Moonlight. He's a Kansan like they are and believes in small farmers and doesn't like big ranchers or railroads. With that attitude, Heyes believes he'll last about forty-eight hours in Wyoming. Lom already talked to him about the boys and Moonlight will consider giving them an amnesty. All they have to do is stay out of trouble. In the meantime, though, they'll still be wanted. Heyes wants to know, "That's a good deal?"

GUEST CAST

LANE BRADBURY	ELLEN ANDERSON
BRETT HALSEY	ED STARR
WARREN VANDERS	CURLY RED JOHNSON
JOHN RUSSELL	LOM TREVORS
ROBERT NICHOLS	MR. MAGRUDER
JEFF COREY	GEORGE W. BAXTER
ROBERT DONNER	CHARLIE TAYLOR
CHARLES DIERKOP	CLAYTON CREWES
SONNY SHIELDS	BLACK HENRY SMITH

With only four more episodes to the series, Ben Murphy and Roger Davis had a great script to work with, one that showcased their talents, both as actors and as the characters Curry and Heyes. Heyes's silver tongue and Curry's fast draw are used to great advantage at the outlaws' camp. Elation at getting the amnesty leads to disappointment then to resignation as they begin anew working toward the pardon with the replacement governor. In telling the story for Dick Nelson, Roy Huggins observed that this one would answer the question "Why do our boys call themselves Smith and Jones?"[42]

Many historical references add to the realism of the episode. Fort Morgan, as Nelson and Huggins wrote in the teleplay, "is a small middle-of-nowhere town in the flat, prairie country of Northeastern Colorado. It has among other things, a saloon and a telegraph office."[43] The real Red Sash Gang – the sash being just a piece of clothing and not used specifically to identify members[44] – though not officially recognized or well organized, controlled much of Johnson County, Wyoming, in the 1880s.

Huggins had fun with the Red Sash Gang members. According to descriptions he inserted into his story, Clayton Crewes was "cadaverously skinny and has a face that belongs on the label of an iodine bottle. Black Henry has beady eyes, shaggy black hair and a scraggly beard, and his mouth is in a permanent tight-lipped grimace . . ." Being a taciturn man, his favorite phrase was "I'm a man of few words and if it don't suit you, I'll kill you" and the actor playing Black Henry is given this line in the script. As for Curly Red, he was "as bald as an egg . . . the only thing curly and red about him is his nose."[45] As for Charlie Taylor, he is described as having a gap-toothed grin and being "*ugly*. He's a big, strapping fellow – as the saying goes, not much for looks but Hell for stout."[46]

An inveterate history buff, the inordinately rapid turnover of Wyoming Territorial governors caught Huggins's attention. Francis E. Warren served from February 1885 to November 1886. Many petitions for pardons can be found among his official papers. George W. Baxter replaced him on November 11 and only served until December 20. It is surprising that Huggins did not then recognize E.S.N. Morgan as acting governor. Thomas Moonlight took over on January 24,

1887. Words scrolling on the screen at the end of the episode indicate the progression of men in the governor's chair, even though the dates shown are slightly off.

What was also off was Governor Thomas Moonlight's name. Huggins had started off with the correct name but at some point, "his first name got changed (to Charles). . . .(T)hat was a sheer accident. . . .When I first found out about him . . . there was something he'd done that was interesting and I used it as a ploy in the story." Huggins wondered if audiences would realize it was a mistake or think that it was changed deliberately. The inadvertent substitution of the wrong name distressed Huggins even thirty years later. "I hated that," he said, "because it started out correct." Somewhere between the story line and the typing, "someone got careless."[47]

Huggins remembered in an interview with the authors that he had made Heyes and Curry cousins in "The Reformation of Harry Briscoe" and had reinforced the relationship in "The Men That Corrupted Hadleyburg." However, he did not recall that for some reason he decided in this episode to change it. Dick Nelson wrote a scene in which Heyes tells Ellen of his and Curry's familial relationship. With no further elaboration, Huggins, in his rewrite annotations for Nelson, noted "We are abandoning the business of Heyes and Curry being cousins. They grew up together in Kansas and they lost their parents within a few weeks of each other during the Civil War."[48]

While they're in camp, in his first draft, Nelson has the boys watching Ed and Ellen playfully flirting. Heyes and Curry react "with distaste" and Curry says, "Isn't that awful?" Heyes agrees it's "disgusting."[49] Huggins corrects Nelson's take. "Our boys are a little too righteous about Ed. They shouldn't be. They are taking a rather Victorian attitude and they don't need to, because they've slept with many girls."[50] Because Curry's role in the charade was to ignore Ellen in deference to Ed, Heyes had to make sure Ellen knew Curry liked her and hoped she would return with them. Huggins viewed this as a "John Alden – Priscilla relationship – 'Why don't you speak for yourself, John?'"[51]

When Lane Bradbury watched the episode with the authors, she was bothered by her performance of thirty years ago. Looking back, she saw superficial acting, not only on her part but with the entire episode. "There's not a lot of inner life going on underneath the dialogue," she observed. Bradbury guest starred on many programs and remembered feeling sorry for the regulars because the guests usually had "all the meat. They just had all the ingredients to be able to get into that character and act it or be it." In her opinion, *Alias Smith and Jones* hardly provided any "meat" even for the guest stars. Ellen was "written one-dimensionally, but as an actress I should have gotten in there and found other dimensions so that she had some kind of inner life that I was playing against. She obviously had run off from her father so she's got a lot of stuff going on. There was no stuff going on, just light, surface acting . . . There really should have been (some inner conflict) and there just wasn't."[52]

The Strange Fate of Conrad Meyer Zulick

"How can you forget how to rob a bank? Nobody forgets something like that!
It's like swimming!"
– Kid Curry

STORY:	JOHN THOMAS JAMES
TELEPLAY:	NICHOLAS E. BAEHR
DIRECTOR:	RICHARD BENNETT
SHOOTING DATES:	OCTOBER 10, 11, 12, 13, 16, 17, 1972
ORIGINAL US AIR DATE:	DECEMBER 2, 1972
ORIGINAL UK AIR DATE:	FEBRUARY 4, 1974

This story was first called "The Seventh Governor."

"The whole escape plan should be involved and it should be exciting without being violent." – Addenda to story, June 5, 1972: 5.

Douglas, Arizona. Hannibal Heyes and Kid Curry enjoy a poker game in the saloon while outside, Bill Meade recruits M.T. Donovan for an important job, apologizing for not being able to explain why it's so vital.

Fallon, a mean-looking man, overplays his two pair, losing to Curry's three kings. Declaring Curry's luck too good to be true, he vows it will soon end and leaves to get his gun.

When Curry exits the saloon, he is challenged by a now-armed Fallon, who demands the money Curry took him for. Curry refuses, pointing out that Fallon is a bad poker player as well as a bad loser. When Fallon goes for his gun, Curry outdraws him, shooting off his holster. Donovan, who has been watching the exchange, is amazed.

After Heyes and Curry ride out of town, Donovan searches through Wanted posters, telling Sheriff Lundy he's just passing time. Finding the posters on Curry and Heyes, he ponders the information.

Playing cards is becoming too dangerous so, as the boys ride along, Curry suggests it's time to give up poker but wonders what money-making opportunities are left since they've already given up banks and railroads. Catching up to them, Donovan interrupts their musings. He was impressed by the nerve they showed dealing with Fallon and offers them a job rescuing Conrad Meyer Zulick, a lawyer being held hostage by disgruntled miners in Mexico. He'll pay them $300 apiece.

Back in Douglas, they discuss the job over drinks. Zulick is being held in Nacozari, a town one hundred miles south. The mining company's managers disappeared with the payroll. When Zulick went to straighten things out, he was taken hostage by the miners who won't release him until they get paid. Heyes remarks that Zulick must be a good friend but Donovan refutes that; he's never met him. He's taken this job because he needs the money. And they won't get paid unless they return with Zulick in four days.

Taking along a wagon full of farm equipment as a cover, Donovan, Heyes and Curry head to Mexico. To meet the deadline they travel at a grueling pace.

That night Donovan reminds the boys that the miners have a right to hold Zulick under Mexican law, so he doesn't want them to get gun-happy. If there's trouble, the boys can shoot back to discourage the miners, but not to kill them. Heyes assures him they've always avoided killing people and they're not going to start now. With a relieved look, Donovan excuses himself and heads to the creek.

After he's out of sight, Curry announces his belief that Donovan knows who they are. Heyes disagrees. If he knew they were Heyes and Curry, he wouldn't be sending them on a $600 job in Mexico; he'd turn them in for the real money. Curry admits it doesn't make sense, but Donovan's whole attitude toward them is wrong. Continuing to worry, Curry reasons that Donovan guessed who they were because of the shootout with Fallon, but his partner rejects that idea. Heyes regrets having to tell Curry he's slowing down.

In the morning, Heyes asks Donovan why he chose them for this job. Was it just because of the shooting in town? After all, Donovan has made it clear he doesn't need a fast gun. Donovan replies that it was the coolness that impressed him, not the speed, and he needed someone in a hurry.

The trio puts in another grueling day on the road. By late afternoon they're outside the mining camp where they'll wait until nightfall to reconnoiter the area. Heyes checks out the main house while Donovan explores the tent area. Curry watches and covers them.

Heyes returns first with news that Zulick is being held on the second floor of the main house. The first floor is full of miners, but no guards are outside. Curry is eager to hear Heyes's plan and points out that Donovan will need help knowing what to do. They should look at the house as if it were a bank and Zulick was the money in the vault. How would Heyes get him out?

Heyes ponders. No dynamite or nitro, in a house full of guards . . . Finally Heyes admits he can't remember. Incredulously, Curry asks how he could forget how to rob a bank. It's been a long time, Heyes reminds him. Disgusted, Curry remarks, "Boy oh boy, the great Hannibal Heyes. You know what they ought to do with you, Heyes? They ought to drop the reward on you." Before Heyes can respond to this latest insult, Donovan rejoins them. Now all they have to do is get in the house and upstairs.

The Mexicans are enjoying poker, music and dancing. The trio finds a likely window and gains entrance to the house, sneaks up the stairs and surprises a guard. Curry demands to know the whereabouts of the *Americano* as Donovan ties and gags the man. The man points to a door, which Heyes opens with a lockpick.

Surprised, Zulick sits up in bed as the three men enter his room. Donovan introduces himself, explains their presence and urges him to get dressed. Zulick resists at first, but finally does as he's told.

Guns made by Monty Laird similar to the ones Kid Curry carried.

Downstairs the music continues, but the poker game breaks up. Three miners head upstairs as Donovan and the boys lead Zulick out. They quickly duck back into the bedroom, bringing the guard with them.

The miners are alarmed to find the guard missing. As they approach the bedroom, Curry jumps out, gun in hand, and waves them into the room. The music below covers the sound of the fight as Heyes, Curry and Donovan overpower them. This time the four men make it downstairs, but run into the singer. Grabbing her before she can scream, Curry suggests they tie up all the miners to give themselves a good head start. Donovan doesn't want to risk it, but Heyes convinces him.

With Zulick hidden inside the wagon, Donovan drives while the boys lead the way on their horses.

The miners have freed themselves and the chase is on. Their only hope of outrunning them is to abandon the wagon. Riding double on the horses, Donovan, Zulick and the boys escape their pursuers and arrive in Douglas tired and bedraggled, but within the four day deadline.

Meade greets Donovan and Zulick happily. He's got a stagecoach to Tombstone waiting for Zulick and he'll explain everything on the way. After Meade pays Donovan, Zulick thanks him, impressed by the way the men rescued him without bloodshed.

Donovan counts out $300 apiece and pays the boys. Then to their shock, he pulls his gun and orders them to raise their hands. "I'm sorry, boys," Donovan apologizes. "No, I'm not just sorry, I'm ashamed." He knew who they were all along, but he needed someone in a hurry so he used them. Now, though, he has to turn them in. Curry figures he's not ashamed enough or he'd let them go.

At the jail, Sheriff Lundy is amazed and wastes no time locking them up, his delight in stark contrast to Donovan's gloom. The sheriff digs through his desk to find the forms for claiming the reward, but Donovan doesn't want the money;

instead it should go to the Sisters of Charity. Heyes and Curry look up in surprise. With one last shamed look at them, Donovan leaves.

Sheriff Lundy regales the boys with his tale of how their capture will help him get re-elected. Eventually, with an admonishment to his deputy not to open the door for anyone but him, he goes home to bed.

Later, Heyes and Curry are asleep when the sheriff knocks on the door. He says he couldn't sleep so he'll take over and the deputy can go home.

As soon as his deputy is gone, Lundy opens the cell door and informs the boys they're free to go. "How come?" Heyes asks suspiciously. Lundy refuses to give a reason and just urges them to leave. Heyes and Curry decline his offer, citing stories of outlaws offered an open door and then shot trying to escape.

Lundy grows desperate. They've got to go. Nobody's going to shoot them. Heyes closes the cell door, locking it and handing Lundy the key. Lundy begs them to go, insisting he doesn't have to tell them why. "Then we don't have go!" Curry retorts. Heyes challenges the sheriff to convince them there's nothing to be scared of. Lundy can't explain, but he returns their guns and offers to walk out the door with them. Finally, with the sheriff between them, they scope out the street. It's deserted and quiet. Apologizing for doubting him, the boys hightail it out of town.

The next morning, Heyes and Curry ponder the mystery as they ride. It makes them nervous.

They arrive in Tombstone to find a cheering crowd gathered around a speaker's platform as Bill Meade introduces the new territorial governor of Arizona – C. Meyer Zulick. The boys are astonished. As Zulick begins speaking, Donovan catches their eyes. He nods, flashing a brief smile, and they decide it's time to quietly get out of Arizona.

As Heyes and Curry ride out of Tombstone, these words scroll up the screen, "C. Meyer Zulick, who was under arrest in Mexico at the time he was appointed Governor of the Territory of Arizona, served from 1885 to 1889. Under him, 'Doc' Donovan became Deputy Marshal of the Territory. During his administration, the strongest criticism made against Governor Zulick was that he had . . . 'pardoned notorious outlaws . . . .'"

Curry feels it's a mistake to leave Arizona now that they have a friend there, but Heyes thinks Zulick will be a better friend if they get out and stay out. With Arizona now out of bounds as well as Wyoming, Curry laments he feels like an outcast. Heyes begins to list all the places they can still go. By the time he reaches Outer Mongolia, Curry has had enough. "I know where we should go, Heyes," Curry interrupts. "In two different directions!"

GUEST CAST

DAVID CANARY	M.T. "DOC" DONOVAN
SORRELL BOOKE	CONRAD MEYER ZULICK
SLIM PICKENS	SHERIFF LUNDY

BERT SANTOS	LOPEZ
JOHN KELLOGG	MEADE
MIKE MIKLER	FALLON
DENNIS RUCKER	DEPUTY
NINETTE BRAVO	GIRL (DANCER)
RICHARD GARCIA	MINER #1
LUIS MORENO	MINER #2
WALT DAVIS	PLAYER #1
LAURIE FERRONE	SALVATION ARMY GIRL

In this episode, Roy Huggins once again turned to his history books and pulled out a quirky fact to hang a story on – the incarceration of Conrad Meyer Zulick in Mexico. With this springboard, he created a story that could very well have been the way the rescue of Zulick really happened.

Conrad Meyer Zulick was born June 3, 1838, in Easton, Pennsylvania. He became a lawyer, was admitted to the New Jersey bar in 1860, then took an active part in Stephen Douglas's presidential campaign against Abraham Lincoln. During the Civil War, Zulick served as adjutant to the 2nd Division of Colored Volunteers. After being discharged from the army, he formed the New Jersey and Sonora Mining Company, whose unpaid debts to the Mexican government led to his arrest in 1885.

President Grover Cleveland, a Democrat, took office on March 4, 1885, and demanded the resignation of the sitting governor of Arizona Territory, Republican Frederick Tritle. Cleveland sent M.T. Donovan to break Zulick out of the Mexican jail and sneak him back across the border, then on May 5, 1885, appointed Zulick as the seventh territorial governor of Arizona, the first Democrat to hold the office. During his administration Zulick was often criticized for his insistence on the humane treatment of American Indians. Although in the minority with this attitude, he was able to keep settlers from attacking the San Carlos Indian Reservation, thus avoiding bloodshed. He remained in office until 1889.[53]

Huggins was always diligent about avoiding stereotypes in his treatment of Mexicans in *Alias Smith and Jones*. In telling the story to writer Nick Baehr, Huggins at one point explained, "Now we have a very suspenseful action sequence where our boys have to be terribly smart and where we don't have to make the Mexicans stupid. We're not going to see any lazy Mexicans lolling back with a bottle in their hand. If we see a Mexican he's going to look like he's got brains and he's going to look clean and he's going to look alert."[54] In addition, the rescue had to be an action sequence, not any sort of con game. Huggins didn't mind the boys out-fighting their adversaries, but he didn't want them to outwit the miners.

The miners are determined to hold Zulick until they're paid, but are uncomfortable in the role of prison guards and hope the situation will soon end. However, as is usual in *Alias Smith and Jones,* the Spanish dialogue is not subtitled, so the poker-playing miner's query about how long they'll have to keep this up and Lopez's response that they'll continue until they get paid can only be guessed at by the English-speaking audience. Several times Donovan reiterates the miners' rights to hold Zulick under Mexican law, and Zulick himself is reluctant to leave at first, insisting that he's not being mistreated. Besides increasing the suspense, this has the added effect of letting the audience know the Mexicans are not the bad guys, despite their being the main obstacle our boys must overcome.

The villain of the piece turns out to be Donovan. Having promised Meade he'd rescue Zulick, Donovan turned to Heyes and Curry for help, knowing that when the job was done he would hand them over to the law. He's torn by his moral code, which demands that he turn them in despite the debt he owes them. Yet his sense of honor also requires that he abide by the deal he made. So he pays them the $600 he promised, but then marches them to the sheriff. Huggins wanted Donovan to be a complex character that would pull Heyes and Curry, as well as the audience, in different directions, sometimes seeming to be a friend and sometimes seeming to be a danger. Describing the scene where Donovan turns the boys in, Huggins said, "At this point our audience isn't liking Doc very well for that. Then when he turns down the reward, when we learn he's a poor man, and he gives the money to the Sisters of Charity – and looks at Heyes as he walks out and says, 'That's the price I'm paying' – then we get character. It's the best part of the script."[55]

Throughout the series, many people have been seduced by the $20,000 reward offered for the capture of Heyes and Curry. Some, such as Charlie Utley in "Stagecoach Seven," have a change of heart and let the boys go. Others, like Curt Clitterhouse in "Jailbreak at Junction City," are brought down by their own greed for the reward. Donovan is the only one to turn them in and refuse the reward. His insistence that he must pay a penance for his actions makes it all the more surprising that Heyes and Curry's release from jail is later orchestrated by Donovan with the help of a grateful Governor Zulick. Donovan's internal struggles between his moral code and his sense of justice are indeed the best part of the script.

McGuffin

"Do you ever get the feeling that nothing right is ever going to happen to us again?"
– Kid Curry

STORY:	JOHN THOMAS JAMES
TELEPLAY:	NICHOLAS E. BAEHR
DIRECTOR:	ALEXANDER SINGER
SHOOTING DATES:	OCTOBER 18, 19, 20, 23, 24, 25, 26, 1972
ORIGINAL US AIR DATE:	DECEMBER 9, 1972
ORIGINAL UK AIR DATE:	APRIL 21, 1975

Hannibal Heyes and Kid Curry are riding along on their way to Dark Springs when they hear cries for help. On the other side of a hill, they find an older man propped against a tree. He claims to be a treasury agent and he's been shot. It's very important that the package in his saddlebags gets to town. He wants one of them to take it there and register in the hotel under his name, Tom McGuffin. The other one needs to go for a doctor. McGuffin will wait there because he can't outrun the three counterfeiters on his trail.

While Curry heads off to fetch a doctor, McGuffin tells Heyes an agent named Peterson will contact him. Heyes is to give him the package after verifying his identification.

At the Dark Springs hotel, Heyes signs in.

When Curry returns with Doc O'Connell, McGuffin is gone. Instead, three men approach with guns drawn, asking about the wounded man. Curry describes him and says his name was McGuffin. One of the men laughs at this originality because McGuffin usually calls himself "Smith" or "Jones." When asked his name, Curry stammers "Hotchkiss." The men warn Curry and Doc that McGuffin is a dangerous counterfeiter and send them on their way.

Doc questions Jones about his name. Curry thought it wouldn't be wise to own up to the name Jones after what the man said. The Doc sees his point.

Back at the hotel, a young woman knocks on Heyes's door. She claims to be McGuffin's daughter and has been expecting her father. She wonders where he is, but Heyes can't tell her anything because McGuffin is a treasury agent. She scoffs at this; McGuffin is not an agent for anybody. Heyes doesn't know what to think now but fetches a chair for the woman. They'd better sit and talk about this.

Curry arrives in town and registers at the hotel as Thaddeus Hotchkiss. Stopping in at Heyes's room, he discovers his partner out cold on the floor. A cascade of water from the pitcher brings Heyes around. He tells Curry that McGuffin is a treasury agent and the girl, who claims to be his daughter, is a crook. Heyes had hidden the package he was to give to Peterson under the mattress and she stole it after she conked him on the head.

Curry informs Heyes that McGuffin *isn't* an agent. The three men following him told Curry that McGuffin is a counterfeiter who sometimes goes by "Smith" or "Jones." The men said they were treasury agents. But Heyes wants to know who the girl is. "What girl?" Curry yells. They decide they are only innocent bystanders to the whole situation and head out of town riding hell bent for leather to Oak Flat where they send a telegram to Lom Trevors asking about news from the governor. A while later, a return telegram notifies them that the Treasury Department is looking for them in every state west of the Mississippi.

Lom no longer considers himself their friend. They argue in heated whispers in front of the telegrapher. What should they do now? Go to Cheyenne and tell Lom they're not involved? How can they prove it? McGuffin is probably dead and the girl a thousand miles away with the plates.

Entering their hotel room, they find McGuffin propped up on the bed. He's nervous and sick and pointing a gun at them demanding the plates. When Heyes tells him Peterson didn't show, McGuffin assumes Heyes still has them. Heyes begins the tale of the girl who knocked on his door and then knocked him over the head. She said she was McGuffin's daughter. Angry now, McGuffin identifies her as Counterfeit Kate, a big problem for the Treasury Department. Seeing their despondent looks, McGuffin assumes they're in trouble now too.

The plates were the finest ever made, done by a printer-publisher in Denver, bitter after being ruined by the mining companies. If they will help him get them back, he'll see that they are cleared with the government. Peterson is the key. He's a chemist who figured out how to bleach out $1 bills. Combined with the plates, the paper produces an undetectable forgery. Kate, who uses the alias Katherine Lewis, will also be trying to contact Peterson. If the boys will go to Forrest City, they can nab them both. McGuffin warns them about Kate – she's an *artiste* at lying.

Outside her house, they wait for Kate to return. Curry tries to understand the situation, questioning Heyes about McGuffin, the girl and the three men. They give her a few minutes after she rides up, then burst in on her. She's waiting for Peterson and is amused to hear herself described as Counterfeit Kate. However, she is glad to hear news of her father, who is *not* named McGuffin but Gordon Lewis. Heyes says next she'll say he was a Denver publisher. Startled, Kate wants to know how he knew that. McGuffin told him, Heyes answers. She insists his name *isn't* McGuffin. She's waiting for Peterson so she can turn him and the plates in together and keep her father from being prosecuted. Heyes and Curry demand she take them to the plates. She hid them about fifty miles from there.

From his hiding place, Peterson watches as the three mount their horses and ride away.

On the train, Peterson passes their seats and takes one further along in the coach. Kate claims to need the restroom but instead she meets Peterson by the open door at the end of the railroad car. She explains to him that the two men with her are treasury agents; she's taking them to the plates and wants him to get her away from them. Peterson wants to see the plates first, *then* he'll get her away from the two men. Kate acquiesces to his plan.

Fifty miles later, they ride on horseback to a stream where the plates are buried under a pile of rocks. The boys strip off boots, socks and gun belts as they wade into the water and begin to dig. Couldn't she have found an easier hiding place? "Like under the mattress?" she smirks.

When they've unearthed the plates, Peterson shows up gun in hand. He orders all three of them to lie down, then ties their hands behind their backs. He leaves with the plates.

Heyes, Curry and Kate struggle to free themselves. "It's your turn to untie," Curry tells Heyes, "I did it last time."

Back in town, the railroad ticket agent verifies that a man answering the description of Peterson bought a train ticket east. The man had inquired about the boat going from Centralia to New Orleans. With no more passenger trains till the next day, the trio hops a freight train. In Centralia they race for the steamboat ticket window.

A very slow, thoughtful ticket agent confirms that a Harold *Patterson* bought tickets for the steamboat. After much more methodical thinking, he identifies Patterson enough that they're certain it's Peterson. They buy three tickets and run to the dock. The paddlewheel churns on the great riverboat and the gangplank is rolled away. They jump on board just in time.

They plan to separate and look for the chemist, but Kate is exhausted. Heyes orders her to stay put while he and Curry search. Running along the decks, they look into the face of each male passenger. Peterson stands on the top deck smoking a cigar and whistling until Heyes and Curry each grab an arm as they come up beside him. Threatening to toss him overboard if he doesn't come up with the plates, they lean him far enough over the rail to see the roiling water. They're in his cabin, he says.

Peterson had hidden them, where else but under the mattress. When the plates are not to be found, Heyes and Curry realize immediately that Kate got there first. They head out the door with Peterson close behind. He doesn't get far before he sees two treasury agents and turns around, but they've already spotted him. Cornered, Peterson swings out over the rail but is hauled back onboard by the agents.

Heyes and Curry search the boat for Kate. When she sees them coming for her, she steps over the deck rail and, without hesitation, jumps into the river. With no choice, the boys follow. All three swim for shore.

Soaked and exhausted, they crawl onto the sandy bank. Curry checks Kate's purse and finds it empty. The plates must have fallen out somewhere in the river. Now they have no way to prove they weren't involved.

Curry wants to know where all the crooks came from. Except for McGuffin, they haven't run into one treasury agent. Kate reiterates once again that McGuffin's name is really Lewis, he's her father, and he's not a treasury agent. But *she* is!

Later, in the office of the Treasury, she tells them that she is on one special assignment. If she can turn in the plates, it will save her father from prosecution. With luck, she may be able to clear them too.

The chief agent enters with Mr. Lewis/McGuffin. The chief is sorry, he tells Kate, but without the plates, her father will go to prison. That was the deal. Weeping, Kate embraces her father.

The two agents who were on the boat enter the office to notify the chief that divers have found the plates. They saw where Kate jumped in. Laughing, Kate embraces her father.

Outside in the street, Heyes and Curry make their goodbyes to Kate and McGuffin. "It's not McGuffin," he tells them, "it's Lewis, Gordon Lewis." If they're ever in Denver, they should look him up.

Later, riding along, Curry is worried. How do they know they're really *out* of trouble with the Treasury Department? That's easy for Heyes to answer. The chief agent told them so. How do they know he was really the chief agent? It said so on the door. But, Curry rebuts, anyone could paint letters on the door of an empty office. Heyes is exasperated and asks one question of Curry – how do they know they were ever *in* trouble with the Treasury Department?

GUEST CAST

DARLEEN CARR	KATE LEWIS
CLARKE GORDON	TOM McGUFFIN/GORDON LEWIS
L.Q. JONES	PETERSON
ALICE NUNN	HOTEL CLERK
JACK MANNING	DR. O'CONNELL
MORT MILLS	1ST MAN
WALTER BROOKE	CHIEF AGENT
JACKIE COOGAN	PASSENGER AGENT
ALLEN JOSEPH	TICKET AGENT
CHUCK HICKS	CARSON
MONTY LAIRD	TELEGRAPHER
X BRANDS	ROBERTS

According to the Oxford English Dictionary, the first usage of the word *McGuffin* (or *MacGuffin*) was recorded in a lecture that filmmaker Alfred Hitchcock gave at Columbia University in March 1939. According to Hitchcock, the term "McGuffin" was coined by his friend, Scottish screen-writer Angus MacPhail, and means something that sets the film's plot in motion. It is merely an excuse, a diversion. A Hitchcock scholar notes "the first tangible appearance of the McGuffin occurs in Hitchcock's 'chase' films of the 1930s." In those it might be a necklace, a kidnapped child or the top-secret plans of a new aircraft engine. The McGuffin became a key device in Hitchcock's films working as a type of red herring: the false clue or the misdirection of the audience's suspicions.[56]

Indeed, when Heyes and Curry (and the viewers) first meet Tom McGuffin, his story seems so straightforward and credible that any diversion from it appears to be a non-truth. It turns out that his version is false and Kate's and the three treasury agents' stories are true. If one has not been playing close attention, by the end of the program, it's possible to be as confused as Curry. One line in the first draft highlights this confusion. Having been sent to Kate's home by McGuffin, Heyes and Curry wait outside, watching for her return. Curry is trying to get the players straight, averring that he's glad they never went in for "this kind of work. At least with banks and railroads, you knew who was who . . . the banks were the bad guys and we were the good guys. Or, uh, – vice versa . . ."[57]

Several changes were made from the first draft of the script to the finished version. When the boys decide they have fallen into a nest of thieves but are only innocent bystanders, they have to telegraph Lom Trevors. The telegram includes the information that they've got jobs in Oak Flat. Between sending the message and receiving one back, they really do get jobs – peeling potatoes for a café. In the early script, instead of Kate concealing the plates mid-stream under a pile of rocks, she's hidden them under a "huge, helter-skelter pile of battered bricks" among some adobe ruins. When Curry helps Heyes move them, it provides him the opportunity to mumble about "a woman with muscles." The boys and Kate have it easier in the aired version as far as catching the departing steamboat. Originally, the boat had already left and they had to ride another twenty miles downriver to board the boat when it came ashore at Whitman's Landing.[58]

Once again, even this late in the series, it's shades of *Butch Cassidy and the Sundance Kid*. When Heyes and Curry see Kate jump over the rail into the water, they know they have to follow. Curry asks his partner if he can swim and before Heyes can answer, Curry has jumped into the water. The problem is that, just like Sundance, Heyes *can't* swim. However, when he sees the Treasury agents bearing down on him, he climbs over the rail and follows Curry into the water. "Did you say 'no'?" Curry asks as he treads water near where Heyes jumped in, "Then what are you doin' here?" Heyes's reply – "Learning how to swim."[59]

WITNESS TO A LYNCHING

"So what do we do now? Get out of Wyoming and write Lom we're sorry we lost his witnesses?"
– Kid Curry

STORY:	JOHN THOMAS JAMES
TELEPLAY:	NICHOLAS E. BAEHR
DIRECTOR:	RICHARD BENNETT
SHOOTING DATES:	OCTOBER 26, 27, 30, 31, NOVEMBER 1, 2, 1972
ORIGINAL US AIR DATE:	DECEMBER 16, 1972
ORIGINAL UK AIR DATE:	DECEMBER 31, 1973

Hannibal Heyes and Kid Curry ride into town and make their first stop the telegraph office. Barely able to scrape up the eighty-five cent fee, they wire Lom for an update on their amnesty. To their dismay, Lom responds with an urgent summons to Nolan's Rising Sun Ranch in southern Wyoming, an area they try to avoid.

Traveling as if a posse were chasing them, the boys head for Wyoming. Lom meets them at the ranch, complains they took their own sweet time, then stalks into the cabin. Puzzled by his manner, the boys follow. Heyes and Curry's arrival is noted by two men with binoculars.

Lom introduces the boys as Joshua Smith and Thaddeus Jones, two of the most competent men he knows, to Doctor Amos Snively and his daughter Cybele. Doc Snively is delighted they'll be with them night and day.

Outside, Lom explains he's got the Snivelys in protective custody and someone is sure to try to get them away from the ranch or even kill them. He figures the boys have the guts and know-how to protect them. If they fail him, they can forget about their amnesty. Then Lom softens and offers them $100 apiece to do the job before continuing the story. Doc and Cybele witnessed a rancher named Rosswell lynch a homesteader for legally settling on a nice piece of range Rosswell claims as his own. He lynched a man before and that time the witnesses suddenly disappeared. Lom doesn't want that to happen to the Snivelys so he's putting them in Heyes and Curry's hands. Rosswell has already tried breaking them out of jail and bribing them. With one last warning that the Snivelys had better be there when he returns to get them for the trial, Lom leaves.

The boys sit down with Doc and wonder how he came to see the lynching. Doc explains they were just passing by in his medicine wagon. Seeing their confusion, Doc wonders if Lom explained he was the famous Doctor Snively. To his disappointment, the boys have never heard of him, so he goes into his pitch.

The group is still being watched.

Over dinner, Doc explains Cybele is responsible for their being there. He was ready to accept Rosswell's lawyer's offer of $5,000 in exchange for leaving Wyoming and never returning, but Cybele wouldn't hear of it. She feels justice should be done for poor Mr. Harvey, the lynching victim. Doc brings out one of his elixirs to toast justice. It's called Cure-Al, he tells them, and is guaranteed to cure alcoholism if taken as directed, which is one full bottle every other day. The boys sniff it dubiously, then Curry asks what's in it. "Fifty-five percent health producing herbs and the juice of a few flowers," Doc says, "and forty-five percent alcohol." The boys raise their cups to justice.

Some time and several bottles later, Heyes announces Cure-Al to be the greatest medicine he's ever taken and Curry admits he'd never take another drink as long as he had the elixir. Doc Snively tells them of the time he sold one hundred seventy-nine bottles in one hour in a town with only forty-six people in it. In four days the alcohol problem was gone – and so was the town! They all dissolve in drunken giggles. Heyes asks what Cybele does. She's the show, Doc proudly explains, drawing a crowd with her dance. Cybele dons her skimpy costume and demonstrates her belly dance for the mesmerized outlaws.

The next morning Heyes and Curry are miserable. Does Doc have anything for a hangover? With great good cheer, Doc pulls another elixir from his bag – Doc Snively's Morning Metamorphosis. But before he can open it, gunshots send them scrambling for cover.

Heyes and Curry take positions at the window. A voice demands they send out Doc and Cybele. Heyes refuses and the men outside resume firing. It's time to leave. Doc and Cybele will hitch up the wagon while Heyes and Curry keep the gunmen at bay. Doc panics, wanting to stay where they are. Heyes insists, knowing the gunmen will take chances at night they won't take in the daylight, so they have to leave now.

Heyes drives the wagon while Curry keeps up a barrage against the men on their tail. Cybele and her father lie on the floor of the wagon, reloading guns for him as fast as they can. Things get too dangerous for the pursuers and they give up the chase.

That night around the campfire, Doc Snively worries that they're not safe. He isn't convinced by Heyes's assurances that the paid gunmen, not interested in being killed themselves, are long gone or by Curry's assertion that they'll see to it that nothing else happens.

In the morning, Cybele pours coffee. Doc is curious about their next move. Heyes tells him they'll ride into town, telegraph Sheriff Trevors and do what he tells them. Heyes trails off, a strange look on his face. As Curry and Cybele watch with concern, Heyes passes out. Curry heads toward him, but collapses on the way. Cybele is first alarmed, then dismayed, as she realizes her father drugged their coffee. Doc says he was wrong not to take the money Rosswell offered. The sheriff can't protect them and neither can these boys. Their only hope is to cooperate with Rosswell.

Heyes is the first to come to. He crawls over to check on Curry who wakes with a groan. Surveying their situation, the still somewhat fuzzy-headed Heyes declares they need horses. Curry agrees, but wants to know how, where and with what they'll get them. "We're deputies, aren't we?" Heyes reminds him. "We'll requisition them."

The boys, scared to tell Lom they've lost his witnesses, decide to track down Doc and Cybele. They figure the two have gone to Rosswell's lawyer, B.F. Simpson.

In Douglas, Heyes and Curry knock on Simpson's door. At the boys' claim of having important information for her husband, his wife informs them he's gone to Lost Spring to catch the train to Nebraska. Heyes takes this as proof Simpson has Doc and Cybele with him because otherwise he would catch the train here in Douglas. Curry points out they can't catch the train in Douglas, either, since Lom's office is only two blocks from the station and they can't afford to be seen.

The boys intercept the train at a water tower. By the time it pulls into Lost Spring, Heyes and Curry are relaxing in the passenger car, faces buried in newspapers. Simpson, the Snivelys, and a gunman enter. Doc stops in consternation at seeing the boys but the group finds seats at the opposite end of the car.

Doc asks Simpson to clarify their arrangement. Simpson explains when they reach Chadron, Nebraska, he'll be paid $5,000 and is free to go anywhere he wishes – except Wyoming. The gunman has come along to protect them. Doc considers this information for a moment, then starts to point out Heyes and Curry, but Cybele interrupts before he can. With a frown, Doc asks for a moment alone with his daughter.

Heyes and Curry keep an eye on the Snivelys from behind their newspapers. As the lawyer and the gunman leave the car the boys wonder if Doc gave them away, but decide not to do anything unless Simpson starts something.

Doc and Cybele argue until finally she agrees to go along with accepting the bribe, providing he doesn't tell Simpson about Joshua and Thaddeus.

Heyes and Curry decide to force Simpson's hand. At the next town, they'll telegraph Sheriff Owen Kimball in Chadron and have him remove the Snivelys from the train.

The train reaches Chadron. When Sheriff Kimball enters the train, Heyes points out the Snivelys and watches with satisfaction as they are placed under arrest.

In the sheriff's office, Simpson loudly protests Kimball's actions. He has no jurisdiction in the matter! Kimball is unmoved. He's familiar with the Rosswell case and intends to keep the Snivelys in custody until he hears from Sheriff Trevors.

Simpson and his gunman return with a writ of *habeas corpus* and Marshal Guthrie to enforce it. Sheriff Kimball refuses to turn the witnesses over, but Doc overhears the conversation and shouts out that he doesn't want to be in protective custody. Simpson is delighted to leave the matter up to the Snivelys. Doc eagerly acknowledges the writ, but Cybele refuses to leave the cell. Simpson is clear on that point. "If your daughter doesn't leave, you don't leave."

After the frustrated lawyer has gone, Heyes and Curry spell it out for the Snivelys. Simpson promised money but Doc will never see it. Instead he'll be dead. The gunman isn't there to protect Doc and Cybele; his task is to protect Rosswell by killing them. Doc resists their argument until Heyes bluntly challenges him. "Are you willing to bet her life that you're right and we're wrong?"

Simpson returns to the sheriff's office, this time with an arrest warrant for Doc and Cybele. Kimball demands to know the charge. "A federal charge," Simpson announces smugly. "Selling whiskey to Indians." Kimball knows what Simpson is up to, but there's nothing he can do. While he berates the lawyer for his shady actions on behalf of the Stockgrowers Association, Heyes and Curry quietly slip away.

Heyes picks the lock on the cell and the boys hustle Doc and Cybele out the back door.

Kimball reluctantly admits he must respect the warrant and leads Simpson to the cell, only to find it empty. Simpson is incensed, but Kimball just shrugs, hiding a smile.

Heyes, Curry, Doc and Cybele ride hard and reach an abandoned line shack. Doc is exhausted and in no shape to continue. Only one witness is needed, so Doc urges them to go on without him. Heyes won't hear of it.

Simpson and Marshal Guthrie lead a posse in pursuit of them.

Heyes and Curry confer in a corner of the cabin. The posse is certain to find them, so the best thing is for Heyes to go for help while Curry stays to protect the Snivelys.

He gets ready for battle as the posse surrounds the cabin. Guthrie calls out, promising there will be no bloodshed if the Snivelys come out. Curry refuses to let them. Guthrie gives him one minute to reconsider; then they'll start shooting. Cybele and Doc take cover and, true to his word, Guthrie and his men begin shooting.

Curry returns fire. Doc apologizes to his daughter for putting her in such danger, but Cybele understands. He was just doing what he thought was best for her. Before a second barrage can begin, Lom and his men arrive.

Simpson questions Lom's presence since he has no jurisdiction in Nebraska. Lom explains he's here to offer the Snivelys safe conduct to Wyoming, if they want it. Simpson produces his federal warrant, but Lom wonders if Simpson, who practices law in Lom's county, really wants to stake his career on that warrant. Giving it some thought, Simpson decides not to interfere. Lom asks the Snivelys to come out of the cabin and walk to whomever they want to leave with.

Inside, Cybele asks her father what he wants to do. They could go to Simpson and get the money because he wouldn't dare do anything to them now. He considers, tempted once more by the $5,000.

Arm in arm, Doc and Cybele leave the cabin. They hesitate as both groups wait anxiously, but finally Doc leads the way toward Lom. Simpson accepts his defeat.

Doc and Cybele travel in their medicine wagon, looking around for some sign of Joshua and Thaddeus. Just as Doc decides they must not be coming, the boys ride up. Doc tells them Rosswell was convicted, but the judge only gave him twenty years. Cybele is curious about why the boys didn't attend the trial. They exchange a glance, then Curry admits it's because he's Kid Curry and Joshua is Hannibal Heyes. Cybele laughs in disbelief. "So you're just not going to tell us, are you?" With fond farewells, the boys ride off.

Leaving Wyoming, Heyes ponders why no one believes them when they say they're Heyes and Curry, and yet also don't believe them when they say their names are Smith and Jones. Curry thinks it's because Heyes has a dishonest face. Heyes insists it would make more sense to say they don't believe him because he's got an *honest* face. It must be Curry's dishonest face that's the problem. Heyes cuts off his friend's attempt at an explanation by announcing there is no answer to the question. "What was the question?" Curry wonders.

Wyoming in the 1880s was a dangerous place unless you were a rich cattleman in good standing with the Wyoming Stockgrowers Association. This era was a shameful example of greed and corruption in the West, but it did provide Roy Huggins with many stories for the series. "Witness to a Lynching" is one of five third season episodes in which Huggins inserted Heyes and Curry into real events in Wyoming history. He based this tale on the lynching of Ellen Watson and Jim Averell, recognizing the dramatic possibilities of following the story of the witnesses. "There were four people who witnessed the real lynching, and all four of them died, mysteriously."[60]

In 1889, the richest cattleman in Sweetwater County, Wyoming, was Albert J. Bothwell. He considered all the land in the Sweetwater Valley his own, despite having no legal claim to it, and when homesteaders began to move in, he was outraged. No homesteaders outraged him more than Jim Averell and Ellen Watson. These two had the temerity to homestead parcels of land that Bothwell considered his best pasture. He decided to get rid of them.

When Bothwell's attempts to buy them out failed, he turned to less savory methods. A stock detective named George Henderson rode through Ellen's pasture and saw cattle with fresh brands. He suggested to Bothwell that could mean Ellen was illegally branding mavericks. Bothwell took the hint. Declaring her to be a rustler, Bothwell and five cohorts abducted her, then went to Jim's homestead and grabbed him, too. Two boys, eleven-year-old Gene Crowder and fourteen-year-old John DeCorey, witnessed the abductions and raced to tell neighbor Frank Buchanan. Buchanan, along with Jim's nephew Ralph Coe, followed the cattleman and arrived in time to see the lynching. Buchanan alerted authorities and murder warrants were issued for the six cattlemen.

Before the trial, however, the witnesses began to disappear. Gene Crowder vanished, although rumor had it that his father took him away to protect him. John DeCorey was said to have moved to Steamboat Springs, Colorado, but he too was never seen again. Frank Buchanan was last seen in protective custody in Cheyenne and Ralph Coe mysteriously died on the day of the scheduled hearing, very likely from poisoning. With no witnesses to testify against Bothwell and the other cattlemen, the charges were dropped. No attempt was ever made to investigate the disappearances of Crowder, DeCorey and Buchanan or the death of Coe.[61]

Huggins created his story from the point of view of the witnesses, putting Doc and Cybele Snively in the wrong place at the wrong time and making Doc just shady enough to be tempted by the bribe Rosswell's lawyer offers. Like Frank Buchanan, the Snivelys find themselves in protective custody and, no matter how desperately Doc wants to deny it, faced with the very real danger of being killed by the ruthless rancher. With another nod to history, the writers use the fate of the witnesses to the real lynching as Curry's argument to convince Doc to testify. Doc and Cybele would disappear and everyone would think they had simply gone to another state, Curry tells him, but in reality they would be dead. Bothwell got away with his lynchings, but such an outcome was unacceptable to Huggins and to the network. "It's contrary to history that the guy would ever go to jail at all. No Judge would ever send Rosswell to jail. But in our story we have to."[62]

Huggins was able to find a believable compromise to resolve the story to the satisfaction of both himself and the network. There's a point at which a lawyer stops doing things for his client and Simpson could realistically decide not to risk his reputation and his career for a man guilty of murder. With a little help from Lom, Simpson sees this way out. Rosswell is brought to justice and Simpson's defeat is made believable.

ONLY THREE TO A BED

"Heyes, blowin' safes sure made a sissy out of you."
– Kid Curry

STORY:	JOHN THOMAS JAMES
TELEPLAY:	RICHARD MORRIS
DIRECTOR:	JEFFREY HAYDEN
SHOOTING DATES:	UTAH – JULY 14, 15, 17, 18, 19, 20, 21, 22;
	STUDIO – JULY 24, 25, 26, 27, 28, 31, AUG. 1, 2, 3, 4, 1972
ORIGINAL US AIR DATE:	JANUARY 13, 1973
ORIGINAL UK AIR DATE:	JANUARY 7, 1974

Hannibal Heyes and Kid Curry hurry down the street with Bronc, an old cowhand attempting to coerce them into joining him in a horse venture. His plan is to cut out twenty ponies from a herd of wild horses and sell them in Cheyenne. He knows the boys have been staying away from the short arm of the law and need a vacation. If they had any reservations about the proposition, the word *vacation* dispelled them.

On the way to Piney Basin, they pass a crude wooden sign advertising a Road Ranch – "Stagecoach stop, baths 50¢, bed 50¢, only three to a bed." They register at the ranch and request they each have a bed. They also ask owner Sam

Haney about renting a corral. Sam charges one dollar per day for that because he expects damages when rancher Mark Tisdale learns the boys plan to round up wild horses he considers his. Piney Basin is open range, public domain; but Tisdale claims it under the rule of customary range. There will be additional charges for nursing if they get shot. The boys wonder what Bronc has gotten them into.

Next day, the wild horses skitter as Heyes and Curry attempt to lasso them while Bronc shouts encouragement. Heyes lassoes one horse which turns, dragging him out of his saddle and along the ground.

At the end of the first day, they're hot, sweaty, and sore and have caught three horses. With six more days of work ahead of them, all Heyes wants is a hot bath and bed. That is, until he spots a beautiful woman on the porch of the ranch house. She is one of the passengers on the recently arrived stagecoach.

At supper served by Belle, the young daughter of the proprietor, Heyes questions the beautiful Beegee, and learns she's a performer who is on her way to an audition, hoping to sing at the Palace in Cheyenne. She's also scouting a husband there. Curry asks Emma Sterling about herself, but her brother squelches his queries as the driver announces it's time to leave for Sheridan. As soon as the stage departs, Heyes's aches and pains return and he heads for bed.

The next day, Heyes and Curry are back at cutting out the horses. Bronc helps some, mostly by shouting support or directions.

At a rifle shot, the horses stampede and the three men drop to the ground. Heyes and Bronc return fire while Curry heads up a steep hill to circle around behind the shooter. The young man who's been firing at them is amazed at Curry's prowess when Curry shoots the rifle from his hand.

Bronc and the boys escort the young man, Mark Tisdale's son, back to his father's ranch. Tisdale stands up for his son, saying he was shooting at thieves. Bronc insists the land is free range, but Tisdale claims the land under Montana's "courtesy of the range." He won't allow even twenty horses to be taken. They're his even though he's never branded them.

When the three partners return to the ranch house, they find the stagecoach passengers have returned because the stage broke down. The driver went on to Sheridan for repairs or a new coach. With all the guests, they will have to double up – Emma Sterling and Beegee to one bed; Heyes, Curry and Bronc to another; and Mr. Sterling to a bed all his own. A dour Puritan, he doesn't sleep with anyone unless absolutely necessary.

But there won't be three to a bed because, with Tisdale riled up, one of them

Coming only three weeks after episodes which placed Heyes and Curry in 1885-1886, in the revised script dated July 26, 1972, another reference verified the time frame. Though the line was cut for the aired version, after Beegee suggests the compromise of $20 per head for the broken horses, Sam Haney calls to Tisdale that he should take it. "We're only fifteen years away from the twentieth century. Accept the deal ... so you can see that century."

Bronc's first name is Oscar and Beegee's name comes from Huggins's identifying her as a good-Bad Girl. — Story notes, May 2, 1972: 2, 9.

will have to guard the corral. Bronc takes first watch. After supper, Curry dances with Beegee and Heyes with Belle to a tune from a music box. When Sam Haney breaks in on Heyes to dance with his daughter, Heyes asks to dance with Beegee. That leaves Curry to seek out Emma who has been watching the dancing while embroidering. Her brother sits nearby with a book. He sternly intercedes when Curry asks her to dance, claiming his sister finds Curry's advances offensive. Curry apologizes and Emma flees the room.

Mark Tisdale watches Bronc through binoculars.

Beegee entertains them with a song. When Bronc comes in with word that it's Thaddeus's turn on guard, Bronc takes up his fiddle and a lively square dance ensues. At its conclusion, Heyes and Beegee are left alone when the others head to bed. They play poker while Beegee tells about running away from her daddy's dry goods store. She's looking for a husband because she's not that good a singer.

While Curry's on guard, Emma approaches to apologize for her rudeness. Curry replies it's his nature to ride into things and he's used to being slapped down. Defending her brother, Emma sees no sin in dancing though it's against their beliefs. Her devout brother watches out for her.

Inside, Beegee wins every hand of poker. Heyes accuses her ever so politely of distracting a man with her pretty brown eyes while she stacks the deck and crimps the cards. Insulted, she claims to need her beauty sleep and heads for bed. From the window, she watches as Emma leaves the barn after seeing Curry.

When it's Heyes's turn to stand guard, Beegee slips out to see him. She asks him for a cigarette but learns he only smokes cigars. She knows nothing else about him, like why he isn't married. He never met anyone worth giving up the cowboy life for, he says. Beegee can't believe he enjoys the life. Surely, he has fond memories of his ma and pa happy at the end of the day sitting by the fire and looking out at the snow? Heyes counters his father hated snow. Beegee has set her sights on Heyes as a possible husband, but Heyes claims he has no land, no ranch. Her prospect with him is as slim as drawing to an inside straight. Still, they enjoy a tender kiss.

On the third day, after cutting out three more wild horses, Heyes and Curry begin to break them. Bronc is too old to risk breaking his neck when Heyes and Curry are natural showoffs, eager to perform before the ladies. That night, while Bronc is on guard and Heyes and Curry sleep, the horses act skittish and nervous. Bronc draws his gun on a shadow but before he can fire, he is hit on the head. Tisdale's ranch hands lead away the ponies.

When Bronc comes to, he sounds the alarm, waking his partners.

At daylight, Heyes, Curry, and Bronc head out to Tisdale's ranch. He's taken back his horses and the sheriff in Billings has deputized some men he's hired. Tisdale instructs the deputies to put the trio under arrest for horse thieving. Curry calmly refutes him. You can't steal something that doesn't belong to anybody and they didn't see any No Trespassing signs. A deputy gets ready to enforce Tisdale's order. That is, until Curry outdraws him. Curry then orders the rest of the deputies to throw their guns into the water trough.

That done, the boys go back to breaking horses. Bronc and Sam Haney cheer them on. Beegee cheers for Curry and when Heyes says he too could use some encouragement, she tells him he is "deaf, dumb and blind" and she's decided he's not the one for her. Disgusted, he slams his hat back on and heads for the corral. Even Emma Sterling is laughing at the sight of the boys on the wild horses until her brother reproves her with a frown.

During the entertainment, the stagecoach driver stops to say the coach couldn't be fixed and he's on his way to Billings to get a new one. He'll be back the next morning.

That evening, Curry is once again on guard when Emma startles him. She's come to say goodbye. When they leave tomorrow, she won't be able to say goodbye the way she wants to because of her brother. He doesn't understand the cowboys, but she has found knowing Mr. Jones to be a wonderful experience.

Curry is glad she came because it might have shocked her brother when Curry kissed her goodbye. He kisses her tenderly then. Curry was worried Emma's brother might scare her off from what life is all about but he's not going to worry any more. He thinks she'll be all right.

He watches her go then sits down again to mend a bridle when he's startled by Beegee's approach. He thinks he's going deaf; she could have had him *and* the horses. She doesn't want the horses but may be making a play for him. Joshua is too stupid, she thinks. Thaddeus has more sense, more maturity. Mocking Emma, she tells him when she says goodbye in the morning, she won't be able to say it the way she wants to, so she's here now. Curry and Beegee kiss long and hard. Spoiling her for all other men, he shows her "how it's supposed to be."

Next morning, Curry watches as Beegee gives Heyes a passionate goodbye kiss. Curry approaches the Sterling siblings and bids a succinct goodbye. He extends his hand to Beegee who thanks him for showing her how it's supposed to be. Curry smirks at Heyes's puzzled look.

After another day on the range, with Tisdale viewing them through binoculars, the boys enter the ranch house to find Beegee back. Heyes and Curry worry they may have said something to raise her hopes. Instead, she says she just likes it there and she's happy.

Before supper, the boys and Bronc gaze contently on their small herd of twenty tamed horses. While eating, Curry suggests they sell the horses in Sheridan instead of driving them all the way to Cheyenne. Mark Tisdale's voice cuts off any reply. He's come to take back his horses and if they still want the animals, the price is his life. Fools in Washington, D.C., made laws which override public domain. Tisdale is of the old school and is taking back his rightful property.

Beegee suggests a compromise. Instead of the three men having to drive twenty horses to Cheyenne, during which trip they might possibly lose all the animals, what if Tisdale paid them $20 a head just for the work they put into breaking them? Tisdale considers for a long moment. He finally agrees and, to save face, will send his men for the animals. He'll be back later to pay them, but insists that nothing be said about the money.

Heyes, Curry and Bronc kiss Belle goodbye and load the stagecoach with their gear. Beegee won't be going along because Sam has asked her to stay.

Curry is surprised at the development, but Heyes is just relieved. Wistfully, Curry adds that she did have a nice little dimple. Heyes remembers he knew a fella once who fell in love with a nice little dimple and made the mistake of marrying the whole girl.

GUEST CAST

JoAnn Pflug	Beegee
Dana Elcar	Sam Haney
Laurette Spang	Emma Sterling
John Kerr	George Sterling
Dean Jagger	Mark Tisdale
Paul Fix	Bronc
Janet Johnson	Belle Haney
Michael Rupert	Tisdale's son
Pepper Martin	Head Gunman
Gary Van Orman	Stage Driver

"Only Three to a Bed" is one of the few episodes hardly relating to the series' premise. The only reference to amnesty is Bronc's acknowledging the boys have been trying to stay away from the law. Curry's fast draw is in evidence when he outdraws Tisdale's gunman but Heyes's silver tongue seems to have disappeared. Curry does most of the talking, attempting to convince Tisdale they have a right to the horses. For someone who didn't need to be told how to handle himself in the clinches in an early episode, Heyes does a poor job of interacting with Beegee. He needs to prove his superiority by pointing out her card manipulations. Even though she's been insulted, she visits him when he's on guard alone but, instead of leveling with her about marriage prospects or using his silver tongue to put her off, he offers lame excuses, joking that if he eats right, he can keep up with the other fellas doing cowboy work. He doesn't play on her sympathy of his having lost his parents at an early age, but defiles her mental picture of a loving home life. It is amusing to speculate on how the same scene would have played out if Heyes had asked Emma to dance and she later defended her brother to him and Beegee had made a play for Curry as Roy Huggins initially planned the story, particularly considering Huggins's idea that "neither one of our boys is sentimental. Curry is a little more conceited about women. Heyes is shrewder, maybe even smarter, maybe a little more sensitive."[63] In the aired episode, these virtues and vices are exchanged.

In a few instances, however, *Alias Smith and Jones* canon tenets surface. The Sterlings are from Kansas as Curry and Heyes are. Curry again demonstrates his rapport with children when he bids goodbye to young Belle Haney, saying sincerely that he'll miss her. Emma Sterling and Sister Grace from Apache Springs have much in common. Both are restricted by the religion they profess but both will be all right in the future after having met the Kid.

Curry had a right to be worried about Emma. John Calvin, considered the founder of the Puritan ethic, prohibited dancing, drinking, card playing, ribaldry, fashionable clothes and other amusements. Critic H.L. Mencken defined Puritans as people "haunted by the fear that someone somewhere may be happy."[64] Puritans who came to America emphasized biblical interpretations considering the human body as inherently impure and depraved. The hardships of life in the American wilderness, combined with bizarre aspects of the Puritan philosophy, made life especially difficult for the women of that time. As early feminist Lillie Devereux Blake said in 1892: "The Pilgrim mothers not only had to endure all that the Pilgrim fathers suffered, but had to endure the Pilgrim fathers as well."[65]

Stuntman Monty Laird remembered that during the filming of the horse roundup, Jimmy Nickerson and Sonny Shields were stunt doubling Ben Murphy and Roger Davis. In one scene, when Heyes ropes a horse, his saddle breaks and pulls him off. He's holding on to the rope and it drags him. The director wanted a close-up scene of Roger being dragged, so Roger went to three of the biggest grips and told them, "'Now when you guys pull me, I want you to really pull me, run just as fast and as hard as you can.' And the director also said, 'Now look, Roger, we don't need you to roll around, just drag straight. That's all you have to do. Drag straight right past the camera. Beyond it, cut, print, we've got it.' Not Roger. Method actor. Boy, they started dragging him, he started rolling and they drug him right into a light stand. . . .and off to the hospital he goes."[66]

Director Alex Singer remembered the mishap from a slightly different perspective. Rocks protruded from a point in the ground. He and Roger talked about it "and the plan was that he would let go a couple of feet before the rocks." He didn't. "When they brought him back from the doctor's, he did the scene again. He was very courageous but . . ." Singer continued, "We were always half between half-screaming and half-laughing and Roger was also. He was pretty good-humored about it, everything considered, but it would drive Ben crazy."[67]

CHAPTER 10

HANNIBAL HEYES AND KID CURRY
WOULD CEASE TO EXIST

In the cutthroat world of American network television, *Alias Smith and Jones* did not fare well. The show was a charming blend of humor and action with occasional flashes of social commentary, but it had trouble reaching a sufficiently large audience to suit ABC. The potential for success was there; tantalizing glimpses of what could be were evident whenever NBC pre-empted *The Flip Wilson Show*. Roy Huggins, with a philosophic shrug, recalled that the episodes screened at Audience Surveys, Inc. always tested well. "We got huge numbers with *Alias Smith and Jones*. People loved the show; they just didn't watch it."[1] Network executives made many decisions based upon ASI scores and the show's positive test numbers helped keep it on the air despite its lackluster Nielsen ratings. During the 1971-72 season, based on twenty-five telecasts, the show garnered an overall rating of 16.3% and a 25 share. In other words, 10,120,000 households were watching the adventures of the two lovable outlaws each week.[2] In that season, *Alias Smith and Jones* ranked fifty-fifth out of seventy-eight programs, yet ABC still appeared to have faith in the show and renewed it for the 1972-73 season.

Frank Price knew the real problem facing the show was its timeslot. *Alias Smith and Jones* had been a mid-season replacement show and had inherited its original 7:30 p.m. Thursday timeslot from *Matt Lincoln*, one of the spate of so-called "relevance" shows which the networks were offering in the hope of attracting a young, hip audience. *Matt Lincoln* premiered on September 24, 1970, and, like most of the other "relevant" programs, immediately sank into obscurity. By the time *Alias Smith and Jones* began airing in January 1971, viewers had developed the habit of tuning in to *The Flip Wilson Show*, and they saw no reason to change.

Price was frustrated by the situation. He knew that if only the show weren't opposite the enormously popular comedian, it would be sure to thrive. For proof one had only to look overseas. While the show struggled in America, it soared in Great Britain. *Alias Smith and Jones* premiered on BBC2 on Monday, April 19, 1971, and was an instant success. Although ratings did not have the same significance for the non-commercial BBC as they did for the US network, the broadcaster was nevertheless pleased with the performance of their new American series. In its 8:00 p.m. timeslot, *Alias Smith and Jones* decisively trounced its competition on BBC1 and ITV, pulling in 20.4% of the viewing audience. In comparison, BBC1's well-respected news magazine Panorama attracted only 8.4% of the audience while ITV's documentary *World in Action* had to be satisfied with 8.1%, although their ratings grew to 15.6% in the second half-hour with the sitcom *For the Love of Ada*. *Alias Smith and Jones's* rating is even more impressive given that only fifty-six percent of UK households were capable of receiving BBC2 broadcasts in April 1971.[3]

In July 1971, the episode "A Fistful of Diamonds" was the subject of a BBC Audience Research Report. The audience for *Alias Smith and Jones* had grown since the broadcast of the pilot three months earlier; the show now pulled in 22.5% of television viewers while BBC1's audience had dropped to 6.3% and ITV's audience averaged 8.7%. Viewers were asked to rate this episode on a five point scale of four dimensions defined by pairs of descriptive phrases: Thoroughly Entertaining/Very Boring; Very Easy To Understand/Very Difficult To Understand; Excellent Plot/Poor Plot; Definitely Out of the Ordinary/Just Ordinary. Seventy percent of the respondents rated the episode "thoroughly entertaining" while only two percent found it "very boring." Fifty-one percent of the audience gave the episode the highest ranking of "definitely out of the ordinary" while another twenty-five percent put it on the second highest point on the scale for that category. The BBC found that "A Fistful of Diamonds" was "a highly enjoyable episode of a series which has consistently given much pleasure." It was very much to the audience's taste with its two delightful heroes, an interesting and entertaining plot, and a nice touch of humor.

Most of those responding to the survey had been fairly regular viewers of the series and were loud in their praise for this "Western with a difference." While a minority of viewers, approximately two percent, felt the show was rather childish and that the films were "much of a muchness," most of the audience recognized *Alias Smith and Jones* had "an indefinable something that set it apart from the others."[4] The British audience proved what Frank Price and Roy Huggins already knew and struggled to convince ABC of – *Alias Smith and Jones* was special. In Britain, *Alias Smith and Jones* reached its full potential, winning a large, loyal and enthusiastic audience and leaving its competition in the dust. The series was then, and has remained, the most popular American import the BBC ever aired.

The *Alias Smith and Jones* audience might not have been numerous enough for ABC, but that was not the only problem. Peter Duel's death had forever altered the show and, while the ratings did not drop significantly when Roger Davis took over the role, for one very important person the magic was irretrievably gone. That person was Barry Diller, Vice President of Program Development for ABC. When Frank Price went to the network in 1972 and once again pleaded for a new timeslot, this time Diller obliged him. For its third season, *Alias Smith and Jones* would air on Saturday night at 8:00 p.m., opposite *All in the Family*, the number one show in America. The implication was clear. Diller had decided to make

Alias Smith and Jones the network's sacrificial lamb on Saturday night. Nothing that had gone up against the sitcom had survived, and the possibility that *Alias Smith and Jones* would buck the trend was remote. Price laments, "We were ill-fated . . . first we had Flip, then we had *All in the Family* and then Peter . . . we know we've got something fabulous but we can't seem to see daylight somehow. We keep getting crushed."[5]

Yet, as of April 1972, production notes indicate that Universal expected to film and deliver a full third season. ABC specifically ordered twelve episodes with an option for eight more. But Diller threw another curve at them. ABC's new martial-arts show *Kung Fu* would initially share the Saturday timeslot, pre-empting *Alias Smith and Jones* every fourth week until mid-season. Then, beginning in January 1973, *Alias Smith and Jones* would once again be the sole occupant of that timeslot and air every week.[6] This tactic did not bode well for the show.

As the 1972-73 season approached, ABC did promote the series, sending Ben Murphy and Roger Davis on a promotional tour in early September 1972. They visited major cities across the nation, appearing on local talk shows, doing radio interviews and visiting ABC affiliates to plug the series. *Daily Variety* was fairly optimistic about the new timeslot, commenting in a review of the new season, "If the young adults continue to fall in with CBS-TV's *All in the Family* and the other folks go for *Emergency* on NBC, *Alias Smith and Jones* may have found its ideal spot on early Saturday night, filling the vacuum for youngsters."[7] But this upbeat assessment didn't take into account the fact that, in most households, parents, not youngsters, were controlling the set. Roger Davis ruefully remembers, "Even *my* parents watched *All in the Family* first, and then tuned in to the last half hour of *Smith and Jones*."[8]

Heyes and Curry struggled against Archie Bunker as the season progressed, but as in their battle against Flip Wilson the year before, they still managed to perform respectably given the circumstances. It wasn't enough for Barry Diller. Jo Swerling recalls, "He didn't like the show as well with Roger as he did with Pete and decided that the show had run out of gas, even though the numbers didn't support that." Swerling, while acknowledging that Ben and Roger didn't share the same kind of chemistry as Ben and Peter had, nevertheless feels the audience was accepting the change. "I think it was a bad call to cancel *Alias Smith and Jones*. I think he should have let it go for at least one more season to see what would happen. [But] he wasn't interested."[9] This lack of interest led Diller to abruptly cancel the show in November 1972. Instead of celebrating the mid-season pickup they were expecting, the cast finished shooting and wrapped up the series with a farewell party on Stage 35 on November 3, 1972.

Beginning January 20, 1973, two new sitcoms – *Here We Go Again* and *A Touch of Grace* – would replace *Alias Smith and Jones*. Ironically, *A Touch of Grace* was based on the British sitcom *For the Love of Ada*, one of the shows *Alias Smith and Jones* routinely outperformed in Britain. These two comedies performed so poorly, they disappeared from ABC's schedule five months later, not even lasting through the summer rerun season. For the next three years, everything ABC put up against *All in the Family* was promptly cancelled. Swerling remembers the bittersweet feeling those successive failures brought. "A considerable time passed before they had anything in that timeslot that performed as well as *Alias Smith and Jones,* so it was a little bit of *schadenfreude* that we were able to indulge in, but it didn't bring the show back."[10]

Barry Diller might have lost interest in *Alias Smith and Jones,* but the BBC hadn't. Roy Huggins recalled *Alias Smith and Jones* was "tremendously popular in the United Kingdom, Australia and New Zealand. It was a big, big hit. And it was such a big hit they wanted to pay to have it produced."[11] In a startling move, when ABC cancelled the series, the BBC began negotiating with Universal to pick up the production costs in an effort to keep the show alive. Frank Price, who personally loved the series, felt the idea was all well and good, but from a business standpoint it was completely impractical. The show was budgeted at approximately $190,000 per episode, money ABC recouped through its advertising rates. The BBC was a non-commercial broadcaster, funded by television license fees paid by taxpayers in Great Britain; there was no way they would be able to afford such a venture. "Therefore that's the kind of thing I put in the category of 'that's very nice' but nothing we can really do," Price regrets.[12] The two companies dickered back and forth, offers and counter-offers being considered and rejected one by one.

At one point, it seemed the BBC might just succeed. Although the production company had been shut down, Roy Huggins gave Roger Davis a heads-up about the imminent resumption of production, urging him not to take any other jobs. "Get packing, we're going to Spain to shoot."[13] However, in the end, Price's assessment was correct: though the two companies came within $50,000 per episode of reaching an agreement, a pittance in Hollywood terms, ultimately the BBC could not afford to produce the show themselves and the deal fell through. The adventures of Hannibal Heyes and Kid Curry were over.

Reminiscing about the show thirty years later, Ben Murphy recalls that, although Peter Duel's death had moved him up to lead, initially he would have rather quit and had the show stop then and there. But when the show went back into production, Ben went to work "because it was always my job, I was under contract." During the first season and partway through the second, though he was getting three times more fan mail than Peter, he had been paid Screen Actors' Guild minimum. Roy Huggins went to the Black Tower and pled Murphy's case. Huggins told them it wasn't fair. "He's working the same hours and he's getting one-tenth the pay."[14] Ben was still not getting rich though he did get the raise after Peter died. But, Ben sadly recalls, "the important issue was Peter was gone and it was going to be changed forever. Period. As far as I was concerned, it was a new show then."[15]

Ben appreciated the tough position Roger Davis found himself in, though they often clashed. Roger believes "neither of us ever had the smarts to come together and go, 'Y'know, we could potentially have a real long run here . . .'"

To Ben that was never possible. "The show depended on being a fun-loving show . . . [and] once someone kills himself, the audience goes, 'Whoa. Not only do we miss him, but these obviously are not fun-loving guys anymore.' . . . [Peter] shooting himself casts a pall on the show. Not only the fact that he wasn't there."[16]

Roger Davis doesn't subscribe to Ben's theory about the show being doomed after Peter Duel's suicide. He knows he gave it his best effort in a bad situation in a bad timeslot and says, "I will always be regretful of it not having been a major success. Yet, I don't know, as Ben said, 'What could you have done about it?' What *could* I have done about it?"[17]

Three years earlier, when Huggins had come aboard, one of the things he did not care for was the premise that the outlaws had only one year in which to prove themselves. If he had had his way, Huggins would have written it so the governor gave the boys five years to earn amnesty. Even given the malleability of television time, he knew from his work on *Run for Your Life,* that when a set deadline has come and gone – in that case the man's death from disease in two years – and the anticipated outcome has not occurred, the audience becomes unwilling to hang on any more and will cease to watch the show. When Paul Klein of NBC notified Huggins the show was about to be cancelled, he didn't credit Klein's argument that "people who watch television are very literal and they would not accept *Run for Your Life* if he's still alive in a fourth year." Huggins wondered about Little Orphan Annie. "You know, she never grew an inch for forty years." Klein acknowledged Huggins's point but argued that Little Orphan Annie was a comic strip, not a television series, and audience expectations were different.[18]

One other concept Huggins kept in mind was how Heyes and Curry were on probation. "As long as they stayed out of trouble, they'd be let alone, go right along, but if they got into trouble, [they'd be sent to] prison for life. . . .They were frequently motivated by a fear that if they did something, they would go back to prison . . ." Knowing he could have sent them to languish in prison or granted them their amnesty, when Huggins was asked what he would have done had he been given the opportunity for a series finale for *Alias Smith and Jones,* he said, "I think if I'd known, I'd want to do something . . . I undoubtedly would have ended this show with their freedom."[19]

The development of "The Day the Amnesty Came Through" began at the end of July 1972 when Huggins told the story to writer Dick Nelson. The story, with the promised amnesty granted to Heyes and Curry and then snatched away, would have allowed the series to continue for realistic and historical reasons – the change of governors. In it, Huggins echoed the pilot dialogue wherein Sheriff Lom Trevors tells them their attempt for an amnesty must remain a secret. Only they, he, and the governor will know about it. The plot mirrors the pilot in their having to begin again to prove their good intentions, but the episode's scheduling was another indication Huggins did not see the cancellation coming. After it aired, four more episodes followed. Even if he had no other plan for a final episode (an unlikely scenario given Huggins's fertile imagination), ending the series with the outlaws being granted amnesty, even if it were rescinded by the new governor, would have made a satisfying closure.

Instead, the show was abruptly cancelled and, as far as the audience knows, Heyes and Curry are still out there, leading quiet lives of desperation awaiting the governor's signature on their amnesty papers. The further adventures of Heyes and Curry remain forever a mystery, but for the actors who played them, life went on, however disparate from the last several years.

When the show was cancelled, Frank Price, who had taken Ben Murphy under his wing, offered Ben his next role as Mike Murdoch, Lorne Greene's sidekick in the short-lived *Griff* series, its concept being "old cop, young cop, both originally cowboys." In late 1974, Ben was back in cowboy costume as Wild Bill Hickok to Matt Clark's Buffalo Bill and Kim Darby's Calamity Jane in *This Is The West That Was. College* students popularized the satirical western drama into a cult movie classic.

(Sagala collection)

Ben Murphy.

Then, Ben was ready for something new. Always into physical fitness and exercise, one day he tried tennis and immediately fell in love with the game. In between filming movies for TV, like *Heat Wave!* and *Sidecar Racers,* and guest-starring in such favorites as *Love, American Style* and *Marcus Welby,* he played tennis. Ben enjoyed the breaks between acting gigs, unlike other actors who constantly hustled to get more work. The game rewarded his tenacity, and he gained proficiency at it. At one time, he was touted to be best in California, playing a consistent serve-and-volley game. A commentator once remarked, "He acts like he's playing Wimbledon."[20] Exertion expended in the game helped Ben deal with his disappointment when he wanted to try for one of the roles in *Starsky and Hutch,* but Universal insisted he abide by his exclusive contract with them and he was not loaned out.

Around this time, Ben began dating a Pan Am airline stewardess. While he was in Chicago performing in a play, his date introduced him to her friend, Jeanne Davis, also a stewardess. When Ben flew to Australia for the role of Jeff Rayburn in *Sidecar Racers,* coincidentally Jeanne was an attendant on the flight. The reunion ignited a spark and they began dating.

In 1976, Frank Price approached Ben and asked for a favor. Michael York was currently doing a pilot for a series called *Gemini Man* and things were not working out. Price wanted Ben to replace York and finish the pilot in order to fulfill Universal's commitment to the network. Ben agreed, thinking it was just a movie. He played the role of Sam Casey, a government agent who, after a freak accident, could become invisible by using a specially designed "wristwatch." When the series sold, however, he found himself in it for the duration, much to his dismay. A take-off on H.G. Wells's *The Invisible Man, Gemini Man* was a tough role for Ben to play because he's claustrophobic. In one sequence, the script called for him to do an underwater scene wearing an old-fashioned bell-type helmet and diving suit. Having to breathe through a hose and having no control was tough on him. He remembers feeling like the man in the iron mask. "I thought I was going to die . . . There's air but, it's that feeling you can't take it off. . . .I literally just would sweat bullets and just had to almost cry and beg them to get the shot as fast as they could . . ."[21]

Ben Murphy with Molly.

In 1978, when his Universal contract expired, Ben devoted more of his energy to tennis, and he married Jeanne Davis. A year later, Ben landed what he considers one of the best, most well-done shows he ever did, *The Chisholms*, a CBS mini-series. As Will Chisholm, oldest son of the frontier family, his was a major role alongside Robert Preston and Brian Keith. Ben read for the part, earning the job on his own talent, a heady victory for him. Shortly afterwards he bought a house high in the hills of Malibu with a gorgeous view of the ocean.

By 1980 Ben realized he was "never meant to be married" and he and Jeanne divorced. More guest star roles came his way in *Fantasy Island, The Love Boat* and *Trapper John, MD*. In another TV movie, *Time Walker*, he played a scientist who discovers an alien found inside an ancient mummy. In 1983, he had an important role as Robert Mitchum's oldest son in *The Winds of War*, one of the highest rated mini-series of all time. After that, even though he had all kinds of acting credits to his name, when NBC producers were casting *The A-Team*, they wanted him to audition for the character Face. He said at the time, "I wasn't used to that and my performance was rotten. As it turned out, the rejection was good for me because it convinced me it was time I turned my life around."[22] In an effort to jump-start his career, he went back to acting class. For years he attended a weekly workshop designed to hone his skills. He enjoyed it because it was a place where "a lot of us older actors go and just work out for free with each other, with cameras and so forth."[23]

The persistence paid off. Ben won the role of Patrick Sean Flaherty, the dashing Irishman who doled out sweepstakes checks on *Lottery!* Though he could still pass for a man ten years younger, Ben told a reporter, "This has to be the first show I've done in seventeen years where I'm not going to be called Kid."[24] Ben fondly remembers *Lottery!* as being the most fun show he's ever done. From then on, he was constantly busy with guest star roles and an occasional TV movie. In *The Cradle Will Fall*, a suspense drama in which Ben played a medical examiner, he shared star honors with Lauren Hutton and James Farentino. Then, as a member of the large cast of *Berrengers*, a nighttime soap opera about the reigning family of a prestigious New York department store, he stood out as the oldest son of the patriarch. The concept, too similar to *Dallas*, was overdone, however, and the series did not last long. Another disappointment occurred a year later when Ben came close to winning a starring role in *Miami Vice*. The show's concept of two south Florida crime-fighters began as a white man paired with a Hispanic. Ben was in the running with Don Johnson. When the producers decided to change the characters to a black man and a white man, they also finalized their decision and cast Johnson.

However, a leading role came along in 1988 when Barry Diller, now head of the new Fox network, tapped Ben to play the lead in *Dirty Dozen*, a World War II series. As Lieutenant Danko, he commanded a troop of twelve ex-convicts promised an amnesty of sorts if they could carry out top-secret missions against the Germans and come out alive. The show was not one of Ben's favorites because it required a lot of hard work and was produced in Yugoslavia, a long way from home. It goes down in the record books, however, as being one of the first programs on the new Fox network.

Since then, Ben has guest starred in shows as diverse as *Dr Quinn, Medicine Woman* and *JAG*. Unfortunately his foray into the movies, *Hanging Up*, ended up on the cutting room floor. Still, he is a happy man; he likes Malibu "because there's no smog, there's a good tennis club and a track at the nearby university where I can run."[25] Very conscious of being physically fit, he exercises and still plays tennis regularly.

After years of renting out the home he bought in the Malibu hills, he decided to move into it and has spent several years renovating it to his taste. Details of wall color, stucco texture and stonework occupied his attention for hours each day. As a segmenter, Ben found the experience both frustrating and fulfilling. "I'm not personally a guy that likes to have eight balls in the air at once. I like to deal with this issue and then I like to go deal with that issue, but I can weave things together," he said. After all is said and done, though, it's his two dogs that make the house "home."

As for his acting career, he's philosophical. "Life is still going to go on. There are still going to be ups and there are still going to be downs. And what is success? I'll tell you this: My career peaked almost at the very beginning . . . with *Alias Smith and Jones*." How does he feel about that? "A little sad maybe. But I've enjoyed life."[26]

Roger Davis, the other half of the Heyes-Curry partnership, continued to keep busy, interspersing his two loves: acting and architecture. He began buying and managing several complexes in Beverly Hills. After losing out on the starring role in *The Way We Were* to Robert Redford, Roger put his architectural education to work by designing and constructing improvements for his properties. In 1974, Roger was hitting the big and small screens once again, appearing in films such as *The Killer Bees* and *The Education of Sonny Carson* and guest starring on *The Rockford Files* premiere.

One day, Roy Huggins phoned almost apologetically. "I have a show that Ben's starring in that I want you to narrate." The show was *This Is the West That Was* and Huggins felt Roger's voiceover would be just the thing to tie the loose ends of the script together. He told him, "I want you to treat it as if you were a character in the show," so, in a way, it was technically the last time Roger and Ben worked together.

In 1975 came the theatrical release of *Flash and the Firecat,* in which Roger's younger brother, Brent, also appeared. It's a "light-hearted, cute movie where I do have a real good time." He was not having a good time at home, however, and around this time, he and his wife divorced.

At the end of 1976, he was at Universal ready to play the romantic lead in the Glen Larson produced show *Bionic Woman* with Lindsay Wagner, when he became seriously ill with a ruptured appendix, peritonitis, and gangrene. For four months he fought for his life. Seven operations later, doctors finally gave him a clean bill of health.

Roger married Suzanne Emerson in the late 1970s, becoming a first-time father to a daughter, Margaret, in May 1981. He continued his acting career with *Nashville Girl* and *Ruby*. Then, in 1976-77, Douglas Heyes was directing a TV miniseries called *Aspen* and talked producer Roy Huggins into hiring Roger. Heyes thought he would be perfect for the rich boy Maxfield Kendrick role. By spring 1980, Roger was on-screen again, guesting on the short-lived sequel to *Battlestar Galactica, Galactica 1980*.

Roger then relocated to Kentucky where he revived his interest in real estate investing and development and built the Louisville edifice known as 1600 Willow. He purchased the 1905 Seelbach Hotel and completely redesigned and restored it. In 1982, he appeared in the movie *The Act* and on television in the late-1980s in *Highwayman*. He is also credited with acting in Larson's TV pilot, *Chameleons*. Larson remained loyal to Roger over a long period of time and used him in several of his shows.

Roger moved back to Los Angeles, divorced a second time, and resumed his real estate business. By this time, he had a collection of antique label art from California's citrus packing days. He decided to use them in a sports line design and opened a tee-shirt manufacturing business, Packing Crate Classics, in Santa Monica, which still thrives and boasts over one hundred employees. But now, about the only time he involves himself with the tee-shirts is to take them to the annual *Dark Shadows* festivals. Roger appears at every convention and still appreciates the undying interest in the show.

He got into the production side of the film industry when he produced and starred in *Beyond the Pale* and is currently developing a film based on the Pinkerton detectives. His most recent real estate projects have taken him to Ventura, Pacific Palisades, and Hollywood Hills, where he is designing and constructing lofts built into the sides of mountains. To do this, he has had to shore up the land with massive retaining walls six stories tall and four hundred eighty feet long, containing twenty-five thousand tons of concrete. He is a far-sighted developer, moving mountains to create new homes.[27]

(Sagala/Bagwell collection)

Roger Davis on the deck of home he built in Malibu.

Thomas Jefferson once wrote, "Architecture is my delight. Putting up and pulling down my favorite amusement." Roger Davis identifies with Jefferson's sentiments because he has "always subscribed to the theory that architecture is an art . . . Ruskin said it better. 'Architecture is an art that so disposes the edifices built by man that they increase his power, his pleasure, his whole state of being.'" Roger believes "if you design a house right, a person gets into it and he feels great, [it's] wonderful to wake up in it every morning."

When a reporter once asked him, "What are you in this for?" he replied, "No matter what I design, no matter how long it lasts, or how upset you may be by it, or how much money it may make in the end . . . I'm an actor. I mean, people have seen [me] as an architect, builder, designer, businessman, all this stuff, . . . and I'm very good at that stuff, and understand the process and everything, every little nuance about building twenty-story high-rises and running a hotel, being that kind of person, whatever. But still, I'm an actor. . . ."[28]

Looking back, Roger wonders, if he had taken another road, how life would have worked out. From the moment Huggins phoned him about replacing

(Sagala/Bagwell collection)

Roger Davis at front door of home he built in Malibu.

Peter, Roger wondered if doing so was the right thing. "I was really putting my career on the line; I was at a point where my stock was real high and I needed to make the right move. It would have been tough for anybody to rise out of [replacing Peter], but I was more motivated by the fact that I really owed Roy not to say no. The potential was that if it didn't work, I could be done for. I think, for the most part, it came to pass." Alex Singer understood his ambivalence and told him that first day on the set, "It's a horrible tragedy; there's nothing to be done for it. If you don't get the job, it doesn't mean that somebody won't get the job or that Peter isn't dead. It's not your fault. You didn't pull the trigger."[29]

Roger's greatest achievement "has always been doing my own thing, working for myself. And there I have had just enormous success and had enormous monetary rewards, [and a] feeling of accomplishment. . . Working as an actor is really working for someone else. It is doing the director's bidding, the producer's bidding, the studio's bidding." Huggins once told him he liked his work as an actor but felt he had the temperament to be a producer. Roger admits, "That bothers me a little bit . . . and it may be, [but] I didn't take that direction in the business."[30]

Ben, too, speculates how his career might have turned out differently, "had I been a smarter businessman," but he knows he would have had to be a completely different person with negotiating and business skills he lacked at the time. Instead, he admits, he never concerned himself with the business end. "I probably could have positioned myself to do better shows than I did. I just usually took what they offered me. Moved on with it. . . .Had I known more and what my powers were, I might have put myself in a better product or held out for better parts. That's poor business on my part."[31]

Roy Huggins, the *producer extraordinaire,* made actors look good with his interesting, well-written stories. With the cancellation of *Alias Smith and Jones,* Frank Price, who had put Huggins in association with Glen Larson, next brought him together with Stephen J. Cannell. Together they created *The Rockford Files* in which Huggins used one of his favorite actors, James Garner, as a slightly disreputable private eye, just the kind of unconventional character Huggins liked to write about. Cannell, who later hired Huggins to serve as executive producer on his show *Baretta*, eulogized Huggins, saying, he "taught me everything that I used in my career on how to create and write and produce a television show."[32] Huggins came out of retirement to produce *Hunter* for Cannell and then concentrated on writing his memoirs. When he was eighty-three years old, he was still involved in filmmaking and had a hand in the movie version of *The Fugitive*, and later received Executive Producer credit on the series remake in 2000. Roy Huggins passed away in April 2002.

Glen Larson, creator of the show, left the production team at the end of the second season. "It was a great experience," Larson says, "but I was happy to leave . . . to move on, because I wanted to be able to create some more things and have them my own way, do them the way I wanted to do them." Larson observes, "[Roy]'s very autocratic . . . We saw a lot of things differently, *especially* the humor." This clash of tastes and styles led to friction between the two men, but Larson readily admits, "I was also learning. I learned a *lot* from Roy." He was often frustrated when Huggins cut out his jokes, but developed an appreciation for the wisdom of such cuts later in his career, when he was the one doing the cutting. "I had to do the same things on occasions later when the writers would want to do something that was funny or precious . . . We get the joke, but we lose the hero."[33] He learned his lessons well. After leaving *Alias Smith and Jones*, Larson took over as showrunner on *McCloud*, then went on to create many more series, among them *Battlestar Galactica, The Six Million Dollar Man*, and *Magnum, PI*. The current nostalgia craze has been good to Glen Larson. Several of his old television shows are in development as feature films, *Battlestar Galactica* was re-made as a mini-series for the Sci Fi Channel in 2003, and in 2004 he returned to his roots as a musician, performing on stage once again as part of The Four Preps in a reunion concert filmed for PBS.

Frank Price pointed out a basic tenet of writing a book about a television series when he observed that getting everyone's viewpoint about a show like *Alias Smith and Jones* was like the blind men and the elephant. In that fable, seven blind men encountered an elephant and as each man felt a different part of it – trunk, legs, hide, tail, tusks – he came away with a different impression of what the whole animal was like. Similarly, each person involved in *Alias Smith and Jones* had his or her perspective on the show. But if any one theme ran through the memories of all those involved, it would be that doing *Alias Smith and Jones* was fun. For each, though the sad memories will always be there, of course, not only for Peter Duel, but also for what might have been had the show gone on longer, the sweet memories survive the bad. In the re-write notes for "The Posse That Wouldn't Quit," Huggins noted a bit of humor in the script he particularly liked: "It's interplay, the fun our two boys have with each other."[34] The good times were not only had by the actors and production team, but by the audience as well.

Alias Smith and Jones was on the air for only two short years. It has now been more than three decades since Hannibal Heyes and Kid Curry roamed the West in search of their elusive amnesty, but they are still fondly remembered by those who enjoyed the show during its original run, and they gain new fans whenever the show reappears on television. Huggins proudly admitted his shows were rare. "They actually are stories that hook you, that surprise you, that hold your interest and then leave you satisfied. They are so rare on television that [*Alias Smith and Jones* is] still your favorite show." The spirit of fun and collection of good stories became the legacy of those two pretty good bad men. But that legacy, as Ben Murphy says, ". . . exists with those fans who love it now. Roy's job is done; my job is done. Those people who love that show are now keeping it alive."[35]

ENDNOTES

NOTES FOR INTRODUCTION

1   James D. Horan and Paul Sann, *Pictorial History of the Wild West* (New York: Crown Publishers, 1954)
     206; Joseph Rosa, ed., *The West* (New York: Smithmark Publishers, 1994) 165.

2   Horan 198, 96.

3   Horan 210.

4   Larry Pointer, *In Search of Butch Cassidy* (Norman, OK: Univ. of OK Press, 1977) 240-250; Jack Cox,
     "Who *Were* Those Guys?" *Denver Post,* Sep 12, 1999: 1F.

5   Cox, *Denver Post.*

6   Horan 217.

7   David Marc and Robert J. Thompson, *Prime Time, Prime Movers* (Syracuse, NY: Syracuse University
     Press, 1992) 172.

8   Roy Huggins, interview by the authors, May 23, 2001.

9   Jeff Greenfield, *Television – The First Fifty Years* (New York: Harry N. Abrams, Inc., 1977) 141.

10   J. Fred MacDonald, *Who Shot the Sheriff?* (New York: Praeger, 1987) 55.

11   Ibid. 48-9.

12   Frank Price, interview by the authors, Feb 25, 2003.

13   www.imagesjournal.com/issues06/infocus.htm, accessed Sep 5, 2003.

14   MacDonald 8.

15   Jeff Gremillion, "Back in the Saddle Again," *TV Guide,* May 23, 2003: 4.

NOTES FOR CHAPTER ONE

1   That's equivalent to $482 million in 2003 dollars. Samuel H. Williamson, "What is the Relative
     Value?" Economic History Services, Apr 2004, URL: http://www.eh.net/hmit/compare/, accessed
     Sep 8, 2004.

2   Leon Claire Metz, *The Shooters* (New York: Berkley Books, 1976) 125; Time-Life Books, *The
     Gunfighters* (Alexandria, VA: Time-Life Books, 1974) 93.

3   Glen Larson, interview by the authors, Feb 19, 2003.

4   Frank Price, interview by the authors, Feb 25, 2003.

5   Contrary to speculation, the name "Hannibal Heyes" was not chosen as an homage to Douglas Heyes.

6   Glen Larson, interview by the authors, Feb 19, 2003, and Apr 29, 2004.

7   Brenda Marshall, "Face In The Mirror. Pete Deuel: Gidget's Brotherly Brother-in-law," *TV Radio Mirror*, May 1966.

8   "Peter Deuel 'I Have To Be The Best' So What Else Would You Expect With Parents Like These?" *Motion Picture*, Aug 1967.

9   Lou Larkin, "Peter Deuel: He Kisses The Girls And Makes Them Cry," *Modern Screen*, Mar 1967.

10   Ibid.

11   Fredda Dudley Balling, "Deuel With Death," *Movie World*, Mar 1967.

12   Kim Darby, interview by the authors, Apr 29, 2004.

13   Swerling interview, 2004.

14   *Modern Screen*, op. cit.

15   Jack Jobes, telephone interview by Sagala, May 10, 2004.

16   Ibid.

17   "From The Private Pasts of Pete & Ben," *Teen Life*, Jan 1972.

18   Dennis Fimple, interview by the authors, Aug 4, 2002; Jack Jobes, telephone interview by the authors, Sep 4, 2004.

19   Harry Castleman and Walter J. Podrazik, *Watching TV: Four Decades of American Television* (New York: McGraw-Hill, 1982) 194.

20   Jo Swerling, Jr., interview by the authors, Aug 8, 2002.

21   Percy Shain, "He Prefers Duel to Deuel," *Boston Globe TV Week*, Feb 14, 1971.

22   Price interview.

23   Bettelou Peterson, "He Was Headed For the Top," *Boston Globe TV Week*. Feb 3-9, 1980.

24   Ben Murphy, phone interview by authors, Dec 12, 2002.

25   Ben Murphy, interview by the authors, Apr 25, 2004.

26   Viola Hegyi Swisher, "Hollywood's Professional Training Ground," *After Dark*, Nov 1970.

27   Percy Shain, "He looks just like..." *Boston Globe TV Week*, Mar 7, 1971.

28   Granada Plus (UK Cable Channel) interview, aired Mar 2002.

29   Swerling interview.

30   Roy Huggins, *25 Years down the Tube*, unpublished autobiography, 37.

31   Huggins interview.

32   Price interview.

33   Ed Robertson, *Maverick: Legend of the West* (Beverly Hills, CA: Pomegranate Press, 1994) 93.

34   John, Thomas and James are the names of three of Huggins's four sons.

35   Swerling interview.

NOTES FOR CHAPTER TWO

1   "Journey From San Juan," Prod. #32615, rewrite notes, Dec 22, 1970: 1.

2   Huggins interview.

3   "The Day The Amnesty Came Through," Prod. #35511, rewrite notes, Sep 5, 1972: 18.

4   "McCreedy Bust: Going, Going, Gone," Prod. #34237, Nov 16, 1971: 40.

NOTES FOR CHAPTER THREE

1   William Goldman, *Adventures in the Screen Trade* (New York: Warner Books, 1983) 470.

2   Huggins interview.

3   Jo Swerling, Jr., interview by the authors, Aug 8, 2002.

4   Jo Swerling, Jr. interview by the authors, Apr 23, 2004.

5   "The McCreedy Bust," Prod. #32614, story notes, Nov 24, 1970; script, Nov 29, 1970.

6   Huggins interview.

7   Robertson, op cit.

8   "Exit from Wickenburg," Prod. #32616, rewrite notes, Dec 3, 1970: 11.

9   Mark Twain, *Life on the Mississippi* (Boston: James R. Osgood & Co., 1883), chapter 22.

10 Ben Murphy, interview by the authors, Aug 7, 2002.

11 "Wrong Train to Brimstone," Prod. #32607, rewrite notes, Nov 23, 1970: 18.

12 "The Girl in Boxcar #3," Prod. #32620, story conference, Dec 3, 1970: 14.

13 http://www.montrealmirror.com/ARCHIVES/1999/100799/book.html;
    http://www.thestranger.com/2000-01-27/books.html, accessed Apr 8, 2003.

14 Joseph R. Weil, as told to W.T. Brannon, *"Yellow Kid" Weil: The Autobiography of America's Master
    Swindler* (Chicago: Ziff-Davis Publishing Co., 1948) 20-25.

15 http://www.salon.com/books/review/1999/08/03/maurer/, accessed Apr 8, 2003.

16 "The Great Shell Game," Prod. #32621, script Jan 11, 1971: 28.

17 "The Great Shell Game," Prod. #32621, script Jan 19, 1971: 53.

18 "Return to Devil's Hole," Prod. #32617, script, Dec 23, 1970: 18, 19.

19 "Return to Devil's Hole," Prod. #32617, script, undated: 12.

20 "Return to Devil's Hole," Prod. #32617, rewrite notes, Jan 5, 1971: 2.

21 Swerling interview, 2002.

22 Denis McLoughlin, *Wild and Woolly. An Encyclopedia of the Old West* (Garden City: Doubleday, 1975)
    480-1; "A Fistful of Diamonds," Prod. #32619, script, Dec 18, 1970: 22.

23 "A Fistful of Diamonds," Prod. #32619, rewrite notes addenda, Dec 22, 1970: 2.

24 "A Fistful of Diamonds," Prod. #32619, rewrite notes, Dec 21, 1970: 9.

25 "Stagecoach Seven," Prod. #32623, rewrite notes, Feb 1, 1971: 13

26 Swerling interview, Apr 23, 2004.

27 www.runestone.org/kmlc.html, accessed Oct 19, 2002.

28 "The Man Who Murdered Himself," Prod. #32622, story conference, Jan 7, 1971: 39.

29 "The Root of It All," Prod. #81438-F-32606, rewrite notes, Nov 19, 1970: 14.

30 "The Root of It All," Prod. #32606, script, Nov 20, 1970: 21.

31 "The Root of It All," Prod. #81438-F-32606, rewrite notes, Dec 28, 1970: 8.

32 "The Root of It All," Prod. #81438-F-32606, rewrite notes, Nov 20, 1970: 13.

33 "The 5th Victim," Prod. #32625, story conference, Jan 12, 1971: 12.

34 "The 5th Victim," Prod. #32625, rewrite notes, Feb 11, 1971: 29.

35 Huggins interview.

36 Ibid.

37 "The 5th Victim," Prod. #32625, story conference, Jan 12, 1971: 35.

38 Huggins interview.

39 "Journey From San Juan," Prod. #32615, story conference, Dec 2, 1970: 40.

40 "Journey From San Juan," Prod. #32615, script, Dec 17, 1970: 16.

41 William Goldman. *Adventures in the Screen Trade* (Time Warner, Co., 1983) 454.

42 Huggins interview.

NOTES FOR CHAPTER FOUR

1   "Latest Nielsen Scores Could Give CBS Pause on Rural Housecleaning," *Variety* Mar 10, 1971.

2   Price interview.

3   Davis interview, Feb 22, 2003.

4   Ibid.

5   Irv Broughton. "Roy Huggins." *Producers on Producing: The Making of Film and Television* (Jefferson, NC: McFarland & Co., 1986) 174, 176.

6   Price interview.

7   Larson interview, Feb 19, 2003.

8   "Round 2 for ABC's 'Alias Smith and Jones,'" *Los Angeles Herald-Examiner* Aug. 7, 1971.

9   Broughton 178.

10   Edgar Penton. "Zany is the word for Smith and Jones," *Muskegon Chronicle* May 9, 1971.

11   Cecil Smith. "Huggins: A Man for Two Seasons, Western and Now," *Los Angeles Times TV Times* Jul 4, 1971.

12   Singer interview, Apr 21, 2004.

13   Huggins interview.

14   Ibid.

15   http://www.caucus.org/archives/93spr_impressions.html, accessed 7/19/03.

16   Dennis Fimple, interview by the authors, Aug 4, 2002.

17   Gloryette Clark, interview by Bagwell, Jun 19, 2004.

18   Huggins interview.

19   Singer interview, Feb 17, 2003.

20   Swerling interview, Apr. 23, 2004.

21   Broughton 168.

22   Broughton 169.

23   Ibid.

24   Swerling 2003.

25   Swerling 2003.

26   Cecil Smith. "Smith and Jones, Just Highwaymen" *Los Angeles Times* Jan. 4, 1971.

27   John Walker. "Pete Closes Ranks with Bobby, David, and Donny," *Chicago Tribune TV Week* Oct 16, 1971.

28   Kay Gardella. "Pete's Not Convinced He's Lucky," *Sunday New,* Apr 25, 1971:S20.

29   *Los Angles Herald-Examiner,* op cit.

30   Dan Yergin. "If They Stay out of Trouble!" *Radio Times* Apr 22, 1971.

31   Murphy interview, Aug 7, 2002.

32   Gardella, op cit.

33   Tom Green. "Filming New Series Hectic," *Rochester Democrat and Chronicle* Jan 17, 1971.

34   Gardella, op cit.

35   Green, op cit.

36   Stone, Judy. "He's Alias Smith or Alias Jones," *TV Guide* May 15, 1971: 32; *Los Angeles Herald-Examiner,* op cit.

37   Fimple interview.

38   Ibid.

39 Richard Dana. "Pete Duel was arrested! Charged with Drunken Hit-and-run Driving," *Motion Picture Magazine* Aug 1971. A reading of .10 percent is sufficient to show a person has diminished capacity in operating a motor vehicle. The scale goes up to .50 where the person is literally "dead" drunk.

40 James Crenshaw. "Scoop! Cops arrest Pete Duel on Three Felony Charges," *TV Radio Mirror* Aug 1971.

41 Fenton Bresler. "Why Peter Duel Blew His Brains Out," *Pageant* January 1975; Brenda Shaw, "His Anguished Plea for Help," *TV Radio Mirror,* Apr 1972.

42 Larson interview, Apr 29, 2004.

43 Ibid.

44 Holliman interview.

45 *Los Angeles Herald Examiner,* op cit.

46 Walker, op cit.

47 Monty Laird, interview by the authors, Aug 5, 2002.

48 Lois Richman. "Shooting star of the month: Ben Murphy," *Screen Stars* May 1971.

49 Murphy interview, 2002; Fimple interview; Bresler, op cit.

50 Murphy interview 2002.

51 Murphy interview 2002.

52 Fimple interview.

53 Marcho Amedeo. "The Fan Letters I Answer First!" *Movieland and TV Time* Jun 1971.

54 "Ben Murphy in London," *Superstar* Jul 1972.

55 Murphy interview 2002.

56 Laird interview.

57 "Don't Shoot" *Superstar* Apr 1973.

58 Fimple interview.

59 Fimple and Murphy 2002 interviews.

60 inger interview 2003.

61 Tom Green. "'Smith and Jones' Nothing Phoney about It," *Rochester Democrat and Chronicle TV tab* Jun 27, 1971.

62 Murphy interview 2002.

63 Green, op cit.

64 *Los Angeles Herald-Examiner,* op cit.

NOTES FOR CHAPTER FIVE

1 Irv Broughton, ed. "Roy Huggins," *Producers on Producing: the Making of Film and Television* (Jefferson, North Carolina: McFarland & Co. 1986) 176.

2 "The Day They Hanged Kid Curry," Prod. #34216, rewrite notes, May 19, 1971:3.

3 "The Day They Hanged Kid Curry," Prod. #34216, rewrite notes, May 19, 1971: 4.

4 "Grandma Curry Comes to Town . . . Ooops, It's Walter Brennan." *TV Guide,* Sep 4, 1971.

5 Benjamin P. Eldridge and William B. Watts, *Our Rival the Rascal: A Faithful Portrayal of the Conflict Between Criminals of This Age And The Defenders of Society – The Police* (Boston, MA: Pemberton Publishing Company, 1897) 57.

6 "How to Rob a Bank in One Hard Lesson," Prod. #34213, story conference, May 14, 1971: 12.

7 Singer interview, Feb 17, 2003.

8 "Jailbreak at Junction City," Prod. #34211, script, Jun 21, 1971: 11.

9   Alex Singer, e-mail to Sagala, Mar 10, 2003.

10 Huggins interview.

11 "Jailbreak at Junction City," Prod. #34211, script, Jun 14, 1971: title page, handwritten note.

12 "Jailbreak at Junction City," Prod #34211, story notes, May 11, 1971: 9, 14.

13 Roger Davis, interview by the authors, Apr 24, 2004.

14 "Smiler with A Gun," Prod. #34220, script, Jun 21, 1971: 59.

15 "Smiler with A Gun," Prod. #34220, script, Jun 21, 1971: 63.

16 Roger Davis, interview by the authors, Feb 22, 2003.

17 "The Posse That Wouldn't Quit," Prod. #34218, rewrite notes, Jul 7, 1971: 19.

18 Murphy interview, Apr 25, 2004.

19 Huggins interview.

20 "The Posse That Wouldn't Quit," Prod. #34218, story conference, Jun 1, 1971: 11.

21 "The Posse That Wouldn't Quit," Prod. #34218, script, Jul 6, 1971: 32; rewrite notes, Jul 7, 1971: 41.

22 www.snowcampdrama.com/gifts.html, accessed Mar 9, 2003.

23 "Something to Get Hung About," Prod. #34221, story notes, Jul 8, 1971: 27.

24 "Six Strangers at Apache Springs," Prod. #43219, story notes, Jun 3, 1971: 2; rewrite notes, Jun 28, 1971: 1.

25 "Six Strangers at Apache Springs," Prod. #43219, story Notes, Jun 3, 1971: 6.

26 "Six Strangers at Apache Springs," Prod. #43219, Rewrite notes, Jul 20, 1971: 23.

27 "Six Strangers at Apache Springs," Prod. #43219, Story notes, Jun 3, 1971: 3, 11.

28 "Six Strangers at Apache Springs," Prod. #43219, Rewrite notes, Jul 20, 1971: 32.

29 "Six Strangers at Apache Springs," Prod. #43219, Rewrite notes, Jun 28, 1971: 10.

30 Swerling interview 2002.

31 Huggins interview.

32 "Night of the Red Dog," Prod. #34222, script, Aug 16, 1971: 33.

33 "Reformation of Harry Briscoe," Prod. #34223, script, Aug 4, 1971: 6; story outline, Jul 20, 1971: 12.

34 "Reformation of Harry Briscoe," Prod. #34223, story outline, Jul 20, 1971: 2.

35 "Reformation of Harry Briscoe," Prod. #34223, rewrite notes, Aug 6, 1971: 9.

36 http://home.earthlink.net/~dcrehr/firsttw.html;
    http://www.ideafinder.com/history/inventions/story097.htm, accessed February 9, 2003.

37 Ed Robertson, *Maverick: Legend of the West* (Los Angeles: Pomegranate Press, 1994) 77.

38 Huggins interview.

39 "Dreadful Sorry, Clementine," Prod. #34215, story notes, May 13, 1971: 9.

40 "Shootout at Diablo Station," Prod. #34224, story notes, Aug 24, 1971:26.

41 "Shootout at Diablo Station," Prod. #34224, story notes addendum, Aug 25, 1971.

42 Swerling interview, 2002.

43 Broughton 168.

44 "Everything Else You Can Steal," Prod. #34212, episode deal.

45 "Everything Else You Can Steal," Prod. #34212, script, Jun 4, 1971:1.

46 Louise Elliot in Baer's first draft.

47 "Everything Else You Can Steal," Prod. #34212, addenda, May 13, 1971: 2, 3, 26.

48 Ibid: 23.

49 "Everything Else You Can Steal," Prod. #34212, story notes, May 11, 1971:2.

50 Larson interview, 2003.

51 http://www.thrillingdetective.com/trivia/huggins.html, accessed Aug 23, 2004.

52 "21 Days to Tenstrike, Prod. #34235, story notes, Oct 14, 1971: 24.

53 Swerling interview, Apr 23, 2004.

54 "The bank robber, THE QUOTE, and the final irony"; http://www.banking.com/aba/profile_0397.htm, accessed Jan 14, 2003.

55 Ben Murphy, Peter Duel interview. *The Merv Griffin Show*, CBS, KNXT-Los Angeles, Los Angeles, Dec 3, 1971.

56 Huggins interview.

57 Singer interview, 2003.

58 "The Man Who Broke the Bank at Red Gap," Prod. #34241, story notes, Oct 28, 1971: 19.

59 "The Man Who Broke the Bank at Red Gap," Prod. #34241, script, Nov 19, 1971: 32-33.

60 "The Man Who Broke the Bank at Red Gap," Prod. #34241, script, Nov 19, 1971: 1.

61 "The Man Who Broke the Bank at Red Gap," Prod. #34241, script, Dec 17, 1971: 1.

62 Larson interview, Feb 2003.

63 "The Man Who Broke the Bank at Red Gap," Prod. #34241, story notes, Oct 28, 1971: 27.

64 Swerling interview, 2002.

NOTES FOR CHAPTER SIX

1 Singer interview, 2003.

2 Swerling interview, 2002.

3 Fimple interview.

4 The Lakers did win the game against the Seattle Supersonics – 122 to 106.

5 Swerling interview, 2004.

6 Laird interview, 2002.

7 Fimple interview, 2002.

8 David D. Burns, MD, *Feeling Good* (New York: Avon Books, 1999) 9.

9 Lou Larkin, "Peter Deuel: He Kisses The Girls And Makes Them Cry," *Modern Screen*, Mar 1967.

10 Dora Albert, "Peter Deuel: We're In Love – But We're Not Getting Married!" *TV Picture Life*, Jun 1967.

11 Morris Townsend, "Peter Duel: He Cared Too Much To Live..." *Silver Screen*, Apr 1972.

12 Ben Murphy, interview on Granada Plus, UK Cable Channel, aired Mar 2002.

13 Swerling interview, 2002.

14 Brooke Scott, "Tormented Peter Duel Commits Suicide: Was He Only Trying To Grab Some Peace?" *TV Radio Talk,* Apr 1972.

15 Swerling interview, 2004; Huggins interview.

16 Murphy interview, 2004; Huggins interview.

17 Singer interview, 2003.

18 Price interview, 2003.

19 Swerling interview, 2002 and 2004.

20 Harry Castleman and Walter J. Podrazik, *Watching TV: Four Decades of American Television* (New York: McGraw-Hill, 1982) 13.

21 Les Brown, *Televi$ion: The Business Behind The Box* (New York: Harcourt Brace Jovanovich, Inc., 1971) 312.

22   Price interview, 2003.

23   Davis interview, 2003.

24   Jobes telephone interview by Sagala, May 10, 2004.

25   Murphy interview, 2004.

26   Davis interview, 2004.

27   Davis interview, 2003.

28   Ibid.

29   Swerling interview, 2004; Murphy interview, 2004.

30   Singer interview, 2003.

31   Singer interview, 2003 and Apr 27, 2004.

32   Murphy interview, 2002.

33   Davis interview, 2003.

34   Swerling interview, 2002.

Notes for Chapter Seven

1   Davis interview, Feb 22, 2003.

2   Singer interview, Apr 27, 2004.

3   Davis interview, Apr 24, 2004.

4   Earl Holliman, telephone interview with Sagala, Mar 12, 2003.

5   Chris Fimple, interview with the authors, Feb 16, 2003.

6   Another exception is the Alcalde of Santa Marta who was played by two different actors because of protests by Hispanic activists. See "The Clementine Ingredient."

7   Huggins interview.

8   Gary L. Roberts, "The Search for Order on the Last Frontier," in *With Badges & Bullets: Lawmen & Outlaws in the Old West*, eds. Richard W. Etulain, Glenda Riley. (Golden, CO: FulcrumPublishing, 1999) 10-23.

9   Gary Topping, "Vigilantism with Honor," in *With Badges & Bullets: Lawmen & Outlaws in the Old West*, eds. Richard W. Etulain, Glenda Riley. (Golden, CO: Fulcrum Publishing, 1999) 94-103.

10   "Don't Get Mad, Get Even," Prod. #34242, story notes, Dec 16, 1971: 1, 6.

11   "Don't Get Mad, Get Even," Prod. #34242, story notes, Dec 16, 1971: 8.

12   "Don't Get Mad, Get Even," Prod. #34242, story notes, Dec 16, 1971: 11.

13   "Don't Get Mad, Get Even," Prod. #34242, script, Jan 24, 1972: 9.

14   "Don't Get Mad, Get Even," Prod. #34242, script, Jan 18, 1972: 37.

15   "Bernhardt, Sarah," "Paganini, Nicolo." *Microsoft® Encarta® 98 Encyclopedia*. © 1993-1997 Microsoft Corporation.

16   Huggins interview.

17   Ed Robertson, *Maverick: Legend Of The West* (Beverly Hills, CA: Pomegranate Press, Ltd., 1994) 61.

18   "How To Change A $10 Bill," Prod. #34240, rewrite notes, Nov 29, 1971: 2.

19   "How To Change A $10 Bill," Prod. #34240, rewrite notes, Nov 29, 1971: 10.

20   Twain, Mark. *The Tragedy of Pudd'nhead Wilson* (American Publishing Co. 1897).

21   Roy Huggins. *25 Years down the Tube* (Unpublished biography) 61.

22   "Bad Night in Big Butte," Prod. #34201, undated script: 35.

23   "Bad Night in Big Butte," Prod. #34201, rewrite notes, Oct 12, 1971: 20.

24   Jack Elam, note to Sagala, Aug 19, 1997.

NOTES FOR CHAPTER EIGHT

1   Swerling interviews, 2002 and 2004.

2   Swerling interview, 2004.

3   Singer interview, 2003 and Apr 27, 2004.

4   Swerling interviews, 2004; Murphy interview, 2002 and 2004.

5   Laird interview, 2002.

6   Davis interview, 2003.

7   Murphy and Davis, interview by the authors, Feb 22, 2003.

8   Murphy interview, 2002.

9   Murphy and Davis interview, 2003.

NOTES FOR CHAPTER NINE

1   The other two are "The Biggest Game in the West" and "What Happened at the XST?"

2   "The Long Chase," Prod. #35508, script, Jun 27, 1972: 2.

3   "The Long Chase," Prod. #35508, script, Jun 27, 1972: 2.

4   "The Long Chase," Prod. #35508, script, May 10, 1972: 30.

5   Huggins interview.

6   Swerling interview, Apr 23, 2004.

7   "High Lonesome Country," Prod. #35503, story notes, Apr 21, 1972: 20.

8   Alex Singer, interview by the authors, Apr 21, 2004.

9   "High Lonesome Country," Prod. #35503, story notes, Apr 18, 1972: 5; Singer, op cit.

10   Buscombe, Edward, ed. *The BFI Companion to the Western* (New York: Atheneum, 1988) 217.

11   "High Lonesome Country," Prod. #35503, script, Oct 11, 1972: 46.

12   Davis interview, Feb 22, 2003.

13   Mike Shiloh, "The Shiloh Files: Death of A Television Genius," Apr 21, 2002, http://www.thelatest.net/shiloh8.html, accessed Dec 16, 2003.

14   "The McCreedy Feud," Prod. #35506, story notes, May 3, 1972: 11.

15   "The McCreedy Feud," Prod. #35506, story notes, May 3, 1972: 2.

16   "The McCreedy Feud," Prod. #35506, story notes, Apr 19, 1972: 1.

17   "The McCreedy Feud," Prod. #35506, script, May 31, 1972: 2.

18   "The McCreedy Feud," Prod. #35506, story notes, May 3, 1972: 23.

19   Huggins interview.

20   Jennie Calder. *There Must Be a Lone Ranger – The American West in Film and in Reality* (New York: Taplinger Publishing Co., 1974) 158.

21   William Goldman. *Adventures in the Screen Trade* (New York: Warner Books, 1983, paperback 1984) 470-1.

22   Huggins, op cit.

23   *Daily Variety,* Aug 16, 1972: 1, 40.

24   Swerling interview, Aug 8, 2002.

25   "Bushwhack!" Prod. #35501, rewrite notes, May 19, 1972: 31.

26   Leon Claire Metz, *The Shooters* (New York, NY: Berkley Books, 1976) 172-174.

27   "Bushwhack!" Prod. #35501, rewrite notes, May 19, 1972: 8.

28   "Bushwhack!" Prod. #35501, rewrite notes, May 19, 1972: 10.

29   "Bushwhack!" Prod. #35501, script, May 17, 1972: 32.

30   "Bushwhack!" Prod. #35501, rewrite notes, May 19, 1972: 24.

31   "What Happened at the XST?" Prod. #35505, script, Jul 3, 1972: 4.

32   "What Happened at the XST?" Prod. #35505, script, Jul 3, 1972: 24.

33   "What Happened at the XST?" Prod. #35505, story notes, Apr 19, 1972: 3; script, Oct 23, 1972: 4.

34   "What Happened at the XST?" Prod. #35505, story notes, Apr 19, 1972: 1.

35   Bruce J Schulman, *The Seventies* (New York: The Free Press, 2001) 96-99.

36   "What Happened at the XST?" Prod. #35505, story notes, Apr 19, 1972: 25.

37   "The Kidnap Story," Prod. #35510, story notes, Jun 1, 1972: 12.

38   Ibid.

39   "The Kidnap Story," Prod. #35510, story notes, Jun 1, 1972: 17.

40   "The Kidnap Story," Prod. #35510, story notes, Jun 1, 1972: 21.

41   Gloryette Clark, interview by Bagwell, Jun 19, 2004.

42   "The Day The Amnesty Came Through," Prod. #35511, story notes, Jul 28, 1972: 2.

43   "The Day The Amnesty Came Through," Prod. #35511, script, Sep 26, 1972: 3.

44   http://www.gunnyragg.com/redsash.htm, accessed May 23, 2003.

45   "The Day The Amnesty Came Through," Prod. #35511, story notes, Jul 28, 1972: 9; script, Sep 26, 1972: 18.

46   "The Day The Amnesty Came Through," Prod. #35511, script, Aug 30, 1972: 17.

47   Huggins interview.

48   "The Day The Amnesty Came Through," Prod. #35511, rewrite notes, Sep 5, 1972: 18.

49   "The Day The Amnesty Came Through," Prod. #35511, script, Aug 30, 1972, 25-6.

50   "The Day The Amnesty Came Through," Prod. #35511, rewrite notes, Sep 5, 1972: 18.

51   The Day The Amnesty Came Through," Prod. #35511, story notes, Jul 28, 1972: 24.

52   Lane Bradbury, interview by the authors, Feb 20, 2003.

53   http://www.sosaz.com/public_services/Arizona_Blue_Book/1999_2000/ch02.htm, accessed Feb 23, 2004; http://jeff.scott.tripod.com/Zulick.html, accessed Feb 25, 2004.

54   "The Strange Fate of Conrad Meyer Zulick," Prod. #35509, story notes, Jun 1, 1972: 7.

55   "The Strange Fate of Conrad Meyer Zulick," Prod. #35509, story notes, Jun 1, 1972: 14.

56   www.labyrinth.net.au/~muffin/faqs_c.html; www.quinion.com/words/qa/qa-mcg1.htm, accessed May 25, 2003.

57   "McGuffin," Prod. #35512, script, Aug 23, 1972: 24.

58   "McGuffin," Prod. #35512, script, Aug 31, 1972: 39.

59   "McGuffin," Prod. #35512, script, Aug 31, 1972: 46-7.

60   "Witness to a Lynching," Prod. #35504, story notes, Apr 24, 1972: 6.

61   http://legendsofamerica.com/WE-CattleKate.html, accessed May 29, 2004.

62   "Witness to a Lynching." Prod. #35504, story notes, Apr 24, 1972: 42.

63   "Only Three to a Bed," Prod. #35502, story notes, May 27, 1972: 14.

64   Stephen G. Hyslop." The Puritans," *The History Channel Magazine*, May/June 2004: 61.

65   http://www.humanismbyjoe.com/Puritans Dark Side.htm, accessed Sep 30, 2003.

66   Monty Laird, interview by the authors, Aug 5, 2002.

67 Singer interview, Apr 21, 27, 2004.

NOTES FOR CHAPTER TEN

1 Huggins interview.

2 E-mail from Jo LaVerde, Nielsen Media Research, to Jo Bagwell, Sep 26, 2001; McDonald, 123.

3 *BBC TV Viewing Barometer,* Week 16, Monday, Apr 19, 1971.

4 "An Audience Research Report," BBC, Aug 17, 1971.

5 Price interview, 2003.

6 Interoffice memo from Steve Heilpern to Roy Huggins, Apr 13, 1972.

7 *Daily Variety,* review of "The Long Chase," Sep 20, 1972.

8 Davis interview, 2003.

9 Swerling interview, 2002.

10 Swerling interview, 2004.

11 Huggins interview.

12 Frank Price, telephone interview, Apr 24, 2004.

13 Davis interview, 2004.

14 Swerling interview, 2002.

15 Murphy interview, 2002.

16 Murphy and Davis interview, 2003.

17 Ibid.

18 Huggins interview.

19 Ibid.

20 *World Tennis,* Oct 1985.

21 Murphy interview, 2002.

22 Jerry Gladman, "After years of lucking out, Murphy wins a lottery," *Sunday Sun Television Magazine* (Toronto, Canada), Nov 20, 1983.

23 Murphy interview, 2002.

24 Gladman, op cit.

25 Rosemary Lord, "I'm a Highly-Paid Bum, I got just what I wanted . . ." Oct 19, 1975.

26 Dutch TV interview with Ben Murphy, aired March 2002; ibid.

27 Diane Wedner, "Driven up the wall," *Los Angeles Times,* Feb 16, 2003: 1K.

28 Davis interview, 2003.

29 Davis interview, 2004; Singer interview, Apr 27, 2004.

30 Davis interview, 2004.

31 Murphy interview, 2004.

32 *Los Angeles Times,* Apr 6, 2002.

33 Glen Larson, interview by the authors, Apr 29, 2004.

34 "The Posse That Wouldn't Quit," rewrite notes, July 7, 1971: 13.

35 Murphy interview, 2002.

APPENDIX A

MAVERICK VS. ALIAS SMITH AND JONES

Roy Huggins said in an interview with the authors that of all the shows he did over the course of his career, *Maverick* was his favorite, partly because of the show itself and partly because of the enormous influence it had over other television Westerns. When Frank Price asked Huggins to take over as showrunner for *Alias Smith and Jones,* he agreed because it offered him the opportunity to remake *Maverick,* but in a format that took advantage of there being two characters who were together all the time. The *Maverick* influence in *Alias Smith and Jones* becomes very apparent when the two shows are compared. The following list shows how often an old story was given new life:

MAVERICK	ALIAS SMITH AND JONES
TWO TICKETS TO TEN STRIKE	EXIT FROM WICKENBURG
ESCAPE TO TAMPICO	JOURNEY FROM SAN JUAN
SHADY DEAL AT SUNNY ACRES	DREADFUL SORRY, CLEMENTINE
POINT BLANK	EVERYTHING ELSE YOU CAN STEAL
THE SAVAGE HILLS	McGUFFIN
GAME OF CHANCE	DON'T GET MAD, GET EVEN

In addition to entire stories being reworked, many small things that were first used in *Maverick* were used again in *Alias Smith and Jones:*

MAVERICK	ALIAS SMITH AND JONES
THE QUICK AND THE DEAD	PILOT

This episode refers to characters named Shields and Kane and a town named Fort Griffin. In the *Alias Smith and Jones* pilot, the two bullies in the walk-off scene are named Shields and Kane, and Kane recognizes Kid Curry from when he saw him in Fort Griffin, "one jump ahead of the posse." This *Maverick* episode was written by Douglas Heyes, who collaborated with Glen Larson on the *Alias Smith and Jones* pilot.

| ROPE OF CARDS | THE McCREEDY BUST AND OTHERS |

This episode was the first to introduce the Five Pat Hands Trick, also known as Maverick Solitaire. In *Maverick,* Bret wins an acquittal for a man on trial for murder by using this trick to get the lone holdout on the jury to change his mind. In *Alias Smith and Jones,* Heyes uses this trick to get even with Big Mac after being taken by the Hoyle Rule.

| ACCORDING TO HOYLE | THE McCREEDY BUST |

Speaking of the Hoyle Rule, this episode hinges on Samantha Crawford's knowledge of an obscure rule in Hoyle – that straights aren't played in stud poker unless announced at the beginning of the game. Samantha beats Bret with a pair of nines; Big Mac beats Heyes with a pair of jacks.

| RAGE FOR VENGEANCE | THE BIGGEST GAME IN THE WEST, WHAT'S IN IT FOR MIA? |

This episode was the inspiration for two *Alias Smith and Jones* episodes and is a prime example of how Huggins's "recycling" resulted in distinctly different stories from the same initial idea, in this case the combination of poker and counterfeit money.

| POINT BLANK | JAILBREAK AT JUNCTION CITY |

Here Bret Maverick arrives in town broke and hungry. He uses the Belt Trick to win $5. The Belt Trick involves rolling up a belt and inviting the mark to stick a pencil through one of the loops so that the pencil is inside the belt when it's unrolled. The trick is that if the belt is unrolled in the opposite direction from that in which it was rolled up, the pencil will always be outside the belt. In "Jailbreak At Junction City," Heyes and Curry arrive in town broke and hungry. Heyes bets the bartender that he can stand an egg on end without cracking the shell. The trick to this is to use salt to provide enough stability to balance the egg. The Egg Trick earns Heyes and Curry $10.

| COMSTOCK CONSPIRACY | THE McCREEDY BUST |

In this episode, John Bordeen bet Maverick that he could cut the Ace of Spades on the first try, then stabbed a knife through the deck. Maverick, however, had palmed the card and Bordeen lost the bet. Bordeen did not take it as well as Big Mac did when Heyes caught him out with the same trick.

THE THIRTY-NINTH STAR   NEVER TRUST AN HONEST MAN

In this episode, Maverick picks up the wrong suitcase and finds himself in trouble with desperate politicians. Heyes picks up the wrong suitcase and the boys find themselves in trouble with a powerful railroad baron.

YELLOW RIVER   21 DAYS TO TENSTRIKE

Maverick joins a cattle drive in which two drovers are stabbed to death. Huggins took this idea and melded it with an episode of *The Virginian* called "50 Days to Moose Jaw," creating a story of a lethal cattle drive on a deadline.

Besides "50 Days to Moose Jaw," he recycled several other stories he created during his tenure as executive producer on *The Virginian*. While "John Thomas James" was his pseudonym of choice on *Alias Smith and Jones*, on *The Virginian* he alternated between "John Francis O'Mara" and "Thomas Fitzroy."

THE VIRGINIAN   **ALIAS SMITH AND JONES**
THE EXILES   WHICH WAY TO THE OK CORRAL?
VENGEANCE IS THE SPUR   RETURN TO DEVIL'S HOLE
STRANGERS AT SUNDOWN   STAGECOACH SEVEN
RUN AWAY HOME   THE GIRL IN BOXCAR #3

APPENDIX B

BLOOPERS

SOMETIMES THE HURRIED PACE OF PRODUCTION RESULTED IN FILMING OR EDITING ERRORS.

PILOT
Wheat refers to "seven sorry lives of crime," but there are only six outlaws.

Deputy Harker collects guns from the five outlaws at the poker table (the sixth was underground digging), but all six go to collect guns from Harker later, and get them.

Heyes and Curry leave Porterville in jackets, but when the posse is chasing them, they are riding in shirt sleeves.

When Harker stops in front of the door to the saloon, Heyes runs into the back of him.

When Heyes gets down to the saloon, he has bangs, then he doesn't. When he's talking to Wheat the bangs are back.

When Harker looks at his watch, it has regular numbers. The next time he checks, it has Roman numerals.

MCCREEDY BUST
There's an electrical cord hanging behind Armandariz's armoire

Heyes's hat and coat go on/off while he's safe-cracking.

A microphone precedes them as they walk in the street after having left Blake in the bar. In the US version, the camera pulls back until you can see their feet along with the microphone, this is not in the BBC version.

Heyes lays out five cards across on the table, but in the next camera angle, there are six across.

Heyes and Curry are dusty and dirty in the saloon. When they leave, Heyes's hat is clean.

EXIT FROM WICKENBURG
Mary says, "Good morning" when Curry is practicing his marksmanship in the alley. Later Heyes tells Curry to forget what he said "this afternoon."

WRONG TRAIN TO BRIMSTONE
The conductor's lantern was unlit, even though he signaled with it at night.

Heyes's hat moves forward and backward on his head when he and Curry are locked in the baggage car.

They asked the man on the wagon about the stagecoach. He said it had already left but there was a train headed east at "8:00 tonight." At 8:00 p.m. it should be dark or getting there. When they go to the train depot to buy tickets, it's dark. When they follow Grant and Gaines into the washroom, it's dark. When they come out of the washroom, the sun is shining, it looks like early morning.

There is an Out of Order sign on the privy. What part of a privy can be out of order?

THE GIRL IN BOXCAR #3
When Heyes is being slapped around, his hair gets suddenly combed.

THE GREAT SHELL GAME
In the scene where Sylvester, Heyes and Grace are at the club, Grace is wearing a cream lace dress with a hat. In the next scene, presumably after Dr. Sylvester has downed a few drinks, they are half-dragging him through the hotel corridor. She is in a completely different dress – red!

On the way to Texas, Grace mentions they will be in "Laredo" in the morning. But when the coach pulls up at the end of their journey, the driver says "El Paso, folks. Everybody out."

RETURN TO DEVIL'S HOLE
Big Jim was told that Hamilton hit his head on the wall when he fell. He was standing in an open doorway and fell backwards.

When Heyes hits Jim, Jim is holding his glass of whisky. After Heyes has hit him, Heyes is holding the whisky and gives it back to Jim.

When Heyes first dumps a stack of money out of Clara's bag, it appears to be about an inch thick. By the end of the scene, it looks to be about half that.

In the bunkhouse scene, when Heyes tries to tell the gang that Jim is quitting, in the mid-shots Hamilton is wearing a jacket. In his close-ups, he isn't.

FISTFUL OF DIAMONDS
In the last shot, there should have been about thirty-one stones – ten sent to TF Ayers and twenty-one to salt the diamond field with, instead there are only about fifteen.

STAGECOACH SEVEN
Heyes's hair goes from messy to combed and back again.

Nine riders are on the hill ready to hold up the stage. Five of them are shown actually holding up the stage. Seven men ride off after the holdup. They are down to six after riding off to catch Heyes and Curry. Then, they are up to seven.

ROOT OF IT ALL
Heyes's and Curry's pants are soaking wet from being in the water, but when approached by bad guys minutes later, their pants are dry.

When Deputy Treadwell is hurrying to the saloon to gather a posse to chase our boys, he's fumbling around trying to put on his gunbelt, and the gun falls out. He goes into the saloon with the gun still lying in the street, but he comes out of the saloon with it in his holster.

The boys' guns – now you see them, now you don't.

When the stage is first held up, the robbers take their guns. But Heyes and Curry have guns when they catch up. When they're pacing out the map, neither one is wearing guns or gunbelts. When they're held up again, Simpson tells his gang to get their guns. Then, walking back, both are wearing gunbelts, but no guns. Then, at the train, they've got guns again.

Heyes has $1,500 of Leslie's money in his hand when the gang surprises them. Then he turns and raises his hands and the money is gone.

5TH VICTIM
There are colored Polaroids on Helen's dresser mirror.

When Heyes is shot, he flies off the left side of his horse, consistent with being hit on the right side. But when he is in bed, the bullet wound is on the left side of his forehead.

When Curry crawls out of pond, the camera moves around him 180 degrees and the shadow of the cameraman is over him.

JOURNEY FROM SAN JUAN
The table nearly tips when Heyes and Curry sit down with Blanche and Michelle.

When Curry escorts Michelle to her room, he puts his hand on her shoulder. In the next scene, filmed at a different angle, his hand is not on her shoulder

NEVER TRUST AN HONEST MAN
Harlingen's hair goes from being parted on left to the right and back to left again when he's talking to his son about the jewels.

LEGACY OF CHARLIE O'ROURKE
When talking to Charlie, Curry's hand is on the jailbars by his face, in the next shot his hand is down.

At the funeral, they wear string ties. They still have on ties when they are beaten up and when they dunk Harry. In the next scene in the saloon with Harry, the ties are missing. Then they go to Alice's room and Curry has his tie back on.

Charlie buried his treasure not too far from the Mexican border, but Alice had been looking at a map of Wyoming. When they get to the gold, however, it's in Joshua tree forest.

THE DAY THEY HANGED KID CURRY
Curry is leaning on right side of courtroom doorway, then on the left side.

JAILBREAK AT JUNCTION CITY
One bank robber wears little round glasses. Though his hands are tied behind his back, he raises both of them, pushes his glasses back up, then puts his hands back behind his back

SMILER WITH A GUN
Danny Bilson puts a glove on his left hand, then draws with his right.

The guys grew beards and mustaches while at the mine, but their hair did not grow.

During the rattlesnake scene, Heyes says, "Don't anybody move" his lips don't move.

THE POSSE THAT WOULDN'T QUIT
After shooting with the girls, Curry twirls his pistol before putting it back in his holster, but misses.

Bridget shoots all ten cans off the fence. When it's Curry's turn, he shoots six cans that have suddenly materialized on the fence.

The posse is made up of stock footage taken from other shows, a useful device as long as no one is recognizable. However, one shot clearly shows Nick and Heath Barkley of *The Big Valley* leading the chase.

SOMETHING TO GET HUNG ABOUT
Kid Curry enters the hotel after the fight with a dirty shirt. Minutes later, he's wearing the same shirt, but it's clean.

The sound man makes a brief appearance after the fight scene.

When Heyes goes riding off to see Sarah, a cowboy in a vest rides by. An instant later, Heyes has galloped out of sight, the scene switches to the saloon and the same slouching cowboy rides by.

SIX STRANGERS AT APACHE SPRINGS
Heyes wears no hat after the first Indian chase, then the hat appears as they ride into Apache Springs.

Sr. Grace appears behind Fielding *and* behind Mrs. Fielding in the scene at dinner. She is continually polishing the same glass in every scene no matter which angle the camera shows.

In the saloon when chairs and glasses are flying through the air, Curry is suddenly wearing his first season hat.

NIGHT OF THE RED DOG
When Heyes and Curry are panning for gold dust, a hand attached to naked arm and shoulder is seen fingering the dust, but both Heyes and Curry have shirts on.

THE REFORMATION OF HARRY BRISCOE
When Harry comes into their camp with Sam to rob Molly of the $30,000, they show her getting up. She uses her hands to throw the blanket aside and push herself off the ground, but when Harry tells her to tie the boys up, she says "I can't, I'm the one tied up." She raises her hands and they're tied.

DREADFUL SORRY, CLEMENTINE
When Heyes and Curry meet Clem, Heyes's hat is on correctly. After he hugs Clem, his hat falls off. Peter puts his hat on back to front, but carries on with the scene as he calmly takes his hat off, looks at it and places it back on correctly.

SHOOTOUT AT DIABLO STATION
When leaving the cabin to raise the flag, Hayfoot tucks it under his right arm, immediately he steps out through the door and the flag is under his left arm.

How did Curry get in the little hidey-hole with four gunheads in the cabin? All were asleep? Curry can be so quiet? The gang had to pry it open!

Hayfoot's cabin at night is not same as it is during the day; it's two completely different sets.

THE MAN WHO BROKE THE BANK AT RED GAP
Wouldn't Powers have smelled the burned-out candle that the boys used to find their way around his darkened study?

The posse coming to the granary is stock film shot in the daytime, but it's supposed to be 10 p.m.

THE LONG CHASE
The stagecoach doesn't raise any dust with four horses, but the posse creates so much it can be seen for a half mile.

THE CLEMENTINE INGREDIENT
Heyes and Curry each have three different horses while riding to Clem's house.

MCGUFFIN
Curry and Heyes are on the same horses after a fifty-mile train ride.

ONLY THREE TO A BED
For the final confrontation with Tisdale, Heyes leaves the house wearing his gun. When the camera shows him from behind, he's not wearing the gun, but when shown from the front again, the gunbelt's there.

APPENDIX C

TRIVIA

ACADEMY AWARD NOMINEES (* INDICATES WINNER)

JACK ALBERTSON	1969
DON AMECHE	*1985
ANNE ARCHER	1987
WALTER BRENNAN	*1936, *1938, *1940, 1941
BRODERICK CRAWFORD	*1949
SALLY FIELD	*1979, *1984
LOU GOSSETT, JR.	*1982
JOAN HACKETT	1981
BURL IVES	*1958
DEAN JAGGER	*1949
SAM JAFFE	1950
KATY JURADO	1954
SHIRLEY KNIGHT	1960, 1962
ARTHUR O'CONNELL	1955, 1959
ANN SOTHERN	1987
CHILL WILLS	1960

EMMY NOMINEES (* INDICATES WINNER)

ACTORS

JACK ALBERTSON	1975*(two categories, won one), 1976*, 1977, 1982
NOAH BEERY	1977, 1980
SORRELL BOOKE	1964
BARBARA BOSSON	1981, 1982, 1983, 1984, 1985, 1996
WALTER BRENNAN	1959
JOSEPH CAMPANELLA	1968
J.D. CANNON	1975
CONLAN CARTER	1964

Actors (Continued)

Jack Cassidy	1968, 1971
Michael Conrad	1981*, 1982*, 1983, 1984
Wally Cox	1953, 1954
Bradford Dillman	1963
Tom Ewell	1977
Sally Field	1977*, 1995, 2000, 2001*, 2003
Dave Garroway	1956 (two categories)
Will Geer	1973, 1974, 1975*, 1976, 1977, 1978 (three categories)
Louis Gossett, Jr.	1977*, 1978, 1979, 1981, 1984, 1987, 1997
Joan Hackett	1962
Diana Hyland	1963, 1977*
Sam Jaffe	1962
Dean Jagger	1964, 1965
Shirley Knight	1981, 1988*, 1989, 1990, 1992, 1995*(two categories, won both)
Michele Lee	1982
Ida Lupino	1957, 1958, 1959
Juliet Mills	1975*
Robert Morse	1969, 1993*
Diana Muldaur	1990, 1991
Jeanette Nolan	1964, 1966, 1974, 1978
Sheree North	1976, 1980
Susan Oliver	1977
Pernell Roberts	1981
Craig Stevens	1959
Larry Storch	1967
Vaughn Taylor	1952, 1953
William Windom	1970*
Keenan Wynn	1978

Directors

Edward M. Abroms	1970*(film editing), 1972*(film editing), 1973,
Bruce Bilson	1968*
Harry Falk	1975
Alexander Singer	1972*

Writers/Producers

Juanita Bartlett	1979, 1980
Gloryette Clark	1972 (film editing)
Roy Huggins	1958, 1959*, 1968, 1977
Glen A. Larson	1974, 1975, 1978
David Moessinger	1981, 1983

WRITERS/PRODUCERS (CONTINUED)

RICHARD MORRIS	1957
Frank Price	1996
Gene Roddenberry	1967, 1968
B.W. Sandefur	1978
Jo Swerling, Jr.	1977, 1989

MISCELLANEOUS TRIVIA

Number of Gormans – **4**

Number of Harrys – **4**

Number of Tommys – **2**

Numbers in titles – Six Strangers at Apache Springs, Stagecoach Seven, The Girl in Boxcar #3; 5th Victim; How to Rob a Bank in One Hard Lesson; Twenty-One Days to Tenstrike; The Ten Days That Shook Kid Curry; Only Three to a Bed

Number of coin tosses – **7**

Number of times either Heyes or Curry is in jail – **13**

Number of times Red Rock used as town – **5**

Number of times Curry called on to demonstrate fast draw – **22**

Number of times Heyes called on to demonstrate silver tongue – **15**

Number of episodes in which Heyes and Curry play cards – **30**

Number of episodes featuring a cattle drive – **7**

Bankers – Blodgett, Blake, Sterling, Binford, Powers

The name "Hanley" is used for the judge in "Jailbreak at Junction City" and for the horse trainer in "Miracle at Santa Marta."

CLOTHES CARRIED IN THE "MAGIC SADDLEBAGS"

CURRY – brown hat, leather coat with sheepskin collar, tan jacket, leather coat with no collar, white shirt, royal blue shirt, brown shirt, red shirt, light blue shirt, black or navy blue shirt, dark red shirt, red longjohns, white henley, brownish-red henley, green pants, jeans, bandanna, brown leather vest, gray leather vest, gray suit and derby

HEYES – black hat, brown corduroy jacket, gray jacket with black collar, brown suede vest, tan shirt, black shirt, navy blue shirt, white shirt, tan shirt, medium blue shirt, royal blue shirt, blue shirt with white cuffs white longjohns, gray henley, white henley, tan pants, string tie, gray vest, black vest, lapel vest, leather vest, fringed chaps, suspenders, blue or black bandanna, brown suit and derby

MONEY

Heyes and Curry were always interested in money, and often had their hands on a substantial amount, yet somehow never managed to come out ahead. Over the course of the series, the total cash the boys had on hand was $38,178.63. The total amount they were promised by various employers was $464,900. The amount they were actually paid by these employers over the course of the series was $215,967. But in the end, the amount the boys were able to keep was only $23,379.90.

APPENDIX D

MERCHANDISE

Derived from *Alias Smith and Jones:*

Brian Fox novels:

Cabin Fever
Apache Gold
Dead Ringer
Dragooned
Trick Shot
Outlaw Trail

Cigar bands, UK annuals, and trading stamps.

APPENDIX E

TIME SLOTS

SEASON ONE:	ABC THURSDAY 7:30-8:30 P.M. BBC2 – MONDAY 8:00-8:50 P.M.
SEASON TWO:	ABC THURSDAY 8:00-9:00 P.M.
SEASON THREE:	ABC SATURDAY 8:00-9:00 P.M.

APPENDIX F

ROY'S RULES FOR THE WRITERS

Alias Smith and Jones did not have a formal "bible," that is, a written list of character traits and backstory used by the writers to maintain consistency in characterization. But that doesn't mean there wasn't one. The show's bible did exist, but only in the head of Roy Huggins, and he would share his vision of the characters with the writers as he deemed it necessary. Below are the rules for writing about Heyes and Curry as gleaned from story conference notes.

Our boys are trying to build up a record for the Governor. . . .This whole area should be given a reality in the series. Then someday we could build a story around meeting the Governor. *The Root of It All – 11/19/70*

Note: our boys are facing the possibility of being put away as Kid Curry and Hannibal Heyes – which *is* life . . . if it isn't the gallows. *The Root of It All – 11/19/70*

Reward: there should be ten thousand dollars on the head of each one of our boys. Anyone who turns them both in will thus collect twenty grand. *The Root of It All – 11/19/70*

Note: we never refer to them as the Hole-in-the-Wall gang. In the series we will call them the Curry-Heyes gang. *Wrong Train to Brimstone – 11/23/70*

Our boys handle themselves well . . . being Western heroes. They're skilled with guns and they're tough – although they don't look tough. *The McCreedy Bust – 11/24/70*

They tell McCreedy they'll think it over and let him know . . . our boys are too smart to accept any deal like that on face value. They've been around too long and have been crooked too many years to take anything on face value. They are very skeptical, sardonic, cynical guys – although they don't look it. *The McCreedy Bust – 11/24/70*

They've agreed that Heyes will do the poker playing because he's the smart one. Note: part of the humor of this series is that Heyes isn't always the smart one. Curry comes up now and then with better ideas — but our boys always agree that Heyes is the intelligent one. *The McCreedy Bust* – 11/24/70

Note: our boys now have ten thousand dollars apiece and they're going to South America, where they can't be extradited and where they can lie low until their year is up. Then they'll come back. In the meantime, they can live a great life. *The McCreedy Bust* – 11/24/70

Our boys even think about doing something about Sam Finrock — but one of the things they have to watch out for is trouble. They're not really free to be as violent as they might like to be. They might like to take Finrock and tie him up and threaten to kill him if he doesn't tell them — but they don't. *Exit from Wickenburg* – 11/25/70

When our boys first became outlaws, they rode with a guy named Tom Plummer. Almost one of the first robberies our boys were ever in on, they hit a train and got away with thirty thousand dollars . . . Our two boys were there with him that day, a part of that gang. Ten other guys were also a part of that gang – and they're still out there somewhere. *Exit from Wickenburg* – 11/25/70

Our boys tell Plummer that he must not remember them very well. They don't kill people. They never have, and they don't expect to in the future – and they're not going to kill him. *Exit from Wickenburg* – 11/25/70

Heyes and Curry didn't share misspent youths for nothing. They have come prepared. *The McCreedy Bust* – 11/29/70

New approach to the scene: Kid Curry doesn't know Jim Plummer. This all happened nine or ten years ago, before Heyes met the Kid. Heyes was a member of Jim Plummer's gang – and Plummer recognizes him. The Kid never did have to leave town, it was only Heyes . . . but they knew if they wanted to get rid of Heyes, they had to get rid of the Kid too. *Exit from Wickenburg* – 12/3/70

Heyes is in his early thirties – and this all happened when he first started ten years ago. This is the first gang he ever rode with. *Exit from Wickenburg* – 12/3/70

They don't *want* to go back to train robbery. They kind of like this life – it's kind of challenging to be honest . . . and it's also getting very tough *not* to be. They figured out that the time they spent planning a robbery, running from the posse and everything, they made more money doing an honest job — when you put it on a day labor basis. Besides, that Devil's Gorge wasn't exactly the greatest place in the world to live. *A Fistful of Diamonds* – 12/8/70

The Kid and Heyes are still debating, still wondering what to do . . . because they've got that money, and they could leave, go to South America, and they wouldn't have to worry about being nabbed and some other guy blaming a murder on them, etc. But our boys are concerned, too, because it's a violation of their word to the Governor and to Lom. Besides, who wants to live in South America for the rest of his life? This is where they were born – and this is where they want to live. (This is a very important instinct in people, not wanting to be exiled.) *A Fistful of Diamonds – 12/8/70*

Amnesty: our boys haven't got any kind of amnesty. They have been told that if they behave themselves, and really stay out of trouble – stop robbing trains and banks – in a year or so the Governor will consider the possibility of giving them amnesty. Our boys haven't got amnesty partially – they haven't got it at all. All they have is a promise. *A Fistful of Diamonds – 12/21/70*

Neither man is violent. Curry is good with a gun but he's not going to stick it in a guy's face and threaten to kill him if he doesn't tell the truth. *A Fistful of Diamonds – 12/21/70*

Note: we should have no ambiguity about whether our boys are going straight. They are *not* crooks, and they wouldn't be thinking of taking off with that money. *A Fistful of Diamonds – 12/21/70*

General problem: the character of our two boys. In their own rough way, they should be a lot more sophisticated than they are in the present draft. They are more worldly. Curry is just as knowing as Heyes. The writer should go through the script and upgrade the level of sophistication. Our boys should be sharper, smoother. When they're with women, they're much more apt to say things like Cary Grant than like John Wayne. *Journey from San Juan – 12/22/70*

Where money is concerned, Curry doesn't care how it comes. *Journey from San Juan – 12/22/70*

Actually [Michelle] heard all about them wherever they went in the West. Once they got across the Mississippi, people heard all about Heyes and Curry. *Journey from San Juan – 12/22/70*

Curry's first entrance into it is a little angry, because he really doesn't like Downs. But Curry should not be the chip-on-the-shoulder guy. *Stagecoach Seven – 1/7/71*

Note: our boys must *not* get the money, because if they ever got a big sum they would leave the country. They'd go to South America. They can never come out ahead – but they can drive big bargains. *Never Trust an Honest Man – 1/25/71*

Heyes and Curry . . . still have a lot of larceny, self-centered instinct for survival, etc. *Stagecoach Seven* – 2/1/71

He uses the guy as his partner – because Heyes always works with a partner. *How to Rob A Bank in One Hard Lesson* – 4/1/71

Curry – although he's confident – never faces a situation like this (a shootout) with boredom or smiling contempt, because he could come up against someone someday who is better than he is. So he's looking, at the least, neutral, and even possibly worried. *Jailbreak at Junction City* – 5/11/71

They're not free to go around telling people they've been promised an amnesty. They have, in fact, done so. *Jailbreak at Junction City* – 5/11/71

Lom says there's nobody he can think of who could open a Pierce & Hamilton 1878 Model Safe just by turning the dials – except Heyes. Heyes says, "*I can't even do that. I tried it once in the bank in Red Rock and I couldn't do it!*" *Everything Else You Can Steal* – 5/11/71

Note: . . . [Heyes] doesn't think there's anybody who can open a Pierce & Hamilton 1878 Model Safe just by listening. The safe is too good for that. The tumblers are silent. *Everything Else You Can Steal* – 5/11/71

Hannibal Heyes and Kid Curry have been bank robbers, train robbers, and all the rest of it for some time . . . . It's very difficult to do what they used to do – which was without ever having to kill anybody. They had never even shot anybody . . . . Important note: our boys are wanted only in *one* state – Wyoming. *Everything Else You Can Steal* – 5/13/71

Heyes knows how to open [a Pierce & Hamilton 1878 Model Safe.] *Everything Else You Can Steal* – 5/13/71

Heyes is the brain. Curry is cooler, and he's very fast with a gun. He is also more of a ladies' man. *Everything Else You Can Steal* – 5/13/71

Later the *modus operandi* turns out to be very important. Heyes invented this method of robbing a safe. *How to Rob A Bank in One Hard Lesson* – 5/14/71

Our boys are not instant Good Samaritans. They are very reluctant to do anybody a good turn. *The Bounty Hunter* – 6/1/71

Note: Heyes and Curry have no prejudice. They were both born and raised in Kansas – and Heyes should make a point of that. *The Bounty Hunter* – 6/1/71

Note: our boys do any Good Samaritan deed shamefacedly. *The Bounty Hunter –
6/1/71*

Neither Heyes nor Curry have really used rifles very much in their lives. *The Posse
That Wouldn't Quit – 6/1/71*

They're not wanted on any capital offense. They're just wanted for robbery and
they'll get about twenty years. *The Posse That Wouldn't Quit – 6/1/71*

"By the way, young fellow," the Judge says [to Curry], "what states are you wanted in?"
"Just in Wyoming, Your Honor." *The Posse That Wouldn't Quit – 6/1/71*

Note: our boys have really had very little contact with Indians. They're not very
sharp about Indians and Indian attitudes. They don't know how to talk to the
Indians, because neither of our boys speaks very good Spanish. They have picked
up a little, but not very much. *Six Strangers at Apache Springs – 6/3/71*

At its most ordinary, our dialogue is "smart aleck" – and when it isn't that, it's
oblique and witty. (Roy is using this term kiddingly. It really isn't "smart aleck"
he's looking for – it's an oblique and witty view of life, that comes out in the
dialogue of Heyes and Curry.) *The Posse That Wouldn't Quit – 7/7/71*

It is *Curry* who is good with a gun, not Heyes. *The Posse That Wouldn't Quit – 7/7/71*

Curry and Heyes have a relationship wherein they needle each other. *The Posse
That Wouldn't Quit – 7/7/71*

[Drought] is a normal condition in this area, and Heyes knows it. He's a
Westerner. *The Posse That Wouldn't Quit – 7/7/71*

There are no pictures of Heyes and Curry. No one knows what they look like,
and that's why they're able to wander around the way they do. *The Posse That
Wouldn't Quit – 7/7/71*

The Chiricahuas . . . had a tradition of bravery and of independence – which
Heyes could know about. *Six Strangers at Apache Springs – 7/20/71*

"We're from Kansas," . . . Now we learn that our boys are orphans. Their families
lived right next to each other in Kansas, and they grew up together. There were
southern raiders in Kansas during the Civil War. They tell Sister Julia they went
to church before they were ten years old, and their folks had farms next to each
other. Their farms were raided – and both Heyes and Curry were suddenly
orphans. They grew up in what was practically a reform school – a school for kids

who didn't have any parents. They ran away when they were fifteen. After that, they didn't have much time for church. *The Reformation of Harry Briscoe – 7/20/71*

"We almost never take a chance on anything noble," Curry says. *The Reformation of Harry Briscoe – 7/20/71*

"I am Irish," Heyes says.
"No, you're not," she says. "Are you a Catholic?"
"No."
"Then you're not Irish," Daisy says.
"Well, my grandparents came from Belfast," Heyes says. *The Reformation of Harry Briscoe – 7/20/71*

Our boys are equals. Curry does not always defer to Heyes. Curry is just as sharp as Heyes – but he just doesn't scheme as thoroughly as Heyes. He is not as devious as Heyes. Heyes is an expert in figuring out how to rob a bank or how to handle a card cheat. Curry is a specialist in a fast draw. *The Reformation of Harry Briscoe – 8/6/71*

Both of our boys have a degree of sophistication. *The Reformation of Harry Briscoe – 8/6/71*

Our boys never do anything altruistic. *The Reformation of Harry Briscoe – 8/6/71*

"Do you have any idea what it's like to be born to two immigrant Irish Catholics in 1860 in the United States?" Our boys don't know what it's like. *The Reformation of Harry Briscoe – 8/6/71*

Our boys should not sound preachy, because they're not. They're pragmatic. They stopped robbing because it stopped working, not because they got religion. *The Reformation of Harry Briscoe – 8/6/71*

(Re: giving Harry another chance) Even this decision comes out of their essential selfishness. *The Reformation of Harry Briscoe – 8/6/71*

Curry and Heyes are equals in intelligence. Curry is as sensitive as Heyes. *Something to Get Hung About – 8/12/71*

Our boys have had a plan: if they ever got hold of a real hunk of money, they would go to South America. Heyes and Curry have planned this some time ago. *Night of the Red Dog – 8/18/71*

Curry intuitively knows that Heyes wouldn't have said what he said, if he didn't have something in mind. They have a rapport and understanding of each other. *Shootout at Diablo Station – 8/24/71*

"I was hoping it would just make us feel a little better. But I guess maybe it also had to do with the fact that we lost our folks when we were only eleven." *The Men That Corrupted Hadleyburg – 10/18/71*

There is a ten thousand dollars reward on each of our boys. *The Man Who Broke the Bank at Red Gap – 10/28/71*

"Heyes, I don't *want* to live in Australia," Curry says. "This is where I was born and where I've lived all my life – I want to keep *on* living here!" *The Man Who Broke the Bank at Red Gap – 10/28/71*

The writer should find ways to get some of our boys' special kind of humor into the script. The relationship between Heyes and Curry is important in our series. They needle each other, have fun with each other. *The Man Who Broke the Bank at Red Gap – 10/28/71*

The Devil's Hole gang . . . is a gang that used to be led by Hannibal Heyes and Kid Curry before they went straight. The two chief characters in the gang are Wheat and Kyle. They are very friendly toward Heyes and Curry because our boys used to be their leaders. Heyes and Curry do not have their amnesty yet. If they're caught, they're in jail. The Governor cannot, for political reasons, give them an amnesty now because they're too hot. But he has said to our boys – through Lom Trevors, a Sheriff friend of theirs – if they can stay out of trouble for a year or two, he'll give them an amnesty because then it will be politically possible. *The Biggest Game in the West – 10/29/71*

Note: Our boys never refer to themselves as Smith and Jones. Our boys always refer to each other as Thaddeus and Joshua. *What's in It for Mia? – 11/29/71*

Poker game: Heyes would never say he'd only stay in the game as long as his luck holds. Heyes does not believe in luck. *Which Way to the OK Corral? – 12/8/71*

Our boys had a plan to go to San Francisco, get on a boat and go to Australia – where they could live for a long time on eighteen or nineteen thousand dollars, long enough to come back and get their amnesty. They decided they couldn't go to South America because they'd be spotted. But they might be able to blend in, down in Australia. *Don't Get Mad, Get Even – 12/16/71*

Curry, who has never tasted caviar before, suffers terribly when he tastes it. *Don't Get Mad, Get Even – 12/16/71*

The meeting with Clem should be restaged with more warmth. They love each other. *Bad Night in Big Butte – 1/19/72*

We rarely have a scene in our series that isn't told from their point-of-view. Sometimes something is going on and they're not present, but we should avoid this if possible. Almost every scene should be written either from their point-of-view or they're standing right outside, where they might even be able to almost hear what's going on inside. *Bad Night in Big Butte – 10/12/71*

There is this mutual welcome – with each of our boys alone, it would be obviously a lover's embrace. *The Clementine Ingredient – 4/26/72*

Between the Union Pacific and a couple of very big banks and the Wyoming Stockgrowers Association, the numbers of rewards being offered amount to about ten thousand dollars on each of them. They are trying to stay out of the hands of the law and they wander around trying to make a living. Their main goal is to accumulate a big enough hunk of money so they can get out of the country – but they never manage to get that much money. They want to get that money legitimately – and playing poker is legitimate. *Only Three to a Bed – 5/2/72*

Neither one of our boys is sentimental. Curry is a little more conceited about women. Heyes is shrewder, maybe even smarter, maybe a little more sensitive. *Only Three to a Bed – 5/2/72*

We mustn't over-emphasize this difference between Heyes and Curry. . . .It implies that Curry is the second banana and Heyes is in command at all times – which I don't want to do in the series. It isn't necessarily so that it's always Curry who has to go and check to see that everything's safe. Heyes should do it as often as Curry. The difference between them is that Curry shoots faster and more accurately – but they don't have a division of labor. *Witness to a Lynching – 5/30/72*

We should not give Curry lines like "What makes you think that?" and "What now?" He's not really that stupid and he doesn't have to ask Heyes the answer to everything. This is an over-all point in our series. Curry is really as smart as Heyes. He's just not as confident that he's that smart. *Witness to a Lynching – 5/30/72*

Our boys are quite outspoken. *The Strange Fate of Conrad Meyer Zulick – 6/1/72*

Note: we should have *ironic* conflict between Heyes and Curry. *The Strange Fate of Conrad Meyer Zulick – 7/25/72*

Curry should never be petulant. *The Strange Fate of Conrad Meyer Zulick – 7/25/72*

Our boys *could* be briefly stupefied — but they're not going to be so dumb that they remain stupefied for two pages. They're Western heroes, and they don't remain stupefied for five minutes. Maybe fifteen seconds. *The Strange Fate of Conrad Meyer Zulick — 7/25/72*

BIBLIOGRAPHY

BOOKS

Broughton, Irv. "Roy Huggins," in *Producers on Producing: The Making of Film and Television*. Jefferson, NC: McFarland & Co., 1986.

Brown, Les. *Televi$ion: The Business behind the Box*. New York: Harcourt Brace Jovanovich, Inc., 1971.

Burns, David D., MD. *Feeling Good*. New York: Avon Books, 1999.

Buscombe, Edward, ed. *The BFI Companion to the Western*. New York: Atheneum, 1988.

Calder, Jennie. *There Must Be a Lone Ranger – The American West in Film and in Reality*. New York: Taplinger Publishing Co.,1974.

Castleman, Harry and Walter J. Podrazik. *Watching TV: Four Decades of American Television*. New York: McGraw-Hill, 1982.

Eldridge, Benjamin P. and William B. Watts. *Our Rival the Rascal: A Faithful Portrayal of the Conflict between Criminals of This Age and the Defenders of Society – The Police*. Boston, MA: Pemberton Publishing Company, 1897.

George-Warren Holly. *Cowboy: How Hollywood invented the Wild West*. Pleasantville, NY: Reader's Digest, 2002.

Goldman, William. *Adventures in the Screen Trade*. New York: Warner Books, 1983, paperback 1984.

Greenfield, Jeff. *Television – The First Fifty Years*. New York: Harry N. Abrams, Inc., 1977.

The Gunfighters. Alexandria, VA: Time Life Books, 1974.

Heil, Douglas. *Prime-Time Authorship: Works About and By Three TV Dramatists.* Syracuse: Syracuse University Press, 2002.

Horan, James D. and Paul Sann. *Pictorial History of the Wild West.* New York: Crown Publishers, 1954.

Huggins, Roy. *25 Years Down the Tube.* Unpublished biography.

Marc, David and Robert J. Thompson. *Prime Time, Prime Movers.* Syracuse, NY: Syracuse University Press, 1992.

MacDonald, Fred J. *Who Shot the Sheriff?* New York: Praeger, 1987.

McLoughlin, Denis. *Wild and Woolly. An Encyclopedia of the Old West.* Garden City: Doubleday, 1975.

Metz, Leon Claire. *The Shooters.* New York: Berkley Books, 1976.

Pointer, Larry. *In Search of Butch Cassidy.* Norman, OK: Univ. of OK Press, 1977.

Roberts, Gary L. "The Search For Order On The Last Frontier," in *With Badges & Bullets: Lawmen & Outlaws in the Old West,* eds. Richard W. Etulain, Glenda Riley. Golden, CO: Fulcrum Publishing, 1999.

Robertson, Ed. Maverick: *Legend of the West.* Beverly Hill, CA: Pomegranate Press, 1994.

Rosa, Joseph G., ed. *The West.* New York: Smithmark Publishers, 1994.

Schulman, Bruce J. *The Seventies.* New York: The Free Press, 2001.

Topping, Gary. "Vigilantism with Honor," in *With Badges & Bullets: Lawmen & Outlaws In The Old West,* eds. Richard W. Etulain, Glenda Riley. Golden, CO: Fulcrum Publishing, 1999.

Twain, Mark. *Life on the Mississippi.* Boston: James R. Osgood & Co., 1883.

Twain, Mark. *The Tragedy of Pudd'nhead Wilson.* American Publishing Co., 1897.

Weil, Joseph R. as told to WT Brannon, *"Yellow Kid" Weil: The Autobiography of America's Master Swindler.* Chicago: Ziff-Davis Publishing Co., 1948.

ARTICLES

Albert, Dora. "Peter Deuel: We're In Love–But We're Not Getting Married!" *TV Picture Life*, Jun 1967.

Amedeo, Marcho. "The Fan Letters I Answer First!" *Movieland and TV Time*, Jun 1971.

"An Audience Research Report." BBC. Aug 17, 1971.

Balling, Fredda Dudley. "Deuel With Death," *Movie World.* Mar 1967.

BBC TV Viewing Barometer. Week 16. Apr 19, 1971.

"Bernhardt, Sarah," "Paganini, Nicolo." *Microsoft ® Encarta ® 98 Encyclopedia.* © 1993-1997 Microsoft Corporation.

Bresler, Fenton. "Why Peter Duel blew His Brains Out," *Pageant,* Jan 1975.

Cox, Jack. "Who *Were* Those Guys?" *Denver Post*, Sept 12, 1999: 1F.

Crenshaw, James. "Scoop! Cops arrest Pete Duel on Three Felony Charges." *TV Radio Mirror,* Aug 1971.

Dana, Richard. "Pete Duel was arrested! Charged with Drunken Hit-and-run Driving." *Motion Picture Magazine,* Aug 1971.

"Don't Shoot," Superstar, Apr 1973.

"From The Private Pasts of Pete & Ben." *Teen Life,* Jan 1972.

Gardella, Kay. "Pete's Not Convinced He's Lucky," *Sunday News,* Apr 25, 1971: S20

Gladman, Jerry. "After years of lucking out, Murphy wins a lottery," *Sunday Sun Television Magazine* (Toronto, Canada), Nov 20, 1983.

"Grandma Curry Comes to Town...Ooops, It's Walter Brennan," *TV Guide,* Sept 4, 1971.

Green, Tom. "Filming New Series Hectic," *Rochester Democrat and Chronicle,* Jan 17, 1971.

Green, Tom. "'Smith and Jones' Nothing Phoney about It," *Rochester Democrat and Chronicle TV tab,* Jun 27, 1971.

Gremillion, Jeff. "Back in the Saddle Again," TV Guide, May 24, 2003: 4.

Hyslop, Stephen G. "The Puritans," *The History Channel Magazine,* May/June 2004: 60-64.

"Latest Nielsen Scores Could Give CBS Pause on Rural Housecleaning," *Variety,* Mar 10, 1971.

Larkin, Lou. "Peter Deuel: He Kisses The Girls And Makes Them Cry," *Modern Screen,* March, 1967.

"The Long Chase" review, *Daily Variety,* Sep 20, 1972.

Lord, Rosemary. "I'm a Highly-Paid Bum, I got just what I wanted . . .," 19, Oct, 1975.

Marshall, Brenda. "Face In The Mirror. Pete Deuel: Gidget's Brotherly Brother-in-law," *TV Radio Mirror,* May 1966.

McLellan, Dennis. "R. Huggins, 87; Created 'Maverick,' 'Fugitive.'" *Los Angeles Times,* Apr 6, 2002.

Penton, Edgar. "Zany is the word for Smith and Jones," *Muskegon Chronicle,* May 9, 1971.

"Peter Deuel 'I Have To Be The Best' So What Else Would You Expect With Parents Like These?" *Motion Picture,* Aug 1967.

Peterson, Bettelou, "He Was Headed For The Top," *Boston Globe TV Week,* Feb 3-9, 1980.

Richman, Lois. "Shooting star of the month: Ben Murphy," *Screen Stars,* May 1971.

"Round 2 for ABC's 'Alias Smith and Jones,'" *Los Angeles Herald-Examiner,* Aug. 7, 1971.

Scott, Brooke. "Tormented Peter Duel Commits Suicide: Was He Only Trying To Grab Some Peace?" *TV Radio Talk,* Apr 1972.

Shain, Percy, "He looks just like..." *Boston Globe TV Week,* Mar 7, 1971.

Shain, Percy. "He Prefers Duel To Deuel," *Boston Globe TV Week,* Feb 14, 1971.

Smith, Cecil. "Huggins: A Man for Two Seasons, Western and Now," *Los Angeles Times TV Times,* Jul 4, 1971.

Smith, Cecil. "Smith and Jones, Just Highwaymen," *Los Angeles Times,* Jan. 4, 1971.

Stone, Judy, "He's Alias Smith or Alias Jones," *TV Guide,* May 15, 1971: 28-32.

Swisher, Viola Hegyi. "Hollywood's Professional Training Ground," *After Dark,* Nov 1970.

Townsend, Morris. "Peter Duel: He Cared Too Much To Live..." *Silver Screen,* Apr 1972.

Walker, John. "Pete Closes Ranks with Bobby, David, and Donny," *Chicago Tribune TV Week,* Oct 16, 1971.

Wedner, Diane. "Driven up the wall," *Los Angeles Times,* Feb 16, 2003, 1K.

World Tennis, n.p. Oct. 1985.

Yergin, Dan. "If They Stay out of Trouble!" *Radio Times,* Apr 22, 1971.

INTERVIEWS

LANE BRADBURY	FEB 20, 2003
GLORYETTE CLARK	JUN 19, 2004
KIM DARBY	APR 28, 2004
ROGER DAVIS	FEB 22, 2003, APR 24, 2004
DENNIS FIMPLE	AUG 4, 2002
EARL HOLLIMAN	MAR 12, 2003
ROY HUGGINS	MAY 23, 2001
JACK JOBES	MAY 10, 2004
MONTY LAIRD	AUG 5, 2002
GLEN LARSON	FEB 19, 2003, APR 29, 2004
BEN MURPHY	AUG 7, 2002, FEB 22, 2003, APR 25, 2004
FRANK PRICE	FEB 25, 2003, APR 26, 2004
ALEX SINGER	FEB 17, 2003, APR 21, 2004, APR 27, 2004
JO SWERLING, JR.	AUG 8, 2002, APR 23, 2004

OFFICIAL REPORTS

Case Report, Peter Deuel. County of Los Angeles, Dept. of Chief Medical Examiner – Coroner

Medical Report, Case No. 71-13812, Peter Deuel, 12-31-71. County of Los Angeles, Dept. of Chief Medical Examiner – Coroner

Petition for Probate of will. Peter Ellstrom Deuel, aka Pete Duel. Case No. P 579,950.

PRODUCTION NOTES AND SCRIPTS

"21 Days to Tenstrike." Prod. #34235. Story notes Oct 14, 1971, note 24.

"Bad Night in Big Butte." Prod. #34201. Undated script, p. 35; Rewrite notes Oct 12, 1971, note 20.

"The Bounty Hunter" Prod. #34217. Story notes Jun 1, 1971.

"Bushwhack!" Prod. #35501. First Draft May 17, 1972, p.32; Rewrite Notes May 19, 1972, notes 8, 10, 24, 31.

"The Day The Amnesty Came Through," Prod. #35511. Story notes Jul 28, 1972, notes 2, 9. 24; Script Aug 30, 1972, pp. 17, 25-6; Rewrite notes Sep 5, 1972, note 18; Script Sep 26, 1972, pp. 3, 18.

"The Day They Hanged Kid Curry." Prod. #34216. Rewrite notes May 19, 1971, note 3.

"Don't Get Mad, Get Even." Prod. #34242. Story notes Dec 16, 1971, notes 1, 6, 8, 11; Script Jan 24, 1972, p 9; Script Jan 18, 1972, p. 37.

"Everything Else You Can Steal." Prod. #34212. Story notes May 11, 1971, note 2; Addenda to original story May 13, 1971, notes 2, 3, 23, 26, 28; First draft Jun 4, 1971.

"Exit From Wickenburg," Prod. #32616. Rewrite notes Dec 3, 1970, note 11.

"The 5th Victim," Prod. #32625. Story conference Jan 12, 1971, note 12, 35; Re-write notes Feb 11, 1971, note 29.

"A Fistful of Diamonds," Prod. #32619. First draft Dec 18, 1970, p. 22; Rewrite notes Dec 21, 1970, note 9; Rewrite notes Addenda Dec 22, 1970, note 2.
"The Great Shell Game," Prod. #32621. Script Jan 19, 1971, p. 53.

"High Lonesome Country." Prod. #35503. Story notes Apr 21, 1972, note 20; Story notes Apr 18, 1972, note 5; Script Oct 11, 1972, sc. 136.

"How To Change A $10 Bill." ("What's in it for Mia?") Prod. #34240. Rewrite Notes Nov 29, 1971, notes 2, 10.

"The Imperfect Crime." ("How to Rob a Bank in One Hard Lesson"). Prod. #34213. Story Conference May 14, 1971.

"Jailbreak at Junction City." Prod. #34211. Story notes May 11, 1971, notes 9, 14; Script Jun 14, 1971, p. 1; Script Jun 21, 1971, p. 11;

"Journey from San Juan," Prod. #32615. Story conference Dec 2, 1970, note 40; First draft Dec 17, 1970, p.16.

"The Kidnap Story." ("The Ten Days Shook Kid Curry") Prod. #35510. Story Notes Jun 1, 1972, notes 12, 17, 21.

"The Long Chase." Prod. #35508. Script May 10, 1972, p. 30; Script Jun 27, 1972, p. 2.

"The Man Who Broke the Bank at Red Gap." Prod. #34241. Story notes Oct 28, 1971, notes 19, 27; First draft. Nov 19, 1971, p.1; Script Dec 17, 1971, p.1.

"The Man Who Murdered Himself," Prod. #32622. Story conference Jan 7, 1971, note 39.

"The McCreedy Bust." Prod. #32614. Story Notes Nov 24, 1970; Script Nov 29, 1970.

"The McCreedy Bust: Going, Going, Gone," Prod. #34237. Script Nov 16, 1971, p. 40.

"The McCreedy Feud." Prod.#35506. Story Notes Apr 19, 1972, note 1; Story Notes in Teleplay Format May 3, 1972, pp. 2, 11, 23; First Draft Script May 31, 1972, p. 2.

"McGuffin," Prod. #35512. First draft Aug 23, 1972, page 24; Script Aug 31, 1972, Sc. 31, 199.

"Miracle at Santa Marta." Prod. #34233. Story notes Sep 16, 1971.
"Only Three to a Bed." Prod. #35502. Story notes May 27, 1972, note 14.

The Posse That Wouldn't Quit." Prod. #34218. Story conference Jun 1, 1971, note 11; Rewrite notes Jul 7, 1971, notes 13, 19, 41; First draft Jul 6, 1971, p. 32.

"Reformation of Harry Briscoe." Prod. #34223. Story outline Jul 20, 1971, note 2; Rewrite notes Aug 6, 1971, note 9.

"Return Devil's Hole" Prod. #32617. Story Conference Jan 5, 1971.

"The Root of It All," Prod.#81438-F-32606. Rewrite notes, Nov 19, 1970, note 14; First draft script Nov 20, 1970, p. 21; Rewrite notes Nov 20, 1970, note 13; Rewrite notes Dec 28, 1970, note 8.

"Shootout at Diablo Station." Prod. #34224. Story notes Aug 24, 1971, note 26; Story notes addendum Aug 25, 1971.

"Six Strangers at Apache Springs." Prod. #43219. Story Notes Jun 3, 1971, notes 3, 6, 11; Rewrite notes June 28, 1971, note 10; Rewrite notes Jul 20, 1971, notes 23, 32.

"The Strange Fate of Conrad Meyer Zulick." Prod. #35509. Story Notes Jun 1, 1972, notes 7, 14.

"What Happened at the XST?" Prod. #35505. Story notes Apr 19, 1972, notes 1, 3, 25; Script Jul 3, 1972, sc. 4, 37; Script, Oct 23, 1972, sc. 5.

"Witness to a Lynching." Prod. #35504. Story notes April 24, 1972, notes 6, 42.

"Wrong Train to Brimstone." Prod. #32607. Rewrite notes Nov 23, 1970, note 18.

INDEX

Huggins, Roy: 8, 14, 22-3, 24, 25, 26, 27, 28, 29, 30, 51-3, 56, 57, 60, 61, 65, 70, 74, 75, 78, 79, 83, 85, 87, 88, 92, 93, 96, 97, 98, 101, 102, 103, 106, 107, 110, 111, 113, 114-9, 122, 126, 127, 134, 135, 136, 140, 141, 142, 145, 146, 147, 155-6, 158, 161,162, 163, 166, 167, 168, 169, 172, 173, 177, 178, 179, 182-3, 187, 188, 189, 193, 194, 197, 198, 203-4, 209, 214, 218, 219, 220, 223, 229, 232-3, 234, 235, 236, 246, 247, 252, 253, 254, 257, 258, 262-3, 268, 269, 270, 283, 287, 288, 292, 293, 298, 299, 300, 303, 304, 308, 309-10, 313, 314, 315, 319, 320, 321, 324, 325, 330, 331, 337, 341, 342, 346, 348, 349, 351, 352, 356, 357, 358-9, 360

Jaffe, Sam: 135, 184

"Jailbreak at Junction City": 61, 127, **142-7**, 331

James, John Thomas, See also Huggins, Roy: 25, 51, 110, 145, 166, 287

Jobes, Jack: 16, 17, 120, 233-4

"Journey from San Juan": 29, **98-102**

Laird, Monty: 89, 123, 126, 127, 147, 153, 226-7, 273, 274, 276, 277, 321, 347

Larson, Glen: 6, 8, 12, 13, 14, 15, 22, 23, 24, 29, 42, 47, 116, 134, 135, 136, 145, 183, 197, 203, 219, 229, 232, 234, 253, 268, 356, 358, 359

Lee, Michelle: 252, 268

"Legacy of Charlie O'Rourke": **107-11**, 112

"Long Chase, The": 271, **282-8**

"Man Who Broke the Bank at Red Gap, The": **215-20**

"Man Who Murdered Himself, The": **84-8**

Maverick: 8, 14, 23, 24, 25, 27, 30, 53, 98, 114, 115, 182, 183, 194, 204, 252, 254, 262, 269

"McCreedy Bust, The": 26, **49-53**, 218, 219, 299

"McCreedy Bust – Going, Going, Gone, The": 31, **210-15**, 225, 299

"McCreedy Feud, The": 107, **294-300**, 320

"McGuffin": 271, **331-6**

"Men That Corrupted Hadleyburg, The": **220-4**, 325

Minardos, Nico: 304

"Miracle at Santa Marta": **199-204**, 225, 304

Murphy, Ben: 15, 18, 19, 20-22, 42, 48, 60, 61, 69, 115, 120-1, 122, 123-6, 127, 148, 151, 156, 192-3, 209-10, 214, 228, 229, 234, 237, 238, 240, 246, 258, 273, 276, 277-9, 293, 294, 315, 321, 324, 347, 350, 351-2, 353-5, 356, 358, 360

Music: 7, 31, 75, 118, 141, 156-7, 224, 311, 327-8

"Never Trust an Honest Man": **103-7**

Nickerson, Jimmy: 126, 273, 347

"Night of the Red Dog": 35, **169-73**

"Only Three to a Bed": **342-7**

"Posse That Wouldn't Quit, The": **152-7**, 359

Price, Frank: 9, 13, 14, 18, 19, 22, 23, 24, 112, 113, 114, 229, 230, 231-2, 234, 239, 348, 349-50, 351, 353, 354, 358, 359

Production credits: 40-1, 128-9, 280-2

Ray, Diane: 123, 225

"Reformation of Harry Briscoe, The": 155, **174-8**, 325

"Return to Devil's Hole": **71-75**

"Root of It All": **88-93**

Sheinberg, Sid: 13, 112

Shields, Sonny: 273, 321, 347

"Shootout at Diablo Station": 172, **184-8**, 310

Singer, Alex: 115, 117, 127, 141, 146, 214-215, 225, 229, 233, 234, 237, 238, 239, 242, 246, 272-3, 274-5, 292, 293-4, 347, 358

"Six Strangers at Apache Springs": **163-8**

"Smiler with a Gun": 37, **147-52**, 237

"Something to Get Hung About": **157-63**, 220

"Stagecoach Seven": **79-84**, 172, 315, 331

"Strange Fate of Conrad Meyer Zulick": 29, 271, **326-31**

Swerling, Jr., Jo: 16, 18, 22, 25, 51, 61, 75, 111, 116-9, 145, 168, 192-3, 214, 225, 226, 228, 229, 230, 232, 233, 239, 252, 258, 270, 271, 272, 273, 274, 304, 350, 351

"Ten Days that Shook Kid Curry, The": 35, 188, **315-21**

Twain, Mark: 32, 33, 60, 159, 178, 203, 220, 223, 258, 267; *Life on the Mississippi*: 32, 60, 159, 160, 161, 223

Universal: 14, 18, 19, 21, 47, 51, 65, 80, 112, 113, 114, 117, 119, 120, 122, 146, 197, 228, 229, 230, 233, 239, 240, 270, 274, 304, 350, 351, 353-4, 356

Virginian, The: 9, 15, 62, 65, 205

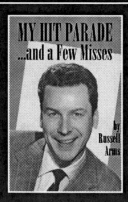

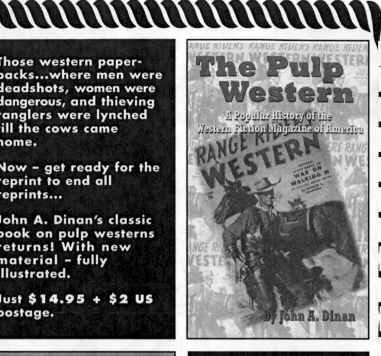
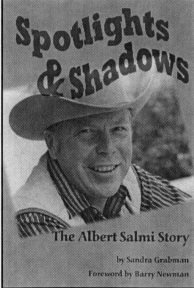

Printed in the United States
113065LV00008B/70-72/A